2/07

THE PASTORA GOLDNER SERIES
in Post-Holocaust Studies

The Pastora Goldner Series in Post-Holocaust Studies explores questions—ethical, educational, political, spiritual—that continue to haunt humanity in the aftermath of Nazi Germany's attempt to destroy Jewish life and culture. Books in this series, addressing the most current and pressing issues of our post-Holocaust world, proceed from scholarship undertaken by the Pastora Goldner Symposium, whose membership—international, interdisciplinary, interfaith, and intergenerational—is committed to dialogue as a fundamental form of inquiry. The symposium and the series are generously supported by Pastora Campos Goldner, who has devoted much of her life to working toward *tikkun olam,* the healing of our world, and whose vision and courage inspire the participants in the symposium who contribute to this series.

THE PASTORA GOLDNER SERIES
in Post-Holocaust Studies

*After-Words: Post-Holocaust Struggles
with Forgiveness, Reconciliation, Justice*
Edited and Introduced by
David Patterson and John K. Roth

*Fire in the Ashes:
God, Evil, and the Holocaust*
Edited and Introduced by
David Patterson and John K. Roth

*Open Wounds: The Crisis of Jewish Thought
in the Aftermath of Auschwitz*
David Patterson

Testimony, Tensions, and Tikkun: *Teaching
the Holocaust in Colleges and Universities*
Edited and Introduced by
Myrna Goldenberg and Rochelle L. Millen

OPEN WOUNDS

The Crisis of Jewish Thought
in the Aftermath of Auschwitz

DAVID PATTERSON

UNIVERSITY OF WASHINGTON PRESS
Seattle and London

University of Washington Press
PO Box 50096, Seattle, WA 98145
www.washington.edu/uwpress

Library of Congress Cataloging-in-Publication Data
Patterson, David, 1948–
Open wounds : the crisis of Jewish thought
in the aftermath of Auschwitz / David Patterson.
p. cm.—(Pastora Goldner series in post-Holocaust studies)
Includes bibliographical references and index.
ISBN 0-295-98645-x (hardback : alk. paper)
1. Holocaust, Jewish (1939–1945)—Moral and ethical aspects.
2. Holocaust, Jewish (1939–1945)—Influence.
3. Judaism—20th century.   4. Judaism—Doctrines.
5. Holocaust (Jewish theology).   I. Title.   II. Series.
D804.3p3776 2006   940.53'1814—dc22   2006016887

The paper used in this publication is acid-free and 90 percent recycled from
at least 50 percent post-consumer waste. It meets the minimum requirements of
American National Standard for Information Sciences—Permanence of Paper
for Printed Library Materials, ANSI z39.48–1984. ♾ ♻

Illustration (jacket, p. i): *First Station: Auschwitz-Birkenau*, by Arie Galles
(1998, 47½ × 75 in., charcoal and white Conté on Arches with barbed wire-impressed
wrought-iron frame), from the suite of fifteen drawings *Fourteen Stations/Hey Yud Dalet
(Hashem Yinkom Daman)*, the latter phrase meaning "May God avenge their blood."
The title of the suite refers both to the Stations of the Cross and to the fact that the
Nazi concentration camps and killing centers were near railroad stations. Galles's
drawings are based on Luftwaffe and Allied aerial photographs of those sites. Within
this drawing and all the others are invisibly embedded, hand-lettered phrases
from the Kaddish, the ancient Jewish prayer for the dead.

FOR

Emil L. Fackenheim,

with gratitude,

AND FOR

Tomás Daniel Cortest,

an innocent soul who has

ascended to the upper realms

CONTENTS

PREFACE ix

ACKNOWLEDGMENTS xiii

1 Introduction: The Open Wounds of Jewish Thought 3

2 The Bankruptcy of Modern and Postmodern Thought 32

3 Ethical Monotheism and Jewish Thought 63

4 The Holocaust and the Holy Tongue 91

5 The *Sifrei Kodesh* and the Holocaust 116

6 The Muselmann and the Matter of the Human Being 144

7 Jewish Thought and a Post-Holocaust *Tikkun Haolam* 173

8 Mystical Dimensions of Post-Holocaust Jewish Thought 201

9 Though the Messiah May Tarry 230

10 Conclusion: No Closure 253

NOTES 259

BIBLIOGRAPHY 305

INDEX 327

PREFACE

In this book, I undertake a Jewish response to the Shoah. Unlike most other authors who have engaged a similar task, I offer a view of what makes a Jewish response Jewish. As with the determination of any definition, the attempt to define what is "Jewish" in a Jewish response to the Shoah entails drawing some lines of distinction. The distinctions, however, are intended more to establish a spectrum of shades of Jewish thinking than to determine an absolute delineation. Of course, like any definition, my understanding of what makes Jewish thought Jewish excludes some responses to the Shoah and includes others. But I do *not* take the term *Jewish* to be a synonym for "valid" or "insightful," any more than it can be a synonym for "Orthodox" or "Chasidic." Nor do I believe the question of what makes a Jewish response to the Shoah Jewish to be a question of what makes a Jew a Jew. But I do maintain that a Jewish response to the murder of the Jews is needful. And if a Jewish response is needful, then the question of what makes it Jewish must be raised.

Further, I proceed from the premise that the Nazis' assault on the Jews included an assault on the Torah that has defined the Jews for three thousand years. Indeed, the Nazis themselves understood this point. Therefore, I turn to the Torah slated for annihilation in the Shoah in my response to the Shoah. In keeping with centuries of Jewish teaching, I take the term *Torah* to include both the Written Torah and the Oral Torah, that is, both the Five Books of Moses and the texts of Mishnah, Gemara, Midrash, and Kabbalah, as well as commentaries ranging from Rashi to Schneur Zalman of Liadi. Just as I draw on a variety of Jewish thinkers, so do I draw upon a variety of what are termed *sifrei kodesh*, or "sacred texts," in order to take my thinking about the Shoah to new levels.

I do not regard one set of sacred texts to be more legitimate than another; the textual tradition consists of an interweaving of biblical, tal-mudic, midrashic, and mystical sources, each of which has its place in Jewish thinking and Jewish life. To be sure, one cannot divorce one aspect of Torah from another without undermining the substance of the whole teaching. As my bibliography indicates, I do not privilege the mystical over the talmudic or the biblical over the midrashic in my effort to respond to the Shoah; rather, I take each of these categories to be interwoven with the others, and not isolated or unrelated to one another. This method, in fact, reflects an age-old Jewish method of seeking according to four levels of understanding: the literal *(pshat)*, the allegorical *(remez)*, the homiletical *(drash)*, and the mystical *(sod)* levels.

While modern and postmodern thinkers may balk at a response to the Shoah that contains mystical elements, the mystical perspective per-vades Jewish philosophy and Jewish religious life. Maimonides, for instance, begins Part III of *The Guide for the Perplexed* by saying that his primary objective throughout the book has been to expound on the *Maaseh Bereshit* (Deeds of Creation) and *Maaseh Merkavah* (Deeds of the Chariot); in other words, his aim, as he states it, is to connect the mystical teachings with his philosophical inquiry. With regard to our daily lives, from the moment when we thank God for returning our soul to this world in the morning to the moment when we ask God to fill our eyes with light, lest we "sleep the sleep of death" at night, our days are filled with texts, teachings, and customs from the mystical tradition.

When Elie Wiesel insists that what took place in the Holocaust took place in the soul, he opens up a mystical consideration of the event, par-ticularly since he still identifies himself as a Chasid. When Emil Facken-heim considers whether the Divine image in the human being can be destroyed, he introduces a notion that has mystical implications, even though he was not a mystic. When Primo Levi refers to the Divine spark that was snuffed out in the Muselmann, he invites a consideration of what that spark is, which is a mystical question, despite the fact that he was not a religiously observant Jew. I do not see how we can take our understanding of the assault on the Jewish soul to a deeper level without considering Jewish teachings on the soul. And as soon as we turn to Jewish teachings on the soul, on the Divine image, or the Divine spark, we are knee-deep in mysticism. In fact, the statement of purpose for the Pastora Goldner Series in Post-Holocaust Studies uses a key term from the mystical tradition to articulate what this series sets out to accomplish: it is *tikkun haolam,* which is a "mending or healing of the world." Shall we use this mystical term without considering the tradition that gives rise to it?

Again, I do *not* maintain that a Jewish mystical approach is the only valid approach to the Shoah. My thinking is deeply influenced and informed by philosophers such as Emil Fackenheim, Emmanuel Levinas, and Abraham Joshua Heschel, none of whom invokes much of the mystical tradition in his thinking, and all of whom I take to be deeply Jewish thinkers. Nevertheless, I do maintain that if a distinctively Jewish response to the Shoah incorporates the written and oral traditions of Torah, those traditions include the mystical teachings.

In the spirit of the Pastora Goldner Series in Post-Holocaust Studies, I welcome any dialogical engagement that may arise from the pages that follow.

DAVID PATTERSON
Memphis, Tennessee

ACKNOWLEDGMENTS

I would like to express my deepest gratitude to Pastora Goldner for her generous and conscientious support of the Pastora Goldner Symposium on Post-Holocaust Studies and for the Pastora Goldner Series in Post-Holocaust Studies published by the University of Washington Press. My thanks go to John K. Roth, my coeditor-in-chief of the series; to Leonard Grob, without whom neither the symposium nor the series would exist; and to Naomi Pascal, whose leadership at the University of Washington Press has made the series a reality. Also at the University of Washington Press, Marilyn Trueblood and Xavier Callahan deserve my deepest gratitude for their excellent work on the volume. I would also like to acknowledge the University of Memphis Arts and Humanities Research Grant Program, whose support helped to make the completion of this volume possible, as well as the University of Memphis College of Arts and Sciences for granting me a Faculty Development Assignment to work on this book.

Finally, the generous support and friendship of three people have helped to make this book possible: Dr. W. Harry Feinstone, Bert Bornblum, and his brother David Bornblum of blessed memory.

OPEN
WOUNDS

I

Introduction

The Open Wounds of Jewish Thought

These are the rents of mourning not to be sewn up: the death
of a father or a mother; the death of a teacher who taught one
Torah; the death of a people's leader; the death of the head of a
rabbinic court; upon hearing evil tidings; upon hearing God's
name blasphemed; upon the burning of a *Sefer Torah*; upon
seeing the cities of Judea in ruins; upon seeing the Temple
in ruins; upon seeing the ruins of Jerusalem.
—Talmud Bavli, *Moed Katan* 26a

In his commentary on the Torah, the great thirteenth-century rabbi Nachmanides makes the following prophecy: "The children of Esau [Chris-
tendom] will not formulate a decree against us designed to obliterate our
name entirely, but they will do evil to some of us in their countries."[1]
Unfortunately, the sage was mistaken: although he knew very well the
slaughter of the Crusades, he had no conception of the Shoah that would
befall his people seven hundred years later. Indeed, how could he? The
Shoah was a devastation unprecedented in its scope and singular in its
implications. It cut a wound into the body of all of Israel, and not just
those who fell victim to the catastrophe. As it is written, "the people of
Israel are compared to a lamb. What is the nature of the lamb? If it is
hurt in one limb, all its limbs feel the pain."[2] Taking the matter to a deeper

level, the *Midrash Chinukh* says that if a single human life is taken, the victim's blood raises an outcry that reverberates throughout the universe.³ What, then, must be the outcry of a sea of blood? The cry, indeed, is deafening. If we cannot hear it, it is because it is unceasing, a dissonance that has drowned out the music of the spheres.

The blood poured out in the murder of European Jewry continues to surge in the blood of every Jew—indeed, of all humanity. And, since the level of the soul known as *nefesh* is in the blood (Genesis 9:4), it is not just the body of Israel but its very soul that has been wounded.⁴ Here, too, in the depths of the soul, each Jew is tied to the other, as well as to God. Each soul, said the Baal Shem Tov, founder of Chasidism, is "a limb of the Shekhinah," which is the Divine Presence in this world, so that "a sorrow caused to one affects all."⁵ As Yitzhak Katznelson asserts in his *Vittel Diary,* "it is against the great Beth Hamedrash [the dwelling place of the Shekhinah], the spirit and soul of East European Jewry, that the nations have set this Horror."⁶ This attack upon the spirit and soul of Israel lies in the calculated destruction of Jewish cemeteries and synagogues, of Jewish texts and sacred artifacts, of Jewish homes and families— all of which was planned according to the Jewish calendar of holy days. And all of which came to an assault on the Holy One Himself.

Herman Kruk leaves no doubt as to whether the Nazis understood the religious and metaphysical implications of their actions against the Jews. In his diary from the Vilna Ghetto, he often refers to the Gestapo's "Jew Specialists," such as the infamous Dr. Pohl, director of *Judenforschung ohne Juden,* that is, "research on Jews without Jews."⁷ It was the responsibility of certain Nazis to be thoroughly familiar with Jews and Judaism, with Jewish teachings and traditions, and to use their knowledge to destroy Jewish souls and the testimony that enters the world through the Jewish people. Kruk points out, in fact, that the press in Germany and Nazi-occupied Poland referred to the war as the "Jew War" or the "War against the Jews," suggesting that the *complete* annihilation of the Jewish people and Jewish testimony was not a mere side agenda but was Germany's prime directive in waging war.

Why did the Nazis target the Jews in particular? It is more than a matter of ancient prejudice. According to Ignaz Maybaum, it was because Hitler "knew that the Jew, historically and existentially, even without any choice, stands for justice, mercy and truth. He stood for everything which made every word of Hitler a lie. The Jew, without opening his mouth to utter a single word, condemned Hitler."[8] While Maybaum was wrong in his conclusion that the Shoah was "progress through sacrifice,"[9] he was right on this point. The Nazis did not target the Jews because some Jews may have prospered during an economic depression; in that case, it would have been enough to impoverish them. Nor was it because the Jews were an easy scapegoat for social problems; in that case, it would have been enough to rid only Germany of its Jews.[10] No, it was because the Jewish presence in the world signifies a testimony—a Torah—on the ineluctable sanctity of every human being. Such a teaching, so fundamental to Torah, is fundamentally at odds with Nazi thinking.

In the Nazi worldview, the Jews were not an economic or political or social problem but a cosmic, *ontological* evil that had to be eradicated, a point that Oskar Rosenfeld makes very clear in his diary from the Łódź Ghetto. Noting, for instance, that the teachings in the *Pirke Avot,* a classic from the Talmud forbidden in the ghetto, are diametrically opposed to Nazi ideology, he sees that there is not enough room for Nazis and Jews to dwell in the same universe.[11] The Nazis fought the Jews because, according to their infamous ideologist Alfred Rosenberg, the Aryan "race has been poisoned by Judaism," and not merely by Jewish blood, for the *-ism* is *in* the blood.[12] Therefore, Rosenberg insisted, all Jews are prone to think talmudically, "whether they are atheistic Bourse-speculators, religious fanatics, or Talmudic Jews of the cloth."[13] As Julius Streicher, the notorious Nazi publisher of *Der Stürmer,* stated it in 1936, whoever fights the Jew fights the devil, and whoever masters the devil conquers heaven: to get rid of the Jews, in other words, is to assail heaven and thus get rid of the Holy One, which was the Nazis' ultimate aim.[14] And the Nazi philosopher Martin Heidegger complained of the "Jewification of the German *Geist,*"[15] that is, the German "mind" or "spirit," suggesting a metaphysical aspect to the Jewish threat to German humanity. As Yehuda Bauer has correctly argued, "to the Nazis, the 'Jewish problem' was a problem of cosmic importance,"[16] something that far transcended the economic, ethnic, political, social, or cultural reasons behind the hatred of the Jews.

If we turn to Rashi, the great commentator of the eleventh century, for a deeper insight into this point, we realize that the Holocaust is not reducible to a case of genocide but is a singular case of deicide. Stating the principle at work here, Rashi wrote, "Whoever attacks Israel is as though he attacks the Holy One, blessed be He."[17] If we recall a teaching articulated by the Koretzer Rebbe, a disciple of the Baal Shem Tov, this point will become even more clear: "God and Prayer are One. God and Torah are One. God, Israel, and Torah are One."[18] And all were slated for annihilation.

Since God, from a Jewish standpoint, is the ground of all thought and meaning, this assault on God entails an assault on thought: thought itself has been *wounded,* and not just challenged or confused. It is not that we merely lack the imagination or the intellect to respond to this devastation of God and humanity and therefore do not know *what* to think. Beyond that, we do not know *how* to think. This wounding of thought itself is the reason why, in the words of Steven Katz, "Auschwitz has become an inescapable *datum* for all Jewish accounts of the meaning and nature of convenantal relation and God's relation to man."[19] Because Jewish thought is wounded through the Holocaust, it is in a state of crisis. At stake in addressing this crisis is the future of the Jewish people, for without the categories of Jewish thought to guide our Jewish thinking, we lose our Jewish doing and therefore our Jewish being. And we must summon all our abilities to determine how Jewish thought might respond to the Nazi assault on Jewish being, or else the Nazis will have their victory, and history will be done with the Jews.

Indeed, what Arthur Cohen maintained in 1981 is still the case today: "It is an unresolved predicament of Jewish thought to speak correctly about the relationship of the Jew to history, the Jewish people to the nations, the eternal vortex into which God inserted Torah and the inescapable obligation of the Jew to be citizen among citizens and neighbor among neighbors."[20] In his anthology of philosophical responses to the Holocaust, Michael Morgan points out "how slim are the really superior Jewish contributions to the enterprise of rethinking Judaism after Auschwitz."[21] The difficulty, however, with the post-Holocaust "rethinking" of Judaism is not that it has failed to go far enough or deep enough; rather, it has failed to be Jewish enough. There lies the crisis. And it has cosmic dimensions. Rabbi Adin Steinsaltz identifies four cosmic crises in the history of heaven and earth: the "Shattering of the Vessels" at the time of creation, which opened the door to evil; the Sin of the Tree of Knowledge of Good and Evil, which damaged all of creation; the Sin of the Golden Calf, when the Jew people were nearly lost; and the Destruction of the Temple, when God's presence was nearly lost.[22] With the Shoah, we have a fifth crisis.

The Nazis attempted to purge the world of the Jews, and with them the commanding presence of the Holy One. Similarly, a certain line of philosophical development has tried to purge thought of anything and everything Jewish. Some thinkers who happen to be Jewish have been part of this process; others have failed even to address the issue. But before we delve further into this question, let us briefly consider what until now has been the Jewish response to the Shoah.

THE JEWISH RESPONSE TO THE SHOAH THUS FAR

As in every other disaster that has befallen the Jewish people, the rabbis responded to the Holocaust from the very depths of the destruction. In most cases, however, this response did not fall into a category of Jewish philosophical thinking about the implications of the event for our relation to God and humanity. Rather, as in other times of catastrophe, it took the form of answering halakhic questions (questions of Jewish law) that arose from the event. Of course, these rabbis also attested to the horrors taking place all around them. One recalls, for example, the ingenious efforts undertaken by Jewish leaders such as Rabbi Ephraim Oshry of Kovno, who ruled that Kaddish can be said on a Righteous Gentile;[23] by Rabbi Yitzhak Nissenbaum of Warsaw, who declared to the Jews that in those days of destruction, *Kiddush Hashem* (the "Sanctification of the Name," usually understood as martyrdom; see *Ketuvot* 111a) meant doing everything possible to survive as Jews;[24] and by Rabbi J. M. Toledano of Kovno, who bore witness to the Nazis' special satisfaction in "killing women, particularly if they were pregnant, and when women were there with children they were dashed in pieces."[25] While such rulings and observations are laden with philosophical implications, none of these sages pursued those implications. Indeed, they hardly had the luxury to do so.

In the post-Holocaust era, however, many Jewish thinkers have tried to develop a philosophical and theological response to the event. Their attempts have been anthologized in volumes such as Arthur Cohen's *Arguments and Doctrines,* Dan Cohn-Sherbok's *Holocaust Theology,* Steven Katz's *Interpreters of Judaism in the Late Twentieth Century,* Michael Morgan's *A Holocaust Reader,* Alan Rosenberg and Gerald E. Myers's *Echoes from the Holocaust,* and Bernhard H. Rosenberg and Fred Heuman's *Theological and Halakhic Reflections on the Holocaust.* Steven Katz divides the various Jewish responses to the Holocaust into nine categories, according to the thesis that guides each one:

1. The Holocaust is essentially the same as all other Jewish tragedies (for example, Eliezer Berkovits, *Faith after the Holocaust*).
2. The Holocaust is a punishment for the Jewish sin of complicity in the project of modernity (for example, Bernard Maza, *With Fury Poured Out*).
3. Israel is the suffering servant who was afflicted for the sins of humanity (for example, Ignaz Maybaum, *The Face of God after Auschwitz*).
4. The Holocaust is a modern *Akedah,* a binding of Isaac, and is a test of our faltering faith (for example, Irving Greenberg, "Cloud of Smoke, Pillar of Fire").
5. The Holocaust is a temporary eclipse of God (for example, Martin Buber, *Eclipse of God*).
6. The Holocaust means that God and His Covenant with the Jewish people are dead (for example, Richard Rubenstein, *After Auschwitz*).
7. God chooses to be powerless for the sake of human freedom, and the Holocaust is the price paid for that freedom (for example, Hans Jonas, *Mortality and Morality*).
8. The Holocaust is a moment of revelation and a call for Jewish survival (for example, Emil L. Fackenheim, *God's Presence in History*).
9. The Holocaust is an inscrutable mystery and eludes all thought (for example, Elie Wiesel, *One Generation After*).[26]

Katz's categories are quite helpful in identifying the issues and the positions that have characterized Jewish thinking about the Shoah thus far. His book *Post-Holocaust Dialogues,* where he presents these categories, also contains excellent analyses of some of the major philosophical respondents to the horror, including Richard Rubenstein, Ignaz Maybaum, Eliezer Berkovits, and Emil Fackenheim. Other must-read studies of what have passed for Jewish responses to the Holocaust include Michael Morgan's *Beyond Auschwitz,* which also contains analyses of Hannah Arendt, Irving Greenberg, Arthur Cohen, and Elie Wiesel, and Zachary Braiterman's *(God) after Auschwitz,* which focuses on Rubenstein, Berkovits, and Fackenheim. None of these scholars, however, raises the questions that drive this volume: What makes a Jewish response to the Shoah distinctively Jewish? What might that Jewish response be? And what is at stake in responding Jewishly to the annihilation of the Jews?

I shall not go into a lengthy analysis of the works written by the Jewish respondents to the Shoah. The scholars mentioned above have already accomplished that task. In order to set the context for the investigation of the questions raised here, however, a few words should be said about some of the key problems, as well as some of the key insights, that have characterized the Jewish response to the Holocaust.

PROBLEMS AND INSIGHTS IN THE
JEWISH RESPONSE TO THE SHOAH

One of the most disturbing difficulties with what has been deemed a "Jewish" response to the Holocaust is that the principles guiding the response sometimes resemble those that contributed to Nazi thinking. We have already pointed out that a defining feature of the Holocaust lay in the Nazis' assault on God, Torah, Covenant, Divine commandments, human holiness, transcendent truth, absolute ethical responsibility— everything the Jews represent by their very presence in the world. Such an assault against the Jews is perfectly in keeping with a philosophical tradition that understands freedom in terms of autonomy, authenticity in terms of resolve, and humanity in terms of contingency; that displaces God with the thinking ego and takes "rational" conclusions, rather than Divine commandments, to be the basis of morality; and that has removed all height and holiness, all absolute truth and meaning, from thought. Such thinking is characteristic, for example, of Hannah Arendt and Richard Rubenstein. As I shall argue, not only are their responses to the event not in keeping with what I shall define as Jewish thought, but they are antithetical to Jewish thought.

Arendt's influences, for example, were Aristotle and Kant, to say nothing of Heidegger, and not Moses or Akiva, so that her thinking about God and evil is not based on anything Jewish.[27] Here, it is worth noting that Kant maintained that "the euthanasia of Judaism is the pure moral religion,"[28] and Heidegger insisted that "the *Führer* himself and he alone *is* the present and future German reality and its law."[29] As for Rubenstein, chief among his influences are Freud, Tillich, Sartre, and Arendt, all of whom maintain that, in a sense, the Jews themselves are to blame for anti-Semitism inasmuch as they insist on being a people apart, a Chosen People. Although Rubenstein says that the Torah is "sacred," he insists that in no sense is it from God and that Jewish religious life possesses no "superordinate validation."[30] In other words, the Jews are not chosen, and there is no Covenant. Rubenstein sees in Judaism no more than a therapeutic value, as Morgan correctly points out.[31] Basing the future of the Jews on an arbitrary "peoplehood"[32] and a pagan "return to the cosmic rhythm of natural existence,"[33] Rubenstein's "Jewish" response to the Holocaust amounts to an abrogation of the defining essence of Jews and Judaism. To be sure, he maintains that ultimately there is no future for the Jewish people and no meaning in human life.

Rubenstein says, for example, contrary to all Jewish teaching, that "there is only one Messiah who redeems us from the irony, the travail, and the limitations of human existence. Surely he will come. He is the Angel of Death. Death is the true Messiah and the land of the dead the place of God's true Kingdom."[34] Recalling an insight from Rabbi Steinsaltz, one realizes that no view could be more anti-Judaic. "In Judaism," Steinsaltz writes, "holiness is first and foremost the sanctity of life. Where life abounds, holiness is at hand. 'Life' is a synonym for all that is most exalted in Creation. One of the names of God is 'the God of life.' The Torah is described as 'the Torah of life.' The Torah itself speaks of 'life and goodness' as of one and the same thing."[35] Contrary to the Torah's injunction to choose life (Deuteronomy 30:19), Rubenstein's words call to mind something akin to the Nazi cult of death as described in Yvonne Karow's *Deutsches Opfer* (German Sacrifice).[36] Certainly not the same as the Nazis, but similar to them, Rubenstein would have the Judaism of Torah go away, to be replaced by the pagan worship of Eros and Thanatos. Embracing the ideas of the Nazis' pagan precursor Friedrich Nietzsche, Rubenstein holds that life has no inherent meaning and that human "dignity" is merely a derivative of power.[37] In what sense, then, is Richard Rubenstein a *Jewish* thinker?

In contrast to Rubenstein, but just as shocking, Maybaum sees the murder of most of Europe's Orthodox Jewry as a *necessary evil,* if not as a good thing. After the Holocaust, he argues, "the medieval organization outside which God was not supposed to be found has been destroyed. You can be a Jew outside the *din* [judgment], outside the religious organization as defined in codes."[38] In other words, according to Maybaum, one is a Jew apart from anything that over the centuries has defined what it means to be a Jew; therefore, one is free of the traditional obligations that come with being a Jew—a position that distinguishes Maybaum's thinking from the halakhic view that no matter how far a Jew has strayed from his or her Judaism, he or she remains a Jew subject to the Covenant and the commandments of Torah. What, then, does it mean to be a Jew, from Maybaum's standpoint? Answer: nothing in particular, or at least nothing pressing. And Maybaum sees that as a good thing.

Katz correctly notes that, as a classical Reform Jew, Maybaum takes the obliteration of the shtetl—that is, of the *Talmud Jude*—to be an "enhancement," and Hitler to be God's unpleasant but desirable agent.[39] Maybaum sees the Holocaust as horrific, yes, but nonetheless as progress,[40] since it frees the Jews not only of Torah and Talmud, as already noted, but also of Zionism, which perpetuates the "myth" of the Jews as a "people apart."[41] The implication is that the Jewish people are better off without the revealed Torah and the State of Israel, since he sees these as the greatest impediment to a future in which Jews can be "like everyone else." What makes that future Jewish in any meaningful way, and not just in an incidental way, is unclear. Like most Reform thinkers, Maybaum views Jews in Kantian terms, that is, in terms not of a sacred testimony for which they are chosen but in terms of the merely accidental. What counts most for Maybaum is that Jews are "rational beings," a term that appears nowhere in Torah. In what sense, then, is Ignaz Maybaum a *Jewish* thinker?

With regard to those whose thinking might seem more Jewish, one may call to mind Arthur Cohen, who underscores the inscrutable mystery of God and the Shoah through his invocation of the *mysterium tremendum*. But this term is not a Jewish or a Hebrew term; it is a Latin term taken from the Christian theologian Rudolph Otto. Cohen is quite right, however, when he declares that "to assert God's death in the interest of self-liberation" is "a trifling narcissism" and "an already well-established irrelevance."[42] Unlike Rubenstein and Maybaum, moreover, Cohen recognizes that the Holocaust "ended once and for all" the "dreams of the project of enlightenment and emancipation and the surge of moralist progressivism which dominated the liberal strain of European Judaism."[43] And yet he buys in to two key terms that came out of the Enlightenment when he explains that the "bridge" he attempts to cast "over the abyss" of the Holocaust "is one that sinks its pylons into the deep soil of human freedom and rationality,"[44] the very notions that have been so seriously undermined by the Holocaust. Thus Cohen's thinking is Jewish to a point, but not as much as it might seem at first glance, because he takes his key terms from Christianity and the Enlightenment thinking that contributed to the Holocaust.

Among the Orthodox rabbis known for their responses to the Shoah are Irving Greenberg and Eliezer Berkovits. Greenberg's response to the Shoah comes to this: "No statement, theological or otherwise, should be made that would not be credible in the presence of the burning children."[45] It is taken from his essay "Cloud of Smoke, Pillar of Fire," the title of which invokes ways in which the Shoah has challenged Jewish thought. The title refers, of course, to the smoke and the fire of the Divine Presence as it guided the Israelites through the wilderness. The smoke and the fire, however, have now taken on quite a different presence: they are the smoke and the fire that rise from the pits in which Jewish children were burned alive. Contrary to watching over us, moreover, the smoke and the fire haunt us. The Midrash relates that when the Egyptians threw the children into the Nile, God raised the children up from the Nile, saved their lives, and laid them in the desert (*Pirke de Rabbi Eliezer*, 42). But in the time of the Shoah, they were left to the desert of ash and flame. And, as Elie Wiesel has said, "these children / Have taken your countenance, / O God."[46] What once signified the presence of God now signifies His eclipse. The ashes that have rained down from the cloud of smoke and the pillar of fire now cover the earth—that is where the eclipse of God takes place: not in the heavens but on the earth. If "the earth is the Lord's," as it is written (Psalms 24:1), the Lord Himself, the Infinite One, is covered with these ashes that breach infinity.

And yet, despite the power of his images—perhaps *because* of that power and those images—I have never been sure what to make of Greenberg's statement. Is it supposed to render us mute? After all, what *can* be said in the presence of burning children? Dare one speak at all? Dare one remain silent? "Woe to me if I speak"—one recalls the lament of Rabbi Yochanan ben Zakkai—"woe to me if I do not speak" (*Kelim* 17:16). Sara Nomberg-Przytyk, in her remembrance of a children's transport that arrived one night at Auschwitz, offers a hint of what might be said: "Suddenly, the stillness was broken by the screaming of children, . . . a scream repeated a thousand times in a single word, 'Mama,' a scream that increased in intensity every second, enveloping the whole camp. Our lips parted without our being conscious of what we were doing, and a scream of despair tore out of our throats. . . . At the end everything was enveloped in death and silence."[47] Has Jewish thought, then, been reduced to a scream of despair that tears itself from our throats? Shall our thoughts now be enveloped in death and silence? That seems to be Greenberg's recommendation. But apart from appealing to our emotions, which is perhaps needful, our being silenced by the burning children does not take us any closer to a Jewish understanding of the Shoah or to a future for Jewish thought.

Greenberg's recommendation leads him to the view that any faith we may muster after the Holocaust is at best a "moment faith,"[48] for in the Holocaust we collide with an evil so great that none of the categories that shape our faith and our thinking can accommodate it. This evil sends us back into an arena where we wrestle with our faith, for our faith, with God, against God. Greenberg's point about faith, however, is not so innovative as it may seem. If prayer, or *tefillah*, is also a form of wrestling, as its cognate *naftulim* suggests, then the task of wrestling from our souls and from God a deeper faith is as a old as the name *Yisrael*, which means "he who strives with God." Nor does Jewish teaching demand faith so much as it demands study, prayer, and deeds of loving kindness. And Greenberg knows very well that we cannot afford "moment kindness." To be sure, he sees that the only viable response to the burning children is to reaffirm meaning and value in life "through acts of love and life-giving,"[49] as commanded by Torah, whether we feel up to it or not. And that, certainly, is very Jewish.

This insistence, however, does not jibe with his conclusion concerning the covenantal relation between God and the Jews after the Holocaust. Here we are left with what Greenberg calls a "voluntary covenant." During the Holocaust, he maintains, the Covenant's "authority was broken, but the Jewish people, released from its obligations, chose voluntarily to take it on again."[50] The difficulty I see with this idea is that if the Covenant is voluntary—if we are free to choose *not* to enter into the Covenant—then we are also free not to reaffirm life through acts of love and life-giving kindness, which is what Greenberg urges. True, Greenberg insists that "after the Holocaust one *must* challenge the absolute claims of a secular culture that created the matrix out of which such a catastrophe could grow."[51] And he is absolutely right. But how can this *must* be voluntary for a Jew? For if we are not bound, as Jews, by the Covenant, then we are not bound by the commandments, from the prohibition against pork to the prohibition against murder. Without the Covenant that chooses us *prior* to any choices we make, we have no real obligation, and our choices have no ultimate meaning.

To help Greenberg a bit, we could recall a teaching from the Zohar, where it states that the various nations rejected the Covenant of Torah before the Jews "voluntarily" accepted it (see *Zohar* III, 192a–93a); but there is also the talmudic teaching that God held a mountain over the Israelites gathered at Sinai and warned them that they would be buried under the mountain if they did not accept the Covenant (*Shabbat* 88a; *Avoda Zarah* 2b). The point, however, is not that God threatened the Jews, saying, "Accept the Torah, or else I'll crush you." No, it is that without Torah, humanity is buried under the might of a strictly material world, lost in a hopeless struggle that no one can win, where power is the only reality and weakness the only sin. We may have a choice. But it is, in a sense, a choiceless choice. As Emmanuel Levinas has rightly said, "the Good is good precisely because it chooses you and grips you before you have had the time to raise your eyes to it."[52] So it is with the Covenant. The mountain that compels us to choose *Hael Hatov*, "the God who is the Good," is not the mountain of might; it is the mountain of the Good itself. If there is no Mount Sinai and the Covenant is voluntary, then it is also voluntary for God, so that our outcry, our outrage, and our questioning of God are rendered as meaningless as they are groundless.

Like the cloud of smoke and the pillar of fire, however, the mountain that threatens to bury us assumes a new significance in the post-Holocaust era: it is a mountain of ashes. Not only does the mountain hang over us, it abides within us, as literally and as graphically as the mountain of ashes under the concrete dome at Majdanek. For the winds have spread a mountain of ashes—the ashes of six million Jews—over the face of the earth, east to west and pole to pole. The ashes inhabit the ground that yields our bread. They curl up in the crumbs we place in our mouths. If, as the talmudic sage Rabbi Ammi once taught, he who eats from the earth of Babylon is as though he ate the flesh of his ancestors (*Zevachim* 113b), what shall we say of this bread that we now harvest from the ashen earth? As we are made of that bread, so are we—all of humanity—made of those ashes: we are the grave to those denied a grave.[53] The only thing we have as an alternative to the mountain of ashes is the Covenant of Torah that the Nazis tried to reduce to dust, even if we must seek the black fire and the white fire of Torah among the embers of those ashes (see, for example, *Tanchuma Bereshit* 1).[54]

One Jewish thinker who understands the exigency of the Covenant, both for God and for humanity, is Eliezer Berkovits. Although Berkovits describes "the system of the planned dehumanization" of the Jews as "uniquely German,"[55] he maintains that there is nothing essentially unique in the dilemma posed by the Holocaust.[56] He further insists that in Judaism faith demands that we question God in the aftermath of such a catastrophe.[57] And, invoking the passage from Isaiah 42:15,[58] he is aware of a very important tension that characterizes Jewish thinking about God and humanity: "That man may be, God must absent Himself; that man may not perish in the tragic absurdity of his own making, God must remain present."[59] Therefore, Berkovits rightly understands, the aim of Jewish thought is not to settle matters with the fixed formulas and ready answers of theodicy; as Shmuel ben Nachman teaches in the Talmud, "whoever holds that someone is suffering due to his sins is in error" (*Shabbat* 5a).[60] The aim, rather, it is to maintain the tension of a strife of the spirit, which can be maintained only through an adherence to Torah,

Talmud, and Covenant.[61] Without that adherence, we lose both the grounds and the meaning of any objection to evil; indeed, we lose the very notion of evil. Therefore, even in evil—"at the very doors of the gas chambers," as Berkovits points out[62]—we encounter God.

The problem I find with Berkovits is not so much with what he brings out as with what he leaves out, for what he leaves out shows that the Jews are in fact faced with an unprecedented dilemma. The dilemma, as Emil Fackenheim expresses it, is this: during the time of the Third Reich, Jews were murdered not because they abandoned Torah but because their grandparents adhered to it.[63] The newness of the dilemma does not demand that we abandon Torah, Talmud, and Covenant—just the opposite: it demands that we take our Jewish thinking and our Judaism to even deeper levels. Berkovits misses the defining singularity of the assault not only against the Children of Israel but also against the God of Israel. When the Christian crusaders slaughtered the Jews, world Jewry was faced with a dilemma, but it was not the same dilemma. A Christian could object to the slaughter and still remain a Christian; a Christian could say, "We are going too far," and still remain within the teachings of Christianity. With a Nazi, however, there was no "going too far"; indeed, when it came to murdering Jews, a Nazi could not go far enough. Out to eliminate the Divine prohibition against murder through the murder of God Himself,[64] the Nazis had no limiting principle, no Divine injunction, to curtail their actions. What the Nazis perpetrated against the Jews, then, was not unimaginable—it was everything imaginable, for the imagination was the only limit to their actions. Thus, undertaking an assault on the Infinite One, their evil approached the infinite: it was as infinite as the imagination.

Among the most profound and most genuinely Jewish thinkers to respond to the Holocaust is one of the most neglected in these contexts: it is Emmanuel Levinas.[65] His friend Maurice Blanchot rightly recognized Levinas as a post-Holocaust Jewish thinker when he wrote, "How can one philosophize, how can one write within the memory of Auschwitz . . . ? It is this thought that traverses, that bears, the whole of Levinas's philosophy."[66] Like Rubenstein, Levinas rejects theodicy. Unlike Rubenstein, who takes being to be something neutral and meaningless and rejects the Divine commandments of Torah, Levinas is a Jewish thinker who insists, "Being has meaning. The meaning of being, the meaning of creation, is to realize the Torah. The world is here so that the ethical order has the possibility of being fulfilled. The act by which the Israelites accept the Torah is the act which gives meaning to reality. To refuse the Torah is to bring being back to nothingness."[67] Thus Levinas sees arising from the Holocaust not just the injunction to survive as Jews but also the demand for an ethical absolute, which derives not from the landscape of being but from what is "otherwise than being," from the "exigency of holiness"[68]—in a word, from the Torah that only Jewish thought and Judaism can transmit.

As early as 1934, Levinas recognized that National Socialism "stems from the essential possibility of *elemental Evil* into which we can be led by logic and against which Western philosophy had not sufficiently insured itself."[69] Indeed, Western philosophy could not insure itself against National Socialism, because Western philosophy could not think in terms of the holy. Unlike some of the thinkers we have considered so far, Levinas understands the holy to be a key category not only for Jewish thought but also for ethics as first philosophy. "To renounce after Auschwitz," he writes, "the God absent from Auschwitz—no longer to assure the continuation of Israel—would amount to finishing the criminal enterprise of National Socialism, which aimed at the annihilation of Israel and the forgetting of the ethical message of the Bible, which Judaism bears, and whose multi-millennial history is concretely prolonged by Israel's existence as a people."[70] And by *Judaism*, Levinas understands the Judaism of Torah and Talmud, as evidenced in his studies of the Talmud.

As a distinctively Jewish thinker, Levinas has made his most significant contribution to Jewish thought by exposing the complicity of Western ontological thought in the Nazi enterprise—something that most other Jewish respondents to the Holocaust have failed to do. He accurately states, for example, the implications of the ontological thinking that begins with Kant and culminates in Heidegger: "A philosophy of power, ontology is, as first philosophy which does not call into question the same, a philosophy of injustice. . . . Heideggerian ontology, which subordinates the relationship with the Other to the relation with Being in general, remains under obedience to the anonymous, and leads inevitably to another power, to imperialist domination, to tyranny."[71] Grounding freedom in autonomy and authenticity in resolve, this strain of the speculative tradition situates freedom beyond the Law and is therefore lawless. It is, as Levinas correctly argues, "the outcome of a long tradition of pride, heroism, domination, and cruelty" that "continues to exalt the will to power."[72] The exaltation of will and power, moreover, is characteristic of postmodern thought, which, in its absolute rejection of all absolutes, is diametrically opposed to Jewish thought. This is perhaps the most crucial insight that we have from Levinas. To be sure, in the response of Levinas to Heidegger we have a Jewish response to Nazi thinking.

Among the Jewish thinkers who have wrestled with a philosophical response to the Holocaust, the one who most thoroughly and most profoundly engages the event is Emil L. Fackenheim. Unlike most other Jewish philosophers, Fackenheim understands that the impetus behind the Nazis' project to murder world Jewry was not racism, envy, or scapegoating, nor was it economic depression, xenophobia, or the Treaty of Versailles. No, as the Nazis themselves understood, the Nazi hatred of the Jew was a first principle rooted in a metaphysics that shaped their entire worldview. Also unlike other thinkers, Fackenheim finds in Auschwitz not a Divine silence but a Divine commandment, what he calls the 614th Commandment: namely, that Jews must survive as Jews so as to refuse the Nazis a posthumous victory.[73] Contrary to Michael Wyschogrod's reading of Fackenheim, the point of the 614th Commandment is survival not for its own sake[74] but for the sake of a "millennial testimony," a chief component of which is the Divine prohibition against murder. If the Jews should be lost, the prohibition would be lost. If the Holocaust represents a singularity in human history, as Fackenheim maintains, it is not only because of its unprecedented nature, the exterminationist policy of a modern state, the development of technology for purposes of murder, the criminalization of Jewish being, and so on. More than that, its singularity lies in its metaphysical dimensions as an instance of Divine revelation in the midst of a human assault on the Divine.

How do the Nazis undertake that assault? Not just by eliminating the Divine prohibition against murder but also by making murder a defining principle of their own worldview. To be sure, one move requires the other. With an insight that eludes others, Fackenheim sees that "the murder camp was not an accidental by-product of the Nazi empire. It was its pure essence. The divine image *can* be destroyed. No more threatening proof to this effect can be found than the so-called Muselmann in the Nazi death camp. . . . The *Muselmänner* are a new way of human being in history, the living dead."[75] And: "The Nazi state had no higher aim than to murder souls while bodies were still alive. The Muselmann was its most characteristic, most original product. He is a *novum* in human history."[76] Demonstrating the connections between the Nazi assault on God and the Nazi undoing of the human image, Fackenheim opens up implications of the event that no other thinker has breached. He has also implicated modern philosophy in the role it played in the Holocaust through its removal of God from our thinking and the subsequent devaluation of the human being.

As a philosopher, then, Fackenheim recognizes the radical differences between Judaism and modern philosophy. With the denial of Divine otherness in such thinkers as Fichte, Schelling, and Hegel, he rightly points out, "divinity comes to dwell, as it were, in the same inner space as the human self, and this is enough to raise the spectre of a modern, internalized idolatry."[77] Moreover, this outcome of German Idealism ultimately manifests itself in National Socialism: "Because Nazism internalizes divinity, it is an idealism. Yet since it idolatrously identifies finiteness and infinitude, it is an idealism *totally without ideals.*"[78] This modern idolatry is the result of a thinking about human autonomy that in principle renders revelation impossible.[79] Invoking the 614th Commandment, Fackenheim retrieves a notion of revelation and with it the Divine prohibition against murder that is part of that revelation. Without the revealed nature of the prohibition, it is not an *absolute* prohibition. Because the Nazis set out to eliminate the Divine prohibition against murder in the extermination of the Jews, the refusal to allow Hitler a posthumous victory entails a retrieval or mending of the Voice from Sinai that forbids murder.

This notion of mending the world, or *tikkun haolam*, is crucial to Fackenheim's *To Mend the World,* his most notable philosophical response to the Holocaust. Jewishly speaking, what is sought in this mending, in this *tikkun*, is not just the revelation of God's commandment but the recovery of God's life, and with it our own. Fackenheim outlines three dimensions of the *tikkun haolam* with which post-Holocaust Jewish thought is confronted: the recovery of Jewish tradition; the recovery from an illness; and the open-ended nature of the recovery process.[80] The recovery of tradition entails the recovery of the category of the holy in our thinking about humanity. The recovery from an illness is a recovery from the indifference that has rendered humanity deaf to the cry of the other human being. Both of these endeavors are by definition without resolution; after the Holocaust, both remain open wounds. Says Fackenheim, "No religious meaning will ever be found in Auschwitz, for the very attempt to find it is blasphemy. There remains only the possibility of a religious response; this, however, is inescapable."[81] One task undertaken in this volume is to make that response.

Michael Morgan has correctly characterized Fackenheim as a thinker who understands the centrality of Torah to Jewish identity; for Fackenheim, according to Morgan, Torah underlies "the Jewish perspective of each Jew, and neither revelation nor any other event is confronted without it."[82] Indeed, Fackenheim has insisted that "a commitment to Sinai and Revelation" has always been paramount in his thinking.[83] In my view, then, Fackenheim's post-Holocaust thinking does not require correction so much as it calls for elaboration. His notion of *tikkun haolam,* for example, could use a more detailed consideration as a distinctively Jewish concept derived from the sacred texts of the Jewish tradition. His idea of the 614th Commandment could be filled out by pursuit of its implications for our relation to the other 613. The connection between the Muselmann and "postmodern man" could be more fully developed by those of us who are indebted to Fackenheim's efforts.

Finally—and of particular importance to this volume—Fackenheim raises a question that none of the other thinkers raises: it is the question of what makes Jewish thought Jewish. He notes, for example, that in Israel the term *Machshevet Yisrael*—literally, the "thinking of Israel"—"encompasses all 'Jewish thought,' from ancient Midrash to modern Zionist thought, including also Jewish philosophy. *Philosophia Yehudit* [literally, "Jewish philosophy"] is the narrower category of the kind of thought that involves a disciplined, systematic encounter between Jewish heritage and relevant philosophy."[84] What characterizes the project undertaken here is not just an encounter between Jewish heritage and "relevant philosophy"; nor is it simply an investigation of the thinking that has come from the people of Israel, from the prophet Amos to Amos Oz. Perhaps the best term for what we are doing in this work is *Machshavah Yehudit*—literally, "Jewish thought"—particularly since the word for "thought," *machshavah*, may also mean "troubled mind," something that most post-Holocaust Jewish thinkers have in common.[85] And the root of *Yehudit*, the word for "Jewish," is *hodah*, which means "to offer thanks." It would seem, then, that one defining feature of Jewish thought is that it is a thinking at once troubled and grateful—troubled because of how much is at stake in our thinking, grateful precisely because so much is at stake.

TOWARD AN UNDERSTANDING OF
WHAT MAKES JEWISH THOUGHT JEWISH

If we cannot determine what makes Jewish thought Jewish, then the testimony that makes the Jewish people a people apart will be lost. Since the *Divine* prohibition against murder is at the center of that testimony, it too will be lost. And if the prohibition is lost, then murder is no longer evil; it is merely evil *to me.* The issue before us, then, is a matter not just of life and death but of living and killing. If we are to deal with it in any responsible fashion, then Jewish thought cannot be defined by the accidents of nature attached to the thinker: the fact that a Jew has a thought, in other words, does not make it a Jewish thought. There are *essential* differences between the ideas of Karl Marx and the thinking of Menachem Mendel Schneerson.

One other thing must be made clear: *it is not my contention that Jewish thought is better or more legitimate than non-Jewish thought.* Courageous Christians such as Harry James Cargas, Alice L. Eckhardt and A. Roy Eckhardt, Franklin Littell, John Roth, Didier Pollefeyt, and Juergen Manemann have responded to the Shoah with profound insight, and Jews would do well to listen to them. The Eckhardts' reexamination of the Resurrection[86] and Littell's claim that anti-Semitism is the sin against the Holy Spirit[87] are part of a perfectly legitimate and extremely valuable Christian response to the Shoah. Just as none of them would reject the Christ and yet maintain that his or her response is Christian, we cannot reject the Torah and yet maintain that our response is Jewish. Still, I also maintain that a Jewish thinker can learn a great deal from a Jew who has rejected the Torah; few, for example, have attained a deeper grasp of the

Shoah than Primo Levi, and we must ponder his words as well. Nevertheless, whatever we may learn from Christians, atheists, and other thinkers, Jews in a post-Holocaust world cannot buy in to the ontological speculative tradition that contributed to the Holocaust if they are to continue to live in the truth they have represented since the time of Moses. And the key to the truth of the Jew—the key to the identity of the Jew—is the Torah that the Nazis sought to erase from the face of the earth.

Fackenheim rightly declared that "nothing so powerfully makes a philosopher *Jewish* as 'Torah.'"[88] Because the Divine prohibition against murder is revealed in the Torah that defines Judaism, I take that absolute prohibition to be a cornerstone of Jewish thinking. Because the Torah is written in the holy tongue, I take the Hebrew language to be a key to the categories that shape Jewish thinking. And because that thinking has developed over the centuries in the works of the Jewish sages, I take those texts to be among the defining elements of Jewish thought. This does not mean that Jewish thought, over the centuries, has not been influenced by other ways of thinking; but Jewish thinkers have always grounded their thinking in Torah. Maimonides, for example, may have been influenced by Aristotle, but, contrary to Aristotle, he insisted upon the truth of the creation, not at the hands of the "unmoved mover" but from the mouth of the God of Abraham.[89] Jewish thought, then, is a thinking that on some level takes the teachings and commandments of Torah to be absolute, that incorporates Hebraic categories into its thinking, and that is informed by the *sifrei kodesh*, the texts of the sacred tradition. These parameters are much broader than they may seem at first glance, as the history of Jewish thought has demonstrated. Even if one adheres to them very strictly, there is a great deal of room for argument, and argument is essential to Jewish thinking.

Perhaps the category most crucial to Jewish thought is what in Hebrew is known as the *kadosh,* or the "holy." Contrary to most speculative thinking on the topic, the holy is not an extreme degree of goodness, a moral ideal, or a principle of reason. The verbal root of *kadosh* is *kadash,* which means "to be consecrated," "to be made holy," or "to become holy." It is a word that implies setting something apart and making it distinct from everything else in the world, not as a "special thing" among things in the world but as a vessel of what is beyond the world; the holy, therefore, both exceeds and permeates "all there is." As understood in Jewish thought, then, the category of the holy is alien to Western speculative philosophy. When the speculative thinkers address the topic of the holy, it generally has something to do with some ultimate form of being, supreme in morality or might or beneficence or reason. They often see God as distinct from the holy and do not understand Him to be the Holy One. In the *Euthyphro,* for example, Plato argues that the holy is holy not because god loves it; rather, god loves it because it is holy.[90] Similarly, Kant maintains that god is deduced from morality, not morality from god.[91] While it is true that Jewish philosophy has its "rationalists," such as Saadia Gaon, Bachya ibn Paquda, Maimonides, and Gersonides, it must not be forgotten that no matter how much they were influenced by Greek philosophy, these scholars all adhered to Torah-based thinking about holiness. Indeed, most of them, including Maimonides, were mystics.[92]

Viewing the holy as a *who,* and not as a *what,* Torah-based thinking is as foreign to Western ontological philosophy as it is essential to Jewish thought. Ontological thought, viewing god as a concept or category, necessarily sees god as a *what,* a something that cannot come from nothing. Jewish thought, viewing God as a Divine *Who,* approaches God as a Someone, as the Holy One, who emerges from "nothingness" in a movement of creation that is also a movement of relation: a relation with the human being created in the image and likeness of the Holy *Who.* Whereas ontological thought sees god as a first principle of Being, Jewish thought sees God as the One both beyond Being and in the midst of Being, the Creator—not the cause—of all things. Whereas ontological thought sees the world as a composite of natural phenomena and human events, Jewish thought sees the world as a composite of Divine word and Divine will; here there are no accidents or laws of nature, and human events are an avenue of Divine revelation. Whereas ontological thought sees the human being as an animal among animals in the natural world, Jewish thought sees the human being as an emanation of the Divine Presence, as a "breach of being." Hence the holy is most immediately manifest in the human. Which means: every human being is infinitely precious, regardless of color or culture, age or ability, aesthetics or intelligence, or even moral character.

Because our relation to our fellow human being is essential to our relation to God, Jewish tradition teaches that the Sixth Utterance of God,

"Thou shalt not murder," parallels the First Utterance, "I am God" (see, for example, *Zohar* I, 90a). For Jewish thought, then, the question is not "Why is there something instead of nothing?" but, to paraphrase Levinas, "Do I live by murder?"[93] Indeed, it is a question that is articulated in the two questions put to the first murderer: "Where is your brother?" (Genesis 4:9) and "What have you done?" (Genesis 4:10). Because God is the one who asks, God is the one who determines whether and why it matters as to how we respond. That determination, in turn, lies in the fundamental categories of Jewish thought, such as holiness, Torah, Covenant, commandment, chosenness, Messiah, creation, revelation, and redemption. Because Jewish thinking is shaped by multiple categories, identifying a particular instance of thinking as Jewish or non-Jewish is rather like saying whether it is dark or light: it is a matter more of spectrum than of a yea-or-nay resolution. There is a point, however, where so many of the Jewish premises have been eliminated that a thinker may no longer be recognizable as a Jewish thinker. One cannot have Jewish thought without God and Torah, for instance, any more than one can have Christian thought without Incarnation and Resurrection.

Based on the definition here proposed, then, I do not regard Arendt or Rubenstein as Jewish thinkers, even though they are assuredly Jews and even profound thinkers. Since Maybaum takes the Nazis' assault on rabbinic Judaism to be something desirable, I do not regard him as a Jewish thinker; Maybaum engages in a kind of theodicy, and theodicy is highly problematic for Jewish thought. I do take Greenberg, Berkovits, Levinas, and Fackenheim to be Jewish thinkers, but, as I have indicated, there is room for clarification, elaboration, and even correction in their thinking. To that end, this book will draw heavily not only upon the categories listed above but also upon texts of the sacred tradition, including the mystical tradition, as well as key terms from the Hebrew language. Throughout this volume, I shall pursue the task of defining *Machshavah Yehudit*.

THE APPROACH HERE TAKEN

Steven Katz's nine categories of Jewish response to the Shoah are generally attempts to explain the evil of the Holocaust either in Jewish terms or through a departure from Jewish terms. Here, by contrast, the aim is not so much to explain the evil of what happened as to understand what must happen next. An explanation of evil requires an exercise in theodicy, which, it will be argued, is antithetical to Jewish thought. If explanation is suspect, however, understanding is essential. The distinction between the two, viewed in Hebrew terms, is clear. "To explain," *levaer,* is literally to bring "into the light," *beor.* Yet part of what characterizes the open wounds of Jewish thought is the shadow of Auschwitz that extends over all thinking, despite the *Torah Or,* or the "Light of Torah." Indeed, that darkness is what calls for the Light of Torah; from a Jewish standpoint, the light that might transform darkness into light can come from nowhere else, least of all from modern, ontological, or postmodern thought. And it summons us to understand rather than explain.

The Hebrew word for "understanding" is *binah,* which is a matter not of clarifying a concept but of establishing a relation between God and human, between human and human, for the Hebrew verb for "understand" is *lavin*; its root is *bein,* which means "between." Whereas explanation pertains to what is "clear and distinct" by the "natural light,"[94] in the Shoah we confront an unnatural darkness so that we must reject explanation for the sake of entering into a relation of understanding. As the fifteenth-century sage Don Isaac Abrabanel has pointed out, understanding arises not in isolation but in community,[95] for, unlike explanation, understanding requires a human, dialogical relation; it requires a *between* space. The movement toward the other human being required of understanding is what makes understanding an essential feature of *teshuvah,* the movement of return to Torah, as our sages have taught.[96]

Rabbi Joseph Soloveitchik articulates the difference between explanation and understanding very well: "The 'I' of fate seeks a philosophical explanation of evil and finds not, the 'I' of destiny says: 'I am concerned about evil from a halakhic standpoint, like a person who wishes to know the deed which he shall do; I ask one single question: What must the sufferer do, so that he may live through his suffering?' . . . The fundamental question is: What obligation does suffering impose upon man? This question is greatly beloved by Judaism, and she has placed it at the very center of her world of thought."[97] As a matter of thought, the understanding sought by "the 'I' of destiny" is a matter of what must be done: for *Machshavah Yehudit*, thinking and doing are of a piece, where doing is a caring for the other human being. And caring for the other human being is the obligation that suffering imposes upon me: that obligation is my destiny. Here we recall that the Hebrew word for "destiny" is *yiud*; it is a cognate of *edah,* which means both "testimony" and "community." The "I" of destiny is chosen to engage in a certain testimony for the sake of a community; it applies to every human being, Jewish and non-Jewish. Indeed, as the Chosen People, the Jewish people are chosen to transmit to the world the truth that every human being is chosen for a destiny. In order to meet that destiny, our task is not to explain evil but to do something about it. The task undertaken in this volume is to determine what that doing has to do with a distinctively Jewish thinking in the aftermath of the Shoah.

Because the endeavor to define Jewish thought requires an examination of what has become of thinking, chapter 2 explores the bankruptcy of modern and postmodern thought. It begins by clarifying how Jewish thought regards the nature of thinking itself; it then contrasts that view with the ontological identification of thought with being. In the tension between the two lies the key to what I call "philosophical anti-Semitism." One misunderstanding that has resulted from modern thinking about the Holocaust is that anti-Semitism is a form of racism. Approaching anti-Semitism in philosophical terms, and not as a form of racism or religious prejudice, chapter 2 explains what philosophical anti-Semitism is *anti.* Having made this point, the chapter then discusses the specific challenges that face a distinctively Jewish mode of thought in the post-Holocaust era. Thus the next chapter examines the inadequacy of modern and postmodern thought in their efforts both to prevent and to respond to the Holocaust; the nature of philosophical anti-Semitism; and the difficulties facing Jewish thought in its effort to respond to the catastrophe.

Because a primary difficulty facing Jewish thought lies in its engagement with modern philosophy, chapter 3 examines the contrast between ethical monotheism and Jewish thought. The chapter maintains that the same elements of German Idealism that went into the creation of Auschwitz also produced what is known as "ethical monotheism," and that the liberal Judaism that emerged from the combination of Idealism and Judaism is not only inadequate to respond to the Holocaust but may play into the hands of those who want to see the Jews eliminated through assimilation, if not through extermination. In a word, chapter 3 shows that Judaism is not a form of ethical monotheism, and that ethical monotheism cannot, therefore, be construed as a Jewish response to the Shoah. Thus the tension between Auschwitz and Jerusalem is a tension not just between the site where Jews were murdered and the capital of the Jewish State; it is a tension between Athens and Jerusalem. It is not for nothing that the proponents of ethical monotheism were anti-Zionists. Jewish thought, with the Holy City as its symbolic center, must incorporate the category of holiness into its thinking, a category that is alien to the thinking that produced ethical monotheism. Only with Jerusalem as its "philosophical capital" can there be a future for a distinctively Jewish thought.

What it means to regard the Holy City as a category for Jewish thought having been determined, chapter 4, "The Holocaust and the Holy Tongue," considers ways in which the Hebrew language may inform Jewish thought after Auschwitz. While such a consideration is part of the general approach taken throughout this volume, chapter 4 examines some specific terms relevant to the Holocaust itself. The very word *Shoah*, for example, has as its root the word *shav*, which means "nothingness," suggesting that the Shoah entails the imposition of a radical Nothingness upon the Jewish people. Among other key Hebrew terms to be examined here are *toledot, davar, shtikah, raash, kol, olam, musar, brit, shamam, behalah, galut,* and *geulah*—meaning "history," "word," "silence," "noise," "voice," "world," "ethics," "covenant," "to be desolate," "panic," "exile," and "redemption," respectively. The premise is that, given the Nazi assault on language as a defining feature of the Shoah, part of what is demanded of Jewish thought in the post-Shoah era is to consider how the perennial Jewish language might provide some insight into the assault on the Jewish soul. According to Jewish tradition, the soul is made of that language.[98] If the Nazis set out to destroy souls before they destroyed bodies, one step toward the restoration of the soul is a restoration of the Jewish word to Jewish thought.

Since the holy tongue shapes the thinking we receive from the holy texts, chapter 5, "The *Sifrei Kodesh* and the Holocaust," considers ways in which the sacred texts of the Jewish tradition might be incorporated into a Jewish response to the Shoah, especially with regard to the assault on the meaning and value of human life. If Jewish thought is to be Jewish, it must be informed by the holy texts of the sacred tradition, as Franz Rosenzweig has suggested. "A knowledge of Midrash," he maintains, for instance, "is necessary for the understanding of Jewish thought."[99] And a knowledge of Midrash requires a knowledge of Torah, Talmud, Kabbalah, and other bodies of *sifrei kodesh*. This approach, too, belongs to the method behind the entire volume. The aim of chapter 5 is to explain more fully the role of the Book and the meaning of the "holy" in traditional Jewish thinking; how the holy came under assault in the Shoah; and how the holy books may be incorporated into post-Holocaust Jewish thought. Because holiness most immediately manifests itself through the human being, chapter 5 draws upon the *sifrei kodesh* to examine the assault on the most fundamental origins of the human being: the mother, the father, and the child.

Since the Jewish teaching on the holiness of the human being is so basic to Jewish thought, chapter 6 explores more thoroughly the radical tension between a Jewish view of the human being and what the Nazis made of the human being. Titled "The Muselmann and the Matter of the Human Being," the chapter elucidates the idea of the holy within the human, as taught in the Jewish tradition. Because a defining feature of the Holocaust is an assault on the notion of a human being, Jewish thinking in the post-Holocaust era has to address this issue. Chapter 6, then, addresses a definitive philosophical question that emerges from the Holocaust: what is a human being? Or: what imparts value to the *other* human being? After exploring the Nazis' assault on death itself, the chapter elucidates the singularity of the Muselmann and the death camps' walking dead as a distinctively Nazi creation; it also elaborates on why the Muselmann is emblematic of the Holocaust. To that end, the chapter builds on insights from Primo Levi and on Emil Fackenheim's response to Levi. For example, three key points in Levi's exposition on the Muselmann are the Muselmann's loss of time, his loss of words, and his loss of relation. The chapter's thesis is that only the recovery of a Jewish view of the human being can bring about the recovery of a future not just for Jews but also for humanity *as* humanity.

Since the recovery of a future entails a process of mending, chapter 7, "Jewish Thought and a Post-Holocaust *Tikkun Haolam*," draws upon two major post-Holocaust Jewish thinkers to examine the often used and often misused term *tikkun haolam*. Further developing points raised in previous chapters, chapter 7 examines the Jewish origins of the notion of *tikkun haolam* and how the phrase has been misused; key points in the thinking of Levinas and Fackenheim that may inform Jewish thinking about *tikkun haolam*; and the implications for a continuing development of Jewish thinking about *tikkun haolam*. While the term appears in several talmudic texts, it assumes an even deeper significance in a mystical discourse that articulates a certain way of understanding world and reality, God and humanity, Torah and Covenant. In chapter 7, then, I open up a discussion of Jewish mysticism that is developed more fully in the subsequent chapter. One point to be made here is that there must be a mending of the Jewish concept itself—a *tikkun* of *tikkun*—if there is to be a post-Holocaust future for Jewish thought.

With the mystical aspects of *tikkun* outlined in chapter 7, chapter 8 proceeds to a further exploration of the mystical dimensions of post-Holocaust Jewish thought. What is meant here is not that there are already mystical categories at work in post-Holocaust Jewish thought but that a consideration of this dimension of Jewish thinking might add to our understanding of the Holocaust. Because the mystical teachings run throughout Jewish prayers and practices, a consideration of them is essential to an understanding of what makes Jewish thought Jewish. Key points developed in chapter 8 include the mystical view of God and humanity, the relation between God and evil, and the structure of creation. With this groundwork established, the chapter then examines a mystical response to the Holocaust that comes from the midst of the event itself: it is the *Esh Kodesh (Sacred Fire)* of Rabbi Kalonymos Kalmish Shapira, Rebbe of the Warsaw Ghetto. On the basis of Shapira's text, I consider whether we may be living in an *Olam Shoah,* a World of Shoah, that is made of the shell of Jewish ashes that now cover creation. One crucial concern here is to show that theodicy has no place in post-Holocaust Jewish thought. Another important concern is to consider avenues of return from the *Olam Shoah,* not in a movement backward, to how things were, but in a movement forward, approaching a redemption whose seeds lie in exile itself.

The matter of redemption, then, brings us to chapter 9, "Though the

Messiah May Tarry." After clarifying views of the Messiah in Jewish tradition, chapter 9 examines the Hebrew notion of *emunah*, or "faith," and how waiting for the Messiah entails acting on his behalf; the meaning of *brit*, or "covenant," for a post-Holocaust Jewish thought that awaits the Messiah; ways in which the Infinite is manifest in the messianiac hope; and the meaning of the Messiah for post-Holocaust Jewish thought. One key to the development of these points is the question of how a certain outrage with God or a questioning of God might be part of the messianic enterprise. Another key is a consideration of what all of this means for the possibilities of human care and human dwelling in the world. Indeed, these—outrage and care—are two dimensions of the waiting for the Messiah that is also a doing. Here, too, an examination of mystical concepts and Hebrew terms will be central to the next step for Jewish thought in the aftermath of Auschwitz.

Finally, in chapter 10, "Conclusion: No Closure," we come to the realization that theodicy is not an issue for Jewish thought. For a Jewish response to the Holocaust, the crucial question concerns our relation to Divine sanctification, not the absence of Divine intervention. In order to enter into a process of sanctification, we must enter into the flames of Torah that could not be consumed by the flames of Birkenau. And where Torah is concerned, there is neither conclusion nor closure.

The quote from the Talmud that opens this introductory chapter refers to the tearing of clothing as an act of mourning. In the time of the Shoah, the Jewish people endured such losses—and more—on unprecedented scales, both physically and metaphysically. The mystical tradition teaches that God too has "clothing," or *levushim*: God's clothing consists of thoughts, words, and deeds.[100] Like an invisible man who can be "seen" only when clothed, the hidden God is revealed only when He is veiled— revealed precisely as the Hidden One, revealed through our thoughts, words, and deeds. In the aftermath of Auschwitz, the world has witnessed the tearing of deep wounds, in our deeds as well as in our words. Murder, for example, is now called "martyrdom." Children with stones shield men with guns. Those who seek peace are butchered. And no one knows what to think.

If our words and deeds are in such a state of crisis, so also is our thought.

It, too, has been torn in the wake of the Shoah; it, too, is wounded.[101] This clothing, however, we have torn not in mourning but in submission to the temptation put to the first human being: the temptation to become as God, not only knowing but also devising, and thus perverting, good and evil. Therefore, the god we would become is not, in fact, the God of Torah, who is loving, forgiving, and long-suffering. It is, rather, the ego made into a god, for this "knowledge" of good and evil is *daat,* a word that also means "joining together," so that the "knowledge" of good and evil becomes a confusion of good and evil. This tearing of God's clothing, then, comes in a collapse of good and evil into a sameness. As the great mystic of the sixteenth century, Rabbi Chayyim Vital, has said, "This is the sin that came about through the Tree of Knowledge of Good and Evil: it caused a mixing and confusion [of good and evil] throughout all the worlds" (see Chayyim Vital, *Shaarei Kedushah,* part 1, gate 1). Thus, according to the Gerer Rebbe, Rabbi Yehudah Leib Alter, this "mixing of evil with good" was the meaning of the serpent's temptation that "you will be as God" (Genesis 3:5).[102] And this primordial collapse runs throughout modern and postmodern thinking.

Striving to become as god, we have lost our connection to God. Thus "torn," we are "alone," both of which are meanings of the Hebrew word *badud.* And so, in the tearing of our deeds, words, and thought, we languish in the isolation of an open wound. Locked inside the solitude of our being, we have wounded our soul. Indeed, according to the Jewish mystical tradition, the three levels of the soul[103] that are manifest in this world correspond to these three kinds of "garments": *nefesh* ("soul") corresponds to deeds, *ruach* ("spirit") to words, and *neshamah* ("living soul") to thoughts (see, for example, *Zohar* III, 101a; see also Yaakov Yosef of Polnoe, *Toledot Yaakov Yosef, Bereshit* 5). What this wounding of the human soul and human thought means in the post-Holocaust era for the Jewish people, as well as for humanity, is what we now proceed to explore.

2

The Bankruptcy of Modern
and Postmodern Thought

When Ben Damah, the son of Rabbi Ishmael's sister, asked when
he might study the wisdom of the Greeks, the Rabbi answered,
"Go find a time that is neither day nor night and then learn the
Greek wisdom."—Talmud Bavli, *Menachot* 99b

What does the phrase "bankruptcy of thought" mean? How, indeed, can
thought become "bankrupt"? Thought enters "bankruptcy" when it no
longer operates in the categories that might reveal something about thinking, and, more important, when it is unable to determine the absolute
sanctity of one's fellow human being. It loses its value, in other words,
when it cannot determine that the other person has an absolute value
beyond contingency and context. Once bankrupt, thought can no longer
think that, in any given thought, something more than thought might
be revealed, something that would declare the life of a human being to
be not just valuable or worthy of respect but *holy*. Indeed, once bankrupt, thought cannot see past itself. The Western ontological tradition
has led to just such a bankruptcy of thought.

From the standpoint of Jewish thought, by contrast, there is no thinking without the revelation of something more than thought: the holiness of human life. Indeed, the Chasidic master Nachman of Breslov
taught that deeds of loving kindness are essential to any understanding

that thought might attain.[1] What, then, is the nature of Jewish thinking about thought, as opposed to thought in the Western ontological tradition, and how may it be contrasted with the bankruptcy of modern and postmodern thought?

JEWISH THINKING ABOUT THOUGHT

According to the Greek thinking that gave rise to the speculative tradition, the aim of wisdom is to "know thyself." According to Jewish thinking, as stated by the twelfth-century scholar Bachya ibn Paquda, the aim of wisdom is to "become cognizant of the Creator," who shows Himself in the very phenomenon of thinking (Bachya ibn Paquda, *Chovot Halevavot* 2:5). If Jewish thought is both troubled and steeped in gratitude, as suggested in the previous chapter, it is because the thinking of Another, of One who sanctifies thought itself, overshadows and disturbs human thought. As the disciple of the Baal Shem Tov, Rabbi Yaakov Yosef of Polnoe, states it, "the thought above awakens the thought below."[2] And the Bahir, an ancient mystical text, describes this higher thought as "a king that is needed by all things that were created in the world, both above and below";[3] in his commentary on the Bahir, Aryeh Kaplan adds, "The [Jewish] concept of thought is like that of 'up.'"[4] Jewishly speaking, there is no human thought without this "up," which is a higher "thinking" that situates the life of a human being in a dimension of height.

Emmanuel Levinas alludes to this higher presence when he declares that "the psyche in the soul is the other in me, a malady of identity, both accused and *self*, the same for the other, the same by the other."[5] This other that is the soul is an emanation of the Divine Light who thinks me into being and, in thinking me, commands me to attend to the need of the other human being. Hence one of the expressions for "God" in Hebrew is *Baal Machshavot*, the "Master"—or the "Ground"—"of Thoughts." It is not merely that God knows our innermost thoughts but rather that God is the origin of thinking itself. Thus the formula for the Jewish outlook is not "I think, therefore I am," but rather "God thinks, therefore I am." Which is to say: "I am summoned for the sake of another, therefore I am." If, in the words of Adin Steinsaltz, "the soul of a [person] is the Divine speech that speaks the [person],"[6] then the soul is more than a speech act: it is the manifestation of a creative Divine thought that thinks in the imperative mood: Thou shalt. . . . The thinking soul is made of the Divine imperative.

Created from the "flames" of God's "intellectual fire," as the medieval mystic Solomon ibn Gabirol puts it,[7] the soul thinks under the *chupah*, or "canopy," of Divine thought. A *chupah* is, of course, a wedding canopy. The word suggests a marriage of human and Divine thinking; it suggests that thinking harbors an aspect of prayer,[8] as when a Jew wraps the *tefillin* (phylacteries) around his finger and says, "I betroth myself to You forever; I betroth myself in righteousness and justice, in kindness and in mercy. I betroth myself to You in faithfulness: and you shall know Hashem" (from Hosea 2:21–22). When the Jew then begins the morning prayers, the first words to come from his mouth are: "I take upon myself the commandment *v'ahavta l'reakha kamokha,* 'you shall love your neighbor as yourself'" (Leviticus 19:18). And when, according to Jewish law, is it light enough to lay *tefillin?* When it is light enough to behold the face of your neighbor (R. Solomon, Ganzfried, comp., *Kitsur Shulchan Arukh* 10:2). There is no prayer, no genuine thought, without this orientation toward the other human being, this vision of the face of the other person.

To be sure, a better rendering of *kamokha,* translated from Leviticus as "as yourself," would be found in the phrase "You shall love your neighbor, for loving the other *is* your self": that loving is the *who* that you are in the depths of your being.[9] Therefore, we have the teaching that this love for the other human being is the foundation of Torah (Yaakov Yosef of Polnoe, *Toledot Yaakov Yosef, Korach* 2). Says the Chofetz Chaim, "He who only occupies himself with Torah study and not with kindness is as if he has no God."[10] Where lies the meaning of Torah? Not just in the word or even between the words: it lies in the relation to the other human being. Oriented toward Torah, then, Jewish thought is oriented toward the other human being.

Inasmuch as such thinking about thought takes thought to be a mode of prayer, God is never the object of thought but rather is the thinking subject. This distinctively Jewish view of thought is a theme that runs throughout the work of the distinctively Jewish thinker Abraham Joshua

Heschel. He says, for example, that "God-awareness is not an act of God being known to man; it is an act of man's being known by God. In thinking about Him we are thought by Him."[11] Thus "we approach Him, not by making Him the object of our thinking, but by discovering ourselves as the objects of His thinking."[12] In the words of a *tsadik*, "men believe they pray before God, but this is not so, for the prayer itself is divinity."[13] Which means: if thinking is akin to praying, then there is something *more than* thought that permeates thought, something *more than* all there is. Operating within the category of this *more*, Jewish thought manifests more than ontological thought can accommodate.

Levinas is helpful in this connection: "The Infinite affects thought by devastating it and at the same time calls upon it; in a 'putting it back in its place' it puts thought in place. It awakens it."[14] It sobers it up. And it troubles it. Here we see a deeper implication of the point that *machshavah* means not only "thought" but also "troubled mind." For Jewish thought, the mind is troubled because Another troubles it. It is troubled because a matter of infinite importance is at stake in its thinking; indeed, the word for "important," *chashuv*, is a cognate of *machshavah*. A matter of importance issues from the canopy of thought that commands us to love our neighbor, which is a commandment to be who we are, that is, to be what God creates us to be. It lies in what is more than a thinking that equates itself with being, in what Levinas describes as the "otherwise than being."

What can be more than thinking, stemming from something other than the neutrality of being? It is "rejoicing," or *simchah*, which is an anagram of *machshavah*. Therefore, says the Chasidic master Rabbi Dovid Chernobler, *Machshavah Yehudit* is thought steeped in joy, despite its wounds.[15] Indeed, at times joy can enter only through an open wound. Steeped in joy, Jewish thought is steeped in the Divine Presence, for the Divine Presence (the Shekhinah), says the Talmud, abides neither "in levity nor in vain pursuits, but only in rejoicing" (*Pesachim* 117a). Why? Because, as Nachmanides declares, in rejoicing alone can we get rid of the self.[16] The rejoicing that ignites our thinking, then, is the opposite of enjoyment, which, inasmuch as it is focused on the ego, is thoughtless.[17] Rejoicing comes with the realization of matters of weight: life becomes heavy, as Martin Buber says, "but heavy with meaning."[18] Therefore, like the weighty tablets of Torah that bore Moses down the mountain (*Pirke de Rabbi Eliezer*, 45), thought steeped in joy is *up*lifting.

We lie back and enjoy. But we rise up and rejoice. And here we find a striking contrast between Hebrew and Greek perspectives, between Jewish thought and speculative thought. It is said, for example, that Socrates once stood perfectly still for twenty-four hours as he struggled to work out a philosophical conundrum, so intense was his concentration. Moshe Leib of Sassov, by contrast, once declared, "When someone asks the impossible of me, I know what I must do: I must dance!"[19] For Jewish thought, the dance is a mode of thought, because in the dance the spiritual descends and the physical ascends to arrive at levels of insight otherwise unattainable. That is why the "dance," the *machol*, is a means of praising God (see, for example, Psalms 150:4); and it is a means of "reconciliation" with God, which is another meaning of the root *machal*. Thus Rabbi Barukh, the son of the Great Maggid of Mezeritch, once exclaimed to Rebbe Leib, the Shpole Zeide, "What you achieve by dancing, others do not attain by praying."[20] The image of the leaping Chasid is the opposite, say, of Rodin's *The Thinker*, a figure that is seated, frozen in reflection. The dance is the opposite of that paralysis.[21]

The joy that is more than thought, and that is, as the Chernobler suggests, the essence of Jewish thought, brings us back to the Jewish view of thought as a mode of prayer. Rejoicing thought is an emanation of Hashem; therefore, says the Chasidic master Rabbi Levi Yitzchak of Berditchev, one cannot know "the Light of Hashem" through thought alone, but only through thought that is more than thought: through thought that is steeped in joy and prayer.[22] In thought's ontological mode, there is no room for prayer; who, indeed, among the great speculative thinkers of the last three hundred years is known for his or her treatise on prayer? Like Immanuel Kant, most of them have only contempt for prayer[23] except, perhaps, as a psychological balm for the feebleminded. For an ontological thinker— whether Kant or Descartes, Hegel or Heidegger—prayer cannot be construed as thought. "To the [speculative] thinker," Heschel correctly notes, "God is an object; to the man who prays, He is the subject."[24] Which is to say: the speculative thinker takes himself to be autonomous and generates his own commandments from his own thinking, whereas the Jewish thinker knows himself to be heteronomous and generates his thinking from a Divine commandment. Therefore, from the viewpoint of Jewish thought—and contrary to Descartes—I am not a *res cogitans,* not a "thinking thing."[25] I am, rather, a "thought thing" and therefore a "commanded thing."

This relation between God and thought is not to be confused with the Neo-Platonist view of thought as an emanation of the transcendent logos,[26] or with the Cartesian claim that the concept of the infinite comes from the Infinite One.[27] Understood in terms of the Cartesian concept or in terms of the Greek logos, God is not the Creator of heaven and earth but is, at best, the Supreme Being, the Unmoved Mover, the First Cause, or the First Principle. The Jewish notion of creation, Heschel correctly notes, transcends causality; suggesting the presence of a Creator with whom we have a relation, "it tell us how it comes that there is causality at all."[28] The causal, ontological god of the philosophers, by contrast, is utterly indifferent to the human being and therefore utterly alien to Jewish thought. Such a god, understood as sheer perfection, is in need of nothing: as Aristotle asserts, it neither loves nor is in need of love.[29] Nor does it have a name: we do not cry out, "Father!" to the First Principle. And it does not ask what God asks Adam and each of us: "Where are you?" The logos is not the Creator who summons us to rejoice, who is swayed by prayer, who in His love for us commands us to love others, and so on. In a word, the logos of the philosophers is not a *who* at all.

The first name for God that appears in the Torah, by contrast, is *Elohim,* a name that is a manifestation of the *Who,* as the Zohar explains:

When the most Mysterious wished to reveal Himself, He first produced a single point which was transmuted into a thought, and in this He executed innumerable designs, and engraved innumerable engravings. He further engraved with the sacred and mystic lamp a mystic and most holy design, which was a wondrous edifice issuing from the midst of thought. This is called *Mi,* or "Who," and was the beginning of the edifice, existent and non-existent, deeply buried, unknowable by name. It was only called *Mi.* It desired to become manifest and to be called by name. It therefore clothed itself in a refulgent and precious garment and created *Eleh,* or "These," and *Eleh* acquired a name. The letters of the two words intermingled, forming the complete name *E-l-o-h-i-m* (*Zohar* I, 2a).

As understood by Jewish thought, the very presence of a *Who* in the midst of being is a transcendence of being. The prayer of *mi khamokhah,* "who is like You," which Moses prayed upon crossing the sea (Exodus 15:11), is not just a rhetorical question but also an affirmation: precisely the *Who* is what resembles God. Hence every encounter with a *Who* is an encounter with God.

If thought is to avoid bankruptcy, it must not forget that all thinking is measured in the light of a higher thought. This being measured lies at the core of what it means to be created—and commanded: we are *accountable* for our thoughts. Indeed, a cognate of *machshavah* is *cheshbon,* which means "accounting" or "reckoning," as in the phrase *cheshbon nefesh,* a "reckoning of the soul." There is no *Machshavah Yehudit* without this reckoning before the *Baal Machshavot.* According to Bachya ibn Paquda, that accountability is precisely the light of enlightened thought, "the sun which illuminates the depths of your inner being."[30] Where it is not bankrupt, thinking is an accounting in the light of having been questioned; it is a response in the light of having been implicated by the *Who,* both as God and as neighbor. Hence, Jewishly understood, all thought is dialogical; it unfolds not in the monological solitude of my being but in a movement toward another being, a movement sanctified and commanded by One who is otherwise than being.[31] The modern and postmodern bankruptcy of thought lies in the collapse of this realization and of this responsibility, which is a collapse of the *Who.*

What is the nature of this being commanded that is so central to Jewish thought? It is a state of being connected. Contrary to the Jewish understanding of the *mitzvah,* or "commandment," which Heschel describes as "a prayer in the form of a deed,"[32] both modern and postmodern thought view commandments as orders or rules to follow, and not as "connections," which is the meaning of *tsavta,* the Aramaic root for *mitzvah.* Says Rabbi Chayim ben Attar, "Every *mitzvah* is meant to close a gap that may exist between man and God."[33] The importance of the *mitzvah,* Rabbi Steinsaltz points out, "lies not in its content or efficacy, be it material or spiritual, but in the fact that it constitutes a point of contact with the Divine."[34] Jewishly understood, a commandment is a portal that opens up a pathway to the manifestation of holiness and goodness in the world. Jewishly understood, all thinking constitutes a similar opening, for all thinking transpires in the light of having been chosen *by* the holy *for* the good—transpires, that is, in the light of having been thought.[35]

Says Levinas, the good "is not the object of a choice [in thought], for it has taken possession of the [thinking] subject before the subject had the time—that is, the distance—necessary for choice. There is no subjection more complete than this possession by the Good, this election."[36] And, Jewishly understood, there is no freedom more profound than this subjection. By contrast, and in keeping with the cry of Eliade that "man cannot be free until he kills the last god,"[37] modern thought seeks to escape this subjection in its pursuit of a counterfeit freedom and an illusory autonomy. This is, in the words of the Nazi philosopher Alfred Rosenberg, "freedom in the German sense," a Kantian freedom that "consists of an inner independence."[38] But if such a freedom "is to be the essence of man," as Franz Rosenzweig has rightly pointed out, then "it will pay dearly for such pretensions."[39] The result of this paying dearly has been a bankruptcy of thought that is a bankruptcy of the good, for once the last god has been eliminated, so has the holy that chooses us for the good. Thus, taking ourselves to be unaccountable, we are of no account.

In the nineteenth century, Rabbi Samson Raphael Hirsch commented on this bankruptcy by pointing out, "Men who believed themselves the possessors of the knowledge which the commandments had been designed to teach, thought themselves now absolved from the fulfillment of the commandments."[40] Thus, in the wake of the modern and postmodern denial of the Holy One, we are reduced to the "atheist being" to whom Levinas refers when he says, "Only an atheist being can relate himself to the other and already *absolve himself* from this relation,"[41] for the atheist pretends to rid himself of the *Who*. Indeed, that is precisely the atheist project. Ridding ourselves of the Divine *Who*, we reduced ourselves and others to an *it*. Reduced to an *it*, we are of neutral value and a matter of indifference so that each can be replaced by another, and all are expendable. As the last two hundred years have demonstrated, to think God out of the picture is to think the other human being out of the picture. Ontological philosophy eliminates both God and humanity by situating the *I* at the center of all consciousness and concern, thereby reducing the other to the same, that is, to a moment of *my* experience, and not God's experience of me. We complain about the absence of God, but, as Heschel has noted, "God did not depart of His own volition; He was expelled. *God is in exile*."[42] Concerned solely for itself, the thinking ego has elbowed Him out of the way.

In the Heideggerian *Sein zum Tod*, or "being toward death," for example, the death that concerns me is *my* death.[43] For the Jewish thinker, the death that concerns me is the death of the other human being—the widow, the orphan, and the stranger, who are of no concern to Heidegger. "The fear of God," Levinas puts it, "is concretely my fear for my neighbor."[44] Therefore, he says, "the Divine can be manifest only through my neighbor"[45]—and my neighbor *is* neighbor only through the Divine, for my neighbor is my *neighbor* inasmuch as through him I encounter the Divine commandment to care for him. This concern for the other human being is, in the words of Levinas, "how a thought thinks more than it thinks."[46] It thinks more than it thinks because it thinks in the light of having already been commanded not to murder, both from on high and from the face of the other human being.[47] It thinks more than it thinks because it is not a thought *of something* but a thought *for someone*.[48] Thought becomes bankrupt when it can no longer think for the sake of another. And that comes about when it no longer thinks in the light of the absolute, Divine prohibition against murder. The bankruptcy of thought blinds us to the face and thus leads to the bankruptcy of relation, to the illness of indifference. This indifference toward the other human being is the outcome of the ontological project to "think being" and thus equate being with thinking.

"To think being," says Levinas, "is to think on one's own scale, to coincide with oneself. And the way the ability to say *I* was understood in that adequate knowledge which equaled itself in equaling being, without being able to remain outside that adequate knowledge to weigh it down, was called freedom. But on that royal road as well, [some] philosophers found they had been duped."[49] Rosenzweig's indictment of philosophy's reduction of the world to the "perceiving self"[50] is even stronger: "Corresponding to the Copernican turn of Copernicus which made man a speck of dust in the whole is the Copernican turn of Kant, which, by way of compensation, placed him upon the throne of the world, much more precisely than Kant thought. To that monstrous degradation of man, costing him his humanity, this correction without measure was, likewise, at the cost of his humanity."[51] Refashioning himself after his own image, the human being loses his human image and ultimately dehumanizes the *other* human being, for he loses the holiness that defines the human. Thus we have the bankruptcy of modern thought and the postmodern confusion.

More than postmodern, this bankruptcy of thought is primeval: it is the "confusion," the *bilbul,* that characterizes the confusion of tongues at the Tower of Babel, which is literally the Tower of Confusion. Contrary to the popular misconception, the tale of the Tower of Babel is not intended to explain how the multitude of languages came to be. In his thirteenth-century commentary, the Baal HaTurim says that the confusion was there even when the people "had one language with unique words" (Genesis 11:1), for this phrase means their words were "empty and void."[52] According to the fourteenth-century sage Ovadiah Sforno, the confusion lay in the supposition that the people could "make a name" and therefore generate a meaning from their own autonomous selfhood: they had no knowledge of the Name of the Holy One, from whom all names issue, as it is written in the Zohar.[53] Confusion also lay in the fact that, through building a tower to the heavens, the people thought they could define their own dimension of height.

The Midrash reveals the consequence of this confusion: when a man fell to his death during the construction of the Tower of Babel, no one even noticed; but when a brick was dropped and broken, a great lamentation went up, and the people cried out, "When will another come in its stead?" (See *Pirke de Rabbi Eliezer,* 24.) Hence we have the reading of Genesis 11:7 from the eighteenth-century sage Rabbi Yaakov Culi, who notes that in the phrase *navlah sham sfatam,* "let us confuse their tongues," the word *navlah* (a cognate of *bilbul*) may also be read as *nevelah,* which means "corpse."[54] Read in this way, says Rabbi Culi, the verse means "let us make their speech produce corpses."[55]

And so it has come to pass. As modern and postmodern thought have developed, words have been reduced to culturally fashioned systems of signs and thus torn from any ultimate or absolute meaning that transcends the system. With this tearing of the ultimate from the word there has been a corresponding tearing of sanctity from the human being. The Nazis never spoke of killing people but only of "resettlement," "special treatment," and "processing units." Thus in modern and postmodern times our speech has produced corpses.

THE HORROR OF ONTOLOGICAL THOUGHT

The history of humanity over the past two hundred years has made at least one thing clear: the Enlightenment brought no enlightenment. In a word, the Enlightenment was a lie. The lie was exposed in Auschwitz, where the character Harry Preleshnik, modeled after his author Ka-tzetnik 135633, discovered the corpse of his friend Marcel Safran, a Jew who had been transformed into that distinctively Nazi creation: the Muselmann. "Prone before his eyes," writes Ka-tzetnik, "he saw the value of all humanity's teachings, ethics and beliefs, from the dawn of mankind to this day. . . . He bent down, stretched out his hand and caressed the head of the Twentieth Century."[56] Thus the inmate of Auschwitz finally put his finger—and his hand—on what modern thought has made of the human being. Nor has postmodern thought done any better. Indeed, Gillian Rose has shown that postmodernism, despite its opposition to modern logocentrism, "marshals in the service of its arguments the very methods of [modern] critical reason it finally wishes to abolish."[57] The point at which modernism and postmodernism meet is their shared ontological egocentrism.

One understands why the Talmud warns us to keep our children away from speculative philosophy (*Berakhot* 28b; *Bava Kama* 82b). One also understands why the shift from modern to postmodern thinking is accompanied by a profound sense of horror and desolation. Before the onset of Auschwitz, we see it in the famous dying words of Kurtz in Joseph Conrad's novel *Heart of Darkness*—"The horror! The horror!"—as well as in T. S. Eliot's famous poem "The Waste Land."[58] Recalling that in Hebrew the word for "wasteland," *shemamah,* also means "horror," we realize that the state of desolation in which modern thought finds itself is a state of horror. Reflecting further on this horror that comes with the modern desolation of the soul, Buber writes:

> When man is for once overcome by the horror of alienation and the world
> fills him with anxiety, he looks up and sees a picture. Then he sees that

the I is contained in the world, and that there really is no I, and thus the world cannot harm the I, and he calms down; or he sees that the world is contained in the I, and that there really is no world, and thus the world cannot harm the I, and he calms down. And when man is overcome again by the horror of alienation and the I fills him with anxiety, he looks up and sees a picture; and whichever he sees, it does not matter, either the empty I is stuffed full of world or it is submerged in the flood of the world, and he calms down. But the moment will come, and it is near, when man, overcome by horror, looks up and in a flash sees both pictures at once. And he is seized by a deeper horror.[59]

The time of which Buber speaks, when both the substance of the world and the sanctity of the soul vanish with the erasure of good and evil—the time of the deeper horror—has long been upon us. It is the time of the postmodern pretense that has resulted from the modern presumption.

The desolation and the horror of *shemamah* can be seen in the loss of all value, all substance, all meaning. In such a state, we go "mad," *shimem* in Hebrew, which is a cognate of *shemamah*. Can the megamurderers of the twentieth century—Hitler, Stalin, and Mao, to name a few who took themselves to be autonomous and self-legislating—be called anything else? And what does modern thought have to recommend in the way of something comparable to the Divine, absolute prohibition against megamurder? The horror is that we have lost the prohibition, for the soul cannot live without the Divine prohibition. That is why we are so disturbed.

It is also why Rosenzweig claims that, ultimately, the Western ontological tradition can recommend only suicide, a horrifying conclusion that thinkers such as Søren Kierkegaard and Leo Tolstoy had reached well before Rosenzweig.[60] It is surely why Albert Camus opens *The Myth of Sisyphus* with one of the most famous lines in modern philosophy: "There is but one truly serious philosophical problem, and that is suicide."[61] Having thought God out of the picture, philosophy thinks itself into suicide. But Camus's answer to the problem—the individual's revolt, freedom, and passion—is no answer. Revolt in the name of what? Freedom to do what? A passion ignited by what? No, in the existentialists we have a revolt that is mounted only against the void, a freedom that is free to do *anything* one can will, and a narcissistic passion that is only for the sake of the elusive self, which thought has equated to being and, in so doing, has reduced to nothingness.

Contrary to the themes of suicide that haunt modernity, in Hebrew there is no precise equivalent for the term *suicide*. Although we have the modern Hebrew word *hitratsach,* which, like the Latin-based word *suicide,* means "to murder oneself," this verb does not appear in the holy tongue—that is, the biblical Hebrew—that informs Jewish thought. Nevertheless, there are Hebrew terms for "suicide" that are quite revealing. In the *Kitsur Shulchan Arukh,* for example, the phrase meaning "to commit suicide" is *ibed atsmo*: literally, "to lose oneself" or to lose one's "essence," one's "substance," one's "strength" *(otsem),* the very "bone" of one's being (Ganzfried, comp., *Kitsur Shulchan Arukh,* 201:3). And what is the substance of the human being? It is the soul that emanates from the Divine Being. There is no self-murder because there is no autonomous, independent "self." Another phrase for "suicide" in the *Kitsur Shulchan Arukh* is *ibed atsmo ladaat*: literally, "to lose knowledge of one's essence" (ibid.), as if a person could take his own life only if he had lost all knowledge or understanding of life and of who he is.

This loss of knowledge is the madness of modernity, a madness whereby we begin by killing God, proceed to killing our neighbor, and end with killing ourselves, all in a single movement.[62] And yet this distinctively modern condition is anticipated in the ancient story of Cain, who set out to kill God by killing his brother, and, in killing his brother, killed his very substance and identity, his *otsem.*[63] This single, suicidal movement—in which God, soul, and the other human being are eclipsed by a counterfeit "I"—is rooted in the equation of thought with being.[64] In this movement, Levinas points out, evil is unmasked: it is the ego. "Evil," says Levinas, "claims to be the contemporary, the equal, the twin, of the Good. This is an irrefutable lie, a Luciferian lie. It is the very egoism of the ego that posits itself as its own origin, an uncreated sovereign principle, a prince."[65] Here, the "self" is all—and nothing—so that the madness of modern and postmodern thought has become "the end and the beginning of everything," as even the postmodernist Michel Foucault understood: "Not because it is a promise, as in German lyricism, but because it is the ambiguity of chaos and apocalypse."[66] But it is an apocalypse without redemption. It is the apocalypse of the eclipse, the chaos of collapse; in a word, it is the radical evil that postmodernity cannot recognize because it does not have the categories.

Hannah Arendt maintains that "it is inherent in our entire philosophical tradition that we cannot conceive of a 'radical evil.'" Unable to accommodate the Nazi evil, as well as other evils in our time, writes Arendt, all we can say is that "radical evil has emerged in connection with a system in which all men have become equally superfluous."[67] Nothing could better describe the postmodernist thinking that has emerged from modern ontological thought. To be sure, Arendt opens our eyes not just to the failure or inadequacy of modern and postmodern thought; wittingly or not, she leads us to the realization of a certain evil about such thinking. It is what Levinas has called a "philosophy of injustice."[68] And yet *injustice* seems to be an inadequate term for a way of thinking "in which all men have become equally superfluous." Injustice is evil, yes. But from the standpoint of ontological thought, the term *evil* is unintelligible except as a social norm or cultural convention. Justice has become what Thrasymachus declared it to be in Plato's *Republic,* "nothing else than the advantage of the stronger."[69] In many "intellectual" circles, the corollary to this axiom is now a self-evident platitude: power is the only reality, and the will to power is the only justification. Hence weakness is the only sin. Which means: the oppressor can never be in the wrong.

Here, a passage from Levinas referred to in the previous chapter is worth quoting at greater length: "Heideggerian philosophy," where the modern and the postmodern meet, "precisely marks the apogee of a thought in which the finite does not refer to the infinite (prolonging certain tendencies of Kantian philosophy: the separation between understanding and reason, diverse themes of transcendental dialectics), in which every deficiency is but weakness and every fault committed against oneself—the outcome of a long tradition of pride, heroism, domination, and cruelty. Heideggerian ontology subordinated the relation with the other to the relation with the neuter, Being, and it thus continues to exalt the will to power, whose legitimacy the other alone can unsettle, troubling good conscience."[70] To posit this troubling of good conscience is already to take a religious stance, and that is just what Heidegger sought to overcome.

In 1922, the Nazi thinker proclaimed that what attracted him to philosophy was "the full-blown antireligious attitude of the German *Geist* ripened from German Idealism."[71] And in the *Introduction to Metaphysics* he maintains that "it was not German Idealism that collapsed; it was the era that was not strong enough to match the stature, the breadth, and the originality of that spiritual world."[72] In the Nazis Heidegger saw the strength necessary to match the stature, the breadth, and the originality of the original idea. Thus, as rector of the University of Freiburg, he wholeheartedly embraced National Socialism. In his infamous Rectorial Address, delivered on May 27, 1933, at the University of Freiburg, he extolled the "magnificence and greatness" of Nazism[73] and declared that "all abilities of will and thought, all strengths of the heart, and all capabilities of the body must unfold *through* battle, heightened *in* battle, and presented *as* battle"[74]—where any contemporary German listener would immediately associate the word *battle,* or *Kampf,* with *Mein Kampf,* the "sacred text" that provided the ideological warrant for the Nazi genocide.

But how, exactly, does the antireligious stance "ripen" from German Idealism? It begins with Kant.[75] Paul Gruyer has rightly said (but perhaps without realizing the ramifications of what he was saying) that "at the philosophical level of the transformation of the Western concept of a human being from a mere spectator of the natural world and a mere subject in the moral world to an active agent in the creation of both, no one played a larger role than Immanuel Kant."[76] Once the human being is the "active agent" in the creation of nature and morality, God becomes superfluous, as Kant himself understood: "All that does depend upon the direct will of God," he writes in his *Universal Natural History,* "is the creation of matter."[77] Contrary to being defined by the Divine commandment, the human being is "determinable," says Kant, "only by laws which he gives to himself through reason."[78] Thus Kant's rationalist theology opposes revealed religion. God becomes meaningless not only as Lawgiver and Redeemer but also as Teacher and Father. Losing the fatherhood of God, we lose the brotherhood of humanity: once God is superfluous, so is every human being equally superfluous.

Like Kant, Hegel was a rationalist who associated freedom with human autonomy.[79] Although, unlike Kant, he viewed revealed religion as the highest form of consciousness, he maintained that revealed religion is superseded by the absolute knowledge of reason.[80] Thus Hegel denied the otherness of the divinity, so that, as Fackenheim explains, "divinity comes to dwell, as it were, in the same inner space as the human self."[81] The perceiving self that had appropriated the world now appropriates God, both as creator and as destroyer. The "life of the Spirit," says Hegel, "is not the life that shrinks from death and keeps itself untouched by devastation, but rather the life that endures it and maintains itself in it."[82] Thus the stage for totalitarian devastation is set.

With the Neo-Hegelian Ludwig Feuerbach, God is reduced to nothing more than a projection of one's own psyche.[83] Under the influence of Feuerbach, Bruno Bauer issues a "moral demand for the Jew's voluntary self-dissolution," which in turn becomes the " 'moral' right to exterminate him."[84] Joseph Soloveitchik rightly observes that the path of development here is one on which the philosopher sees God as no more than "an infinite ideal to which he aspires. His philosophical religiosity is anthropocentric and anthropocratic. The point of departure is not God but the universal experience (of Him), which is considered creative, redeeming, and inspiring—the maximum bonum of mental life. He is absorbed in his own self rather than in a transcendent God."[85] Hegel's "spirit" is now a synonym for "self." Inasmuch as I am absorbed in this "spirit," the other human being does not summon my responsibility but rather threatens my freedom. With the advent of Nietzsche, then, God is what one aspires to become in a self-apotheosis into the *Übermensch*,[86] and other human beings are mere *Untermenschen*.

While this is admittedly a simplification, it is not an oversimplification. History has demonstrated that, as thinking is identified with being, the divinity is internalized and finally replaced, in Fackenheim's words, "by a humanity potentially infinite in its modern 'freedom.'"[87] Because it is infinite, "modern freedom" eliminates the Infinite One so that human beings may do whatever they have the will to do. Indeed, they are justified by will alone. Thus the God of Abraham is dead, as Nietzsche declared.[88] Here, Edith Wyschogrod reveals a telling connection between Hegel and Nietzsche, despite all their differences: "The intellectual implications of Hegel's radical vision [of the internalized God] are first realized in Nietzsche's depiction of the madman who not only declares the death of God, but makes the equally important and unthinkable claim that man is the killer."[89] "Man," here, is first the modern, enlightened man, who engineers the killing of God, only to shrink in terror at the abyss that remains;

later he is the postmodern man, who glorifies and wallows in the nothingness that yawns upon the elimination of absolutes, for that abyss is the abyss of postmodern freedom,[90] beyond any law, resolute and decisive. It is the abyss of our own nothingness, when we understand our being—and our thinking—in terms of the will to power.

"The expression 'will to power,'" says Heidegger, "designates the basic character of beings; any being which is, insofar as it is, is will to power. The expression stipulates the character that beings have as beings."[91] Just as Nietzsche's will to power defines the *character* of beings, so does Heidegger's resolve define the *authenticity* of beings. "Dasein *is its own self,*" Heidegger maintains, "in the original isolation of silent resolve,"[92] for resolve is the height of autonomy and freedom. Here, as Hans Jonas points out, "decision in itself is the greatest virtue. . . . [Heidegger] identified the decisiveness (of the Führer and the Party) with the principle of decisiveness and resoluteness as such. When I realized, appalled, this was not only Heidegger's personal error but also somehow set up in his thinking, the questionability of existentialism as such became apparent to me: namely, the nihilistic element that lies in it."[93] In its Heideggerian form, existentialism means that what is mine is mine by virtue of my resolve. It means that what is mine is mine, and, if I have the will, what is yours is mine, which, says the Talmud, is a manifestation of evil (see *Pirke Avot* 5:10). It is the Nazi evil. It is the Heideggerian evil. It is the postmodern evil.

One of the central features of the Heideggerian thinking that characterizes both Nazi ideology and postmodern thought is the elimination of the other human being from its concern. "Das Dasein existiert umwillen seiner," Heidegger declares: "*Dasein* exists for the sake of itself."[94] As Jacques Taminiaux points out, this means "that Dasein is always engaged in the care of itself, and of itself alone, and that Dasein wills itself alone."[95] The ethical concern for the other human being—any concern for the other human being as a being who is infinitely dear—becomes not only superfluous but harmful. Says Heidegger, "If one takes the expression 'concern' . . . in the sense of an ethical and ideological evaluation of 'human life' rather than as the designation of the structural unity of the inherently finite transcendence of *Dasein,* then everything falls into confusion and no comprehension of the problematic which guides the analytic of *Dasein* is possible."[96] The "ethical . . . evaluation of 'human life'" requires a capacity for having one's thinking disturbed by a concern for another, a capacity for hearing the cry of the victim. But, as John Caputo has shown, the victim is a matter of indifference for Heideggerian thought.[97] And Wyschogrod has correctly noted that anything involving a caring human relation, such as love or friendship, "plays no part in Heidegger's analysis."[98] Therefore, Heidegger's concern over falling into confusion is an expression of what is itself the modern and postmodern confusion.

This concern, a concern for thought, is the opposite of the human concern. It is once again the confusion—and the horror—of Babel, in which the value of the other human being is lost. It is the loss of what Buber calls the "You." If, as Buber says, "only as the You becomes present does presence come into being,"[99] then the postmodern project has resulted in a radical erasure of presence, both human and Divine. This undoing of the You is the outcome of the undoing of the Holy One, a point that becomes clear when we note the Zohar's interpretation of *Bereshit bara Elohim et-ha . . .* , the opening line of the Torah. Instead of reading it as "In the beginning God created the . . . ," the Zohar reads it as "In the beginning God created the *alef, tav, hey* of *atah*: You." Says the Zohar, "The word *et* consists of the letters *alef* and *tav*, which include between them all the letters, as being the first and last of the alphabet. Afterwards *hey* was added, so that all the letters should be attached to *hey*, and this gave the name *atah* (You)" (*Zohar* I, 15b). Losing the human You, we lose the Divine You; losing the Divine You, we lose the human You, for "in every You," as Buber has said, "we address the eternal You."[100] In the postmodern abyss of freedom, there is no one to address other than the "Same" or the self, which, in the words of Heschel, is a self-deception.[101] And, like Narcissus, we languish before the illusion.

Thus with the postmodern elimination of absolutes comes the elimination of presence, the elimination of God as *Hamakom,* the One who is present here and now, in this place. And where is God most radically absent? In Auschwitz: Auschwitz is where the modern and the postmodern meet. It is where we hit bottom, without even knowing it, for once we hit bottom, we no longer have the capacity to realize what has taken place. Recall, in this connection, an insight from Levinas: "The contemporary world, scientific, technical, and sensualist, sees itself without exit—that is, without God—not because everything there is permitted and, by way of technology, possible, but because everything there is equal. . . . Everything is absorbed, sucked down and walled up in the Same."[102] Auschwitz is precisely the manifestation of the Same, a realm in which there are neither madmen nor criminals, as Primo Levi has said,[103] a place where the distinction between the living and the dead has collapsed, a nonplace that is the opposite of *Hamakom,* the One who is called "the Place." Such a realm, Rabbi Steinsaltz reminds us, is the "world of *tohu,*" of the chaos and the void overcome by creation, "a world where nothing is delineated."[104] And who is most radically sucked down and walled up in this nonplace, this anticreation? The Jew.

PHILOSOPHICAL ANTI-SEMITISM

Just as Christianity has been theologically anti-Semitic, so is modern thought, as well as its postmodern outgrowth, philosophically anti-Judaic if not anti-Semitic. Inasmuch as Jewish thought has been influenced by modern thought, part of the crisis facing post-Holocaust Jewish thought lies in its having been infected by implicitly anti-Judaic thinking, which is manifested not so much as Jew hatred as in the categories of ontological thought itself. In order to clarify some of the challenges facing post-Holocaust Jewish thought, then, we must first consider the nature of this anti-Judaic thinking.

Rabbi Jonathan Sacks exposes a good deal of what characterizes modern thought and its philosophical anti-Judaism, which at times is sheer anti-Semitism, when he observes that

almost all the great continental philosophers of the eighteenth and nineteenth centuries—Voltaire, Kant, Hegel, Schopenhauer and Nietzsche— delivered sharp attacks on Judaism as an anachronism. Voltaire described it as a "detestable superstition." Kant called for its euthanasia. Hegel took Judaism as his model of a slave morality. Nietzsche fulminated against it as the "falsification" of all natural values. . . . Martin Heidegger, the greatest German philosopher of his time, became an active Nazi. Modern Western philosophy, promising a new era of tolerance, manifestly failed to extend that tolerance to Judaism and the Jews. Against this background, the transition from Enlightenment to Holocaust is less paradoxical than it might otherwise seem.[105]

Indeed, there is nothing paradoxical about it.

Modern thought has made God irrelevant by situating the thinking ego at the center of being. This movement alone is enough to make modern thought anti-Semitic. It is not for nothing that we have come to preach tolerance for everything except biblically based religion, beginning with Judaism. As Berel Lang has pointed out, "there are few figures of the Enlightenment in fact who in their common defense of toleration do not qualify that principle where the Jews are concerned. This fact alone would be significant for assessing the Enlightenment in relation to its ideals; it becomes still more significant in the light of evidence that this attitude toward the Jews was not accidental or simply the recrudescence of earlier prejudices, but was engendered by the doctrines of the Enlightenment itself."[106] And he explains: "The Enlightenment provided a 'justification' for anti-Semitism that went well beyond the rejection of Christianity as such, a justification based on the principle that motivated the Enlightenment reaction against the unenlightened past as a whole: that with the possibility of freedom and equality that was now open to [the Jews], all citizens of the new regime had an obligation to commit themselves to those ideals by renouncing the differences that had characterized (whether as cause or effect) their previous tutelage."[107] Here, too, the Jews, like everything else in ego-centered thinking, were to be "absorbed, sucked down and walled up in the Same," to cite once again the words of Levinas. To be sure, that was the meaning of Clermont de Tonnerre's famous assertion before the Assembly of the French Revolution: "To the Jews everything as individuals but nothing as a people." Bottom line: assimilate or die.

The philosophical anti-Semitism spawned in the Enlightenment has its roots in earlier philosophical projects that have characterized Western ontological thought. Jean-François Lyotard has rightly pointed out, for example, that the Jews were murdered in Auschwitz not because of their race but because of their constant reminder to Western thought of its miserable failure in the effort to deny human dependence on the Holy

One. "'The jews,'" as he puts it, are for this reason "the irremissible in the West's movement of remission and pardon. They are what cannot be domesticated in the obsession to dominate."[108] And if they cannot be domesticated, they must be annihilated. Thus Lyotard outlines the history of anti-Semitism: "One converts the Jews in the Middle Ages, they resist by mental restriction. One expels them during the classical age, they return. One integrates them in the modern era, they persist in their difference. One exterminates them in the twentieth century"[109]—which is the final, postmodern solution to the Jewish Question.

Ever since the Enlightenment, as Fackenheim has said, "the denial of the living God was an essential aspect of man's scientific and moral self-emancipation. If man was to be fully free in his world, God had to be expelled from it. . . . The living God had to become a mere 'Deity,' a 'Cosmic Principle'—remote, indifferent, and mute."[110] And: "The moment the living God became questionable, Jewish existence became questionable."[111] Why? Because the essence of Jewish existence, like the essence of Jewish thought, lies in the living presence of the Divine, which is manifest in Torah, Covenant, Hebrew prayers, Sabbath observance, and so on. Without God, such things are empty, and if such things are empty, Jewish life is meaningless.

The living God, moreover, became questionable as soon as the revealed Word became questionable; with the advent of the Enlightenment, both came under assault. As Rabbi Sacks has rightly understood, "the assault on the Word could not but be an assault on the Jewish God. Nor can we escape reflection on the fact that within a century, the culture which had reduced the book of the Covenant to fragments had reduced a third of the people of the Covenant to ashes."[112] In those ashes we have the most radical deconstruction of the Word. Indeed, according to Jewish teaching, the Jew is made of the Word—is made of Torah—body and soul,[113] and the talmudic sages refer to the soul as a *Sefer Torah*, or a "Torah scroll" (*Yoma* 85a). Thus what began as a philosophical assault on Torah led to the ideological assault not just on the body of Israel but on the very soul of the Jew: pursuing this logic to the end, the Nazis *had* to kill Jewish souls before they killed Jewish bodies. It was the only way they could be philosophically consistent.

Inasmuch as Jewish thought is rooted in the Word—that is, in the

Torah—it affirms the human heteronomy that lies in the human dependence on the Holy One. In its modern contexts, then, as Henri Crétella correctly says, "the adjective *Jewish* does not designate an ethnic group. On the contrary, it signifies that there is no true humanity without being related to divinity—as the Jews have shown us. In other words, it is not blood and soil which properly define us, but rather the possibility of emancipating ourselves from this very blood and soil."[114] Taking the Divine spark within every human to be derived from one God, Judaism represents a view of God, world, and humanity that is diametrically opposed to the Nazi *Weltanschauung,* which shares elements of the modern as well as the postmodern worldview. Hence the Nazi economist Peter Heinz Seraphim insisted that National Socialism was based on much more than prejudice or racial hatred; the racial foundations, he maintained, were rooted in an all-encompassing philosophical outlook, not in ethnic or religious difference.[115] Which is to say: the Jew is not the "other"; the Jew is the "evil": the Jew represents the ultimate threat to modern autonomous freedom, insisting as he does that freedom lies not in autonomous reason and resolve but in heteronomous adherence to Torah (see, for example, *Avot* 6:2). To be sure, either the Jew is evil or modern thought is evil—and those who have the will and the power to act upon the philosophical implication will do so.

Hence, as Fackenheim has argued, the Nazis were not anti-Semitic because they were racists. It is just the reverse: they were racists because they were anti-Semitic.[116] The Jewish teaching concerning the human being is, first, that each one is created in the image and likeness of the Holy One; second, that each one has his or her origin in a single one, in Adam; and, third, that each is bound to the other through blood and through a common tie to God. Nothing could be more opposed to Nazi ideology or to Western philosophy. The Nazis were anti-Semitic for the same reason that Western ontological thought is anti-Semitic. Who among modern and postmodern thinkers can affirm that the Holy One creates every human being in the image of holiness? Who among them can declare that each of us is tied to all through a transcendent tie to the Creator of all human beings? Who among them can insist, with the Jew, that this interweaving of human and divine relation into a single relation is *the truth*? And so we see what the anti-Semite is against.[117]

It has been argued that Western ontological thought, both in its modern and in its postmodern modes, is distinguished by the thinking ego's appropriation of God, world, and the other human being. It is what Levinas describes above as being "absorbed, sucked down and walled up in the Same." The anti-Semitism that is a necessary part of such thinking is a walling up of the one who declares the ontological walling up of the other person to be evil: it is the walling up of the Jew. Hence, in the words of Levinas, "the anti-Semitic remark is like no other. Is it therefore an insult like other insults? It is an exterminating word, through which the Good that glorifies Being sees itself brought to unreality and shrivels up in the deepest recesses of a subjectivity."[118] Which is to say: the Jew who attests to the glory of the Holy One is interred in the Same. Anti-Semitism, therefore, has nothing to do with biology, as Levinas correctly points out; "anti-Semitism," he says, "is the archetype of internment."[119] This internment, of course, finds its extreme and most logical manifestation in the extermination camp, where the Jew has been removed from the world and relegated to the antiworld—*not as a form of punishment,* as Primo Levi realized,[120] but as a burial of the Jew in the abyss of nonbeing, which is the abyss of the Same.

The internment of the Jew persists even within the walls of the camp itself: in the camp, says Levi, every Jew was "desperately and ferociously alone."[121] This condition of utter isolation manifests itself—from Nazi legislation to the ghetto to the camp—as a refusal of sustenance, of bread and hospitality, a refusal of a place to dwell. Indeed, the Talmud teaches that three things deprive a man of his senses and of the knowledge of his Creator: idolaters, an evil spirit, and oppressive poverty (*Eruvin* 41b). All three went into the Nazis' internment of the Jew in the time of the Shoah. The "evil spirit," says Fackenheim, was the "all-too-spiritual anti-Spirit that affirmed the modern identity of the divine nature and the human in an unprecedented, enthusiastic, self-sacrificing celebration of hatred, degradation, and murder."[122] And, as he has pointed out, the idolaters were the children of the Enlightenment.[123] Bringing to bear all the evil of their idolatry, the Nazis imposed upon the Jews not just an oppressive poverty but a murderous deprivation of everything, down to the hair on their heads.

This walling up of the Jew in the nothingness of the Same is a consumption, in which the Jew is consumed in flames and as raw material, transformed into soap, fertilizer, and lamp shades. And it is an internment without refuge. "I spend every night there—every night!" Fania Fénelon cries out.[124] "I am still totally immersed in the nightmare of yesterday," declares Bertha Ferderber-Salz.[125] And Charlotte Delbo, who is not Jewish but who articulates with terrifying eloquence the Jewish condition, nears the end of her memoir only to lament, "We have lost our memory. None of us will return."[126] The question that remains is: Can Jewish thought think its way out of this internment? Can Jewish thought return from the concentrationary universe, in a movement that is truly a *teshuvah*? Or shall it mimic the shibboleths of its oppressors?

THE CHALLENGES FACING JEWISH THOUGHT

Michael Morgan identifies three challenges that confront post-Holocaust Jewish thinkers: "(1) to encounter the death camps and the destruction of European Jewry honestly and seriously; (2) to oppose unconditionally the evil and negativity of that event and all the evil it represents; and (3) to go on as a Jew, to continue to live Jewishly in the contemporary world."[127] Each of these challenges is tied to the others. A Jew cannot encounter the death camps seriously without opposing the evil they represent; and a Jew cannot oppose that evil *as evil* without living—and thinking—Jewishly.

What we shall do throughout this volume that Morgan does not do, however, is to address exactly what it means not only to live Jewishly but also to *think* Jewishly. The chief difficulty facing post-Holocaust Jewish thought is to refuse to think in the same categories that led to the attempted extermination of the Jewish people. In keeping with the project to collapse everything into a sameness, modern and postmodern thought would make not only Jewish existence but also Jewish thought merely incidental or accidental, and not particularly distinctive. But if Jewish thought is merely accidental—if any Jew who has a thought, from Rabbi Akiva to Karl Marx, from Sigmund Freud to the Lubavitcher Rebbe, is a Jewish thinker—then being Jewish becomes accidental. And if it is accidental, then it is incidental. Which is to say: the designation of thinking as Jewish is meaningless. And that means: the designation of a life as Jewish is meaningless. What we face now more than ever is the pressure to assimilate not only culturally but also philosophically: having been pressured to think in modern terms, we are now pressured to think in postmodern terms. The postmodernist would have us let go of this business about being a people apart, having a Jewish State, adhering to the covenantal commandments, and so on. We must be "the same as everyone else," citizens of the global village. In short, we must disappear.

Fackenheim has correctly pointed out that the impetus to collapse Jewishness into a being the same as "everyone else" is itself a form of anti-Semitism.[128] And in their desperation to fit in, no matter what the current intellectual fashion or fad, Jews are often duped into becoming unwitting accomplices to the anti-Semitism of postmodernism. In the contexts of modern and postmodern nihilism, says Eugene Borowitz, "the old hope of serious values without commitment to God is increasingly untenable. . . . Yet the primary model most people use in their thinking remains the Cartesian one of the detached self seeking truth without preconceptions or commitments. This has particular appeal to Jews since it immediately releases them from Jewish attachment in accordance with the social pressures on any minority to assimilate to the majority."[129] The temptation to assimilate, of course, lies not only in the social status of the Jew but also in the philosophical and religious status of the Jew. Since the Holocaust was the extreme manifestation of a certain way of thinking, Jews must refuse not only the social pressure to fit in but also the philosophical pressure to accommodate their thinking to modern and postmodern categories.

The situation we face is very much like the one Rabbi Akiva describes in the Talmud by means of a parable. A fox, he related, once went for a walk along a riverbank. Suddenly he came upon a school of fish that were frantically trying to get away from something.

"What are you fleeing from?" the fox asked them.

"We are fleeing from the nets that the fishermen have cast into the river," they answered.

"Why don't you come up onto the land?" the fox suggested. "You can live with me and follow my ways. You will be safe."

Said the fish to the fox, "If we are threatened in the water, which sustains our lives, how much more so would we be threatened on the land, where we would surely perish!"

So it is with the Jews, said Rabbi Akiva: if there is danger in our devotion to Torah, the very substance of our lives, how much more danger is there in the abandonment of Torah? Where, then, would we turn when evil is upon us (see *Berakhot* 61b)? Still, many are tempted to assimilate and follow the ways of the fox.

One place where the temptation to assimilate in thought can be seen is in the rise of liberal Judaism in the nineteenth century, a rise that continues into our own time (we shall take a detailed look at this phenomenon in the next chapter). And one of the key categories in liberal Judaism is the Kantian category of autonomy. But "autonomy," says Fackenheim, "if carried to its logical conclusion, once made the central concept of liberal Judaism, must necessarily destroy Judaism."[130] Why? Because only "the God of traditional Judaism can be present *to* man. If man is autonomous then God can be present only *in* man, as 'conscience' or 'insight' or 'creative genius.' But to accept this is in the end to fall prey to idolatry."[131] Idolatry, too, is a challenge facing post-Holocaust Jewish thought. Here, too, we have the confusion of Babel, for atop the tower, the Midrash tells us, there was to be an idol with a sword in his hand to wage war with God (*Bereshit Rabbah* 38:6). Just so, modern thought wages war with God. Once we fall prey to this idolatry, we fall prey to the thinking that led to Auschwitz, which, in Fackenheim's words, is "*the* modern idolatry because, being unsurpassable, it reveals all that idolatry can be in the modern world."[132] And idolatry is chief among the three sins we must refuse, even on pain of death, in the act of martyrdom known as *Kiddush Hashem*.[133]

We must cross a bridge, therefore, that leads from the extermination of the Jewish people to a future for the Jewish people, from modern and postmodern thought to Jewish thought. And we must keep in mind what is written in the Talmud: "When do human beings come under the judgment? Said Resh Lakish: When they pass over a bridge" (*Shabbat* 32a). Jewish thought is faced not just with the task of responding to the Shoah but also with the task of testimony, with a *Kiddush Hashem*. But in the post-Holocaust crisis of Jewish thought, the call to a *Kiddush Hashem* must be understood as Rabbi Yitzhak Nissenbaum of Warsaw understood it: the "Sanctification of the Name," usually understood in terms of dying as Jews, now means doing everything possible to *live as Jews*.[134] Jewishly understood, living as Jews in the post-Holocaust era—in the age of the hegemony of postmodern thought—is itself a kind of martyrdom, for postmodern thinkers are no less hostile toward the absolutes of Torah than were their modern predecessors.

Here, we recall a Jewish thinker's reply to Camus's assertion that the one truly serious philosophical problem is suicide: the one truly serious philosophical issue, says Heschel, is martyrdom.[135] André Neher explains: *Kiddush Hashem* "is the negation of the absurd. Everything receives a meaning through the ultimate testimony of the man who accepts that meaning to the very limit. Everything is oriented in relation to that testimony. Everything becomes *sanctified* through it. Jewish tradition calls the *sanctification of God* martyrdom, which has found its first historical examples in the *lives* of the prophets"—and not in the ruminations of the philosophers.[136] Jewish thought is faced with the challenge of finding expression in Jewish life; just as there can be no prayer without deeds, no Torah without observance, so can there be no thinking without living—*as Jews*.

Addressing the difficulty facing Jewish thinkers in the post-Shoah age, Fackenheim writes, "Either the whole, long history of Jewish faith—one of no mere theoretical affirmations but of untold devotion, sacrifice, and martyrdom—rests, in the end, on a fundamental and tragic mistake or else there is a need for a radical turning—a turning to the ancient God in the very midst of modernity."[137] Here we have the meaning of the word *teshuvah,* a word often mistranslated as "repentance" (which in Hebrew is *charatah*): *teshuvah* actually means "return" as well as "response." So essential is *teshuvah*, not only to human life but also to all the rest of creation, that, according to the Talmud, it is among the seven things that preceded the creation (*Pesachim* 54a).[138] This return to the ancient God is a return to Torah and to the community of Israel, since, in the words of the Koretzer Rebbe, "God and Torah are one. God, Israel, and Torah are one."[139] It is a return to the *mitzvah,* not as a "good deed" but as a Divine commandment, for the ancient God dwells precisely in the *mitzvah*: it is a vessel of holiness, a portal through which the Holy One enters the world.[140] It is, in the words of the thirteenth-century mystic Rabbi Joseph Gikatilla, the return of the soul *(nefesh)* to "the place from which it has been uprooted."[141] Therefore, said Nachman of Breslov, a human being, prior to making *teshuvah*, has only a counterfeit existence, an existence that allows no room for holiness, hence no room for reality.[142]

Further, just as Jewish thought—*Machshavah Yehudit*—is steeped in thanksgiving, so, say the rabbis, is *teshuvah* wrapped in gratitude (see, for example, *Orchot Tsaddikim*, gate 26). It is gratitude in the midst of disturbance, gratitude for the disturbance itself. "Modern Jewish consciousness has become troubled," Levinas realizes. "It does not doubt its destiny but cannot calmly be witness to the outrages overwhelming it. It has an almost instinctive nostalgia for the first, limpid sources of its inspiration. It must once again draw its courage from that inspiration and again rediscover in it the certitude of its worth, its dignity, its mission."[143] "Rediscover" means *teshuvah*; according the Chasidic master Elimelekh of Lizensk, it is the one means we have of preventing the loss of memory.[144] The outrages overwhelming Jewish thought include the postmodern thinking that would have the Jews either forget or "deconstruct" the sources of Jewish thought and thus render *teshuvah* meaningless. Postmodernism overwhelms the Jewish thinker not only with this outrage but also with the temptation to forget what makes Jewish thought Jewish and the Jewish thinker a Jew. In this matter postmodernism is not only canny—it is foxy.

Here, we recognize a very important feature of the devastation of egocentric thinking that belongs to modern and postmodern thought: it is lapse of memory, for nothing gets in the way of memory more than the ego. Therefore, we must *hizkir*, or "offer up" the ego "in sacrifice" if we are to *zakhar*, "remember." Which means: the soul must return to the memory of God that is its essence. Earlier we cited a line from Charlotte Delbo's *None of Us Will Return*: "We have lost our memory. None of us will return." And so we understand what Judaism has always taught, namely, that memory is central to *teshuvah*. Memory of what? Not just of what happened. More than that, the memory at the core of *teshuvah* is a memory of why it matters. It is the memory of God, Torah, and Covenant, if only to engage God in an argument: how, indeed, shall we confront God with our argument and outcry, if we know nothing of His teaching? How can we accuse Him of abandoning the Covenant if we have done the same? And if we forget the teachings and the testimony of the sacred tradition, we shall forget both the means and the grounds for arguing with God. That is why the sages teach that memory is essential to the very existence of the world (see, for example, *Orchot Tsadikim,* gate 19): there are times when, unless we draw upon Torah and Covenant to oppose the Creator, creation will revert to nothingness, for, as Elie Wiesel has rightly said, there are times "when only those who do believe in God will cry out to him in wrath and anguish."[145] Without the Covenant, we forget how to cry out. Without the Torah, we forget why.

God, Torah, and Covenant, for a Jew, are most fundamentally remembered in the remembrance of the Sabbath, where the commandment first to remember (Exodus 20:8) and then to observe (Deuteronomy 5:12) is actually a single commandment: *zakhor veshamor bedibur echad,* "remember and observe—remember and watch over—were given in a single word" (*Rosh Hashanah* 27a). According to the Midrash, the observance of this commandment is equivalent to the observance of all the commandments (*Shemot Rabbah* 25:12; see also *Zohar* II, 47a). Why? Because, says Rabbi Chayim ben Attar, Sabbath observance is the highest repudiation of idolatry.[146] And, as Nehemia Polen has correctly noted, the Nazis' idolatry was manifest in their determination to destroy the Sabbath.[147] One way, then, to state the most fundamental challenge facing Jewish thought is to say that it must be a thinking that remembers and watches over the Sabbath. Which means: a Jewish thinker's thinking is informed by concrete, active Sabbath observance, for the point of this remembrance and observance, as it is written in the Torah, is to make room for holiness in the world. If Jewish thought is to recognize the evil of the Shoah as evil, then the Jewish thinker is faced with thinking in terms of the holy that is manifest in Sabbath observance: to think Jewishly is to think "Sabbathly." And to think Sabbathly is to live in a certain manner—*as a Jew.* This *does not* mean that only one who observes the Sabbath is a Jew; rather, it means that only a Jew is commanded to observe the Sabbath.

Influenced by the speculative, ontological tradition, Jewish thought must remind itself on a regular basis that thinking in terms of the holy is contrary to thinking in terms of the ontic and the ontological. Heschel states it well when he says, "To the philosopher the idea of the good is the most exalted idea. But to the Bible [that is, to Jewish thought] the idea of the good is penultimate; it cannot exist without the holy."[148] Again, thinking in terms of the holy entails thinking in terms of the Sabbath, which is thinking in terms of the Holy One; *Sabbath,* indeed, is one of the names of the Holy One (see *Zohar* II, 88b; see also the commentary on Exodus 20:8 in Chayim ben Attar, *Or Hachayim*). As the Maharal of Prague, Rabbi Yehuda Loeve, has taught, the six days of creation correspond to the six directions of space in the material world; the seventh day corresponds to the holy, which gives meaning to the other six.[149] And each week the passage through the cycle of the six is a return to the seventh: each week we undertake *teshuvah.* Rabbi Benjamin Blech points out in this connection that the word *Shabbat* asks us a question: *Shavta?*—"Have you returned?"[150] Now more than ever, Jewish thought must find a way to respond to this question couched in the Sabbath.

Perhaps here we have the key to a prayer that we say every Sabbath during the morning services. Praying Psalm 34, we recall the time when King David feigned madness in order to save himself from the Philistine king Avimelekh. The psalm opens with the words *leDavid, beshanoto et tamo,* "A Psalm of David, when he feigned madness." The literal translation of *beshanoto et tamo,* however, is "when he changed his understanding," that is, when he altered his "judgment" or "discernment." David feigned madness in order to escape being trapped and murdered by the Philistines. In the postmodern world, we too may feign madness or alter our discernment in order to make our way in a world gone mad. But on the Sabbath we recite King David's psalm so as to remind ourselves of that madness.

There are times, however, when we have gone mad without realizing it—that is the difference between us and King David: we have come to think like the Egyptians, the Philistines, the Greeks, and the Romans, without noticing. Taking on their cleverness, we suppose we are crazy like a fox, when in fact we are merely crazy. It is not for nothing that central to the remembrance of the Sabbath is the remembrance not only of the creation but also of the deliverance from Egypt. The difficulty facing the Jewish thinker is to come out of the Egyptian darkness, in which "a man could not see his brother" (Exodus 10:23), and think in the mode of Sabbath, for we live in a realm where we have lost the Sabbath, and the madness that overcomes us is no longer feigned. We have become "like the others," enamored of the postmodern deception. The crisis of Jewish thought is the "Judaicide," as André Neher calls it, that we can no longer recognize, as we are no longer a people apart: "Judaicide is the ultimate conclusion of the Jew wanting his Jewishness to be 'like the others,' for the others draw the Jew into their nets in order to make him disappear from the scene of history."[151] One way to avoid the nets of postmodernity and to initiate the movement of return to Jewish thought is to see where it was first infected with the madness of modernity. Thus we come to the next matter of concern.

3

Ethical Monotheism
and Jewish Thought

Should a person tell you there is wisdom among the nations,
believe it. . . . But if he tells you there is Torah among the
nations, do not believe it.—*Eichah Rabbah* 2:9:13

From what was said about the movement of return in the previous chapter, it should be clear that, if *teshuvah* is a return from exile, then exile is
not just a geographical category. In addition to the geographical exile, there
is an exile of the soul and of thought. Just as a Jew might wander in an
alien land, so might a Jew be lost in an alien thinking. Such, indeed, is
the exile of Hashem, so that the ultimate purpose of *teshuvah* is to draw
God Himself out of exile, as Rabbi Adin Steinsaltz has maintained.[1] And
most alien to Jewish thought—the orb that most radically eclipses the light
of the holy—is the ego, as the Chasidic master Yechiel Mikhal of Zlotchov
has taught.[2] Lost in the lie of our "egoism," of our *aniyut,* as it is called
in Hebrew, we cry out in the "lamentation" or the *aniyah* of our exile. In
this condition, we never live but only hope to live. In this condition, we
fail to realize that it is better to want what you have than to have what
you want. In this condition, we merely want. Situating the ego at the center of being robs a human being of the capacity for joy, for the ego would
always have more. Yet it is beggared by its abundance. And so, in our not
so quiet desperation, we ask: Where do we go from here—*anah*?

The philosophical exile that confronts the Jewish soul is an ancient one. The Talmud relates, for instance, that the apostate Elisha ben Avuya used to secretly study Greek philosophy before he abandoned Torah (see *Chagigah* 14b, 15b). To be sure, in the epigraph to the last chapter we have a talmudic text that expresses a concern over the adverse effects of Greek wisdom on the Jewish soul. That concern follows Jewish thinkers into the Middle Ages, when Bachya ibn Paquda complained that great "was the destruction of their own understanding. . . . [E]ach of them thought that his evil was the good way, and his erring path the right direction. This view they turned into a statute and moral principle. . . . What had been strange in their world became known to them, while the right way was strange to them" (Bachya ibn Paquda, *Chovot Halevavot* 9:2). Bachya's point will strike a chord in anyone familiar with the modern Jewish flirtation with ontological thought. Leo Baeck, for example, wrote, "At one time it [Judaism] believed that biblical wisdom was contained in Greek philosophy and Greek truth in the Holy Scriptures. It was a naïve belief."[3] Why naïve? Because, says Baeck, "what Greek philosophers lacked above all was that idea of ethical *command*,"[4] delivered from on high, and not merely deduced from reason.[5] Why naïve? Because Greek speculative philosophy—and its modern ontological outgrowth—could never deliver on its promises of truth, meaning, and morality. If the Holocaust has not demonstrated that, it has not demonstrated anything.

Like the serpent of old, speculative philosophy appeals to what is "pleasing to the eye" (Genesis 3:6)—and to the *I*—from Philo, who attempted to "correct" the Scriptures by changing the voice of God to a vision of God,[6] to Edmund Husserl, who declared that "if phenomena have no nature, they still have an essence, which can be grasped and determined in an immediate seeing."[7] Not only was the Jewish enthrallment with speculative thought naïve, it was destructive. One of Baeck's students, Emil Fackenheim, recognizes as much when he registers this complaint over the Jewish product of German Idealism, namely, liberal Judaism (despite his affiliation with that movement). In liberal Judaism, he says,

> Jewish prayer, once *between* a "subjective" self and an "objective" God, is
> viewed as the self's disport with its own feelings, conducive to aesthetic

or therapeutic benefit. Halakhah, once a way walked *before* God, is reduced to "custom and ceremony," performed for the sake of warm emotions within or wholesome relations without. Judaism, once a covenant involving a singling-out God and a singled-out Israel, is seen as a man-made civilization, created by Jewish genius in its human solitariness. And the human person, who once believed he *actually* mattered to God, is now engineered into the mere *feeling* that he matters, on the ground that such feelings banish anxiety and alienation.[8]

Of course, the result is just the opposite: the more Jews have tried to "fit in" socially, culturally, and philosophically, the more alienated and anxiety-ridden they have become. Indeed, it could not be otherwise. For this "fitting in" is a copping out that requires a Jew to renounce his essence and identity as a Jew.[9]

Jewish alienation and anxiety, then, are not so much the outcome of the Gentile's rejection of the Jew as of the Jew's rejection of what lies at the core of his or her own being.[10] It lies in the effort to share in the payoff from worshiping alien gods. This new idolatry is the "new test" that Samson Raphael Hirsch referred to when he wrote, "I bless it, if Israel will regard emancipation not as the goal of its vocation, but only as a new condition of its mission, and as a new test, much severer than the trial of oppression."[11] As Adin Steinsaltz expresses it, the true horror of the exile in Egypt "was that the slaves gradually became more and more like their masters, thinking like them and even dreaming the same dreams. Their greatest sorrow, in fact, was that their masters would not let them fulfill the Egyptian dream."[12] And their greatest wretchedness, like our own wretchedness, was that they saw no harm in dreaming the Egyptian dream, a dream of power and possessions, of pleasure and prestige, a nightmare in which more is better but never enough. Examining the Hebrew word for "Egypt," *Mitsraim,* Rabbi Steinsaltz notes that it is a cognate of *metsar,* which means "narrowness" or "anguish." Says Rabbi Steinsaltz, "Egypt symbolizes narrow-mindedness. Ancient Egypt and its paganism form the model for the individual who fabricates an entire system to refute real knowledge. The system upholds its false reality in the face of Divine reality. Egypt is the prototype of a world that proclaims itself to be autonomous and announces that it owes nothing to others because it is self-sufficient."[13] It is also the prototype of ethical monotheism.

In many circles, both lay and academic, there is some confusion about the term *ethical monotheism*. Indeed, the term itself can be rather puzzling. Does it mean that I embrace God because, through my autonomous reason, I have determined that it is the ethical thing to do? If so, then I am as God, knowing good and evil. And if that is so, then in the end I do not need God: I can get along perfectly well with the just the "ethical," without the myth of "monotheism," and certainly without the myth of Judaism, with all of its archaic and inconvenient rites, rules, and regulations. Or does *ethical monotheism* mean that God is the First Principle of ethics, nothing more than the ultimate concept of the ultimate good? If that is the case, then how am I to pray to or argue with a principle? Indeed, since I stand in no dialogical or covenantal relation with a principle, the principle is precisely *not God* but, at best, merely the *concept* of God. Once again, in the end I have no need of the "monotheism" in ethical monotheism. What, exactly, is meant by the term itself, then, can be unclear if not contradictory. It *is* clear, however, that many people mistakenly take the term to refer to any monotheistic religion—Judaism, Christianity, or Islam, for instance—that has some set of ethical norms to guide human behavior.

Ethical monotheism is a term initially used among nineteenth-century Jewish philosophers as a way of apologizing for Judaism before the court of reason, which amounts to a way of replacing Judaism with reason. It is reminiscent of the situation Fackenheim describes in the time of the Maccabees. In 167 B.C.E., he points out, Antiochus' decree prohibiting Jewish observances "owed its inspiration to Hellenizing Jewish leaders who, long bent on 'accommodating traditional Judaism to the times,' at length enlisted non-Jewish government force. In their own eyes, these leaders were not traitors or apostates. They were a 'reform party,' concerned not to destroy Judaism but rather to preserve it. Yet had their efforts succeeded, they would have destroyed Judaism from within far more thoroughly than any external enemy."[14] In Jewish philosophical circles, ethical monotheism was a companion to Reform Judaism that arose in the wake of the German Enlightenment in an effort to overcome an intellectual embarrassment over the revealed Judaism of Torah and Talmud.

Then as now, many Jewish thinkers were quick to reject such nonrational teachings as those pertaining to diet, clothing, and liturgy without first considering the rationale behind those teachings—or the implications of their rejection. They were comfortable with the idea that God forbids murder; but when it came to the question of whether God buried Moses, they would fidget in their seats. And so they sought a reasonable accommodation in ethics.

As Michael Wyschogrod puts it, however, "ethics is the Judaism of the assimilated,"[15] for what was designated as "ethical monotheism" was not the traditional, rabbinic Judaism grounded in Torah and Talmud but a counterfeit confined to the conceptual limits of reason and subjected to the investigative methods of science, as if Judaism were some sort of science project. Thus the proponents of ethical monotheism based their thinking not on the *sifrei kodesh* or on the Revelation at Mount Sinai but on the methodology of *die Wissenschaft des Judentums,* that is, "the scientific study of Judaism." These thinkers sought the truth of ethical teaching while at the same time rejecting the Divine authority behind the teaching, an authority that transcends reason and that can be affirmed only through the "metaethical" commandments that lie outside the ethical dicta.

At the heart of "the scientific study of Judaism" is the premise that "the Torah is not from heaven," which, from the viewpoint of talmudic teaching (for example, *Sanhedrin* 98a–98b), makes *die Wissenschaft des Judentums* idolatrous. As Emmanuel Levinas correctly points out, such a premise does not open the Scripture to endless interpretation of the infinite Word of Hashem; rather, it closes it, in such as way as to have the last word at the end of a philosophical syllogism.[16] Indeed, this exegetical internment in the text is a form of the anti-Semitism that Levinas defines as internment.[17] It is the opposite of the "incompleteness that is the law of love,"[18] that is, of the Torah given in an act of love from On High. With *die Wissenschaft des Judentums,* one engages the Torah with scientific curiosity, perhaps even with academic urgency, but not with a loving concern for the One who has given it and who in turn commands us to love.

The movement's leading figure, Leopold Zunz (1794–1886), aspired to make Judaism more "reasonable" and therefore more attractive to the many educated Jews who were abandoning the tradition of their fathers and mothers for Christianity.[19] "More attractive" and "more reasonable," of course, amounted to "more lucrative" and "more culturally accept-able," "more about me and how I see it." Zunz, therefore, tried to have it both ways: you can give up the Jewish tradition, he seemed to say, but you do not have to give up being Jewish. But he did not pose the most critical question: if "being Jewish" is no more than a cultural or ethnic affair, then how can it have anything more than a superficial meaning? And if that is the case, what is the interest in retaining a "Jewish iden-tity?" To be sure, many did not. Among the seven Hegelians who founded the *Verein für die Kultur und Wissenschaft der Juden* in 1819, its leader, Eduard Gans, as well as Heinrich Heine, converted to Christianity. After the society collapsed, five years later, only Zunz continued to pursue mod-ern Jewish scholarship.

Zunz was interested more in aesthetic beauty than in philosophical profundity, more in literary sensitivity than in religious piety. With his major works including *Die gottesdienstlichen Vorträge der Juden* (*The Litur-gies of the Jews*, 1832) and *Die Literaturgeschichte der synagogalen Poesie* (*The Literary History of Synagogue Poesy*, 1865), Zunz focused on the hermeneutics of Jewish literature, liturgy, and homiletics, and not on the covenantal relation between the God of Abraham and the children of Israel.[20] Long before postmodern "textual analysis," Zunz treated prayers as artistic texts created with a certain agenda in mind. Still, Zunz was hardly a deconstructionist. Taking a philological approach to the texts of the tradition, he was concerned with their historical evolution as cul-tural creations, and not with what they might reveal about the Holy One, the Covenant, Redemption, and so on.[21]

Other contributors to *die Wissenschaft des Judentums* applied the meth-ods of reason to the study of various cultural aspects of Jewish tradition. Nachman Krochmal (1785–1840), for instance, produced impressive stud-ies of Jewish history and philosophy. His *Moreh Nevuchei Hazman* (*Guide for the Perplexed of the Time*, 1851) followed the model of Maimonides' *Moreh Nevuchim* (*Guide for the Perplexed*) to demonstrate Judaism's com-patibility with rationalism.[22] The French thinker Salomon Munk (1803–1867), also influenced by Maimonides, laid important groundwork for the scientific study of medieval Jewish thought with his critical edi-tion of the *Moreh Nevuchim* in its original Arabic. Missing both from Krochmal and from Munk, however, was the Rambam's devotion to the

Written and Oral Torah as the revealed word of the Holy One, as was his engagement with mysticism. Although their scholarship was seminal, their approach was not Jewish, as they all but omitted the dimensions of the Rambam's thinking that made him a Jewish thinker. Reading the *Guide* without the *Mishneh Torah*, for instance, is like learning the grammar of a language while ignoring the meaning of its words.

At least two other works by leading thinkers in the German Jewish Reform movement contributed to the emergence of ethical monotheism from *die Wissenschaft des Judentums*. Those works are *Die Religion des Geistes* (*The Religion of Spirit*, 1841) by Solomon Formstecher (1808–1889), and *Die Religionsphilosophie der Juden* (*The Religious Philosophy of the Jews*, 1842), by Samuel Hirsch (1815–1889).[23] Although neither Formstecher nor Hirsch developed a systematic exposition of Jewish ethics, they set the stage for such an endeavor: having brought about an apparent reconciliation of Jewish thought with German Idealism, they established the basis for ethical monotheism.[24] Buying into the philosophical "system," however, many Jewish thinkers are like the man who saw a FOR SALE sign in front of a beautiful establishment and went inside to inquire, only to discover that it was merely the sign itself that was for sale.

Let us consider, then, the development of that inquiry, which traded Torah for autonomy, and the reasons why ethical monotheism is contrary to Jewish thought—to *Machshavah Yehudit*.

TRADING TORAH FOR AUTONOMY

The first major figure to draw upon the moral philosophy of German Idealism in an effort to articulate a "Jewish" ethical monotheism was Moritz Lazarus (1824–1903). In *The Ethics of Judaism* (1898), Lazarus incorporates the thinking of Immanuel Kant into an examination of the moral teachings of Judaism with the aim of showing that the ethics of Judaism meets the standard of autonomy required by Kant's moral philosophy. According to Kant, a rational moral agent is an autonomous agent inasmuch as he or she is self-legislating.[25] And to be self-legislating is to derive one's own moral principles from one's own reason, in keeping with the dictates of the categorical imperative: always act in such a way that a universal maxim can be derived from your action without your entering into a contradiction, where "contradiction" means not so much a logical contradiction as your acting in a manner contrary to your self-interest.[26] Murder, for example, cannot be moral, because making murder into a universal maxim would jeopardize your own life. Thus already lying outside the scope of Kant's ethical principle is a teaching essential to Judaism, namely, that I must choose to be murdered rather than commit murder, not because it is in my rational self-interest but because it is a Kiddush Hashem, a sanctification of the Creator of every life. And because it is *commanded* by Hashem.[27]

Prefiguring ethical monotheism, Kant departs even further from the Creator's commanding Voice by arguing that the *concept* of God derives from the moral idea.[28] And the moral idea is a derivative of human reason, not Divine commandment. To be sure, it may be a maxim. It may even be an imperative. But it is not a commandment, not a *mitzvah* or a connection *to* God that comes *from* God. Indeed, with Kant the human being has no connection to God; it is precisely this absence of any connection to God that constitutes the individual's autonomous "freedom." Of course, one may view one's autonomy in terms of the Divine commandments; but if that is the case, Kant maintains, one must understand those commandments as duties that any rational agent would accept *as his own.*[29] Bottom line: Who needs God?

Lazarus agrees and disagrees with Kant. Like Kant, he proceeds from an insistence on the autonomy of the rational being who acts as a free moral agent; unlike Kant, he holds to the premise that the ethics of Judaism, where the commanding Voice of God is the source of the moral imperative, falls into the category of autonomy, and not heteronomy.[30] Lazarus must reject as least a portion of the Kantian position, however, since Kant views Judaism as a slave religion. Why? Because Judaism takes God, not one's own reason, to be the source of the commandment. "Neither Torah as revealed command nor halakhah," Jonathan Sacks correctly notes, "is translatable into the terms of Kantian ethics. Kant himself was in no doubt about this."[31] Hence the Kantian call for the "euthanasia of Judaism."[32] Although he does so unwittingly, Lazarus undertakes precisely the euthanasia program that Kant calls for through his adherence to the Kantian proposition that what God commands is good not because He commands it; rather, He commands it because it is good *as reason would define what is good,* as if God were Himself subject to a categorical imperative. To be sure, for Kant as for Lazarus there is no "as if" here. Setting out to justify the God of Abraham before the god of the philosophers, Lazarus subjects the God of Abraham to the dictates of reason.[33] With this move, however, the God of Abraham is eclipsed by the dictates of reason. Therefore, as many have demonstrated, the God of Abraham is the contrary of the god of the philosophers.

As for the ritual and liturgy prescribed by Torah and Talmud—such as fasting on Yom Kippur—Lazarus saw it merely as a therapeutic tool for engendering positive emotions such as sympathy and compassion.[34] Thus he presents the basic features of ethical monotheism as a hybrid of Kantian Idealism and Jewish moral teaching, in such a way as to displace traditional, Torah-based Judaism: with the adjustment of Judaism to Idealism, the religion of reason displaces the religion of revelation. Justifying Judaism before Kantian moral philosophy, Lazarus renders Jewish thought and Jewish religion unrecognizable to Jewish tradition, where the commandments concerning rite, ritual, and daily routine are as crucial and authoritative as the commandments regarding moral relations. To be sure, each is interwoven with the other. Recall here Abraham Joshua Heschel's statement that a *mitzvah* is "a prayer in the form of a deed": from the standpoint of Jewish thought, there is no ethical action disconnected from the ritual of prayer.[35] Rite and ritual affirm the authority and the *holiness* of the One who commands the moral relation, and holiness is beyond the scope of reason: it is revealed as a presence that exceeds all that resides in the realm of being. That is the meaning of *kadosh,* the Hebrew word for "holy."

Signifying what is "separate," *kadosh* refers not to an object or a principle set apart from other objects or principles; rather, it refers to what is altogether *other* than anything in the landscape of being, to what Levinas describes as "otherwise than being."[36] The holy is, moreover, a *living* presence, a *who* to whom we can pray; by contrast, no philosopher born of the Enlightenment ever uttered a prayer to reason. As a *who,* the Holy One is a living presence with whom we have a covenantal relation inasmuch as He demands that we enter into a relation with those who are created in His image and likeness. Most fundamentally, He commands us to pursue *tsedek,* which is "righteousness" or "justice" (see, for example,

Deuteronomy 16:20).[37] Justice, moreover, is *tsedakah,* which is "charity" or giving without expectation of reciprocation and therefore without self-interest. Lazarus, by contrast—and in keeping with Kant—is primarily interested not in justice but in freedom.[38] Ethics, with Lazarus as with Kant, deals with the laws of freedom as a self-legislating autonomy, and not with the Divine demand for justice understood as righteousness and charity. For ethical monotheism, freedom defined as the autonomy of the self—rather than as justice grounded in charity toward the other—becomes the pivotal concern.

Here one sees a fundamental distinction between ethical monotheism and Torah-based Jewish thinking. With the latter, the ethical relation derives not from rational reflection but from a Divine revelation that surpasses reason to sanction the human relation, a relation that reason may justify but cannot *sanctify.* Thus in the Mishnah we have the commentary on the verse "And the tablets were the work of God, and the writing was the writing of God, graven [*charut*] upon the tablets" (Exodus 32:16): "Do not read *charut* or 'graven' but *cherut* or 'freedom,' for no human being is free save one who is engaged in the study of Torah" (*Avot* 6:2; see also *Eruvin* 54a; *Avot d'Rabbi Natan* 2:3; and *Bemidbar Rabbah* 10:8). Studying Torah, we are charged with a mission to do good. We are not free to choose the good; rather, we are free because we have been chosen by the Good before we make any other choices. As Levinas states it, "the Good is not presented to freedom; it has chosen me before I have chosen it."[39] Therefore, in the words of the medieval sage Judah Halevi, true freedom lies in our servitude to God (*Kitav al khazari* 5:25). That is what makes all of our other choices *matter.*

Further, because the *tsedek* that is righteousness is not a category of reason, it cannot be a category for ethical monotheism. Wherever righteousness is an issue, the human being refrains from murder not because it may endanger his own life but because God commands it. In Jewish thought, *torat hamidot,* the Hebrew term for "ethics," is based more on piety than on reason, more on the Torah of tradition than on the law of contradiction. The phrase literally means "the Torah of character," "the Torah of principles," or "the Teaching on character." By contrast, ethical monotheism is rooted in the methods of reason, and not in the commandments of Torah or the teachings of the sages. Indeed, its aim is to supersede the "outdated" religion of the Jews, who base their beliefs on the revelation at Mount Sinai as transmitted through their rabbis and their holy books. Hence Fackenheim questions whether Judaism can be construed as "ethical monotheism," since the commandments that define Judaism are reducible neither to the ethical nor to the universal.[40] He calls ethical monotheism an "empty abstraction" that "mistakes Jews for members of the *Kant-Gesellschaft.*"[41] And so it is.

The Kantian who made the most profound attempt to keep his ethical monotheism without giving up his Judaism was Hermann Cohen (1842–1918). The founder of the neo-Kantian Marburg School, Cohen had devoted his adult life to a study of Kant's philosophy until something happened that turned his attention to the religion that, as a thinker, he had all but ignored. In 1880 the anti-Semitic German historian Heinrich von Treitschke attacked Judaism as the antiquated religion of an antiquated tribe that was alien to the German people.[42] Cohen responded by writing *Ein Bekenntnis zur Judenfrage (A Reflection on the Jewish Question),* in which he argued (as if it were a defense of Judaism) that Reform Judaism was essentially the same as German Protestantism; rooted as each was in the basic principles of the Enlightenment, each, according to Cohen, had overcome the dark irrationalism of religious myth to become a rational, civilized *Kulturreligion.*[43] Over the years that followed, Cohen authored a series of writings on this view of Judaism; those writings comprise his three-volume *Jüdische Schriften (Jewish Writings).*

The essays in the *Jüdische Schriften* expound upon several ideas that are central to Cohen's ethical monotheism. First of all, in the *Jüdische Schriften* Cohen posits the *concept* of God or the God *idea* not as the origin but as the outcome of ethics. Ethics, says Cohen, "has ultimately no other recourse but to hypothesize the idea of God,"[44] a position in keeping with the Kantian view that God is not the source of morality—He is derived from morality. If God is "holy," it is because He constitutes the moral ground hypothesized by ethics; similarly, man's holiness lies in his sense of morality. To love God is to know God, and to know God is to comprehend morality. Thus Cohen sees transcendence not in terms of a relation to God but in terms of a relation to the moral good, as determined by reason, not as willed by God. And yet, since God's will is at one with the God idea conceived by reason—since His essence lies in the concept of morality—God is precisely the One who wills the Good in accordance with reason. From Cohen's standpoint, He cannot do otherwise. His oneness is a oneness with reason; His uniqueness is the uniqueness of moral perfection.[45]

Further, because God's uniqueness is moral, it is meaningful; hence God's uniqueness, says Cohen, becomes manifest as Divine providence,[46] a concept that is central to a life instilled with meaning, and not with just a *sense* of meaning. God, understood as providence, creates every human being with a moral mission. Thus expressing His love for His human creation, He becomes the Father to all, making each human being the brother to the other. The Jews' status as a people apart, then, is abrogated for the sake of forming a universal community of humankind. The aim of the messianism associated with Cohen's ethical monotheism is not the return of the Jewish people from a geographical or spiritual exile; its aim, rather, is social justice for all humanity, where "social justice" means that each person should enjoy that same autonomous freedom (thus ethical monotheism is distinguished from Christianity, which preaches personal salvation through faith in Christ; those who lack that faith are excluded from salvation). According to Cohen's ethical monotheism, and contrary to Judaism, the Messiah is not a person; rather, the Messiah is the realization of morality in the world. With the ultimate establishment of a universal morality grounded in reason, the spirit of God and the spirit of man merge to form the Holy Spirit, which is the Messiah. Therefore, Cohen maintains, God does not want rite and ritual; He wants deeds for the sake of the messianic age of social justice.[47]

Cohen took the ideas expressed in his *Jüdische Schriften* and developed them into a sophisticated system of ethical monotheism in his most profound work, *Religion of Reason out of the Sources of Judaism* (published posthumously in 1919). Here Cohen views his task to be similar to the one that Maimonides undertook in *The Guide for the Perplexed*, namely, the marriage of philosophy and Judaism. Whereas Maimonides would reconcile Judaism with Aristotelian Rationalism, Cohen would reconcile Judaism with German Idealism. To be sure, Cohen viewed Maimonides as a major forerunner of ethical monotheism, for Maimonides states that God is knowable only through His actions or attributes,[48] which Cohen translates into *moral* actions. Contrary to Cohen and the other ethical monotheists, however, Maimonides was concerned not only with the moral codes that promote social justice but also with the Divine law that revealed the essence of all reality, the law that shapes rite and ritual, prayer and religious observance, as prescribed by Torah.[49] Significant to Maimonides' interest in Divine law, moreover, was the fact that he was an adherent of the kabbalistic teachings,[50] something that Cohen found scandalous in the Jewish tradition.

In *Religion of Reason out of the Sources of Judaism,* Cohen replaces revelation with reason by equating the two, which in turn leads him to equate Divine holiness with moral goodness. Inasmuch as morality derives from reason, says Cohen, the "revelation" of reason is the "revelation" of the Holy One as *der Gute* or "the Good One," in contrast to *das Gute* or "the Good."[51] Because reason is universal in its scope, its aim is precisely God's aim: to establish the universal reign of ethical law and social justice, which is also the aim of the autonomous individual created in God's image. "In autonomy alone," asserts Cohen, "lies the power to assert human morality. It is due to the power of autonomy that the I rises to totality. There is no other goal and no other means for ethics."[52] Nor is there any other goal for ethical monotheism: centered on the "I" of the "I think," its aim is to "think" and thereby control the sum of reality. The aim of Judaism, by contrast, is not to control reality through a religion of reason but rather to sanctify reality through a religion of *mitzvot*.

Examining Cohen's *Religion of Reason out of the Sources of Judaism,* one realizes that ethical monotheism is a reversal of Judaism. In a move that amounts to an apotheosis of ethics, Cohen asserts that "ethics knows neither man nor God; it begets these concepts through its method."[53] As the great "begetter," ethics itself poses as god rather than as what is commanded by God. In the Judaism of Torah and Talmud, neither ethics nor its method begets a "concept" of God, but rather God begets a concept of ethics, as well as a concept of humanity, by entering into a relation with humanity. Whereas ethical imperatives and moral concepts disclose only themselves, the commandment discloses both the law and the Giver of the law.

Further, while Cohen ascribes only a symbolic and therefore contingent validity to the Talmud, traditional Judaism regards the Talmud as the Oral Torah that Moses received from God and whose moral teachings are therefore based on Divine authority. In an attempt to lend some credence to the Talmud—and in keeping with Kantian thinking—Cohen cites the Oral Torah to show that one must obey the dictates of reason without any eudemonic self-interest: "Better is the one who acts because he is commanded than the one who is not commanded but acts" (*Bava Kama* 38a). Although he recognizes the threat to autonomy in this teaching,[54] Cohen fails to acknowledge that the rabbinic intent is to affirm the Divine authority, not the authority of reason. Like Lazarus, Cohen tries to have something both ways that cannot be had both ways: he appeals to the authority of the Talmud while at the same time arguing that it has no authority. This use—or misuse—of the Talmud makes it clear that talmudic Judaism is not compatible with ethical monotheism. And since talmudic Judaism is a distinguishing feature of Jewish thought, ethical monotheism is at odds with that thinking.

With regard to the significance of something as fundamental to Judaism and Jewish thought as Sabbath observance, Cohen does not see it in terms of drawing the eternal into time or ascending ever higher through the gates of prayer; rather, the Sabbath, he maintains, as a day of rest, has the ethical significance of annulling the class distinctions created by labor.[55] Cohen, in fact, all but equates poverty with piety and takes the view of the poor man as pious man to be "the high point of ethical monotheism."[56] As one may gather from the previous chapter, however, the Sabbath is not a "day off." As a remembrance of the Creation and of the Exodus from Egypt,[57] the Sabbath is not about labor or class distinctions; no, it is an opening through which the holiness that gives meaning to the world may enter the world. Hence Heschel maintains that "what *we are* [as Jews] depends on what the *Sabbath is* to us."[58] While it is true that central to Sabbath observance is an orientation toward our fellow human being, the *meaning* of the Sabbath lies in what makes that orientation *matter.*

Just as Cohen views the Sabbath in terms of social justice, so does he regard prayer in terms of moral action; for Cohen, prayer is the connection "between religion and morality in general,"[59] and not between man and God or man and his soul or man and his fellow man, as Jewish thought might view it. While it is true that, Jewishly speaking, prayer is not prayer until it is transformed into acts of loving kindness, this transformation is possible only in the light of the higher relation that is prior to the moral relation. Similarly, Cohen's discussion of the *Mitmensch,* or "fellow human being," in chapter 8 of *Religion of Reason out of the Sources of Judaism* may resemble Judaism's testimony regarding one's fellow human being, but his Kantian outlook cannot bring him to the Jewish idea that the other human being is not equal to but *higher* than oneself.[60] Heschel makes this point by showing that the Kantian dictum to treat a rational being as an end, and not as a means, undermines the martyrdom required to affirm the sanctity of God and humanity, since there is no reason not to regard oneself as an absolute end.[61] Indeed, according to Kant, an action that would lead to any harm to myself cannot be a moral action.

Thus couched in the categories of equality, universality, autonomy, and morality, ethical monotheism stands over against Jewish thought. Because ethical monotheism presented itself as a kind of Judaism made rational, however, it drew a response from some of the twentieth century's major Jewish thinkers. The question that must now be considered is: What was the relation between ethical monotheism and Jewish thought in the twentieth century?

MODERN MOVEMENTS OF RETURN

Chief among the Jewish thinkers to respond to the German Idealism that formed the basis of ethical monotheism is Hermann Cohen's most famous student, Franz Rosenzweig (1886–1929). In his most important philosophical work, *The Star of Redemption,* Rosenzweig situates the concrete life of Judaism over against the abstract reasoning of Idealist philosophy. In contrast to Cohen's discourse of causality, rationality, and morality, Rosenzweig's key terms are *creation, revelation,* and *redemption.* Further, whereas speculative thought would reduce God, world, and humanity to concepts, and therefore to derivatives of one another, Rosenzweig insists upon distinct differences among these realities. To set up these differences, he calls for a new method of thinking: in contrast to the abstraction and isolation of thought ruled by the law of contradiction, Rosenzweig posits the concrete, time-bound interrelation of human beings through what he calls the "new thinking" or the "speaking thinker," a move that draws the human being out of the abstraction of thought and into an active, concrete relation to the other human being.

In an essay titled "The New Thinking: Some Afterthoughts on *The Star of Redemption*," he explains that in the new thinking the method of speech—of dialogical interaction with another person—replaces the isolation and speculation of philosophical idealism. Resting on a relation with *this* human being—and in keeping with *Machshavah Yehudit*—the new thinking unfolds in a specific time and is grounded in a concrete, dialogical relation to one who bears a name, rather than an essence.[62] Thus, in accordance with Jewish teaching,[63] Rosenzweig sees the human being less as a thinking being than as a speaking being. Thought and speech, as the "clothing" through which God makes Himself manifest, are crucial to drawing holiness into the world through deeds. To be sure, the word is itself a deed of Divine utterance so that the "being" of the human being is no longer equated with thought; rather, it transpires in the utterance and in the action that draws the human being into the *between space* of human relation. What was said in the previous chapter about the meaning of the commandment to love one's neighbor (Leviticus 19:18) applies here: the human being *is* that commanded love that draws him or her into this between space.

In another work, *Understanding the Sick and the Healthy: A View of World, Man, and God,* Rosenzweig contrasts Jewish thinking with the speculative thought that shapes ethical monotheism. Here, the "sick" view of God, world, and humanity reduces all three to the perceiving, conceptualizing self by equating thinking with being. Over against the "concept of God" so crucial to Cohen's thought, Rosenzweig invokes the *name* of God—the name of the One who is known as Hashem, as the Name—through which the world acquires a sense and human beings acquire a meaning.[64] Unlike the One who is a concept, the One who is the Name is One with whom we enter into a relation, who can put to us a question and summon from us a response. Because God is Hashem, in other words, He is not conceived or hypothesized by the human mind; rather, God calls every human being *by name* and summons each one to the task for which he or she was created. Similarly, Rosenzweig argues, the human being has no concept of the world from which an essence could be derived: we do not conceive of the world; we interact with it. Just as the name of God is a bridge to the names of people, so is the word a bridge between human and world. "The word is not part of the world,"

Rosenzweig maintains, "it is the seal of man."[65] As for the human being, he asserts that "mankind is always absent. Present is a man, this fellow or that one,"[66] in his concrete flesh and blood, thus making concrete the question God puts to every person: Where are you?

Rosenzweig, however, did not develop his own extended reflection on ethics. His significance lies more in his critique of Kant and Hegel than in the development of an alternative moral philosophy (unless a return to the commanding Voice of Mount Sinai can be regarded as a moral philosophy, which is doubtful). Just as those who tried to incorporate German philosophy into Jewish thought influenced the most profound proponent of ethical monotheism, Hermann Cohen, so did Rosenzweig raise the questions that influenced the most profound ethical thinker among twentieth-century Jewish philosophers: Emmanuel Levinas. While the scope of this chapter on ethical monotheism and Jewish thought does not allow for an exhaustive analysis of Levinas's work, we should consider a few key points in the context of the opposition between ethical monotheism and Jewish thought.

Levinas's ethical philosophy is a response to the general ontological thinking that equates thought with being and that characterizes ethical monotheism. In the equation of thought with being, he sees an equation of the autonomous thinking "I" with being, so that even "ethical" understanding becomes a pretense for appropriating and ultimately oppressing the other. To the extent that ethical monotheism seeks a moral totality based on the principles of reason, as Cohen maintains, it falls into the category of ontological thought. Placing the thinking "I" at the center of being, ethical monotheism degenerates into ethical humanism, which in turn becomes moral relativism, since each thinking "I" has just as much authority as the other. And once moral relativism is installed, morality becomes irrelevant, as one can see among the postmodernist thinkers from Heidegger onward. What does become relevant at that point is the will to power.

In contrast to the association between morality and autonomy that characterizes ethical monotheism, Levinas sees the ethics of Judaism as an "ethics of heteronomy that is not a servitude, but the service of God through responsibility for the neighbor, in which I am irreplaceable."[67] Or perhaps better: the service of the *commanding* God, who requires of us not only a responsibility for the neighbor but also the prayer and Torah study that would sanction such a responsibility. Contrasting the God of the Bible with the god of the philosophers, Levinas maintains that ethics is neither a moment in being nor conceived by thought.[68] Rather, it is otherwise or better than being: it is the Divine *ought* that enters being as a commandment from beyond being, before being.[69] Similarly, God and humanity do not share a moral essence; rather, each is beyond essence, for each is *irreplaceable.* In a word, God and the one created in His image and likeness are *holy.* As an ethical being, therefore, the human being is a "breach of being," manifest not in the thinking "I" but in the divinely commanded movement toward the other for the sake of the other.[70]

At first glance, it might seem that, since he is a monotheist who views ethics as "first philosophy," Levinas is a proponent of ethical monotheism. Hermann Cohen, for example, might agree with Levinas's statement that "to know God is to know what must be done."[71] For Levinas, however, coming to a knowledge of God means having received a Divine commandment, a *mitzvah,* while for Cohen it means having made a rational deduction concerning a moral formalism. Levinas, by contrast, insists that the *mitzvah* "is not a moral formalism" but is rather "the living *presence* of love,"[72] which is manifest precisely in the *commandment* to love.[73] Levinas, therefore, is not a proponent of ethical monotheism. Whereas ethical monotheism derives God from the moral principle, Levinas sees God as the source of the ethical commandment and manifest *in* the commandment.[74] Whereas ethical monotheism emphasizes the autonomy of the self, Levinas focuses on responsibility for the other.[75] Whereas ethical monotheism is interested in freedom, Levinas insists upon the pursuit of justice.[76] In short, whereas ethical monotheism takes revelation to be the revelation of reason, Levinas views it as the revelation of love.

Like Rosenzweig, and contrary to Kant, Levinas maintains that love can be commanded; like Rosenzweig, and contrary to Cohen, Levinas embraces not a "reformed Judaism" but a Judaism grounded in Torah and Talmud.[77] Emphasizing the concreteness of Jewish tradition over the abstractions of the "spiritual" religion-in-general of nineteenth-century Reform Judaism, Levinas insists upon the primacy of the *mitzvot* that lie at the heart of Jewish life.[78] God is the source of those commandments, which we receive not through reason but through the face of the other human being, through *this* person who is here before me *now*. "The face," says Levinas, "is what forbids us to kill."[79] To encounter the face is to encounter Torah; it is through the face that Torah enters this world. Through the face, Torah commands us to be there for the sake of another. Therefore "the presence of the Other is a presence that teaches."[80] It is a Torah that teaches us something about the God who "is welcomed in the face-to-face with the other, in the obligation towards the other."[81] And the obligation precedes the situation: I do not enter into a situation and then derive my universal maxim; no, the "maxim" is already commanded by the Creator.

Levinas views the welcome or the greeting extended to the other person as the core of Judaism and Jewish thought.[82] Because greeting the other person is incumbent upon *me*—because I cannot wait for the other to say hello—I share no equality with the other human being; rather, he or she always comes first. Therefore, I have one responsibility *more* than the other, namely, the responsibility to die rather than inflict death upon the other: the death that concerns me, as Levinas states it, is the death of my fellow human being—not *my* death.[83] And I must attest to that concern even at the cost of my own life, in a Kiddush Hashem. An ethical monotheism grounded in reason cannot deduce this radical inequality. For reason, all equations must balance. For reason, everyone is the *same*—not equally holy, but merely the same, so that in the end nothing really matters, because nothing is really holy. Which means: every life is replaceable.

Opposing the German Idealism that seduced their Jewish forerunners, Rosenzweig and Levinas pose a challenge to an ethical monotheism grounded in reason by reaffirming an "ethical Judaism" grounded in Torah and Talmud. The contexts of their challenges, however, are quite different. Although Rosenzweig did much of his work during and after the devastation of World War I, Levinas did much of his work in the shadows of the Shoah. While the catastrophe of World War I must not be underestimated, Rosenzweig lived in a time when the current ethical urgency was yet to be felt; there are no major works, for example, on the question of ethics after Verdun. There is, however, substantial discussion of the question of ethics after Auschwitz. And Levinas is a major part of that discussion. We cannot close this discussion of ethical monotheism and Judaism, then, without addressing the situation after Auschwitz.

THE EMPTINESS OF A POST-AUSCHWITZ ETHICAL MONOTHEISM

From the depths of the Shoah, Rabbi Kalonymos Kalmish Shapira cried out to his fellow Jews:

> Before Amalek came to fight with you, there were among you servile people who esteemed the very thinking championed by Amalek. You were impressed with the superficial culture in which Amalek takes such pride. As a result, your response to Jewish culture and the wisdom of Torah was chilly [cf. Deuteronomy 25:18]. You were sure that Amalek was very cultured, that his philosophy was quite as good as anything. To be sure, it had its ethics, and there is profit to be had from it in this world. What did God do? He brought you face to face with Amalek.[84]

What Rabbi Shapira so astutely describes from his hovel in the Warsaw Ghetto is the illicit love affair between Judaism and ethical monotheism. (His views on God's connection to the Holocaust we shall examine in chapter 8.)

Like any illicit affair that must end quite differently from the way it began, this one has left us, in the words of Rabbi Joseph Soloveitchik, with postmodernism's "autonomous philosophical apprehension of reality," which "is anti-intellectualistic and hostile to critical thinking. It is pretentious and arrogant. It claims to transcend the boundaries of relational scientific knowledge and to reach into super-noesis. There, it maintains, reality is revealed intimately to the daring mind; subject and object, mind and absolute Being merge."[85] Indeed, arrogance is characteristic of the postmodernists, as one can see in their adulation of Nietzsche. Says Rabbi Soloveitchik, "Dionysian mystic wisdom versus 'decadent' Socratism are the philosophical Armageddon of our age. 'The society of life affirmers,' whose task was the reestablishment of 'superabundance of life,' brought havoc and death."[86] What began as a freedom based on the autonomy and resolve of the individual ended in the formula "Nothing is true and everything is permitted," for those who have the daring and the will.

Inasmuch as ethical monotheism equates freedom with autonomy, it is part of the ontological tradition expressed in Heidegger's equation of authenticity with resolve. Ethical monotheism, then, is implicated by Levinas's attack on Heideggerian ontology. Bound to a concept, even to a concept of God, and not to a person, ethical monotheism ultimately subordinates the relationship with *this concrete human being* to a universal principle imposed upon all of humankind, at which point it collapses both as ethical and as monotheistic. The face of the other person fades from our field of vision so that we grow deaf to the cry of our neighbor and to the commandment from on high that requires us to come to the aid of the other.

Insisting as he does on the *idea* of God and humanity, Hermann Cohen was once asked how one can love an idea; he answered that one can love only an idea.[87] But one cannot be *commanded* to love an idea; one cannot snatch the bread from one's own mouth and offer it to an idea. Nor does an idea suffer without our love. An idea does not demand that I answer the first question put to the first human being: Where are you? An idea does not have a face. An idea does not cry out, as did the children whose screams became the voice of Auschwitz, screams ignored by a world enamored of ideas, screams that shouted in unison, "Mama!" in a deafening echo of the suffering God—screams that drive home the realization that if God does not suffer, then there is no Divine prohibition against murder, for that prohibition arises from love, and not even God can love without suffering. Thus Auschwitz demonstrates the failure of ethical monotheism.

Recognizing the possibly murderous outcome of the abstractions of ethical monotheism, Emil Fackenheim urges his readers to reject Cohen and return to the concrete care for the concrete person commanded by "the ancient God of Israel."[88] Cohen opposed Zionism in the name of a universal humanism, which he thought he had found in Judaism; what he found unacceptable in Judaism is the decisively Jewish teaching that the Jews must remain a "nation of priests" and "a people apart"—that the Jews must be something *particular* and *concrete*. When the Jews are no longer a people apart, however, Judaism becomes superfluous—even dangerous—to the universal humanism that characterizes ethical monotheism. Because ethnic particularity is incompatible with ethical universality, Cohen maintained that ethical monotheism requires the elimination—or at least the radical reformation—of Torah-based Judaism as well as the ultimate assimilation of the Jews. What he did not understand, despite his genius, is that the universalism of Jewish thinking rests precisely upon its particularism, and that its particularism is defined by its universalism.

The Jewish people are chosen, in their particularity, to attest to the universal chosenness of every human being. *Each* human being is singled out to assume an absolute responsibility to and for *all* human beings. Thus the first paragraph of the *Shema,* the "Hear, O Israel" prayer, is recited with the singular "you": *Vehayu hadvarim haeleh asher Anokhi metsave*kha *hayom al levave*kha, "And you [singular] shall lay these words that I command you [singular] this day upon your heart" (Deuteronomy 6:6). And the second paragraph is recited with the plural "you": *Vehayah im shema tishmeu el mitsvotai asher Anokhi metsaveh et*khem *hayom . . . ,* "And if you [plural] hearken unto these commandments that I command you [plural] to do this day . . . " (Deuteronomy 11:13). In the spirit of this simultaneous universality and particularity, Abraham is chosen for the sake of all nations (see Genesis 12:3). In the spirit of this simultaneous universality and particularity, the Ten Commandments, or the Ten Utterances, of God are given in the singular "you," for the sake of every "you." Whereas ethical monotheism can think only in terms of the universal— and therefore *must* propose a totalitarian assimilation and oppose the Zionist aspiration—Jewish thought thinks in terms of this particularity and universality manifest in a single movement of thought.

Admittedly, looking back is easier than looking forward. Still, after Auschwitz, Fackenheim, for one, realizes how and why ethical monotheism unwittingly plays into the hands of the Nazis in a post-Holocaust world. Therefore, he finds an option such as ethical monotheism abhorrent, dangerous, and simply impossible, for it turns out that this option is not only otherwise than Judaism—it is the enemy of Judaism, something that leads to the demise of Judaism and that plays into the hands of the creators of Auschwitz. In *God's Presence in History,* therefore, Fackenheim argues that in a post-Holocaust world "Jewish opposition to

Auschwitz cannot be grasped in terms of humanly created ideals but only as an *imposed commandment*. And the Jewish secularist, no less than the believer, is *absolutely singled out* by a Voice as truly *other* than man-made ideals—an imperative as truly *given*—as was the Voice of Sinai."[89] The Voice that is *otherwise* than man-made ideals—the Voice that is neither deduced nor hypothesized and that commands Jews to be a people apart—is "otherwise than being." Only if the Jews are a people set apart by a Voice that is other than human can Auschwitz be understood as *evil* and not simply immoral. Therefore, Fackenheim rightly insists upon the urgency of maintaining the Jewish State, not merely because the Jews have no haven without a homeland but also because the world has no revelation of holiness without the Jews.

As Fackenheim sees it, what is required for a mending of the world after Auschwitz is precisely Judaism's revelation of holiness, and not ethical monotheism's identification of revelation with reason. What is required is the commanding Voice that judges the soul, and not the rational deduction that merely assesses a concept, for the living soul, like the living God, is not a concept—it is an emanation of God.[90] The history of ethical monotheism, then, is the history of what passes for modern Jewish thought attempting to accommodate itself to the rational idealism born of a world that set out to destroy Judaism and the Jews. Recall Jean-François Lyotard's insight mentioned in the previous chapter: "One integrates them in the modern era. . . . One exterminates them in the twentieth century."[91] With Zunz, Lazarus, and Cohen, ethical monotheism arises in an attempt to justify Judaism before German Idealism; with Rosenzweig, Levinas, and Fackenheim, it falls apart as the teachings of Judaism expose the ultimate moral bankruptcy of German Idealism. Thus ethical monotheism has been utterly discredited in the post-Holocaust age. Where it leads after Auschwitz we have seen in thinkers such as Richard Rubenstein, who rejects the God of Abraham for a kind of neo-paganism, and Ignaz Maybaum, who regards the destruction of the Jews devoted to the God of Abraham in terms of a positive development. Both are left not with ethical monotheism but with an ethical relativism that is powerless to respond to the Nazi horror.

As for the postmodern position on Judaism and Jewish thought after Auschwitz, Josh Cohen, for instance, calls for a "rethinking of the

Absolute,"[92] but his Absolute is not the Divine *Who* with whom we may enter into a covenantal relation. At best, it is a philosophical *What* generated by the thinking subject. Zachary Braiterman also represents the postmodern position on Jewish thought and Judaism. Defining Judaism in terms of "tradition-based social forms," he reduces it to "signs (texts, beliefs, social institutions, literary figures, and ritual observances) that form into a semiotic web of interlinking pieces. By signs we also mean affective states of consciousness brought about by ecstatic experience and catastrophic event."[93] Left only with signs and social forms, we lose word and meaning, since the word, Levinas rightly asserts, bears "an implication of meaning distinct from that which comes to signs from the simultaneity of systems."[94] When we lose the word, we lose our humanity, our sanctity, and our meaning. Left only with signs and social forms, not only do we lose the living presence of the Holy One, we also lose any absolute authority for the ethical imperative. Thus the postmodern response to the Shoah comes to little more than what Braiterman calls "expressions of hurt."[95] What is required after the Nazi horror is not an expression of hurt but the action by which we *help* those who are hurt. What is required is a movement to the inside, even if there is terror inside, as it is written in the Talmud (see *Bava Kama* 60b). What is required is both a physical and a philosophical return to Jerusalem.

FROM AUSCHWITZ TO JERUSALEM: A RENEWED CENTER OF THOUGHT

Jerusalem, open to all humanity only since it came under Jewish rule in 1967, exemplifies the simultaneous universality and particularity of Jewish thought. In the previous chapter, we saw what this means in terms of time: Jewish thinking is informed by a living orientation toward the Sabbath. Here we shall see that, in terms of space, Jewish thinking is informed by a living orientation toward Jerusalem. To be sure, each orientation is interwoven with the other. The Chasidic master Elimelekh of Lizensk, for example, teaches that the six branches of the menorah signify the six days of the week, while the center branch is both Sabbath and Shekhinah *(Noam Elimelekh, Behaalotcha)*.[96] Just as the Shekhinah dwells in the time of the Sabbath, so does she dwell in the space of Jerusalem, as the mystics have noted: using *gematria* (interpretation based on numerical values of Hebrew letters), they note that when the letters of the word *Shekhinah* are spelled out, the word has a numerical value of 596, which is the same numerical value as the word *Jerusalem*.[97] And in the Talmud it is written, "Rabbi Shmuel bar Nachmani said in the name of Rabbi Yochanan: 'Three are called by the Name of the Holy One, blessed be He, and they are the righteous, the Messiah, and Jerusalem'" (*Bava Batra* 75b). Jerusalem, then, represents precisely what the Nazis attempted to destroy at Auschwitz: the Commanding Voice of the Divine Presence as She dwells in the world.

Just as the Shekhinah is identified with Jerusalem, so is She associated with the community of Israel (see *Zohar* II, 98a). The assault on the body of Israel, then, entails an assault on the Shekhinah and her dwelling place, Jerusalem. Similarly, just as Auschwitz symbolizes the Nazi assault on the light of the world, so too, says Rabbi Steinsaltz, does "harm done to Jerusalem" and to those who dwell there strike "at the light of the world."[98] And striking at the light of the world—at the Jewish people, who are a "light unto the nations" (Isaiah 42:6)—is harm done to Jerusalem. As the site where the Temple stood, Jerusalem signifies the presence of Torah in the world, and Torah signifies sanctity in the world. To be sure, the Midrash teaches that the windows of the Temple were designed not to let light in but to allow the light of Torah to radiate into the world (*Tanchuma Tetsaveh* 6). It is no accident, therefore, that Elie Wiesel compares the annihilation of the Jews in the Holocaust to the burning of the Temple.[99] At Auschwitz the Temple was itself placed upon the altar.

Inasmuch as Auschwitz was designed to reduce the body of Israel to ashes, it was designed to reduce Jerusalem to ruins. As we recall from the epigraph to this volume's introductory chapter, the tearing of garments at the sight of the ruins of Jerusalem is among those rents of mourning not to be sewn up (*Moed Katan* 26a). Such wounds remain open wounds. And, just as exile can be both physical and metaphysical, so can the ruins of Jerusalem, for there is a Jerusalem above and a Jerusalem below (see, for example, *Bava Batra* 75a–75b; see also *Pesikta de-Rab Kahana,* suppl. 5:4). There is no "Heavenly Paris," no "Heavenly Tokyo," nor even a "Heavenly New York." But who has not heard of the Heavenly Jerusalem? That is the meaning of the holy in the Holy City.

The notion of the holy in the Holy City, moreover, is not to exclude the human being. Just the opposite. Insisting upon the sanctity of every human being as well as on the interconnectedness of each to the other, Jewish teaching maintains that every human being is tied to the holiness of the Holy City. In the *Tanna debe Eliyyahu,* for instance, it is written that the site where the altar stood in Jerusalem is "the place whence Adam's dust was taken" (*Tanna debe Eliyyahu,* 411; see also *Bereshit Rabbah* 14:8; *Pirke de Rabbi Eliezer* 11). Adam, the one through whom each human being is bound to the other, is made not only of dust but also of the light of the Holy One. As Adam is created in the image and likeness of the Holy, so is Jerusalem. Therefore, in our daily prayers, we acknowledge God as the *Boneh Yerushalayim,* the "Builder of Jerusalem." As the *Boneh Yerushalayim,* moreover, God is the *Shokhen Yerushalayim,* "the One who dwells in Jerusalem" (see, for example, Psalms 135:21). Therefore, in our prayers, we refer to Jerusalem not as "our city" but as "Your city." The Jews make no claim to Jerusalem; rather, Jerusalem lays claim to the Jews. That is why Jerusalem signifies the light of the world.

Signifying the light of God and Torah, Jerusalem signifies the *height* that is the metaphysical dimension of Jewish thought. And in that dimension of height, thought and prayer intersect. "The gate of heaven," says the Midrash, "is in Jerusalem" (*Midrash Tehillim* 4:91:7). In Jerusalem, therefore, stands the gate of prayer, which, for the Jewish thinker, is the gate of thought.[100] As we face Jerusalem when we pray, so must we face Jerusalem when we think, for God and Jerusalem are interconnected, as the sacred texts maintain. The Jewish tradition teaches, for example, that just as there are seventy names of God and seventy names of Torah, so are there seventy names of Jerusalem (see *Yalkut Shimoni, Naso*): just as the living God is a category necessary for Jewish thought, so is the Holy City indispensable to thinking Jewishly. If Jewish thought is informed by Torah, moreover, it is informed by Jerusalem, "for the Torah goes forth from Zion and the word of Hashem from Jerusalem" (Isaiah 2:3), which is to say: the Torah that originates above finds expression as the word of Hashem that emanates from Jerusalem.[101]

For the Jewish thinker, to borrow again from Rabbi Steinsaltz, "it is not only that one thinks in terms of Torah, but also that the Torah thinks within oneself. It is an object that becomes a subject, capable of expressing itself in one's own thoughts and actions."[102] For the Jewish thinker, what Rabbi Steinsaltz says of Torah may also be said of Jerusalem: Jerusalem herself thinks in the thinking of the Jewish thinker. Jerusalem herself is a mode of thinking. I realized the truth of this point the last time I saw Emil Fackenheim in Jerusalem; it was in 2002, a few weeks before his last trip to Germany. "I go to Germany," he told me, "not as a German but as a Jew whose home is Jerusalem." In saying this, Fackenheim the philosopher was one with Fackenheim the resident of Jerusalem. That is how a Jewish thinker thinks *concretely.* God, Torah, and Jerusalem, *concretely* essential to Jewish thought, are among the ten things that, according to the Talmud, are distinguished by the word *living* (see *Avot d'Rabbi Nathan* 34:11).[103] From a Jewish standpoint, then, they are among the things necessary for *life.* The world—and not simply the Jews—can no more do without Jerusalem than it can do without God and Torah. Indeed, Jerusalem is not only the capital of Israel—it is the center of the world.

There is a talmudic text that illustrates this point: "Abba Isi ben Yochanan said in the name of Shmuel Hakaton: This world is likened to a person's eyeball: the white of the eye [corresponds to] the ocean which surrounds the whole world; the iris to the [inhabited] world; the pupil of the eye to Jerusalem; the face in the pupil to the Temple" (*Derekh Erets Rabbah* 9:13). What is the face in the pupil, the face reflected in Jerusalem? It is the face—or the trace—of the Holy One, who gazes at the world as the world gazes at Jerusalem. Jerusalem is like a "peephole" in the gate between heaven and earth. As we peer through the gate, the face in the pupil reveals to us the face reflected in our own pupil, the face of the other human being. It is the face that *concretely* puts to the Jewish thinker the question it puts to the one made of the dust of Jerusalem: Where are you? Here, too, we see the simultaneous universality and particularity of Jewish thought.

The murder of the Jews at Auschwitz, body and soul, was the murder of Jewish particularity and universality. It was the murder of the specific, concrete human being and of the general principle of human accountability. It was the murder of women and babies, old men and boys, who by their very presence in the world signify the light of a testimony bestowed upon all humanity. It was the murder of the human being and of humankind. Without the concrete Jewish reality of Jerusalem, we have only the Jewish abstraction of Auschwitz, for in Auschwitz the Jews were murdered as an abstraction, not as husbands and wives, parents and children, not as human beings with names but as units with numbers. That is why the Nazis could speak only of "processing units" and never of murdering human beings.

The tension between Auschwitz and Jerusalem, therefore, is a tension not just between the site where Jews were murdered and the capital of the Jewish State; it is a tension between the abstract thinking born of Athens and the concrete *Machshavah Yehudit* born of Jerusalem. With the Holy City as its symbolic center, Jewish thought incorporates the category of holiness into its thinking, a category as concrete as the Jerusalem stones and utterly alien to the abstractions of ethical monotheism. Only with Jerusalem as its "philosophical capital" can there be a flesh-and-blood future for Jewish thought as *Machshavah Yehudit*, for Jerusalem signifies not just a point of view but also a mode of thinking in accordance with the divinely revealed Torah. Torah says: give *this* person *this* piece of bread *now*. Reason says: always act according to this universal maxim. Without the Torah that goes forth from Zion and the Word that issues from Jerusalem, people go hungry. And when people go hungry, there can be no Jewish response to the evil that is Auschwitz.

We began this chapter with the opposition between ethical monotheism and Judaism; it has led to an opposition between Auschwitz and Jerusalem. The tension between the two lies in a tension between Nazi ideology and Jewish thought. While the former is informed by the ontological tradition, the latter is shaped by the *sifrei kodesh*, the holy texts of Jewish teaching and thinking. We shall consider how those texts may add to our understanding of the Shoah and how they may contribute to Jewish thought after the Shoah. But first let us consider the basic building block of those texts: Hebrew words.

4

The Holocaust
and the Holy Tongue

Hebrew words describe not only an object but also its very
essence.—Rabbi Yehuda Loeve, *Maharal of Prague: Pirke Avos*

We have seen that the Holocaust is characterized by an assault on the
sanctity of the human being. So radical is this assault that it eludes language, as Primo Levi has said: there is no word "to express this offense . . . :
the demolition of a man."[1] There is no word for this offense because the
demolition of a man is the demolition of the word, which was, indeed,
a defining feature of the Holocaust. Sara Nomberg-Przytyk makes this
point when she asserts, "The new set of meanings [of words] provided
the best evidence of the devastation that Auschwitz created."[2] In place
of the word filled with meaning we have the bleeding wound that remains
after the word has been torn from its meaning, like the bleeding word
Jude branded into the forehead of Shlamek's father in Ka-tzetnik's *House
of Dolls,* "as though it were quite natural that the word *Jude* should give
blood."[3] After Auschwitz, Jewish thought is steeped in the blood that
flows from the open wound of this bleeding word: Jew.

THE WOUND OF THE BLEEDING WORD

When meaning is torn from words, life is bled of its substance, and the
world is transformed into a wasteland. That is when the world as *Mishkan,* as a dwelling place for holiness, is in need of mending, even as the

Holy of Holies in the Temple (which was also called a *Mishkan*) on occasion required repairs. The Talmud relates that whenever the Holy of Holies required mending, a craftsman would be lowered into the sacred enclosure in a *tevah*, or "box." There were openings in the box just large enough for the craftsman to see what had to be repaired and to do his work so that he would not be tempted to feast his eyes upon the glory of the Shekhinah (*Midot* 37a). Now the word *tevah* signifies not only a vessel; it also means "word." Entering the vessel of the holy word, we may descend into the post-Shoah world to undertake the task of restoring it as a holy place. Only through such a repair—only through such a *tikkun*—can we restore our souls.

To be sure, Matityahu Glazerson points out that, according to Jewish teaching, the word "is not merely a vehicle for making known the speaker's intent. Nor is the *alef-beit* a set of symbols or conventions. Rather, the words and letters shape the soul."[4] Rabbi Adin Steinsaltz elaborates: "Beyond our creations, words are also our creators. . . . 'The soul is full of words,' . . . so much so that people believe that each person gets an allocation of words for a lifetime, and once it is used up, life ends."[5] If we come into being through an utterance of the Holy One, our being is also sustained—or threatened—by our own utterances. As Jews entrusted with the care of our Jewish souls, we are entrusted with the care of the holy tongue. What is at stake in this task is inscribed in the face of Shlamek's father, the face of the Jew under assault in a radical assault upon the word—the face disfigured by the bleeding word.

The challenge confronting Jewish thought in the post-Auschwitz era is to answer, as a Jew, to this assault on the word manifest in the assault on the face. "The face speaks," as Emmanuel Levinas has said. "It speaks, it is in this that it renders possible and begins all discourse."[6] And because what speaks from the face comes from an absolute that is beyond the face, "the face is signification, and signification without context. I mean that the Other, in the rectitude of his face, is not a character within a context. . . . All signification in the usual sense of the term is relative to such a context. . . . Here, to the contrary, the face is meaning all by itself."[7] What does the face say? What is the fundamental word that makes possible all discourse? It is this: *Lo tirtsach*, "Thou shalt not murder" (Exodus 20:13).[8] That is the commanding word that instills every word with meaning. Received through Torah, it "is received outside any exploratory foray, outside any gradual development," to borrow another insight from Levinas.[9] The prohibition against murder does not evolve— it is revealed. It is not deduced—it is commanded. Indeed, it cannot be deduced. It is the premise, the absolute a priori, that is the Holy One.[10] This a priori is the word that the Nazis would obliterate from the face of the human being.

For, inasmuch as the Nazi assault on the image and essence of the human being is an assault on the face, it is an assault on the Divine prohibition against murder. And so we see what is undone in the tearing of meaning from the word: when the bond between word and meaning is broken, the prohibition against murder is obliterated. Here we have a key to the Baal Shem Tov's commentary on Genesis 6:16: "You shall make a window *(tsohar)* in the ark *(tevah)*." According to the Baal Shem, this means that one should bring light *(tsohar)* to each word *(tevah)* we speak.[11] Which means: the meaning we connect with the word is the light of sanctity that we attach to life, a light that emanates from the face of the human being. Once word is severed from meaning in the confusion of tongues, the language of the antiworld inserts itself into creation in a darkening of creation. Thus Primo Levi remembers that Auschwitz, whose essence was murder and darkness, was filled with a "sound and fury signifying nothing: a hubbub of people without names or faces drowned in a continuous, deafening background noise from which, however, the human word did not surface."[12] And there is no word for this offense, which is an assault not only upon the human being but upon the very meaning of creation.

According to Jewish teaching, the language of creation is Hebrew (see *Sefer Yetzirah* 1:1). Indeed, "the Holy One," teaches the Gerer Rebbe, Yehudah Leib Alter, "created everything through the twenty-two letters."[13] Michael Munk explains: "That the twenty-two letters of the *Aleph-Bais* [alphabet] were used to create the world is alluded to by the *gematria* of the first three words of the Torah [*bereshit bara Elokim*], 'in the beginning God created' (1202), which is the same as the *gematria* of [*bekh"v otiot bara*], 'with 22 letters He created' the world."[14] Jewishly understood, then, Hebrew is not *in* the world; rather, the world issues from the Hebrew language of the Divine utterance.

Pursuing the implication that the holy tongue appears before the creation of heaven and earth, the Midrash relates, "When the Holy One, blessed be He, gave forth the Divine word, the voice divided itself into seven voices, and from the seven voices passed into the seventy languages of the seventy nations" (*Midrash Tehillim* 2:68:6).[15] What language does God speak when He brings forth the Divine word? It is Hebrew, as the talmudic commentary on Betsalel suggests: he was chosen to oversee the building of the Holy Tabernacle because he knew the secret combinations and meanings of the Hebrew words and letters that God uses at every instant to do the work of creation (*Berakhot* 55a).[16] And the Baal Shem Tov taught that the letters of the Hebrew alphabet "are not mere symbols but the expression of metaphysical realities. They are the counterpart on earth of God's creative processes and are themselves endowed with creative power."[17] Jews chant their scriptures and say their prayers in Hebrew not only because of the pristine nature of the holy tongue but also because doing so is a means of participating in the Divine creation that unfolds at every instant. It is no accident that the Nazi assault on the soul entailed the obliteration of holy texts and Hebrew prayers.[18]

From what has been said, we can see that the Nazi assault on the holy tongue was an assault on the very essence of creation. Indeed, when the sanctity of the human being is under attack, so is the sanctity of the world. And it is a sanctity that pertains not just to the Jews but also to the very notion of humanity. Hence, according to the Midrash, when Moses reviewed the teachings of Torah, just before the Israelites entered the Holy Land, he taught them not only in the holy tongue but also in all the seventy languages of the world (*Tanchuma Devarim* 2).[19] From the beginning, then, we have the affirmation that, in their adherence to Torah and the holy tongue, the Jews are to be a light unto the nations, and that the sanctification of the human being that issues from Torah pertains to all humanity. God's aim, says the *Sefat Emet*, is "to bring all nations near to Him by means of Israel."[20] And, because the Divine utterance gives life, everything harbors a spark of life. Contrary to the neutrality of being that characterizes the views of the Western ontological tradition, in Hebrew there is no neutral gender. Every noun is masculine or feminine and therefore harbors a kind of soul, a living presence. Everything that has a name has a voice.

Indeed, the Baal Shem Tov teaches that "in each and every letter there are worlds and souls and divine powers that both interconnect and join together" (*Keter Shem Tov* 1). Expounding on this idea, Rabbi Yitzchak Ginsburgh explains that each of the twenty-two letters of the Hebrew alphabet possesses three creative powers known as *koach, chiyut,* and *or*— "energy," "life," and "light"—corresponding to physical matter, organic matter, and soul, respectively. The Hebrew letters, says Rabbi Ginsburgh, function as "the energy building-blocks of all reality; as the manifestation of the inner life-pulse permeating the universe as a whole and each of its individual creatures . . . ; and as the channels which direct the influx of Divine revelation into created consciousness."[21] If Hebrew words and letters shape "created consciousness," the Hebrew language can certainly inform Jewish thought. To be sure, this tie to Hebrew is one of the things that makes Jewish thought Jewish.

Tradition teaches that God creates not only world and consciousness but also each soul from the letters of the holy tongue. He puts those letters together to form an utterance so that, in the words of Adin Steinsaltz, "the soul of a [person] is the Divine speech that speaks the [person]."[22] The soul, therefore, is more an action than an object: it is a *speech act* of the Holy One. What we make of our souls lies in whether and how we join our speech to that Divine speech through our thoughts, words, and deeds. Says Rabbi Abraham Isaac Kook, "The soul is full of [Hebrew] letters that abound with the light of life, intellect and will, a spirit of vision, and complete existence."[23] What is the Divine speech that is the substance of the soul? It is Torah. Hebrew is the holy tongue not because it is the language of Torah; rather, Hebrew is the language of Torah because it is the holy tongue. Inasmuch as the Nazis' annihilation of the Jewish people entailed a radical assault on the soul and the Torah of the Jewish people, it was an assault on the holy tongue. If Jewish thought is to recover the spark of life from the ashes of death, it must turn to the holy tongue. The very life of the Jewish soul is at stake in this turning, in this *teshuvah*. This is not to say that Jewish thought must be in Hebrew, but it is to maintain that Jewish thought should be informed by Hebrew.

Thus one question before the Jewish thinker in the post-Holocaust era is: How might a consideration of some key terms from the holy tongue enlighten Jewish thinking about the Shoah in the Jew's effort to recover from that abyss a life and a soul, a future and an identity?

HOLOCAUST AS SHOAH

In the introduction to this volume we made a couple of points concerning what the word *Shoah,* the Hebrew term for the Holocaust, reveals about the event. It was noted, for example, that the root of *Shoah* is *shav,* a word that means "nothingness" as well as "lie." This root tells us first of all that if the term *Holocaust* is a synonym for *Shoah,* then it is not a synonym for "catastrophe," "horrific suffering," or even "genocide." More than an attempt to exterminate the Jewish people, the Shoah is the imposition of the *tohu-vavohu,* the chaos and void, of nothingness upon humanity. It is the creation of an antiworld in the midst of the world, an undoing of creation in a rain of ashes that have found their way into every human being. "The world around us," as Levi recalls his emergence from Auschwitz, "seemed to have returned to primeval Chaos, and was swarming with scalene, defective, abnormal human specimens."[24] These "specimens" reflect the image not of the Creator but of the chaos of the Nazi anti-Creator; these are the inhabitants of the land that the Germans had made of Europe—indeed, of the world. There, says Levi, "it was more than a sack: it was the genius of destruction, of anti-creation, here as at Auschwitz; it was the mystique of barrenness."[25] The Italian word translated as "barrenness" is *vuoto,*[26] which means "emptiness" or "void." The anticreation is the creation of nothing out of something, a return to the abyss of what strives to overcome the abyss.[27] It is Shoah.

The word *Shoah,* in fact, means "abyss." It is fathomless. It is an assault on the Infinite One, an assault that assumes an infinite aspect. And it is primal, cosmic, ontological terror. What we have in the Shoah is not just the abyss that is the Holocaust but also the Holocaust, this "thing," that is the abyss. It is as much a singularity in its devastation as a black hole whose gravity is so great that it swallows up light, space, and time itself. The cognate verb *shaah* means "to become desolate" or "to be devastated"; the *hitpael* form, *hishtaah,* is "to wonder," "to be astonished," or "to gaze in wonder or awe."[28] What is the Holocaust? Exceeding the parameters of genocide, it is the calculated, carefully implemented imposition of the abyss upon the world, beginning with the Jews, complete and cataclysmic. It is the lie made truth, the unreal made real, the return of the world to the nothingness, to the *shav,* that Jewish thought now struggles to overcome. It is the astonishment not over what is unimaginable but over everything imaginable.

The crisis of Jewish thought lies in the difficulty of trying to think one's way out of the abyss, the nothingness, and the devastation of consciousness that belongs to the Shoah. Committing every act imaginable, the Nazis did the unthinkable, as Charlotte Delbo suggests: those sent to the anti-world, she says, "expect the worst—they do not expect the unthinkable."[29] Approaching the Holocaust as Shoah, then, we realize that post-Holocaust Jewish thought must begin with the unthinkable, for when words are torn from meaning, thought is torn from the soul. Regaining thought is a matter of regaining the soul, which in turn lies in restoring meaning to the word, beginning with this word—*Shoah*—that means the annihilation of meaning. We have no other way of returning to life and returning to the world—no other means of *teshuvah*. As Shoah, the Holocaust transforms the world itself into a "concentrationary universe," a realm not only in which "there are no fathers, no brothers, no friends"[30] but also in which there are neither criminals nor madmen.[31] Thus we have inherited a world in which murderers pass for martyrs, terrorists are honored as militants, and tyrants are treated as victims.

Have we, then, seen the end of history? Did it get swallowed up in the black hole of the Shoah? For if it is to be intelligible—if, in fact, it is to be *history*—then history must have some meaning, some aim, some basis for distinguishing horror from happenstance, and good from evil. If Jewish thought is to draw meaning from this history and thus posit a future for the Jewish people, as well as for humanity, then it must think Jewishly about history, and not in the categories we have inherited from a past whose history culminated in the Shoah; to be sure, it was in the Shoah that history came to a halt. How, then, might a Jewish sense of history be regenerated? And what, exactly, makes a Jewish sense of history Jewish? Here, too, Hebrew can help.

TOWARD A HEBREW UNDERSTANDING OF HISTORY

"The dramatic struggle which is illustrated in Hebrew words," says André Neher, speaking of the Bible, "describes not only an object but its very essence by the symbolism of marital love: the pathetic and dialogical encounter of God and Israel gave universal history a meaning. The history of mankind *receives its meaning* by the intimacy of God and Israel."[32] The metaphor of marriage is not accidental: history as such happens in the intimate, covenantal relation between God and humanity, beginning with the Jews, whereby humanity receives a seed from the Father that it must now nurture into a living presence if humanity is to have a history. Hence "the human situation in history," writes Neher, "begins with the covenant."[33] The seed of the Father, indeed, lies in the Covenant so that the Chosen must choose between "life and good, death and evil" (Deuteronomy 30:15)—for the sake of history. History thus understood is a process of bringing forth life: the God of history summons us to choose life (Deuteronomy 30:19). The Hebrew word often loosely translated as "history," then, is *toledot* (strictly speaking, there is no Hebrew word for "history"). It has the same root as *yeled,* the word for "child," the one who imparts meaning to life and to words by drawing from above the memory and continuity that go into the making of a life.

The child, then, is the flesh-and-blood fulcrum of "history" as *toledot.* In their efforts to remove Jews from the Covenant, and therefore from history, the Nazis created realms in the camps and ghettos that were devoid of Jewish children. George Salton, for instance, remembers that when he was liberated from Wöbbelin he saw children for the first time in six years. "I had forgotten how they looked," he comments on his first sight of the German children who lived near the camp. "The Jewish children had all been gassed. Probably by the fathers or uncles of these children here."[34] If all of creation is sustained by the breath of little children, as it is written in the Talmud (see *Shabbat* 119b), so too is history upheld by that breath. Within every infant are gathered not only eons of genetic coding but also millennia of human history, of *toledot.* Here, the implications of the Nazis' first-targeting of children in their murder of the Jews are apparent: the assault on the little ones was an assault on the Holy One, who, through His intimacy with Israel, gives birth to history. It was, in a word, an assault on *toledot.*

While most thinkers who respond to the Holocaust make much of history, few if any adopt a specifically Jewish view of history as *toledot.* What most respondents to the Shoah have in mind by "history" is a chronology of political and cultural events that unfold over the ages—

what Leo Baeck describes by saying, "History is the ruin heap of power, and to work for its triumph is to work for ruin."[35] Even distinctively Jewish thinkers, such as Emil Fackenheim and Emmanuel Levinas, say nothing of the Hebrew *toledot*. Still, Fackenheim correctly describes the notion of history in modern thought as "the self-realization of human freedom, a process which redeemed itself,"[36] and for which God became superfluous. "Whereas to the liberal, history was a self-redemptive process," he writes, making a crucial distinction, "Jewish tradition maintained that history, to fulfill its meaning, requires the incursion of God."[37] That incursion of God is manifest as the *Covenant* with God. And the Covenant with God requires bearing children into the world.

To be sure, according to the Midrash, the children at Mount Sinai agreed to serve as sureties that the Covenant would endure (see, for example, *Tanchuma Vayigash* 1; *Shir Hashirim Rabbah* 1:4:1). At Auschwitz, however, the children had no voice in the matter of whether they might serve as sureties for the Covenant. Therefore, the question for Jewish thought is infinitely more pressing: What shall we make of the Covenant placed in our hands? It is a question that comes to us from the face of history, for history has a face: it has the face of a child. That face asks us how we shall answer for what has been placed in our care. The child, guarantor of the Covenant of Torah, is the guarantor of history—the *yeled* is the guarantor of *toledot*. As a "guarantor," or *arev*, the child situates us at the *erev*, or "eve," of history, making history into what is *about to* come but is *not yet* decided. Jewish thought moves along the edge of this *not yet*. That edge—that "eve"—has a name: it is *birth*. What the Covenant means to a Jewish understanding of history, therefore, can be seen from another meaning of *toledot*: it is "generations," which are "brought forth" (from the verb *yalad*, meaning "to give birth").

Once again, Jewishly speaking, history is something to which God and humanity *give birth* in a covenantal union. Like the birth of a child, the birth of history requires the participation of God (compare Talmud Bavli, *Kiddushin* 30b). As the continual unfolding of creation, history is a continual process of giving birth, from above to below, a process that, mystically speaking, transpires through the Supernal Mother (see *Zohar* I, 22b):[38] it is she who gives birth to history. The Supernal Mother, in turn, is the source of justice, of the *tsedek* discussed in the previous chapter: history is the history of justice. Once we have lost a sense of justice, we lose a sense of history. And, once we have lost a sense of *sacred* history, we have lost a sense of justice.[39] Even in the nineteenth century the Jewish philosopher Elijah Benamozegh was conscious of this point. "The justice of God," he maintains, "is the beginning of history."[40] The Jewish return into history entails the reestablishment not only of the Jewish State but also of the Jewish sense of justice, of *tsedek,* understood in its Hebrew sense as "righteousness" and "charity."

Abraham Joshua Heschel makes a similar point. Viewed Jewishly, "history is the encounter of the eternal and the temporal," he writes. "Just as the Word is a veil for revelation and a sign for prayer, so history may form a vessel for God's action in the world and provides the material out of which man's doing in time is fashioned."[41] Again, "man's doing in time" is the opposite of "doing time"; to "do time" is to languish in the emptiness of timelessness. "Man's doing *in* time," by contrast, is a doing rooted in purpose; it consists most fundamentally of bringing life into the world and, in the process, returning meaning to the word. Therefore, according to the Hebraic view, history is not the narrative of the past; it is an orientation toward the future, a hidden narrative that derives its meaning from a meaning and a redemption yet to unfold: *toledot* is *messianic.*

This meaning is to be attained not in space, as Heschel rightly points out, but only in time: "It is in the realm of history that man is charged with God's mission,"[42] which is always *yet to be* attained. Hence the movement toward the future constitutes the history of the past, as Elie Wiesel has suggested. "The opposite of the past," he writes, "is not the future but the absence of future; the opposite of the future is not the past but the absence of past."[43] If the Holocaust is a breach in Jewish history that divorces us from our past, then it divorces us from the Holy One. And if it divorces us from the Holy One, it divorces us from the Promised One, from the Messiah, in whom our future abides. Finally, if our youth have no sense of history, it is not because they do not read; rather, they do not read because they have no sense of history. And they have no sense of history because they have no sense of future. They have lost the Messiah at the gates of Rome.[44]

But the Messiah no longer languishes at the gates of Rome. No, he abides within the gates embossed with the sardonic ARBEIT MACHT FREI.

He peers at us through the barbed wire, whose touch is deadly. And he cannot get out. There lies the crisis of Jewish thought after Auschwitz: how to release the Messiah from Auschwitz and thus come to the *after*,[45] to the *acharei*, through a movement toward the *acher*, the "other" human being. This is where we attain the "responsibility," the *acharayut*, that is also a "future," or *acharit*. The Messiah will not deliver us. No, just the opposite: we must deliver him. Not through power but through loving kindness toward the other, through the justice and righteousness that are *tsedek*, through the *teshuvah* that takes us back to Torah, back to the Covenant, back to history—back to the future. For "the generations"— the *toledot*—"are made of the righteous and their good deeds," as the Rimanover Rebbe, Rabbi Menachem Mendel, has taught.[46] Which is to say: history is made of *mitzvot*.

Contrary to the claims of most historians and philosophers of history, says Heschel, "human power is not the stuff of which history is made. For history is not what is displayed at the moment, but what is concealed in the mind of the Lord."[47] Concealed in the mind of the Lord is the *mitzvah* that will release the Messiah from Auschwitz. And it may be the very next one. Concealed in the mind of the Lord is the name of a certain child who is yet to be born. And that child may be the very next one. History, *toledot*, is not what has been; it is what might be. It is the history of the Messiah, not merely as the one whom we await but as the one whose coming we work to hasten. That is how the eternal finds its way into history: in our labor to hasten the coming of the Messiah through the *mitzvot* we perform. In the *mitzvot* that go into the making of history God lies hidden. That is why Eliezer Berkovits asserts that God "can only hide in history."[48] Where does He hide? In the messianic future that abides in the child.

Here, the matter of determining Jerusalem to be the philosophical capital for Jewish thought, as discussed in the last chapter, becomes all the more pressing, for Jerusalem and the State of Israel signify the remnant of hope for a continuation of history, Jewishly understood—and for all humanity. Just as history is possible only with the incursion of God, so too, in the words of Levinas, the State of Israel, "in accordance with its pure essence, is possible only if penetrated by the divine word."[49] Not only is the State of Israel possible—it is actual. More than that, it is, in the words of Levinas, a *category*. Commenting on what has become of history in this connection, he writes:

> There is no longer any difference between day and night, between out-side and inside. Do we not smell here, more strongly than a while back, beyond all violence which still submits to will and reason, the odor of the camps? Violence is no longer a political phenomenon of war and peace, beyond all morality. It is the abyss of Auschwitz or the world at war. A world which has lost its "very worldliness." It is the twentieth century. One must go back inside, even if there is terror inside. Is the fact of Israel unique? Does it not have its full meaning because it applies to all human-ity? All men are on the verge of being in the situation of the State of Israel. The State of Israel is a category.[50]

Inasmuch as history is a category essential to a Jewish response to the Shoah, so too is the State of Israel such a category. It is the category that returns the Jewish people to history, to the birth of a future called *tole-dot*. It is the category that returns what is *Jewish* to Jewish thought.

That birth, that return, is the aim of *tikkun haolam,* which is the mend-ing of word and world accomplished through Covenant, Torah, and *mitzvot.* If Jewish thought is to participate in the mending of the world, it must take up a mending of the word reduced to silence. Here, too, the holy tongue can help us to better understand not only a key aspect of the Holocaust but also how Jewish thought might respond to it.

WORD REDUCED TO SILENCE

We have seen what the word *toledot* can add to a Jewish understanding of history. Another Hebrew term for "history" is *divrei hayamim*—literally, the "affairs of the days" or the "words of the days." Indeed, days are made of words. The destruction of words brings about the destruction of days. Because words on planet Auschwitz were torn from their meaning, as Ka-tzetnik puts it, days "on planet Auschwitz revolved around the cog-wheels of a different time-sphere."[51] If history is made of the conceal-ment of God, on planet Auschwitz nothing was hidden—everything was *stark.* Which is to say: on planet Auschwitz there was no history, no *tole-*

dot. Therefore, any attempt to decipher the stark unreality only served to undermine the human being: there was nothing behind the cipher.[52] Thus the "words of the days" were consigned to the ovens of the crematoria. They ascended into the heavens on columns of smoke, along with the bodies and souls that were made of them. In the Torah it is written that we shall live in the Covenant with the Holy One, and He shall live in the Covenant with His Chosen, *kiyemei hashamayim al haarets,* "as long as the heavens are above the earth" (Deuteronomy 11:21). But when meaning is torn from the word—when a word is no longer a word, and the divine spark is extinguished from the human being—the heavens are no longer above the earth. The proof? At Auschwitz the sky was transformed into a cemetery.

For post-Holocaust Jewish thought, part of the restoration of the word entails a return to the Hebrew word for "word," to the word *davar,* from the phrase *divrei hayamim.* If the soul is a Divine speech act, then the soul is made of the word; that is, it is made of its name. "You must watch over your name and your soul," says Rabbi Nachman of Breslov,[53] for they are one and the same, as it is written: "as his name is, so is he" (1 Samuel 25:25). Therefore, in their assault upon the soul of the Jew, the Nazis undertook an assault upon the word that bespoke the essence of the Jew: the Jew's name. Once a Jew received a number, he or she was known by no other word, no other name. "I became A-7713," says Elie Wiesel. "After that I had no other name."[54] "I looked at my number: 7,115," says Alexander Donat. "From that moment I ceased to be a man."[55] "We ceased to be human beings with family names," says Moshe Sandberg. "In my metamorphosis I was No. 124753."[56] In fact, in order to receive his ration, the Jew had to show his number and recite it in German: showing the number in exchange for food, the prisoner declared his namelessness and his nothingness in an alien, unholy tongue as he wasted away on the meager fare.

If "death is silence," as Neher has said,[57] in Auschwitz it is the silence that follows in the wake of the assault on names and words. It is the "silence" that in Hebrew is *shtikah,* a cognate of the word *shituk,* which is a "paralysis" manifest as wordlessness. It is the silence of the Angel of Death, a silence that haunts the soul and the memory of the assault on the soul. In the post-Auschwitz era, the Angel of Death—the Angel with a Thousand Eyes, as yellow as the star that Nazis stamped on the Jews[58]—has been the constant companion of the Jews. Only this time the Angel comes not to take us but to leave us with new eyes, through which we gaze into our harried soul. And through which the Angel puts to us a question, in keeping with the ancient Jewish legend. According to the legend, when we lie in the grave the Angel of Death comes to us so that he might bring us into the presence of the Holy One. But in order to draw nigh unto the Divine Presence, we must correctly answer a question. And so, with his thousand eyes gazing upon us, the Angel breaks his silence and poses the fearsome question, the question he put to Jacob when they wrestled till dawn (see Genesis 32:25-31): "What is your name?"[59]

But what, indeed, do we know when we know our name? To know our name is to know the names of those who confer a name upon us, the names of our mother and our father. It means knowing a tradition borne by those who have borne our names before us; it means knowing a teaching that harbors our future and our mission in life, as inscribed in our name; it means recognizing that we are called by name and must answer to our name. Asking our name, the Angel establishes something about our being that is intimately tied to our doing: knowing our name—like knowing God, from whose Name our names derive—means knowing what we must *do*.[60] To be sure, in the Talmud the rabbis refer to the transmission of Torah from one generation to another as a "handing down of names" (see *Kiddushin* 71a). If, as Edmond Jabès has said, Auschwitz is "the wound of an unsayable name rather than the name of an unhealable wound,"[61] then the return of the Name lies in our own movement of return, in our ability not to say His Name but to affirm our own name in a moment of answering that is never over with. After Auschwitz, Jewish thought must retrieve the memory and the name couched in the *davar* that belongs to the Jew.

In Hebrew, *davar* means not only "word" but also "thing." As the word is torn from meaning, so is the thing torn from its reality. So are the days, *hayamim,* torn from our lives, for the days of our lives are gathered into the things that belong to us, in a pair of shoes, an old sweater, a wedding ring, a watch, a photograph, a book. But just as the Jews were denied the word, so were they forbidden anything that might signify who they were, including their hair. Recall, for example, the deportation scene that Wiesel describes in *Night*: "The street was like a market place that had suddenly been abandoned. Everything could be found there: suitcases, portfolios, briefcases, knives, plates, banknotes, papers, faded portraits. All those things that people had thought of taking with them, and which in the end they had left behind. They had lost all value."[62] Like words that have lost their meaning, these signs of so many lives now signify nothing.

Or better: they signify the nothingness that remains after the loss of the soul, as Livia Bitton-Jackson makes clear in her description of a bonfire built in the middle of a Hungarian ghetto: "Volumes of the Bible, leather-bound Psalms, phylacteries turn and twist and burst into myriad fragments of agony. Pictures and documents. . . . Our soul. Weightless speckles of ash rising, fleeing the flames into nothingness."[63] Into nothingness: as though being were itself consumed in those flames. As the texts containing the Holy Name go up in flames, the name and the essence, the very life, of the Jew also ascend on the column of smoke and ash: photographs— the images of the Jew and of his memory—are burned with his books. Just as the Nazis set out to murder the memory couched in the word, so did they attack the memory lodged in the thing. This, too, is a reason why we must be very careful with words like *Jewish* and *thought.*

As a verb, the word *davar* means "to speak." It designates precisely the capacity that distinguishes the human being from an animal or an object and is the indicator of the Divine within the human. As one created in the image and likeness of God, the human being is a *medaber,* that is, a "speaking being," and not a "thinking thing."[64] Informed by Torah, Jewish thought divides the world into four components: mineral, vegetable, animal, and *medaber* (see, for example, Chayyim Vital, *Shaarei Kedushah,* part 1, gate 2),[65] which tells us that, from the standpoint of Jewish thought, a human being is not an animal. "That thing which is called man," teaches Maimonides, for example, "consists of life and speech" (*Moreh Nevuchim* 1:51).[66] Maimonides, of course, bases his insight on the Targum, where Onkelos renders the phrase "living being" in "man became a living being" (Genesis 2:7) as "speaking spirit." In the time of the Shoah, the assault on life was an assault on speech in a radical reduction of the *medaber,* of the speaking being, to a state of silent nonbeing.

One word for "silence" in the holy tongue is *demamah.* A cognate that also means "silence" or "stillness" is *dumah,* which is the name of the guardian angel of the dead, who sits in judgment over the souls of Gehinnom.[67] The implication? That the judgment of Hashem lies not so much in pronouncing a sentence as in refraining from pronouncing anything: to be judged for our sin is to receive the Divine silent treatment. But Auschwitz is not Gehinnom. Gehinnom is a place of judgment and purification through the word; Auschwitz is a place of desecration and destruction through silence. Here, we are reminded that the verb *damam* means not only "to be silent" or "to be mute" but also "to bleed": once again we have the image of the bleeding word *Jude,* of the open wound, that is at the heart of this silence. Hence the verb *nadam,* which is "to be silenced" or "to be rendered mute," also means "to be destroyed." When God enjoins us to choose life over death (Deuteronomy 30:19), He summons us to choose word over silence—or a word that transmits silence—by offering a word in response to His word as well as to the Nazis' silencing of that word. That is the task facing Jewish thought in the wake of the Nazis' silencing of the word.

Another Hebrew word for "silent" is *ilem* (with an *alef*); it also means "mute." In this word, we have a silence that is opposed to the eloquent silence of the Divine utterance. More than a condition of suffering, it is a state of nonbeing that the Nazis imposed upon the Jews through a radical *alimut,* which is a cognate of *ilem*; it means "violence" or "terror." This is the connotation that should be kept in mind when we read, for instance, the 39th Psalm, where King David gives voice to this silence and this terror, crying *neelamti dumiyah,* "I was mute, silent" or "I was struck dumb with silence" (39 :3). *Ilem,* explains Rabbi Kalonymos Kalmish Shapira, is a silence that overcomes a person "so broken and crushed that he has nothing to say; who does not appreciate or understand what is happening to him; who does not possess the faculties with which to assess or assimilate his experiences; who no longer has the mind or the heart with which to incorporate the experience. For him, silence is not a choice; his is the muteness of one incapable of speech."[68] Because this muteness is the muteness of a human being, however, within it lies hidden an outcry. Indeed, the muteness itself "stands erect," as Rabbi Shapira says, like Joseph's "sheaf," which, in a play on *ilem,* is *alumah.*[69] The muteness of *ilem* is more than deafening; it is defiant and accusing. It announces a certain dialectic between word and silence.

One illustration of what this word reveals about the imposed silence of the Shoah can be found in this passage from Josef Bor's *Terezín Requiem,* a novel about the camp at Theresienstadt:

> The silence had penetrated here, Schächter realized, from outside, from above, from everywhere, and now it spread throughout the room, strident and imperative; it overwhelmed everything, froze the walls into dumbness, maimed the people; not even a quiver of air moved here now. The murmur is silenced, the hum of everyday life, which at other times flows everywhere, in the streets, in the house, even in yourself, though you are solitary. . . . And suddenly the hum has ceased. At first you don't even realize that something has happened. There is only a chill somewhere in the marrow of your bones, as though the coldness of the dark night had touched you. As though the breath of death itself had wafted over you. . . . Then suddenly you are aware of the silence.[70]

It is worth noting that the Czech word here translated as "strident" is *křičí,* which means "screaming" or "shrieking."[71] The silence we address here—the silence of the Shoah—is not the quiet that one might ordinarily associate with silence. Like its characteristic darkness and death, the silence of the Shoah is a veil that hides the light and the life of the word, a point to which other witnesses attest.

George Topas, for instance, cannot forget that when he took his first steps in Majdanek, "a mournful, eerie silence pervaded the descending darkness."[72] Wieslaw Kielar remembers the silence with which he wrestled through nights emptied of time, as he was forced to stand in the narrow confines of the *Stehbunker,* or "standing bunker," at Auschwitz. He writes, "This silence stirs me up. . . . I began to sing, I stamped my wooden clogs; in a word, I began making a lot of noise if only to chase away this damned silence which fills me—I don't know why—with fear."[73] And Nathan Shapell recalls the "deathly silence, screaming silence" that permeated the Sosnowiec Ghetto after the final roundup of the Jews for deportation.[74] In these examples we discover the dimensions of the silence of the Shoah; it is a silence that issues from the absence of the word, from the vault of the universe, and from the depths of the soul. Fear and darkness are the very stuff of the silence with which Jewish thought now does battle. It is the fear of a voicelessness that drains the human being of his soul; it is the darkness of an anticreation pitted against the light created upon the first utterance in the creation of the world.

While the silence that distinguishes the Shoah is this radical voicelessness of the *medaber* reduced to nothingness, it is not a mere blank. The absence of the word is the absence of sense, not of sound. On the contrary, it is a sound and fury signifying nothingness, a silence ridden with the din of screeches and screams, of barking and bellowing, of flames and furnaces. It is silence manifest as *raash,* which translates not only as "noise" but also as "earthquake," a shifting of ground in which the ground of meaning crumbles with the crumbling of the *medaber.* More horrifying than the roar of an earthquake, it is the deafening silence that is the roar of the heavenquake, for this *raash* of the deafening silence cracks the heavens to the core. The opposite of *raash*—what Jewish thought must now retrieve from the silence—is the word that abides in the *kol,* which translates not only as "sound," as in the phrase *kol shofar* or "the sound of the shofar" (Psalms 98:6), but also as "voice": from the standpoint of Jewish thought, every sound *is* a voice because every thing is a word. And within every word there is a Voice other than our own, as the sixteenth-century mystic Meir ibn Gabbai has taught: "There is no uttered word that does not have a 'Voice.'"[75] Laden with meaning and message, the *kol* that is both sound and voice cries out for a word, a thought, and a deed in response to the Divine word that speaks in the silence within every word.

Abiding within the word, the Voice within the silence—the Voice in the mode of silence—speaks from the depths of the cosmos, as Neher has said: "The silence of the cosmos is simply the most eloquent form of the Divine revelation."[76] Silence, therefore, is not the absence of sound, any more than darkness is the absence of light. Indeed, it is the ground of world and creation, the vessel of sound and sense. In the post-Shoah world, Jewish thought must participate in that creation and seek out that sense—or else be implicated in its destruction.

WORLD AND ANTIWORLD IN THE POST-SHOAH EXILE

In Hebrew there are many expressions for God that associate the Holy One with His world. Among them are *Yichud Shel Olam,* or the "Unique

One of the World"; *Chey Haolamim,* or the "Life of the Worlds"; *Tsadik Haolamim,* or the "Righteous One of the Worlds"; *Ziv Haolam,* or the "Glory of the World"; *Adon Olam,* or the "Lord of the World"; *Melekh Haolam,* or "King of the Universe"; *Gavhuto Shel Olam,* or the "Height of the Universe"; and *Kadmono Shel Olam,* or the "Origin of the World." One implication of these expressions for our understanding of the Shoah is that, as an assault on God, the Shoah transpires not just *in* the world but also *against* the world. On the most basic level, the world occupies space and time. But the Nazis destroyed Jewish time through the obliteration of memory and anticipation; they destroyed Jewish space through the erasure of any human *between space* in ghettos, camps, and trains, where one hundred people were forced into spaces designed to hold ten. Thus we have the antiworld: no space, no time. No Jew.

There can be no undoing of God and humanity without the undoing of the "world" designated by the Hebrew word *olam.* If the post-Holocaust world is a world in crisis, exactly what is this world, this *olam,* that is in such a state of crisis? Once again, the holy tongue can add to our understanding of what the Shoah is and what is at stake in our response to it. The word *olam* refers to the sum of the universe. It signifies the expanse of the universe, as in the phrase *olam umlo'o,* meaning "the world and all its fullness" (for example, in *Pesikta Rabbati* 28:3); it signifies the duration of the universe, as in the expression *leolam vaed,* meaning "forever and ever." "World," in this instance, is space-time, encompassing both what is and what is *not yet,* all that falls within every event horizon. *Olam* exceeds the limits of "being" as construed by much of ontological thought. To use a metaphor from Franz Rosenzweig, whereas Western ontology is but a cup of water drawn from the river, *olam* is the river itself.[77] One implication of these possibilities of meaning for *olam* is that the ultimate is rooted in the fundamental. And the Nazis set out to transform both in their assault upon creation.

Shaping the space and time that constitute *olam,* the light summoned upon the first utterance of the world's creation exceeds all there is, to include what is yet to be realized, that is, what is *better.* Therefore, the first utterance of creation, "Let there be light," draws into being what is more than being, what is *better* than being. This *better* is the "shall be" of the *Ehyeh,* or "I Shall Be," by which God identifies Himself when He enters the world and instructs Moses: "So shall you say to the Children of Israel, 'I Shall Be has sent me'" (Exodus 3:14). This is the point at which the Jewish people, *as* a people, enter history because this is the point where they are summoned to ascend to a future, to the Good that imposes upon them the mission to become better and thus overcome their enslavement under what simply is. The "God Who Is the Good," *Hael Hatov,* is the God who is the *better.*

The issue of what is better comes to bear when we consider the other meanings of *olam:* "humanity" and "community," where the fundamental and the ultimate merge in the ethical. The ethical is precisely what is *better* than all there is, without which neither the transcendent nor the imminent is meaningful. Now the Hebrew word for "ethics" is *musar,* a word that also means "fetter" or "bond." What is fettered by ethics is not the human being but the darkness of chaos, of *tohu-vavohu,* overcome through the light of Torah, which includes the light of the ethical. What is fettered, in other words, is the forbidden, as we see from the word *asur,* which means both "fettered" and "forbidden"—forbidden not for the sake of some arbitrary authority but because it threatens the *olam* called into being. Ethics, then, forges the bond that holds humanity together as community. It is the bond that sets us free, for freedom lies not in doing whatever we want to do but in the realization of what we *must* do. The Nazis had no ethic; just as they created an antiworld, so did they create an anti-ethic, an antigood that was beyond good and evil, for which, as we have seen, there is no going too far. For the Nazis, nothing was bound up: there was no *musar.*

One Jewish response to this absence of any limiting principle lies in a cognate of *musar*: it is *masoret,* or "tradition." If we consider the related term in the expression *mesirat nefesh,* meaning "self-sacrifice," the tradition that may answer to the Nazis is a tradition in which the self is emptied of ego, not in the sense of *laying* down a life but in *handing* down a life through a forgetfulness of the self. Self-sacrifice in this sense is a giving that is teaching and testimony, and there is no tradition, no *masoret,* without *mesirat nefesh,* for the meaning of the root verb *masar* is "to transmit" or "to hand down." The tradition handed down from generation to generation—the tradition slated for annihilation in the Nazi assault upon the Jewish generations—is not only the link that connects each to the other but also the substance that holds each one together. And what is handed down through tradition, through the *masoret,* is a *meser,* or "message," with regard to what there is to hold dear and what must be done.

While the ethical injunction concerning what must be done is the tie that binds humanity into a community, it is a hidden bond. It is hidden in the silence of the *alef* that precedes the *beit* of creation, which is the first letter of the Torah; it is hidden in the ineffable absolute that commands ethical action. That is why *alef* is the first letter in the first utterance of the Ten Commandments, where the Hidden One reveals Himself to sanctify the world with His commandments in a saying of *Anokhi,* the divine utterance of "I." Which brings us to a cognate of *olam*: it is the verb *ilem* (with an *ayin*), meaning "to hide" or "to conceal." In his commentary on Edmond Jabès, Josh Cohen writes, "The demand of thinking after Auschwitz would be above all to expose and to bear witness to this silence at the heart of language."[78] But it is not merely the silence of language that places the demand on Jewish thinking. It is the silence hidden in the holy tongue, which is, in a very important sense, otherwise than language. It is the silence of the *alef,* the letter that has no sound, hidden in every letter of the holy tongue (see *Keter Shem Tov* 45), and that signifies the *Anokhi* of Sinai. It is the silence of what Fackenheim calls the Commanding Voice of Auschwitz (which we shall examine in chapter 7).

In the Midrash it is written that the Torah begins with the letter *beit* because *beit* has a numerical value of 2, indicating that two worlds were created: the world that meets the eye and the hidden world (*Bereshit Rabbah* 1:10). The hidden world gives meaning to the material world. For the hidden world is the *olam-haemet,* the "world of truth," which is both to come and in our very midst, invisible as the Holy One is invisible (see *Tanchuma Bereshit* 5). The Holy One is invisible not as the air is invisible but as the absolute is invisible, like "the invisible in the Bible," which Levinas identifies as "the Good beyond being."[79] It is what cannot be gauged or confined to a definition, invisible as the love of a father or the meaning of a life is invisible.

Here we see another, deeper implication of a point made earlier, namely, that in the Nazi antiworld nothing was hidden; all that was there was starkly there. It was a realm full of facts and empty of truth. Which means: there was no *Anokhi,* no Invisible One, no "Who" or "I," to speak either the word of creation or the commandment of revelation. Indeed, each is tied to the other: the Ten Utterances of Creation parallel the Ten Utterances of Revelation, as Rabbi Shapira has taught: "God's word at the creation of the world and God's word at the giving of the Torah are the same, one word. . . . The word of the ten statements [of creation] and the word of the Ten Commandments are also one word, because He and His word are One" (see also *Pesikta Rabbati* 1:3–2:18).[80] Inasmuch as a covenant, or *brit,* was affirmed at Mount Sinai, so was it affirmed in the *bara,* the word "created" in the opening line of the Torah; as Nachmanides has noted, the two words are interrelated.[81] Answering the Nazi anticreation, Jewish thought must look for ways to participate in the creation; one way to do that is to think in terms of covenant, if for no other reason than to determine a ground from which we may confront God.

But in the post-Shoah exile, that is precisely the ground we have lost, the ground that has crumbled from beneath our feet, the ground knee-deep in the ashes of the dead. It is not so much the collapse of the Covenant as it is the collapse of our ability to *think* in terms of the Covenant. The crisis of Jewish thought? To break free of Auschwitz thinking and emerge from the antiworld into the *olam* of creation and Covenant. Remember the words of Fania Fénelon: "It's not me who's doing the thinking—'it' thinks *for* me. . . . I spend every night there—every night!"[82] Just so, the Jewish thinker is faced with spending every night there. Liberation from the post-Shoah exile would entail a liberation from the dominating voice of the *it* of Auschwitz. It is a liberation that requires a movement not just out of a geographical or historical "Egypt" but out of the "Egyptian" thinking that characterizes our exile. Jewish thought must free itself, in other words, by becoming *Jewish.* And one way to do that is to attend to the voice of the holy tongue. Thus thinking Hebraically, we are in a better position to free ourselves *as Jews* from the anticreation, from the desolation, of Auschwitz.

In chapter 2, we pointed out that the Hebrew word for "desolation," "wasteland," or "horror" is *shemamah.* Here, we note that the cognate verb *hishtomem* means "to be horrified" or "to become desolate." The state of desolation that defines the post-Shoah exile is indeed a state of horror. Once again we see that exile does not designate a mere geographical condition: creation itself, reality itself, reels in a metaphysical exile, and we are caught in the maelstrom. The horror of the post-Shoah exile is that it passes for a state of normality, yet it is a calm haunted by an underlying panic. Thus we seethe in a state of *behalah,* which is "fright," "panic," or "confusion." We bolt from diversion to diversion, from fad to fad, not only in our popular culture but also—and much more perversely—in our intellectual culture. *Behalah* is a condition that at first seeps through and then overwhelms the makeshift bulwark that we erect against it. This is where we encounter what modern philosophy calls "the absurd," where the fixtures prove to be not just so many props but part of the crumbling dam itself. And as the waters rise, we suck air.

A cognate of *behalah,* the verb *nivhal,* applies very well to this state of desperation; it means "to be terrified" or "to be disturbed." In this state, we are constantly *bahul,* that is, "worried" or "puzzled," words that are very apt descriptions of post-Holocaust Jewish thought to date. Another word for "worried" or "troubled" articulates this exilic condition. It is *mutrad,* which also means "banished," from the verb *tarad,* meaning "to drive out" or "to expel" as well as "to trouble" or "to distress." In the post-Shoah exile, we are banished to Auschwitz, our thinking clouded by worry and distress so that we suffer lapses of memory and cannot find our way home, back to Jerusalem, back into the Covenant and creation, *as Jews.* The title of Charlotte Delbo's memoir is all but prophetic: *None of Us Will Return.* We live in a chronic state of flight, rushing from one philosophical game to another, desperately trying to escape "it." Yet we cannot escape "it," any more than we can escape our own shadow. We are *its* shadow.

If we are exiled to Auschwitz, however, we can, with the help of the holy tongue, find a key to the gate leading out of Auschwitz. This brings us to one last point in this brief consideration of the Holocaust and the holy tongue.

EXILE AND REVELATION AFTER AUSCHWITZ

In the Midrash it is written that the Jews must promise not to jump the walls of Jerusalem to make their return before it is time, and the Gentiles must promise not to be too severe in their treatment of the Jews (see *Shir Hashirim Rabbah* 2:7:1). After the slaughter of the Shoah, however, the Jews have been forced to jump the walls of Jerusalem, lest the Jews cease to exist altogether. Nevertheless, since the post-Shoah exile is a metaphysical and not a geographical condition, one can be in exile even within the walls of Jerusalem. To be sure, in the Book of Lamentations the city itself is said to have become a *nidah,* or "wanderer" (see Lamentations 1:8): like the Shekhinah, Jerusalem herself follows us into exile, even as we flock into Jerusalem, so that the movement from Auschwitz to Jerusalem leads in a direction that does not go back out but rather penetrates deeper into the core of exile. Perhaps within our very exile the One we long for cries out to us in His own great longing, for it may be that in the midst of the "wilderness," of the *midbar,* is the *davar,* the word, that we seek.

The Hebrew word for "exile" is *galut,* from the verb *galah,* meaning "to wander" or "to go into exile." It also means "to discover" or "to reveal" and is a cognate of the noun *gilui,* "revelation," as in *gilui Shekhinah,* "Divine Revelation" or "Revelation of the Shekhinah." As stated by Rabbi Yehudah Leib Alter, the true meaning of *galut* is *hitgalut,* or "revelation," so that "the glory of God's kingdom [may] be revealed in every place."[83] The difficulty with the post-Shoah exile, however, is that there is no apparent revelation of God's glory. And if there is, it comes at too high a price. Looking at this exile, from within this exile, one cannot help sharing in the remark that Gregor makes to the Rebbe in Wiesel's *The Gates of the Forest*: "I tell you this: if their death has no meaning, then it's an outrage, and if it does have a meaning, it's even more so."[84] And yet there is too much at stake in the post-Shoah exile to simply walk away and say, "It is meaningless." If this murder is meaningless, then humanity is meaningless.

One implication of the possibilities of meaning found in the word *galah* is this: from the standpoint of Jewish thought, revelation is not just a word that we receive—it is a condition in which we live, the condition that makes life possible in that it makes possible the movement of return homeward. To the extent that we are aware of our exiled condition, we come to a certain realization about the need to emerge from that condition: living in the *galut,* we do not simply live somewhere else— we live *away from home.* In that realization, perhaps, lies the seed of redemption. "What is the difference between *galah* and *geulah,* exile and redemption?" asks Rabbi Benjamin Blech. And, echoing a teaching from Rabbi Isaac Meir of Ger, he answers: "The letter *alef* of *Anokhi,* the One representing God," who is the source of revelation—whose utterance of *Anokhi* (Exodus 20:2) *is* the Revelation.[85] Those of us who are blind to our exile are deaf to the revelation that reverberates from within the depths of that exile, deaf to the *davar* in the midst of the *midbar.* What renders us so blind and deaf? It is the ego that eclipses the divine "I"-saying, the *Anokhi,* of Hashem. In this eclipse, we slip into the most insidious exile, which is the comfortable, complacent exile. That is where our eyes grow so used to the dark that we no longer notice the darkness, our ears so deaf to the word that we ignore the deafening outcry of an anguished God, and our nose so accustomed to the smell that we have lost the scent of the ashes.

The Jewish return to the holy land has brought with it a return to the Jewish word, to the Hebrew word, that might shake us from our sleeping sickness. Similarly, a return to the holy texts of the holy tongue may guide us in this post-Shoah crisis of Jewish thought. To be sure, with the return to the holy land and the holy tongue, the holy books have returned to the world in unprecedented numbers. For, as Levinas has rightly said, "the Shoah re-establishes the link—which up until then had been incomprehensibly hidden—between present-day Israel and the Israel of the Bible,"[86] which is the Israel of the *sifrei kodesh.* Perhaps here, too, is a message. Which brings us to the next matter of consideration.

5

The *Sifrei Kodesh*
and the Holocaust

For the crime of teaching Torah, the Romans wrapped
Rabbi Chananiah ben Teradyon in the Holy Scrolls to
burn him at the stake. His daughter Beruriah wept for
her father and for the Torah that would burn with him.
"Weep not for the Torah, my child," said the sage. "For
the Torah is fire. And fire cannot burn fire."
—Talmud Bavli, *Avodah Zarah* 18a

"The ultimate mystery of the Holocaust," Elie Wiesel has said, "is that whatever happened took place in the soul."[1] The Holocaust was essentially an assault on the holiness of the soul, and the holiness of the soul derives from Torah. To be sure, Jewish tradition teaches that the soul is made of Torah, as we have noted. Therefore, Nazis burned Torah scrolls wherever they went. And among the Torah scrolls consigned to the flames were the "scrolls" of the Six Million. Perhaps this is why Emil Fackenheim insists, "A direct encounter with the naked biblical text, once admitted as a theoretical possibility, becomes for contemporary Jewish thought an existential necessity."[2] Without the biblical text— without the *sifrei kodesh*—Jewish thought cannot exist. The engagement with the *sifrei kodesh* has become necessary for Jewish thought inasmuch as it must address the life of the Jewish soul that came under assault in the Shoah and is now slipping away.

Over the years that I knew Fackenheim, he used to relate to me a story about the Jews who would rush into a burning synagogue in order to save the scrolls of the Holy Torah that the Nazis had consigned to the flames.

"The Nazis maintained that the Jews were rats," he said. "But rats do not run into burning buildings to save Torah scrolls."

We, too, must retrieve the scrolls and the holy books—the *sifrei kodesh*—from the flames of the Shoah. For in order to fathom the event as part of *sacred* history, we must pass through the fire of Torah, broadly understood: that is, through the *sifrei kodesh*—Torah, Bible, Mishnah, Gemara, Midrash, Kabbalah, and the writings of the great sages. It is not the Jewish thinker who brings these texts to the Holocaust; rather, the Holocaust brings these texts to the Jewish thinker, with unprecedented intensity. And we must bear these texts into our response to the Shoah, if it is to be a Jewish response. Indeed, without the *sifrei kodesh,* what is left to determine the meaning of the Jew?

In *What Is Judaism?* Fackenheim recalls an image from his childhood. It is a painting of "Jews fleeing from a pogrom. . . . The fleeing Jews in the picture are bearded old men, terrified, but not so much as to leave behind what is most precious to them. In the view of antisemites these Jews would doubtless be clutching bags of gold. In fact each of them carries a Torah scroll."[3] In the post-Holocaust era, we take philosophical flight from Auschwitz to Jerusalem. As Jews, however, we must take care not to leave behind what is most precious, what is the very stuff of our soul: the Torah made of black fire on white fire, as it is written (*Tanchuma Bereshit* 1; *Devarim Rabbah* 3:12; *Shir Hashirim Rabbah* 5:11:6; *Zohar* II, 226b). Just as Torah is made of fire, so does the soul originate "in fire, being an emanation from the Divine Throne" (*Zohar* II, 211b). Therefore, says the Midrash, when the Angel of Death tried to frighten Jacob by making fire shoot up from the ground, the Patriarch cried, "Do you think you can frighten me with fire? Why, I am made of that stuff!" (*Bereshit Rabbah* 77:2). If we are made of the fire of Torah, then we must fetch that fire from the ashes of Auschwitz; that is where we turn in this time of crisis for post-Holocaust Jewish thought: to the holy Torah, broadly construed as the *sifrei kodesh,* or "holy books," for if we leave that behind, we may have escaped—but the Nazis will have taken our souls.

Recall the words of Franz Rosenzweig: the Jewish people "did not originate from the womb of nature that bears nations, but—and this is unheard of!—was led forth 'a nation from the midst of another nation' (Deuteronomy 4:34). . . . And only he who remembers this determining origin can belong to it; while he who no longer can or will utter the new word he has to say 'in the name of the original speaker,' who refuses to be a link in the golden chain, no longer belongs to his people."[4] That golden chain is made of the *sifrei kodesh.* To divorce our thinking from those texts is to sever our link with the Jewish people, including those who were consumed in the flames of the furnaces. And this amounts to severing our ties to the Holy One Himself. For the Talmud teaches that in the Divine utterance of *Anokhi* we have an acronym for the phrase *Ana nafshi ketavit yehavit,* "I have given Myself to you in writing," which is to say: in the written word of the holy texts, we have an intimate link to the Holy One. That is what makes the golden chain golden. The difficulty facing us with the advent of postmodern thought, however, is not just a refusal to be a link in the chain; rather, it is the absence of any concept of such a "chain" from postmodern thinking itself.

Just as postmodern thought cannot conceive of holiness, so it cannot distinguish one text from another. The postmodernist is like one who, as the Talmud says, "buys a scroll of Torah in the market" and is therefore "as one who has seized a precept in the market" (*Menachot* 30a). Inasmuch as we are dominated by a postmodern outlook, it is as though, after the Nazi assault on memory, we have forgotten the difference between Torah and literature, between Torah and philosophy, between Torah and criticism, between Torah and "texts." Thus, laments Emmanuel Levinas, "We are no longer acquainted with the difference that distinguishes the Book from documentation. In the former there is an inspiration purified of all the vicissitudes and all the 'experiences' that had been its occasion, offering itself as Scripture whereby each soul is called to exegesis, which is both regulated by the rigorous reading of the text and by the unicity—unique in all eternity—of its own contribution, which is also its discovery, the soul's share."[5] This is why rabbinical exegesis is of such importance to Levinas; whereas postmodern philosophy speaks *of* the text, he says, rabbinical exegesis makes the *text* speak.[6] If, after Auschwitz, Jewish thought is to be Jewish—if it is to be *Machshavah Yehudit*—then it must attend to the texts, to the *sifrei kodesh,* that speak to it and that make it speak.

But in order to determine how the *sifrei kodesh* might inform Jewish thinking about the Holocaust, we should first consider the term *sifrei kodesh* itself.

THE *BOOK* AND THE *HOLY* IN THE HOLY BOOKS

Anyone who has seen a scribe at work on a Torah scroll—anyone who has an inkling of the rite and the ritual surrounding the writing of the Book—knows that the *Sefer,* or "Book," is revered among Jews as among no other people. "In each and every letter"—we recall the words of the Baal Shem Tov, cited in the previous chapter—"there are worlds" (*Keter Shem Tov* 1). Those who undertake the task of inscribing the letters of Torah take these words very seriously. More than spatial, the space that the Book engages is the space from which thought emerges and is transmitted, the space opened up by the soul and by the Divine Presence. As vast as this space is the time that the Book encompasses. It is a time exceeding any one person's time, a time that includes a trace of the immemorial and a breath of the yet to be. Exceeding space and time, the Book is space and time *as such,* the space and time of creation and memory, of tradition and future, of teaching and testimony. Thus the Book makes us contemporary with the souls who stand *here* and *now* at Mount Sinai.

Tradition teaches that the Book, the *Sefer Torah,* is the blueprint of all creation: fours times, says Rabbi Shimon bar Yochai, the Holy One looked into the Torah before beginning His work of creation (*Zohar* I, 5a; see also *Bereshit Rabbah* 1:1; *Tanchuma Bereshit* 1; *Avot* 3:14). This teaching is based on the words of the prophet Jeremiah: "If I had not established My eternal Covenant [Torah], I would not have fashioned heaven and earth" (Jeremiah 33:25). Unlike a blueprint, however, the Torah is itself the stuff of creation. This view is central to the ancient mystical teachings found, for example, in the *Sefer Yetzirah,* the Book of Creation, where it is written that Hashem "created His universe with three books *(sefarim)*: with text *(sefer),* with numbering *(sefar),* and with storytelling *(sipur)*" (1:1). Judah Halevi explains: "*Sefar* means calculation and weighing of the created bodies. . . . *Sipur* signifies the language, or rather the divine language, 'the voice of the words of the living God.' This produced the existence of the form which this language assumed in the words: 'Let there be light,' 'let there be a firmament.' The word was hardly spoken, when the thing came into existence. This is also *sefer,* by which writing is meant, the writing of God means His creatures, the speech of God is His writing, the will of God is His speech" (*Kitav al khazari* 4:25). And His speech contains teachings and tales; His speech is Torah.

As Torah, the *sifrei* in the *sifrei kodesh* are not books of philosophy and literature; they are books of teachings and tales. That is what post-Holocaust Jewish thought must attend to: the teaching in the tale and the tale of the teaching. Significantly, the verb *siper* means not only "to tell a tale" but also "to cut," particularly "to cut hair." Mystically speaking, creation entails a process of *nesirah,* or "cutting," the upper worlds from the lower—heaven from earth, light from darkness, land from water, male from female—in order to form the distinction crucial to the *relation* that defines creation. Without this relation, we can relate neither the tale nor the teaching. Indeed, we enter into the relation by "relating" a tale, which is another meaning of *siper.* Torah begins not with a catalogue of commandments but with the tale of creation: as part of Torah, *creation itself is made of the tale of creation.* Thus Moses relates the tale of the Torah to the Israelites in the Book of Deuteronomy: the teaching is not complete without the tale of the teaching. And most crucial to relating the tale of the Torah is a relation both to God and to humanity. If the Book opens up holiness, it opens up the *between* space of these relations that comprise a single relation.

Why does God give Moses two tablets, and not one? Not because He cannot write small enough to get his commandments onto one tablet. No, it is to articulate the *between* space of two realms of relation: the first tablet pertains to the relation *ben adam leMakom* and the second to the relation *ben adam lechevero,* "between human and God" and "between human and human," respectively.[7] And yet *there is only one relation.* What, then, is the holiest space in this world? It is not the Temple Mount, nor even the Temple halls. It is not even the Holy of Holies within the Temple. The holiest space in this world is the space *between* the *cheruvim* facing each other atop the ark that contains the Torah. *Atop* the ark, this *between* space is higher than the contents of the ark. This single space signifies the single realm of relation between God and human, between human and human. That is where the Divine Voice speaks. That is where the human voice answers.

Recall, in this connection, a teaching from the Lubavitcher Rebbe, Rabbi Menachem Mendel Schneerson: "Speaking and saying come from the surface, not from the depth of the soul. The mouth can sometimes speak what the heart does not feel. Even what the *heart* says can be at odds with what the man truly wills in his soul. . . . But 'relating' comes from the depths of a man's being."[8] In "the depths of a man's being" lies the *between* space of relation, and the *sifrei kodesh* sound those depths, for in the depths of the human being abides the Divine Being. Rabbi Schneerson goes on to cite a teaching from the *Sifre* on Deuteronomy 11:22: "You wish to recognize the One who spoke and brought the world into being? Learn Agadah [the tales], for in Agadah you will find God."[9] *Agadah,* says the fourteenth-century sage Rabbi Yitzchak Abohav, deals with "the description of the true nature of the universe and the ideals toward which one should strive. It speaks allusively of mysteries and mysticism. It speaks of ethics and character and human nature. It speaks of purification of the body and sublimation of the soul. These are absolute truths."[10] And what makes these truths absolute is the "Holy," the *kadosh,* revealed in the holy books.

Jewish thought cannot draw the Holy into its thinking without the holy books; the volumes of Western philosophy and literature will not do. The mode of thinking about the Holy is the most crucial distinction between the Western ontological tradition and Jewish thought in their understanding of God, world, and the human being. Since the Holy is most concretely manifest in the human being, the human being, as conceived in the holy books, was the primary target of the Nazi assault. The Nazis banned and burned the holy books, not the writings of Luther or Kant or Goethe, because the holy books voice the categorical difference between Nazis and Jews in their view of the human being, for the human being is the most concrete manifestation of holiness. Thus in the Nazi assault on the very notion of the human we have the concrete assault on the Holy.

Because the category of the Holy lies outside speculative thought— as a kind of noncategory or anticategory—the value of a human being lies outside anything that speculative thought can determine. We can esteem, honor, and admire moral integrity, intellectual acumen, athletic ability, professional accomplishment, courage under fire, and simple loving kindness. But holiness means that the value of a human being lies in nothing that can be weighed, measured, counted, or otherwise established by circumstance or observation. Holiness circumvents all circumstance. From the standpoint of Jewish teaching, a human being has *infinite* value—or rather a human being is *holy*—whether he or she is moral or immoral, intelligent or stupid, strong or frail, brave or cowardly, nice or mean. Therefore, Torah and Talmud teach that we must come to the aid of an enemy before we come to the aid of a friend (see Exodus 23:4–5; *Bava Metzia* 32b): it is God, and not my personal inclination, that determines the dearness of the human being. That Divine Presence speaks from the depths of the *sifrei kodesh* that define the Jewish people. It is what the Nazis set out to murder in the murder of the Jewish people. It is what Jewish thought must seek to revive.

For "at Auschwitz," Elie Wiesel has written, "not only man died, but also the idea of man."[11] A key point of conflict characterizing the Shoah as *Shoah* lies in a fundamental opposition between two views of the value of a human being. According to Nazi ideology, the human being is an accident of nature whose essence is determined by "race" and who therefore has no connection to anyone outside "the race." According to the testimony of Torah, the human being is a child of God created in the image of the Holy One; as it is written in the Talmud, it takes three to create a human life: husband, wife, and the Holy One (see *Kiddushin* 30b). And since God begins His creation of humanity with one human being, each human being is *essentially* connected to all others. Why did God begin with one, and not two? In the Tosefta the rabbis explain: "So that in this world the righteous could not say, 'Our children are righteous, and yours are evil'" (*Sanhedrin* 8:4). So that no one could say to another, "That must come from your side of the family, not my side of the family." There is only one side of the family. And we are all blood.

Failing to address this basic issue, most responses to the Holocaust do not reflect a sufficient understanding of what was slated for destruction in the Event. Most thinkers ignore the human and Divine relation revealed through the Book, and the meaning of that relation sanctioned through the Holy. As an annihilation of the Holy within the human, the Shoah is the calculated destruction not only of Jewish bodies but also of Jewish souls and Jewish prayers, of Jewish teachings and traditions, of the *edah* that is both Jewish "testimony" and Jewish "community." These are the elements that go into the Jewish view of humanity that derives from the *sifrei kodesh*. And that view is shaped by the distinctively Jewish view of the mother, the father, and the child. The interrelationships among these three human figures attest to the value of any human being. In fact, these three—mother, father, and child—embody, respectively, the three categories that shape Jewish thought: Creation, Revelation, and Redemption. If we want to uncover the Holy that came under assault in the Shoah, this is where we must look.

In the introductory chapter it was noted that the verbal root of *kadosh* is *kadash,* which means "to be consecrated," "to be made holy," or "to become holy." The intensive form of the verb, *kidesh,* translates not only as "to hallow" or "to sanctify" but also as "to betroth." Hence the word for "marriage," *kidushin,* is a cognate of the word for "holiness." What are the *sifrei kodesh* most fundamentally about? The marriage of a mother and a father, who join with the Holy One in the creation of a child. Therefore, in the pages that follow, these three—mother, father, and child—shall be the focus of our investigation of how the *sifrei kodesh* inform a Jewish response to the Holocaust. We have seen that the Nazi assault on the Jew was an assault on the "talmudic thinking" that defines the Jew.[12] Therefore, the Nazis, undertaking the murder of the very notion of a human being as articulated in talmudic thinking, murdered not only mothers, fathers, and children but also the very idea of a mother, a father, and a child. It is at this definitive core of the Event that there comes most significantly into play the Jewish response to the Shoah in the context of sacred texts.

SOURCE OF CREATION: THE MOTHER

If we understand the significance of the mother in Jewish tradition, then we may better understand what is targeted for annihilation in the Shoah—and what must be retrieved in its aftermath. What, then, do the sacred texts teach about the significance of the mother in Jewish tradition? In his commentary on the *Sefer Yetzirah,* Aryeh Kaplan points out that the Feminine Essence—the essence of the mother—belongs to the domain of Understanding, or *Binah,*[13] a word that derives its root from *bein,* which means "between." Understanding arises from the difference *between* two; and the mother, as the highest manifestation of the Feminine Essence, transforms the difference that characterizes understanding into the nonindifference of love. The mother, then, is the closest tie that we have to the Creator, who is revealed in the nonindifference of love. Since this Other who is the Creator of heaven and earth is ultimately targeted for extermination in the Kingdom of Night,[14] the obliteration of the mother is among the first principles to rule in that Kingdom, where the essence of Israel was under assault.

"The greatness of Israel," says the Midrash, "is compared . . . to a woman bearing child" (*Shir Hashirim Rabbah* 8:14:1), for a woman bearing child is the embodiment of the origin, the love, and the home that constitute Israel. The Zohar, in fact, suggests a connection between God the Mother and the origin of humanity, declaring, "The [Supernal] Mother said: 'Let us make man in our image'" (*Zohar* I, 22b). Here we see why the concept of the mother appears not just at the origin of the individual's life but in the midst of the six days of creation. Thus the Midrash teaches that the Torah not only precedes the creation (*Bereshit Rabbah* 1:4) but is also the basis of all that is born from the womb of creation. The Zohar expresses it by saying, "First came *Ehyeh* (I shall be), the dark womb of all. Then *Asher Ehyeh* (who I shall be), indicating the readiness of the Mother to beget all" (*Zohar* III, 65b). Jewishly speaking, God as loving and merciful—God as Creator—is God as the Supernal Mother. Thus the Nazis made Jewish birth the most nefarious of crimes, and the Jewish mother the most heinous of criminals.[15]

The Hebrew word for "mother" is *em,* which also means "womb." Another word for "womb" is *rechem*; it is a cognate of *racham,* which means "to love" or "to have compassion" as only a mother can love and have compassion. Noting that the Tetragrammaton (the four-letter Holy Name of Y-H-V-H) ends with a *kamats* vowel notation followed by the letter *hey*—which indicates a masculine noun made feminine—one sees that the love and compassion of the feminine are among the manifestations of Hashem in the world. Joined with *rachamim*—that is, with "love" or "compassion"—the Holy One is the *Av Harachamim,* "the Father of love and compassion" or "the loving and compassionate Father"—the Father who is also Mother. Without the mother we have no access, no relation, to God the Father. As Levinas states it, "*Rachamim* (Mercy) . . . goes back to the word *Rechem,* which means uterus. *Rachamim* is the revelation of the uterus to the other, whose gestation takes place within it. *Rachamim* is maternity itself. God as merciful is God defined by maternity."[16] And since maternity is defined by creation, it forms the basis of Torah itself. As such, it is the target of the Nazi annihilation.

This point—that maternity lies at the heart of Torah—becomes clearer still if we recall that the first letter in the Torah is the letter *beit,* which is also the word for "home," the place where human life first makes its appearance in the world. The letter *beit* is shaped like a womb, from which Torah and creation come into being as a *dwelling place,* and not as a realm into which we are "thrown," to use Heidegger's term.[17] To be sure, a biblical euphemism for "dwelling place" is *em beYisrael,* "a mother in Israel" (see Judges 5:7; 2 Samuel 20:19). The house, moreover, is associated with the Patriarch Jacob, as Rabbi Yitzchak Ginsburgh points out: "At the level of Divinity, the house symbolizes the ultimate purpose of all reality: to become a dwelling place below for the manifestation of God's presence. 'Not as Abraham who called it [the Temple site] "a mountain," nor as Isaac who called it "a field," but as Jacob who called it "a house.""'[18] Since, according to the Talmud, "blessing is found in a man's home only on account of his wife" (*Bava Metzia* 59a), the sanctity of the home is linked with the Jewish woman, the wife and mother, who sees to the care of the household.[19] Thus the mothers, wives, and daughters of Israel are known as the House of Jacob.[20] Thus the Midrash speaks of the mother as the source of creation: "The Holy One, blessed be He, said to His world: 'O My world, My world! Shall I tell thee who created thee, who formed thee? Jacob has created thee, Jacob has formed thee'" (*Vayikra Rabbah* 36:4). Setting out to murder the House of Jacob, the Nazis set out to undermine the world.

If the Torah is the foundation of Creation, the mother, through her tie to the *beit* in which the Torah originates, is the foundation of the Torah itself; she is the origin of the origin. And so it is written in the Zohar: "When a man is at home, the foundation of his house is his wife, for it is on account of her that the Shekhinah departs not from the home" (*Zohar* I, 50a). Rabbi Joseph Gikatilla, moreover, asserts that the Shekhinah "in the time of Abraham our father is called Sarah and in the time of Isaac our father is called Rebecca and in the time of Jacob our father is called Rachel."[21] What enters the dwelling place through the wife and mother? It is the Torah itself. The woman of a household is called an *akeret*,[22] a word that derives from *ikar*, which means "essence," "basis," "foundation," and "origin": the mother is all these things that define Torah. Once again, it is through the mother that we have the Torah.[23] Bearing life into the world, she bears Torah into the world. For the Torah *is* life; it is the *Ets Chayim*, the "Tree of Life" that sustains all life (see, for example, Proverbs 3:18; see also *Berakhot* 32b, *Taanit* 7a, and *Vayikra Rabbah* 35:6). Thus the Talmud compares the Torah to a woman (*Kiddushin* 30b). And the Torah is inscribed in the heart (see Deuteronomy 6:6).

In the sixteenth century, Rabbi Yitzchak Luria, the Holy Ari, asked, "If *Binah* or Understanding, which is associated with the Mother, is a mental process, why is it said to be in the heart, and not in the head?" To which Aryeh Kaplan answers, "The heart is actually the Personification of Imma-Mother, which is Binah-Understanding, where She reveals herself."[24] In the Shema's injunction to love God, the first thing with which we love is "all [our] heart," *b'kol levavkha* (Deuteronomy 6:5). Now, the *lamed* and *beit* of the Hebrew word for "heart," *lev*, are the last and first letters of the Torah. The heart, therefore, contains all of the Torah. To love God with all one's heart is to love God with all the Torah, to love God as God loves, to love as the mother loves, for the mother whom the letter *beit* situates at the origin of the Torah embodies the sum of Torah in her personification as the heart. Personified as the heart, the mother signifies not only the origin of life but also the center of life. The heart bears this significance because it is the seat of the love and teaching of God. And the loving kindness shown by one human being toward another is the highest expression of the Divine love and teaching personified by the mother. Creating a realm in which "everything is hostile,"[25] as Primo Levi puts it, the Nazis purged the world of the maternal Presence in the process of creating the antiworld.

If, as Rabbi Ginsburgh says, "loving kindness is the means through which God's presence is ultimately revealed,"[26] it is originally revealed through the mother. In the *Tanya,* Rabbi Schneur Zalman, the first Lubavitcher Rebbe, maintains that loving kindness in the form of charity is feminine and, by implication, maternal, for "it receives a radiation from the light of the *En Sof* that [like a womb] encompasses all worlds."[27] From a Jewish perspective, therefore, maternal love is not just an instinct or a feeling, not simply a natural or psychological phenomenon; much more than that, it is the manifestation of the Most High. The Scriptures, in fact, compare God's love to a mother's love: "As one whom his mother comforts," says the Holy One, "so will I comfort you" (Isaiah 66:13).[28] When that maternal love is targeted for extermination, as it was in the Shoah, the light of all there is to hold dear, the light that was in the beginning, is assailed. Hence, from a Jewish perspective, the ontological assault manifest in the assault on the mother moves to a metaphysical level in the annihilation of maternal love. Like the light created with God's first utterance, the mother's love is the mainstay of life, even and especially during the reign of death; she reveals to the individual that he is still a human being and that his life *matters.* Revealing to us the dearness of life, she makes it possible to *dwell* in the world, for dwelling is possible only where life has value. And the center of that value is the home.

Which brings us back to the *beit.* If, according to Jewish tradition, the letter *beit* situates the mother at the origin of life, the meaning of the letter *beit* places the mother at the center of the home. "The feminine aspect of the soul," Rabbi Ginsburgh points out, "and, in general, the woman in Judaism is symbolized by the house."[29] The reverse is also the case: the home, which houses life within its walls, is symbolized by the woman, who also houses life within her womb. Other associations and explanations come to mind; one recalls, for example, Rashi's commentary on Numbers 26:62, where he writes, "The decree consequent upon the incident of the spies had not been enacted upon the women, because they held the Promised Land dear. The men had said (Numbers 14:4), 'Let us appoint a chief and return to Egypt,' whilst the women said (27:4), 'Give us a possession in the Land.'" It is the women, in other words, who seek out a home and who thus signify the home. The House of Jacob embraces the promise of a place to dwell. The sum of the Torah lies in the commandment to love, and the commandment to love opens up a dwelling place, a place where children and families may come into the world. As we have seen, the mother is the incarnation of that love; hence the mother is the personification of the home. And the camps and ghettos fashioned by the Nazi Reich are precisely the opposite of the home.

The Kingdom of Night instituted by the Nazis is the Kingdom of Exile. Waging a metaphysical war, the Nazis had to drive the Jews from their homes and thus render them homeless prior to killing them. That was a chief function of the ghetto and the camp: the eradication of the dwelling place. In the Nazi assault on the mother, then, we see the fundamental human problem of dwelling, in its most extreme form: the murder of maternal love, which distinguishes the origin of life, is engineered by the devastation of the home. Once the mother is eliminated, the reign of exile and homelessness is inaugurated. Living in a camp, in a ghetto, or in hiding, *every Jew in Nazi Europe was homeless.*

Of course, there is no mother without a father: with the assault on the Supernal Mother comes the assault on the One we call "*Avinu, Malkenu*—our Father, our King." And this assault is articulated through the murder of the father.

SOURCE OF REVELATION: THE FATHER

We have seen that the mother embodies the origin of life, the love of what is most dear in life, and the home that establishes a center for life. In the father we have the truth that provides a ground for life, the wisdom that underlies an understanding of life, and the law that is the substance of life. Thus, said Micah to the Levite from Bethlehem, "Dwell with me, and be unto me a father and a priest" (Judges 17:10). Similarly, Elisha called his teacher Elijah "father" (2 Kings 2:12). In other words: teach me the truth and be my *moreh* and my *horeh*, my "teacher" and my "father," words that in Hebrew have the same root. And so it is written: "Hear, children, the teaching of a father, and heed his words, that you may know understanding" (Proverbs 4:1).[30] To be sure, the Talmud requires a father either to be a teacher or to find a teacher for his child (*Kiddushin* 29a). Says Rabbi Nachman of Breslov, "When a disciple learns the Torah's laws, his face takes on a resemblance to the one teaching him. This is because the law is the wisdom which makes a person's face shine."[31] Thus, "taking after" our teacher, we are like the teacher's own progeny.

The Talmud, in fact, makes the comparison between one who teaches Torah and a parent, since the teacher participates in giving birth to the student's soul (see *Sanhedrin* 99b).

But when, in the Holocaust, the father's words are swallowed up, truth, wisdom, and law—all the things that constitute a sacred reality—are also swallowed up in the black hole of the Holocaust unreality, for the Nazis are precisely those who are without truth, without wisdom, and without law. In Jewish terms, truth, wisdom, and law pertain to the father's teaching of the truth of tradition as an avenue of revelation; to the wisdom that thinkers such as Maimonides[32] and Gersonides[33] identify with God; and to the law that continually issues from the mouth of the Creator, as transmitted through the *sifrei kodesh*. Hence in the *Sifre* on Deuteronomy we are taught that when a child begins to speak, his father should teach him Torah and the holy tongue; if his father fails to teach the child Torah and the holy tongue, "it is as though he had buried the little one" (*Sifre Ekev* 46). Why as though he had buried his child? Because, Matityahu Glazerson explains, the *emet*, or "truth," of the holy tongue "is the foundation upon which the world stands. If one fails to acknowledge the *alef*, symbolizing God, who is the Chief (*aluf*) of the world, one removes the *alef* from *emet*. What remains is 'dead' *(met)*."[34] Here too we see the importance of the holy tongue to Jewish thought: it is a matter of life and death, especially in the post-Auschwitz era. The father who would impart life to his child teaches him the holy tongue so that the child may receive the nourishment of the truth that abides in the holy tongue and in the texts made of that tongue. This is the truth that concerns Jewish thought, especially after the Nazi assault on the truth, wisdom, and law.

In the post-Auschwitz world, the memory of the father entails far more than the mournful recollection of the head of a household. The Nazi attack on the father is an attack on memory itself. According to Jewish tradition, memory belongs to the father, who is responsible for handing down the teaching on the sanctity of life, just as the nurturing of life belongs to the mother. Regarding the *zachor v'shamor* that pertain to the Sabbath, for example, the Bahir teaches that " 'remember' *(zachor)* refers to the male *(Zachar)*. 'Keep' *(shamor)* refers to the bride" (*Bahir* 182). The male is the bridegroom, who is to become a father in the observance of the commandment to be fruitful and multiply (Genesis 1:28). And "being fruitful" lies in transmitting the teaching of Torah.

In the project to exterminate the Jews, the Reign of Nothingness begins with the undoing of this commandment, and it is this commandment that makes the father who he is. Just as the mother embodies creation from Torah, so the father embodies the revelation of Torah; in the beginning, says the mystic Chayyim Vital, the father "first sowed a seed, a drop of material substance that [became] the letters" (*Ets Chayyim* 5:5). The letters, in turn, became Torah. The father, then, contains the primal seed of Israel, the seed of Torah, in the form of revealed teaching and remembrance. And what befalls him reverberates throughout Israel. In the ontological assault on Jewish being, therefore, it is not enough simply to murder the father. The killing of his body must be preceded by the annihilation of his image, for in his image lies the revelation that the father symbolizes. When the father is in his place, being is itself in place: truth, wisdom, and law are in place. Here, truth is not simply a matter of fact—it is an avenue of return to the Most High, and it lays claim to us before we stake any other claims.

Like the father, the revealed truth commands us to pursue the good prior to our own choosing: revelation is the revelation of the *already.* Without this *already,* there is no truth. This is the meaning of Ezekiel's vision along the river Chevar, literally, the river of the "already" (Ezekiel 1:1; see also *Zohar* I, 6b): beholding the secret of primordial creation, he beholds the secret of immemorial revelation. *Already* we are forbidden to murder; *already* we are commanded to have no other gods. This pre-originary *having been commanded already* links the memory of the father to the good that distinguishes truth. An illustration of this idea can be found in the Midrash, where we find a commentary on Joseph that states, "In all his wisdom a certain woman enticed (him), and when he wished to accustom himself to sin, he saw the image of his father, and repented concerning it" (*Pirke de Rabbi Eliezer* 39). From a third position the father emerges as the figure of the good and therefore as a figure of truth. In the murder of the father the good itself is targeted for extinction. This eclipse of the good characterizes the Nazi evil, which is manifest in the murder of the father and the truth he signifies.

In the Mishnah, Rabbi Shimon ben Gamaliel teaches that truth is one of the foundations of the world (*Avot* 1:18). "Speaking falsehood, then," writes Moshe Chayim Luzzatto, "is comparable to removing the foundation of the world; and, conversely, if one is heedful of the truth it is as if he maintains the world's foundation."[35] With the disintegration of truth, when words are torn from meaning as families are torn apart, the world's foundation crumbles, and the ground of revelation collapses. Hence the tradition transmitted through the father is lost. Again, it is not enough to kill the father; a father killed is still a father, still the one who signifies the truth revealed in the teachings and traditions of Torah and Talmud. In the Nazis' metaphysical assault on the Jews, not only the person of the father but also all he signifies must be destroyed. The relation that makes him a father must be destroyed. Indeed, comprehension itself must be destroyed. Elie Wiesel recalls, "In dying, my father looked at me, and in his eyes where night was gathering, there was nothing but animal terror, the demented terror of one who, because he wished to understand too much, no longer understood anything. His gaze fixed on me, empty of meaning."[36] As the father, however, it falls to him to understand, that is, to comprehend and to *think* what the world poses for thought.

According to Jewish tradition, holiness flows into the world through ten *sefirot,* or points of manifestation of the Divine light. From above to below, they are *Keter* (Crown), *Chokhmah* (Wisdom), *Binah* (Understanding), *Chesed* (Loving Kindness), *Gevurah* (Judgment), *Tiferet* (Beauty), *Netsach* (Victory), *Hod* (Praise), *Yesod* (Foundation), and *Malkhut* (Kingdom).[37] Just as Understanding is associated with the mother, so Wisdom is associated with the father. Further, among the connections between the ten *sefirot* and the parts of the body, Wisdom belongs to the skull or to the mind,[38] that is, to the seat of thought. The night that gathers in the eyes of the dying father darkens the mind that constitutes the father, darkens not just the mind of this particular father but mind as such. Thus we have witnessed the darkening of Jewish thought. And the open wound that remains oozes darkness.

Philosophy pretends to be the love of wisdom; it is the key to the conception of the human being. Looking to the *sifrei kodesh,* we find in Bachya ibn Paquda a Jewish expression of this notion: "Sages declared that philosophy is man's knowledge of himself, that is, knowledge of what has been mentioned in regard to the human being so that through the evidence of Divine wisdom displayed in himself, he will become cognizant of the Creator" (*Chovot Halevavot* 2:5). This claim is based on the premise that the human being is created in the image of the Holy One, a premise that has been assaulted by modern philosophers, postmodern theorists, and Nazi murderers. If this premise is the father's fundamental teaching, then the premise is obliterated upon the murder of the father, for the father is the embodiment of that premise and that teaching.

To the extent that the human being struggles to retain the Divine image and thus to remain human, he or she seeks the wisdom to *comprehend.* One cannot decide not to comprehend, any more than one can decide not to breathe—or not to have a father. In the Shoah, it is not that the reasons for the extermination are obscure or complicated; rather, the "reasons" do not belong to reason or to the rational and the thinkable. Recall the words of Charlotte Delbo, cited in the previous chapter: those sent to the antiworld "expect the worst—they do not expect the unthinkable."[39] They do not expect the nullification of thought itself. And yet thinking continues, in the Shoah, to further undermine the life of the human being. Intelligence and thought themselves become the enemy.

As a tradition of thought, the Jewish tradition is a tradition of commentary, not only on the text of the Torah but also on the world created from the blueprint of the Torah. The function of thought is to read the text of the world as one might read the letters of the alphabet, for a corollary to the premise that creation comes into being through Divine utterance is that every detail of creation is laden with revelation. Therefore, it is written not that Adam "named" the animals but that he "read"—*vayikra*—their names: so profound was the wisdom of the father of all humanity that he could "read" the Divine utterance of which all things are made. Just as the father teaches his child the *alef-beit* by which the Torah is read, so does he signify the "reading" of truth in the world through a process of thought. In the antiworld, however, the alphabet of the world is erased so that the life and light of thought are swallowed up rather than released in the effort to read the revelation. There is no burning bush. There is only the burning.

Contrary to what many have claimed, the breakdown of reality that follows upon the collapse of thought is not a problem for the imagination. On the contrary, once thought collapses—and with it the laws and limitations of reality—imagination becomes unlimited, as noted in the last chapter; everything the Nazis did was imagined before it was done. The result of this collapse of law and limit is a perversion of the real into the unreal. "Existence as such," as Jean Améry states it, "became definitively a totally abstract and thus empty concept. To reach out beyond concrete reality with words became before our very eyes a game that was not only worthless and an impermissible luxury but also mocking and evil."[40] Where reality happens, Levinas reminds us, "the *appearing* of a phenomenon is inseparable from its *signifying*. . . . Every phenomenon is a disclosure or a fragment of a discourse."[41] Every phenomenon, in other words, is revelation. But in the antiworld of Auschwitz, where existence *as such* is an empty concept, the phenomenon does not speak—it overwhelms, silent and indifferent. Thus unreality happens in an erasure of revelation. It happens because the father, who is the sign of giving signs, no longer happens. It happens because the father is murdered (if, indeed, even the very notion of murder still applies).

The appearing of a phenomenon is inseparable from its signifying, because the father has made an appearance and has thus rooted the human being in the real. In the concentrationary universe, it is not that one world has replaced another; rather, the real has broken down so that there is no place—no *Makom*—where a world can make its appearance. That place emerges in the midst of the revelation and the relation that make the father who he is. With the loss of the father, the fundamental relationship that goes into the structuring of the real is overturned. Having already noted the father's association with the sefirah of Chokhmah, we recall that, according to Jewish thought, "Wisdom is the conduit of God's essence."[42] The father, as the guardian of tradition, is the guardian of one of the avenues of God's revelation. There is no murder of the father that does not entail a murder of God the Father. And one profoundly horrifying way in which God the Father is obliterated is through the obliteration of the child.

SOURCE OF REDEMPTION: THE CHILD

In the Jewish teaching and tradition that we have from the *sifrei kodesh,* the child's link to redemption is there from the beginning. Recall, for example, the prophet Isaiah's pronouncement on the coming of the Messiah: "The wolf shall dwell with the lamb, and the leopard shall lie down with the kid; and the calf and the young lion and the fatling together; and a little child shall lead them" (Isaiah 11:6). Here we have the diametric opposite of what the Nazis emulated, the expression of a compassion that is the opposite of the cruelty to which the Jewish children were subjected precisely because the Nazis knew what the children meant to the Jews.[43] Yes, all people love their children. Of course. But not all traditions identify children with the Torah and the testimony that are the keys to redemption. In the holy books they are called the *nachalat Hashem,* the "heritage of the Lord" (see, for example, Psalms 127:3). When we note that *nachalah* also means "stream" or "river," we realize that children signify the living waters of Torah that flow from on high. They represent the flow of time that constitutes the presence of God in the realm of space.

When the Torah was given at Mount Sinai, life was given to the world: in the Jewish tradition, the Torah is life itself, and our children are the guarantors of that life, for in the Midrash Tanchuma it is written, "In the hour when the Holy One, blessed be He, was to offer the Torah to Israel, He said, 'Preserve My Torah.' They told Him, 'We shall.' He said to them, 'Give Me a guarantee that you will keep it.' They said to Him, 'Abraham, Isaac, and Jacob will be our guarantee.' He told them, 'Your fathers themselves need a guarantee.' . . . They told Him, 'Our children will be our guarantee'" (*Tanchuma Vayigash* 1; *Shir Hashirim Rabbah* 1:4:1). And the Midrash on Psalms adds, God "asked the infants and the embryos: 'Will you be sureties for your fathers and mothers so that if I give them the Torah they will live by it, but that if they do not, you will be forfeited because of them?' They replied: 'Yes'" (*Midrash Tehillim* 1:8:4). And so we see what is at stake in our adherence to the *mitzvot.*

This teaching that affirms the dearness of our children is so strongly embedded in the Jewish soul that when Adam Czerniakow, head of the Warsaw Ghetto Jewish Council, was ordered to turn over the children for deportation to Treblinka, he took his own life instead. "After Czerniakow made the last entry in his diary on July 23, 1942," notes Israel Gutman, "he left a note to the effect that the SS wanted him to kill the children with his own hands."[44] Perhaps Czerniakow knew on some level that to participate in this murder of the children would amount to becoming an accomplice in the murder of God, if one may speak in such a manner.

The association between the murder of God and the murder of the child is all too clear in a haunting and horrifying scene from Elie Wiesel's *Night*. When the prisoners of Buna were forced to witness the hanging of a child, a man standing behind Eliezer whispered, "Where is God now?" And we read, "I heard a voice within me answer him: 'Where is He? Here He is—He is hanging here on this gallows.'"[45] What this means for Jewish thought Wiesel makes clear in *Ani Maamin*: "With each hour, the most blessed and most stricken people of the world number twelve times twelve children less. And each one carries away still another fragment of the Temple in flames."[46] As a preeminent Jewish thinker, Wiesel knows precisely the implications of what he is saying. He knows, for example, that one Hebrew phrase designating the Temple is *beit-Hashekhinah,* the "House of the Shekhinah." As the children go up in flames, so does the Divine Presence.

The Temple is the House of the Shekhinah not because it is the site of rite and ritual but because it is the center attesting to the sanctity of human life, beginning with the children. Hence the Tikkunei Hazohar refers to children as "the face of the Shekhinah."[47] A Midrash attributed to Rabbi Yehudah ha-Nasi illustrates the definitive link between the presence of children and the Divine presence: "Come and see how beloved are the children by the Holy One, blessed be He. The Sanhedrin were exiled but the Shekhinah did not go into exile with them. When, however, the children were exiled, the Shekhinah went into exile with them" (see *Eichah Rabbah* 1:6:33). In the Zohar we read, "Who is it that upholds the world and causes the patriarchs to appear? It is the voice of tender children studying the Torah; and for their sake the world is saved" (*Zohar* I, 1b). And, in the name of Rabbi Yehudah, Resh Lakish said, "The world endures only for the sake of the breath of the schoolchildren" (*Shabbat* 119b). Here we see a radical departure from the Greek thinking that understands reality in terms of power: in Jewish thinking, the immense weight of the world rests not upon the shoulders of a mighty Atlas but upon the breath of a child, for upon that breath vibrates the sum of meaning.

In the Zohar it is written further: "From the 'breath' which issues out of the mouth the voice is formed, and according to the well-known dictum, the world is upheld only by the merit of the 'breath' of little school-children who have not yet tasted sin. Breath is itself mixture, being composed of air and moisture, and through it the world is carried on. Esoterically speaking, the breath of the little ones becomes 'voice,' and spreads throughout the whole universe, so that they become the guardians of the world" (*Zohar* II, 39a). The world endures not by might but by spirit (compare Zechariah 4:6), as long as it attends to the "voice" that speaks from within the breath of the children. That voice is just what the Nazis set out to silence; that breath is just what they aimed to suffocate, with intellectual malice and philosophical forethought. At the core of the Nazis' assault on God is the determined attempt to suffocate the breath and to silence the voice arising from the mouths of Jewish children. Thus the suffocating silence of the antiworld.

The suffocation of the children in the Shoah not only came with the destruction of their frail little bodies but also included the perversion of their very being. The children of the Shoah *knew only fear.* The paralyzing effect of knowing only fear appears as a rigor mortis that takes over the soul before the body is cast into the earth or reduced to ashes. And so the children did not move; they did not speak and they did not play: they were not children but only the vanishing shadows of children. In the Riga Ghetto, for example, says the sculptor Elik Rivosh, one never saw "a single child playing. All of them just sit in the gateways or cling to their mothers like hunted animals."[48] Racked with fear, their bodies are all but emptied of life's spirit, which is the spirit of the child, who in turn sustains the spirit of a people and a world.

"Children were old, and old men were as helpless as children," Wiesel puts it,[49] a statement illustrated by the image of two children in a ghetto pushing an old man in a baby carriage.[50] If time is a fundamental horizon of human being, then this collapse of time in children robbed of a future fundamentally alters their being. It steals their life away before they are sent to their death, making them more ancient than the Ancient of Days. These little ones are forced into an awareness of every breath sucked forth from their young souls.[51] The days they live are not the days of their lives but the days of their death. Robbed of their time, they are robbed of their place so that any place they occupy is a nonplace; their presence is out of place and their time out of joint. Thus the ontologi-

cal condition to which the Nazis relegated the child exemplifies an ontological aspect of the assault on the people of Israel. As the Jews were cut
off from the world, the children were cut off from the Jews.

Throughout the ghettos of the Shoah the condition of the child was
such that he or she was removed from the care of all. This absence of
care is a manifestation of the absence of the Holy One so that, once again,
the assault on the child becomes an integral part of the assault on the
Holy One. As ubiquitous as the absence of God, the absence of children
and childhood is the death before death, the slaughter before the slaughter, which is a slaughter of the innocents in their innocence, the slaughter of redemption. If the essence of the Nazi empire is the murder camp,
as Fackenheim has said,[52] the essence of that murder is the murder of
the children. The Nazis were not merely murderers—they were *child murderers* who relentlessly tracked down their prey. They were murderers of
the dimension of height that ordains and sanctifies being. They were the
murderers of redemption.

Echoing a Jewish teaching on the significance of the child, Wiesel's
character Moshe asserts, "The Messiah. We seek him, we pursue him. We
think he is in heaven; we don't know that he likes to come down as a child.
And yet, every man's childhood is messianic in essence."[53] Among the *sifrei
kodesh* to articulate this view of the child as savior is the *Even Sheleimah*
of the Vilna Gaon, the renowned sage of the eighteenth century. There
he writes, "The child redeems his parent from Gehinnom and causes him
to be brought to Gan Eden."[54] The lips of the child, untainted by sin,
carry our prayers to God. Without the children, we do not have God's
ear; without the children, it is as though He were deaf.

The Maggid of Dubno, a contemporary of the Vilna Gaon, illustrates
the significance of the child with a parable about a family that lived in
a house in the forest. Every evening the father would barricade the windows and doors of the house to protect his wife and children from danger. But one night a fire broke out in their home. A heavy stone had fallen
and sealed the door so that they could not get out. Since the windows
were locked from the outside, they had no way of crying out to their
neighbors for help. The youngest child, however, discovered the dormer
window, and, because he was so small, he was able to climb outside and
go for help. The villagers came and rolled away the stone from the entrance

to the house. And so the family was saved, thanks to the courageous efforts of a small child. "Even as this one little boy triumphantly flung open the door of his father's house and thereby saved his family," says the Maggid, "so, too, the study, prayers and tears of our children can open the lofty gates of Heaven and thus bring about the deliverance of their elders."[55] What is slaughtered with the slaughter of the innocents, then, is salvation itself.

Perhaps more than anywhere else, in the figure of the child we encounter what is at stake both in the *sifrei kodesh* and in the Jewish philosophical response to the Shoah. What is at stake in the sacred texts is redemption; what is at stake in the Jewish response to the Shoah is the salvation of redemption. Because the Shoah is about the assault on the human being through the murder of mother, father, and child, a distinctively Jewish response to the Shoah entails a testimony to the holiness of what was slated for destruction. And without the *sifrei kodesh,* we have no sense of that holiness. Indeed, a Jewish philosophical response to the Shoah is about more than philosophy; it is about recovery: the recovery of a sacred teaching and of the human image sanctified by that teaching. That is why Jewish thinkers are implicated by their subject matter, even—or especially—when they retreat to the academic comfort of "the history of the Holocaust" or "postmodern variations on Judaism" or "alternative ways of being Jewish" rather than collide with the fate of mother, father, and child. Where do those collisions take place? In the testimony of those who speak from the core of the Event. Along with the *sifrei kodesh,* that testimony must lie at the core of post-Holocaust Jewish thought.

HOLY BOOKS AND HUMAN VOICES
IN THE JEWISH RESPONSE TO THE SHOAH

A distinctively Jewish philosophical response to the Shoah is in some ways unphilosophical, perhaps even antiphilosophical. Students in survey courses in philosophy never study Mishnah or Midrash, nor do they turn to diaries and memoirs when trying to get at the metaphysical dimensions of historical events. Many Jews who attempt a philosophical response to the Shoah also ignore the holy books and the words of the witnesses. Many of the postmodernists, in fact, insist upon ignoring them. James Young, for instance, argues that Holocaust diarists "necessarily convert experience into an organized, often ritualized, *memory* of experience"; hence it is "difficult to distinguish between the archetypal patterns the ghetto diarist has brought to the events, those he perceived in or inferred from them, and those that exist in the narrative. As raw as they may have been at the moment, the ghetto and camp experiences were immediately refined and organized by witnesses within the terms of their *Weltanschauungen.*"[56] The implication is that the testimony of witnesses is suspect *because they were there.*

If Jewish thought is to be Jewish, it must renounce the absurdity of this postmodern view and attend to the voices of the witnesses, with an eye toward the *sifrei kodesh,* the texts that provide the contexts for Jews' testimony *as Jews* and not just as "victims." Not only would failure to attend to these voices be an outrage, it would add to the assault on these souls, for the diarists recorded their testimonies often at risk of their lives, and the authors of the memoirs revisit the horror to bring us an echo of the outcry of the dead. Let us consider, then, a few examples from diaries and memoirs that illustrate the assault on mother, father, and child as we have discussed it so far.

Because the crime of the Jews was *being,* the mother who brought Jews into being was the worst of criminals. The Nazis, making pregnancy a criminal *condition,* and not just a criminal act, demonstrated the complete, ontological scope of their assault on humanity as it unfolded in their assault on the mother. And the Holocaust diarists thoroughly attest to this assault. On February 5, 1942, the Vilna Ghetto diarist Herman Kruk wrote, "Today the Gestapo summoned two members of the Judenrat and notified them: No more Jewish children are to be born. The order came from Berlin."[57] In his diary from the Kovno Ghetto, Avraham Tory noted on July 24, 1942, "From September on, giving birth is strictly forbidden. Pregnant women will be put to death."[58] And in November 1941 Emmanuel Ringelblum reported that in the Łódź Ghetto "Jews have been prohibited from marrying and having children. Women pregnant up to three months have to have an abortion."[59] Thus the Vittel diarist Yitzhak Katznelson cries out, "These Jewish mothers with babes in their wombs! This murderous German nation! That was their chief joy! To destroy women with child!"[60] It was their chief joy because it was a sublime expression of their primary aim.

Turning to some examples from Holocaust memoirs, we are overwhelmed by the realization that a people and a world are ontologically orphaned, their essence redefined as the essence of the orphan. To be sure, in most cases—and, from an ontological standpoint, in every case—these memoirs are the memoirs of orphans. Sara Zyskind's memoir, for example, begins with the memory of the last Mother's Day that her mother enjoyed[61] before the destruction of all days. Soon she loses her mother to the slow death of ghetto life, and the memory of an outcry rises to the surface of her page: "I don't want to be an orphan, Mother!"[62] In Isabella Leitner's memoir we see what becomes of infants—and of mothers—in a realm where motherhood is a capital crime. Relating how the women were forced to destroy babies born in Auschwitz in order to save the mothers, Leitner addresses a child, saying, "You belong to the gas chamber. Your mother has no rights. She only brought forth fodder for the gas chamber. She is not a mother. . . . And so, dear baby, you are on your way to heaven to meet a recent arrival . . . your father."[63]

Just as Jewish souls were crushed before their bodies were destroyed, very often the image of the father was broken before he himself was taken away to death. Sara Zyskind, for example, recalls a moment of gazing upon her father as he prayed, wrapped in the *tallit,* the prayer shawl of ancient tradition. "It struck me," she relates, "that there was something very strange about Father's praying form, as if it were an apparition from another world. Another world? What am I thinking . . . ? Father was still part of this world, and he was all that I had left here. I gazed at him again. There was nothing about him that recalled the image of my once young and exuberant father."[64] Another example of the fragmentation of the image of the father is Gerda Klein's description of her father's reaction when her brother Arthur was forced to leave their home: "Now he was as helpless as I. An overwhelming feeling of pity and pain swept over me. I embraced Papa. The touch of my arms made him shiver, and a suppressed and terrible sobbing cry rose from his throat, a cry which I will never forget, which had no resemblance to the human voice; it sounded rather like the cry of an animal when it has been stabbed and is dying."[65] He who had been heir to the word—who had conveyed the word to his children—loses the word in the loss of his image, for the word, the human voice, is just what constitutes that image. Elsewhere Klein remembers that her father "had changed so much."[66] Leon Wells notes that his father's hair "had turned gray and he was very thin."[67] And in the opening pages of her memoir, Livia Bitton-Jackson recalls, "My father seemed to grow somewhat slack as winter wore on. His silences became longer."[68] In the ontological assault on Jewish being, it is not enough simply to murder the father. The killing of his body must be preceded by the annihilation of his image, for in his image lies the Jewish tradition that the father symbolizes.

While the mother and the father signify an origin and a tradition, the child represents a future and a redemption, from which the present and the past derive their meaning. What becomes of that future-oriented meaning we see in an entry from the diary of Aryeh Klonicki-Klonymus. "How many times," he writes on July 5, 1943, "would I look at my little child, so handsome and full of life, and it would seem to me that it is not a child I am looking at but a box filled with ashes."[69] This undoing of the image of the child is the first manifestation of the undoing of his essence; where the children are concerned, image and essence are of a piece. And in the Shoah, their essence is fear. Says Hanna Levy-Hass in her Bergen-Belsen diary, "The children know no joy. They know only fear, nothing but fear. These poor, humiliated little creatures stand erect for hours on end, with fear racking their bodies, as they stare in paralyzed anticipation of things that will surely befall them."[70] And in his Warsaw Ghetto diary Hersh Wasser comments on the fate of the children, saying, "The soul of the child grows more and more tainted. The lack of schools, the gutter, absolute demoralization, leave their terrible mark. What sort of generation will grow out of all this?"[71] The answer, of course, is that no generation will grow out of this: these children belong to a generation consigned to the gas chambers. And the authors of the memoirs bear the memory of that generation, a memory that can be truly assessed only in the light of the holy texts that underlie these texts.

In the memoirs of the Shoah, the God who is beseeched to heed the cries of the children is Himself reduced to their outcry—and to their silence. For Issahar's wife, the woman in Wiesel's *A Jew Today* who sees dead children everywhere, "they are God's memory."[72] Because the child is the vessel of all meaning harbored by a living future, the death of the child renders the future dead, turned back on the child himself. Here, the child is no longer the flower of youth but the broken shoot of old age. "For them days were months," Simon Wiesenthal remembers. "When I saw them with toys in their hands, they looked unfamiliar, uncanny, like old men playing with childish things."[73] In the child, the Promise from a past goes out to meet us in the future; in the child abides our redemption. But when the child collapses into old age, time and eternity collapse with him, and the Word of the Promise is lost.

Another symptom of the mutilation of the child's image, then, is the loss of the child's word. "Little Bina," Leon Wells says of his sister, "whom I remembered as a lively child, had completely altered. She went about sad and unhappy, and hardly spoke. . . . She would neither talk nor laugh nor play."[74] In the play of the child lies the play of life, a celebration of the life and meaning signified by the child. When that play ceases, being loses its significance: only where children play does life have meaning. With this in mind, we recall a passage from Alexander Donat's memoir, where he says of his three-year-old son, "The lively child whose nature had been movement and playfulness now sat for hours at a time without moving. Whenever I seemed to be leaving him, his only reaction was to tighten his grip on me, uttering only the single word: 'Daddy.'"[75] This single word not only undoes the father; it announces the ontological undoing of the word, for it is a word that both demands a response and makes all response impossible. It announces the doom that is the opposite of redemption.

Which returns us to the problem of determining a Jewish response to the Shoah. The Midrash relates that "when the Gentiles asked the philosopher Avnimus if they could overcome the Jews, he told them that as long as they heard the sound of Jewish children learning [Torah], they were powerless against the Jews" (*Bereshit Rabbah* 65:12). A Jewish response to the Shoah must attend to the voices of the children learning from the holy books. It must attend to the voices of Jewish mothers and fathers who were murdered in their very essence *as* Jewish mothers and fathers, with all the ramifications that we have seen in the *sifrei kodesh*. It must avoid the temptation to think "philosophically," that is, in terms of postmodern philosophy, which knows nothing of the *holiness* of mothers, fathers, and children. Else the mothers, fathers, and children of the Shoah will be lost. Else creation, revelation, and redemption will be lost.

And so the mother, fathers, and children put to us the question put to the first man: Where are you? (Genesis 3:9). Answering them, we answer to a Voice that commands us to answer, the Voice that speaks to us through the *sifrei kodesh*. If we lose the contexts of the holy texts in our effort to respond to the Shoah, we may not lose the voices that cry out to us, but we lose the Voice that commands us to care. If what Fackenheim terms "the commanding Voice of Auschwitz" commands Jews to be Jews so as to refuse the Nazis a posthumous victory,[76] then we must draw that Voice and its commandment into our response to the Shoah. Without the *sifrei kodesh* and the words of the witnesses, we soon grow deaf to the Voice that commands us both from the holy books and from Auschwitz. And once we grow deaf to the Voice, we grow worse than deaf to the voices of the murdered mothers, fathers, and children: we grow indifferent.

Therefore, Jewish thought must fetch the fire of Torah from the flames, for in that fire lies the Divine spark that constitutes our humanity. And, just as the Nazis attempted to consign the Torah to the flames, so did they attempt to extinguish the Divine spark within the human being. Let's consider more closely this matter of the human being's importance for post-Holocaust Jewish thought.

6

The Muselmann and the
Matter of the Human Being

> The Lord God formed the human being of the dust of the
> ground and breathed into his nostrils the breath of life; and
> the human being became a living soul.—Genesis 2:7

From the standpoint of Jewish thought, the matter of the human being is perhaps the most definitive feature of the Shoah. Therefore, it is of fundamental importance to a Jewish response to the Shoah. The imposed nothingness that characterizes the Shoah *as* Shoah—the assault on the Holy One Himself—lies in the devastation of the Divine breath, the *neshimah* that is *neshamah,* within the human soul. In our prayers each morning, we recite the line from the Talmud: *Neshamah shenatata bi tehorah hi,* "The soul that You have given within me is pure" (*Berakhot* 60b). The adjective *tahor,* "pure," is a cognate of the noun *tohar,* which means both "purity" and "brightness": the *neshamah* is that portion of the soul through which the light of the Holy One illuminates His creation. The soul does not simply live—it *shines.* When God declared, "Let there be light" (Genesis 1:3), He declared, "Let there be soul."[1] As an assault on the One who summons the soul into being with a cry of "Let there be light," the Shoah is an assault on that light as it emanates into the world through the soul.

While this devastation of the soul is a desecration of the Invisible One who invisibly imparts the Divine spark to the human being, it assumes a form that is all too incarnate, for it is manifest in that creature whose being is nonbeing: the Muselmann. "When they could still walk," writes Leon Poliakov, "[the Muselmänner] moved like automatons; once stopped, they were capable of no further movement. They fell prostrate on the ground; nothing mattered any more to them. Their bodies blocked the passageway. You could step right on them and they would not draw back their arms or legs an inch. No protest, no cry of pain came from their half-open mouth. And yet they were still alive. . . . "[2] Still alive. . . . But what can this "still alive" mean? Trapped in their mute paralysis, can they still be alive? Can they still be human beings? And what does this collapse of man into Muselmann say of our own humanity?

Rudolf Vrba describes the Muselmänner as entities "whose eyes were empty, whose flesh had fled, whose blood was near to water."[3] Once again we see that the assault on the soul is an assault on something very concrete: flesh and blood. Jewish tradition, in fact, teaches that not only the soul but also the body is made of Torah: of the 613 commandments that constitute the Torah, 248 correspond to the 248 bones of the body, and 365 to the 365 sinews of the body.[4] With the fleeing of the flesh there is a fleeing of Torah and a draining of life from the blood itself. Empty of the light of life, the eyes are drained of the light of Torah. Those empty eyes announce our own emptiness. That flesh has fled, to invade our own flesh in the ashes that abide in our bread. And the blood turned to water is blood emptied of a soul, for the soul, the *nefesh,* is in the blood, as it is written (Deuteronomy 12:23). Once the soul has been slaughtered, the blood turns to water.

If we cannot answer to the matter of the human being that confronts us in the Muselmann, then our own blood will turn to water. Our own flesh will flee. And our own eyes will be emptied of the Divine spark, of the *neshamah,* that constitutes our humanity. Once emptied of that spark, we become blind not only to our own humanity but, more crucial, to the humanity of our fellow human being. Indeed, for Jewish thought, the matter of the human being is a matter that concerns not my value but my responsibility. It is a matter of what imparts value to the *other* human being.

In this chapter, we shall explore the opposition between man and

Muselmann in the light of a Jewish understanding of humanity and what that means for the future not only of the Jews but of all humanity. Only a recovery of the distinctively Jewish view of the human being—the view that the Nazis sought to erase from human consciousness—can open up a future for humanity *as* humanity. Why? Because only Jewish thought, thinking as it does under the canopy of Divine thought, can determine the invisible and infinite dearness of the other human being. Because only from the Torah that shapes Jewish thought do we have the truth that every human being is created in the image and likeness of the Holy One (Genesis 1:27); therefore, who and what we are lies in the love that we offer our fellow human being (Leviticus 19:18). As we saw in chapter 3, the death that concerns me is the death of my neighbor. But that death is just what was under assault in the Nazi assault on the holiness of the human image.

A MATTER OF LIFE AND A MATTER OF DEATH

For a human being, death is not a natural phenomenon that befalls him after three score and ten years; rather, it is part of the task that he is summoned to engage from the moment he is called into being. For an animal, death is not a task—it is a natural phenomenon, part of a natural cycle in which nature takes its course. An animal does not die the death, and so for an animal neither living nor dying is a matter of testimony. Therefore, Joseph Albo reminds us, the "perfection" of an animal lies in existence itself, whereas for a human being it lies in fulfilling a purpose or a destiny—*unto death* (see *Sefer HaIkkarim* 3:2). The injunction to choose the Good by living the Good makes death an issue for a human being. And it makes death otherwise than a natural phenomenon.

There is an important teaching from the Midrash in this connection. On each of the first five days of Creation (except the second day), God pronounced His labor to be good; but on the sixth day, He declared it to be *tov meod,* that is, "very good" (Genesis 1:31). The word *meod* means "more"; its cognate, the verb *himid,* means "to increase." How can the Good be increased? Through the creation of the human being; the human being is *more* than being. And the sign of his being *more* is his death, which, conceived as a task, becomes his infinite offering for the sake of the infinitely dear. Therefore, Rabbi Meir maintains, the *meod* in *tov meod* signifies death, a category belonging to human life alone (see *Bereshit Rabbah* 9:5; see also *Zohar* II, 103a). To choose life is to choose this *tov meod* that distinguishes the human from the animal, and a living Good from a conceptual good. Choosing the *tov meod* means understanding that the basis of our relation to another human being—underlying the commandment to love our neighbor—is our fear for his death. Only others lie in the cemeteries.

Also among the 613 commandments of Torah is the commandment to choose life (Deuteronomy 30:19). Indeed, to be among the Chosen is to be compelled to make this choice. Choosing life, we do not choose merely to stay alive. The emergence of the State of Israel as a haven for Jews is not about survival alone. It is about engaging in a testimony concerning the holiness of a life that has its origin in the Holy One—that is what we choose when we choose life. Making this choice does not mean that we no longer pass away from this earth. Rather, it means that in choosing life we understand death to be part of the process of sanctifying life, the testimonial outcome of a life steeped in Torah, prayer, and deeds of loving kindness. These are the things we choose when we choose life. Death is not eliminated; rather, like life, it is situated within the contexts of the sacred. Understood in terms of the sacred, death is the culmination, not the negation, of life.[5] It is not opposed to life as darkness is opposed to light; it is a task that confronts us in the course of life. Murder is evil; in itself, death is not. Standing by while people die is evil; in itself, dying is not. But the unthinkable evil—the evil that surpasses evil and paralyzes thought, the evil that is ultimate—is the death that is no longer death. For the death that is no longer death comes to a life that is no longer life; it comes at a time when good is no longer good and evil is no longer evil. It comes in the time of the Shoah.

Obliterated during the Shoah was not only Jewish life but also Jewish death, for living as a Jew entails dying as a Jew. And to die as a Jew is to choose life even in death, speaking even in death the Name of the One who is the origin of life in a declaration of *"Shema Yisrael!"* What transpires in the Nazi's imposition of death upon the Jew is not only the end of Jewish life but also the end of the *Shema Yisrael* that makes death the death of a Jew. This prayer, like all prayer, comes from the Holy One, who breathes His image and likeness into the human being. To be sure, the prayer *is* the image and likeness of the Holy One. "To be a man," as Abraham Joshua Heschel says, is to embrace *"the pre-eminence of prayer."*[6] Hence the Nazi *has* to eliminate the Shema: to stifle the prayer's holy word is to strangle the man's holy image. And if the Shema is to be a Jew's dying words, then the Jew's death will be eliminated in the death camp. How did the Nazis eliminate the death of the Jew? By making the Jew into a Muselmann empty of the image and likeness of the Holy One.

It turns out that the assault on the image and likeness of God entails an assault on death itself. Thus, says Fackenheim, "the divine image in man *can* be destroyed. No more threatening proof to this effect can be found than the so-called Muselmann in the Nazi death camp."[7] Far more than an emaciated human being, the Muselmann is the Nazis' manifestation of the evil that is ultimate, incarnate in a creature whose prayer has been silenced and whose death is no longer death. Informing Fackenheim's insight into the meaning of the Muselmann is Primo Levi's memoir *Survival in Auschwitz: The Nazi Assault on Humanity.* The work's original Italian title states more clearly the driving concern in Levi's book.[8] It poses a question concerning the defining substance of *a* human being. It tells us that the subtitle of the 1996 English translation does not in fact pertain to an assault on *all* human beings; after all, the Germans did not attack the Japanese. Rather, the original Italian title addresses the Nazis' radical undermining of the significance and the substance of *any* human being, whether German, Japanese, or Jew.

Adding Fackenheim's insight to Levi's question, we have further evidence of what we have already maintained: namely, that the question of what a human being is—of what imparts value to the *other* human being—is the question that defines the Nazis' annihilation of the Jews. "The murderers of Auschwitz," Fackenheim makes clear, "cut off Jews from humanity and denied them the right to existence, yet in being denied that right, Jews represented all humanity. Jews after Auschwitz represent all humanity when they affirm their Jewishness and deny the Nazi denial."[9] Through the Jews, the Torah's teaching concerning the Divine spark within *every* human being comes into the world. To be sure, the teaching and the Divine spark—Torah and holiness—are of a piece, and the presence of the Jew in the world signifies both Torah and holiness. Thus the presence of the Jew in the world affirms the infinite dearness of the other human being. Which means: it is precisely the Jew who affirms man, over against the Muselmann.

In his memoir, Levi describes the Muselmänner as "the backbone of the camp, an anonymous mass, continually renewed and always identical, of non-men who march and labour in silence, the divine spark dead within them, already too empty to really suffer. One hesitates to call them living: one hesitates to call their death death."[10] Where Fackenheim invokes the Divine image, Levi refers to the Divine spark. But what is this image or spark of the Divine? It is the trace of the Creator and the Light of Creation. It is the image and likeness of the Holy One that emanates from the Throne of Glory (*Zohar* II, 211b). It is a fire taken from the "the black fire on white fire" that is Torah (see *Tanchuma Bereshit* 1; *Devarim Rabbah* 3:12; *Shir Hashirim Rabbah* 5:11:6; *Zohar* II, 226b). It is the holiness that inheres in the humanity of the human being. In a word, it is the *neshamah* that God breathes into every human being.[11] The Nazi, however, sucks from the Jew the *neshamah* that God has breathed into the Jew and destroys the trace of the holy that makes a human being a human being. Transforming the Jew into a creature "too empty to really suffer," the Nazi robs him even of his suffering—and of his death.

In a very important sense, then, the Nazi does not set out to murder the Jew, since only a human being can be murdered. The Nazi perpetrates something worse than murder: he transforms the Jew into a Muselmann. That is what defines the Nazi, just as the Torah defines the Jew. And that is why Levi sees embodied in the Muselmann "all the evil of our time in one image,"[12] the image emptied of the Divine image. It is why Fackenheim sees in the Muselmann the Nazis' "most characteristic, most original product."[13] If Auschwitz signifies the Holocaust, the Muselmann signifies Auschwitz. The Nazis' transformation of man into Muselmann is a singular phenomenon that constitutes the singularity of the Holocaust, and it makes the Holocaust decisive for all humanity. The Muselmann is not merely the calculated outcome of torture, exposure, and deprivation. Far more than the victim of starvation and brutality, the Muselmann is *the Jew* whose very existence was deemed criminal, whose prayers were regarded as an act of sedition, whose holy days were subject to desecration. He is *the Jew* for whom marriage and childbirth were forbidden, for whom schooling was a crime, for whom there was no protection under the law. He is *the Jew* both widowed and orphaned, forced to witness the murder of his family, and rendered "ferociously alone"[14] before being rendered ferociously faceless.

Fackenheim describes the Muselmann as "a *novum*"[15] or "a new way of human being in history."[16] And yet Levi wonders whether it is a way of *human* being at all: "non-men" he calls them. Not non-Jews, from a Nazi standpoint, but *precisely* Jews, whom the Nazis deemed "non-men." The question before us, then, is this: How might this matter of the human being inform post-Holocaust Jewish thought? In order to address this question, we shall examine more closely some of Levi's remarks about the Muselmann as well as Fackenheim's response to this historical *novum*. Three key points in Levi's exposition on the Muselmann are the Muselmann's loss of a past, his loss of words, and his loss of presence. Three parallel issues to consider, with the help of Fackenheim are time, language, and relation. These are the matters that go to the heart of the matter of the human being, to reveal the unprecedented opposition that not only defines the Holocaust but, after Auschwitz, implicates us in our own humanity.

THE ASSAULT ON HUMANITY AS AN ASSAULT ON TIME

"All the musselmans who finished in the gas chambers," writes Levi, "have the same story, or more exactly, have no story,"[17] that is, they have no *storia,* to use the word from Levi's Italian text,[18] a word that also means "history." In this word that means both "story" and "history," and that suggests both "tale" and "tradition," we come to a deeper insight into the Divine spark and what it is made of. It is made of the human being's tale and tradition; it is made of his story. Where the Divine spark is gone, the story is gone. If the Muselmann has no story, a human being does indeed have a story, both personal and communal. The more intimately we enter into a relation with others, the more familiar we become with their stories. Indeed, where one human being lives *in relation* to the other, each is part of the other's story, just as God and humanity are part of each other's story. When God breathes the Divine spark, the *neshamah,* into the human being, He breathes His story, which is His Torah, into the human being. Thus the human being inherits the tale and tradition that make every human being's story meaningful. And each time the tale is related, the spark is transmitted. With each transmission of the tale, there is an increase of light in the world. And with the extinguishing of each story, there is a diminishing of light.

The story, transmitting a spark of God, opens up meaning. Thus the Zohar makes a distinction between speaking, saying, and relating, where relating entails storytelling, or *agadah* (see *Zohar Vayechi* 234b). *Agadah* is the relating that draws us into a relation, both to God and to our fellow human being. Why does the *Sifre* teach that in order to know God we must know the tales of *agadah,* as noted in the last chapter? Because the tales give voice to the ineffable. In the tales we find the Divine spark that animates life and the memory of life. Relating our tales, we enter into a relation with the tales of others, of all humanity; thus, through storytelling, the holiness of humanity emanates into the world. And memory is the form that it assumes: in our memory lies our humanity. If the Muselmann has no tale, he has no memory.

Like Elie Wiesel,[19] Levi declares that "the entire history of the brief 'millennial Reich' can be reread as a war against memory, as Orwellian falsification of memory, falsification of reality, negation of reality."[20] As a negation of reality, the assault on memory is a negation of creation. If what took place at Auschwitz was an "anti-creation," as Levi describes it,[21] it was the anticreation of the "anti-man," of the Muselmann, undertaken through the erasure of story and the obliteration of memory. This annihilation of story and memory brings us to a startling realization: in the Muselmann the Nazis attain their most absolute victory—a victory over time itself. Once death is no longer death, time is no longer time. And the human being is no longer a human being.

For the Jew, the horizons of time are delineated by a memory that exceeds the horizons of birth and death. It is a memory of the Exodus from Egypt and even Creation itself as well as a memory of the future expressed in the memory of the Messiah. Which means: the eternal is manifest in memory. How? Through the care for another. The duration of human time, says Emmanuel Levinas, assumes "the form of a worrying about the other, a spending without counting, a generosity, goodness, love,"[22] all of which were absent from the antiworld of the Muselmann. This absence is precisely the absence of the memory that is a remembrance of the eternal. Thus we find that where memory is absent, the eternal is absent, meaning is absent, time is absent. All three—memory, time, and meaning—constitute life. And all three come under assault in the Nazi assault on the Eternal One, on eternity itself, for the divine spark that is snuffed out in the Muselmann is made of eternity, that is, of "a future which, without ceasing to be a future, is nonetheless present."[23] Thus we have a basic link between identity and eternity. That link is undermined with the undermining of memory.

When memory is broken, moreover, both identity and direction are lost; what remains is not a dead man walking but the walking dead, their souls erased and their steps aimless—the "shufflers," as Isabella Leitner once described them to me, those who have no walk because they have no place to go. We see in the Muselmann the solitude of an internment that Levinas describes as "not the solitude of a being forsaken by the world with which it is no longer in step, but of a being that is as it were no longer in step with itself, is out of joint with itself, in a dislocation of the I from itself. . . . And this lag constitutes [its] present."[24] Hence the dance of antideath called "the Muselmann shuffle," the lag of one who cannot walk because he is out of step with his own existence. There is no "before" that would signal a direction, no "after" that would determine a meaning. There is only the shuffling lag within the narrow confines of the "now." In this confinement the Muselmann has no horizons: no story means no birth, no death, no time.

Lagging and languishing outside of time, the Muselmann has no awareness beyond the infinitesimal instant, which is to say, no awareness at all. Radically indifferent to his own being, he embodies the radical neutrality of Being, of a duration that does not endure but is simply "there." And yet he is there without *being* there. His is a being there—or a nonbeing there—that is utterly without care and drained of all predicates: the eyes have grown dark, the flesh has fled, and the blood has turned to water. His time has run out, as one may gather from Abraham ibn Ezra's commentary on Isaiah 63:3: "The blood is called *netsach*," he writes, "literally 'time,' because through the blood man lives his time."[25] Time *is* the soul that is in the blood. But the Muselmann is devoid of blood, devoid of time. Devoid of any "being there," the Muselmann is devoid of any "being beyond," hence devoid of the Divine spark of life. That is why his death is not death.

Once his memory is obliterated, moreover, the Muselmann loses his link to the immemorial. And so we see that the war against memory is a war against the immemorial. According to Jewish teaching, a human being who harbors a trace of the Divine being harbors a memory traceable to the immemorial, that is, to the Torah that precedes Creation (see *Zohar* I, 5a; see also *Bereshit Tanchuma* 1). It is the dimension of height that belongs to the Most High, whom we invoke in our daily prayers as *hameromam levado meaz,* the One who "alone is on high from aforetime." The immemorial is the Good that chooses us prior to all time and every context, to make our choices meaningful and thus situate us in time. Obliterating the memory of the immemorial, the Nazis obliterate not only the Divine spark that is made of memory but also the ethical Good that makes the matter of the human being *matter.*

Because the Good that situates us in time is tied to the immemorial, "the attachment to the Good," in the words of Levinas, "precedes the choosing of this Good. How, indeed, to choose the Good? The Good is good precisely because it chooses you and grips you before you have had the time to raise your eyes to it."[26] To have a story—to have precisely what the Muselman does not have—is to have been chosen by the Good for a certain mission that we have *yet* to perform. This is not to say that Hashem has not chosen the Muselmann; rather, it is to illustrate how the Nazis unchoose what Hashem has chosen. Thus where life has meaning— that is, where the human being has been chosen—life has time, for to have a sense of meaning is to have a sense of mission and direction, a horizon that we have *yet* to meet and a task that we have *yet* to accomplish. The story of the past is transmitted for the sake of this meaning yet to be fulfilled. And as long as this *yet to be* is at work in life, memory transcends the boundaries of birth and death. When memory exceeds those horizons, death is once again death and dying a task and a testimony, a legacy that affirms a tradition received from our ancestors and an inheritance bequeathed to our children. The one who has no story— the Jew whom the Nazis transform into a Muselmann in their war against memory—is the one who has no tradition.

Because the Nazi made the Jew into a Muselmann in whom the Divine spark is dead, a Jew today must live as if that Divine spark were alive within him—as if he were *in truth* created in the image and likeness of God. There is no other means of emerging from Auschwitz and setting out for Jerusalem. This movement *forward*, from Auschwitz to Jerusalem, is a movement of memory *back* into tradition. It is memory's summons of tradition back into a present so that the present might once more be made of sacred history and thus aspire to a redemptive future. Here we realize that, inasmuch as time is tied to meaning, time is tied to sanctity. As Heschel states it, "time is the presence of God in the world of space."[27] The sacredness of sacred history is the *time* of sacred history. It derives from God's presence *in* that history so that the recovery of tradition is a recovery both of God and of the *existence* of God. "The existence of God," Levinas argues, "is sacred history itself, the sacredness of man's relation to man through which God may pass."[28] The recovery of tradition, therefore, entails a mending of the human relation through which God may pass from a realm *above* into a reality *between*, where a tale related draws both listener and speaker into a relation. When the relation is lost—when the story and history are lost—the *above* and *between* are lost: God and humanity are lost. Auschwitz signifies this single blow that works the double destruction of the human and the Divine in the Jew made into Muselmann.

Hearing the survivor's story, we receive a summons to return to history in a movement from Auschwitz to Jerusalem. It comes not just from the survivor but from beyond the survivor. Where is that "beyond?" Like memory, it is in the texts and in the prayers of tradition. Even Levi, who refused God in the face of Auschwitz, suggests that the tales of the Shoah might themselves be viewed as the tales of a new Bible.[29] Pursuing one implication of Levi's assertion, Fackenheim maintains that an encounter with the biblical text has become a necessity for post-Holocaust Jewish thought,[30] as the sacred text is a key to any recovery of the sacred tradition that has nurtured Jewish life for centuries. This existential necessity confronting the Jew lies in the nature of the Jewish relation to being. If being has meaning for the Jew, it is, in the words of Levinas, "to realize the Torah. The world is here so that the ethical order has the possibility of being fulfilled. The act by which the Israelites accept the Torah is the act that gives meaning to reality. To refuse the Torah is to bring being back to nothingness."[31] Either Torah or Auschwitz: that is the existential necessity confronting the Jew in the post-Holocaust era. Either the man created by the God of Torah or the Muselmann created by the Nazi assault on God and Torah. After Auschwitz there is no third alternative.

Fackenheim repeatedly confronts us with this inescapable decision in his various expressions of the famous 614th Commandment. He insists, for example, that "Jews are forbidden to hand Hitler posthumous victories"[32] and that every Jew confronts "a commanding Voice heard from Auschwitz that bids him to testify *that some gods are false.*"[33] Simply stated, the 614th Commandment is the commandment to "restore the divine image"[34] (a point we shall consider more closely in the next chapter). Whereas the one created in the image of the true God is man, the one created in the image of the Nazi false gods is the Muselmann. Devoid of any trace of Hashem, he is the one for whom a Kiddush Hashem or martyrdom is impossible. Fackenheim argues that "in making Jewish existence a capital crime, Hitler murdered Jewish martyrdom itself."[35] And how do you murder martyrdom? By snuffing out the Divine within the human, for it is the Holy One within the human being that sanctifies the Name in the act of martyrdom.

We may go further than Fackenheim, however, and say that the murder of martyrdom lies not exactly in making Jewish existence a crime but more specifically in the transformation of the Jew into a Muselmann. The recovery of tradition, and with it the recovery of an inescapable either / or, is a recovery of the possibility of martyrdom—that is the task posed for post-Holocaust Jewish thought. Martyrdom can happen only where there is meaning, that is, only where the holy is at stake in life. And the thing that subjects the martyr to destruction is the indestructibility of the holy texts and prayers of tradition. Because the truth of the sacred tradition is a *living* truth, the testimony of the martyr is *for the sake of life.* Wherever this *for the sake of* arises, life is instilled with time. And where life is instilled with time, death is death, situated within its sacred contexts, for where life is instilled with time, death is *for the sake of another,* which means: death is the renewal and resurrection of life.

In this connection, Fackenheim comments on the image of the dry bones in the Book of Ezekiel: "In Ezekiel's image, the dead have fallen in battle. The dead of the Holocaust were denied battle, its opportunity and its honour. Denied the peace even of bones, they were denied also the honour of graves, for they, the others, ground their bones to dust and threw the dust into rivers. To apply Ezekiel's image of Jewish death to the Holocaust, then, is impossible. The new enemy, no mere Haman, not only succeeded where Haman failed, for he murdered the Jewish people. He murdered also Ezekiel's image of Jewish death."[36] As we have seen, this murder of Jewish death is accomplished most emphatically in the creation of the Muselmann. Without a recovery of Jewish death, Ezekiel's dry bones can never regain the flesh and blood of Jewish life. Auschwitz is "a cemetery without a single grave,"[37] and the Muselmann is the image of Auschwitz, more terrifying than Ezekiel's image of dry bones, for Ezekiel's dry bones have their midrash, whereas the Muselmann has none.

"Midrash was meant for every kind of imperfect world," says Fackenheim, but "it was not meant for Planet Auschwitz, the anti-world."[38] If midrash is to find its way from the antiworld into the world, then perhaps what is needed for post-Holocaust Jewish thought is a kind of midrashic madness, a madness that finds an opening for the Divine spark in a realm where that spark has vanished. Midrashic madness, Fackenheim explains, "is the Word spoken in the anti-world which ought not to be but is. The existence it points to acts to restore a world which ought to be but is not, and this is *its* madness. After Planet Auschwitz, there can be no health without *this* madness. . . . Without this madness, a Jew cannot do—with God or without Him—what a Voice from Sinai bids him do: choose life."[39] With this midrashic madness, then, a Jew must choose life *as a Jew,* bearing Jewish children into the world, despite the fact that the identity that gives them life my well threaten their life, for in the Holocaust, Fackenheim points out, Jews were slaughtered not because they abandoned the Torah but because their grandparents adhered to it.[40] That is why Jewish thought cannot oppose the absolute indifference of the Muselmann without a dose of midrashic madness: after Auschwitz, too, Jewish thought must seek "the Word which ought not to be but is." Which is to say: the mending of time requires the mending of the word, for time is in the word, not the other way around: only where there is a word uttered between two is there a response *yet* to be spoken.

MAKING THE MUSELMANN SPEAK

In Elie Wiesel's *Night,* Moshe the Beadle rises from a mass grave and returns to Sighet to relate the tale of his own death.[41] Yet one who can relate the tale of his own death is one whose death is death. Which means: Moshe the Beadle is not a Muselmann. The singularity of the Shoah lies neither in the mass graves nor in the one who rises from a mass grave to warn others of the death that awaits them, for he has a story to tell, even if it is the story of his own death; he can speak, even if no one can believe or understand him.

The Muselmann, however, has neither a story nor a death. Neither mortal nor immortal, he cannot speak; stranded outside the realm of mortality, he has nothing inside him to express or convey: drained of the Divine image, he is drained of the word. Without a word, he is without a presence; and yet he is not absent. On the contrary: he is all too present, overwhelmingly so. The Muselmann—one recalls Levi's words—is part of a *silent,* "anonymous mass" of "non-men,"[42] who say nothing, not because they have nothing to say but because their words have been reduced to nonwords: *that* is the void that they are. Strictly speaking, they are not even silent—they are silence itself. This mute and faceless mass is not a crowd or even a herd; it is not a body of anything that pertains to "the masses." It is a skeletal river of nonbeing that flows into an ocean of ashes. Having reached what Levi calls "the bottom," this river flows upward, through the chimneys, where the silent, anonymous mass ascends into the silence of the heavens. Indeed, the silence of the heavens is precisely the silence of this anonymous mass.

While Levi describes the Muselmann as a figure "in whose eyes not a trace of a thought is to be seen,"[43] according to Jewish tradition, as we saw in chapter 4, the human being is a *medaber,* a "speaker" and not a "thinker." The ability to speak is a capacity superior to thought and therefore more powerfully defines the human being as the one created in the image of the Holy One. A kind word is more valuable than a profound thought, and Jewish thought must generate a kind word if it is to be Jewish. As a *medaber,* a human being may transcend the blank rumbling of the anonymous mass. Rendered wordless, however, the man becomes a nonman: not a word is to be heard from the parched lips of the Muselmann—that is why his staring eyes are empty of thought. Having the capacity neither for speech nor for thought, the Jew made Muselmann is bled of what defines him as a human being. The point bears repeating: his silence is not the silence of one who does not speak. Nor is it the silence of a mute who cannot speak. Because the Divine image is dead within him, the Muselmann's silence is a *dead* silence. It is the singular silence of the concentrationary universe.

Many memoir writers recall the savage screams and shouts and curses that greeted them when they rolled into Birkenau. They also recall the silence that pervaded the antiworld, both in the ghettos and in the camps. Levi writes that when he arrived in Auschwitz "everything was as silent as an aquarium."[44] There was movement, but it was the muffled movement of another world, where one had to be careful not to drown in the horror and in the silence. Yes, the shouting and screaming, brutal and inhuman, were there. But pervading all of it was the silence. Each time the Jewish thinker faces the Muselmann, he faces this silence that swallows up thought. That is the problem for Jewish thought after Auschwitz: as we gaze upon the Muselmann, nothing responds to us but this silence. One task confronting the Jewish thinker, then, is to make the Muselmann speak.

What constitutes this horrific silence of the Muselmann? According to Levi, it is made of hunger. The Muselmann, an incarnation of silence, is the incarnation of hunger; if the Muselmann is the backbone of the camp, then hunger, says Levi, is its essence.[45] This hunger is not the sensation of having missed a meal or feeling like a bite to eat. The hunger of the camp, of the *Lager,* is no more the hunger between meals than its silence is a silence between words. Like the silence, the hunger is ubiquitous and definitive. It is the hunger of a human being diminished to what Elie Wiesel calls "a starved stomach"[46] that no longer even growls. If, as Levinas insists, "to recognize the Other is to recognize a hunger," the silence of the *Lager* is the silence of the radical nonrecognition of the other human being.[47] The hunger and the silence—the silence of the hunger, the hunger of the silence, and the radical emptiness of both—constitute the essence of the camp and are incarnate in the Muselmann. That is why Fackenheim deems his silence a "terrible silence,"[48] a silence that cannot be breached: it is the silence of the void.

If the human being is created in the image of the Divine, the Musel-mann is created in the image of the void. But this void is full—full of a silence that surpasses terror, a silence that swallows the word in the throat before it can reach the lips. Neither something nor nothing, this void is akin to what Levinas describes as "there is." "We do not grasp it through a thought," says Levinas. "It is immediately there. There is no discourse. Nothing responds to us, but this silence."[49] With the appearance of the "there is," he explains, "the absence of everything returns to us as a pres-ence, as the place where the bottom has dropped out of everything, an atmospheric density, a plenitude of the void, or the murmur of silence."[50] This "murmur of silence" is the "anonymous and senseless rumbling of being,"[51] manifest not as thought but as an absolute indifference. This is the culmination of the equation of being with thought: it is a drain-ing of thought from human being. It is the Muselmann.

The Muselmann's wasted body embodies the "there is." Yet he does not encounter the murmur of silence or the rumbling of being that char-acterize the "there is." Indeed, the Muselmann *encounters* nothing; only one in whom the word still abides can encounter something outside him-self. The "there is" is what *we* encounter—or collide with—in the Musel-mann, and that is where the mending of the word becomes an issue. It is not the Muselmann but *we* who are implicated by a horror that strips us of the "power to have a private existence," as Levinas describes it, the horror that arises from "a participation in the *there is*."[52] Therefore, the emptiness to be overcome in the mending of the word is as much ours as it is the *Lager*'s. From the Muselmann it creeps into the survivor; from the survivor it creeps into us, as it crept from Levi into Fackenheim. It is we who must draw the obliterated word from the wordlessness of the Muselmann. As for the Muselmann himself, there is no "existence" more radically private, more brutally isolated, more ferociously alone than his antiexistence.

Of course, not every inmate in the *Lager* is a Muselmann; even so, not a single inmate in the *Lager* escapes the look in those eyes that look at nothing. And yet, despite its resemblance to what Levinas calls the "there is," one hesitates to call the silence that exudes from that "anony-mous mass" a rumbling of "being." To be sure, in *Survival in Auschwitz* we sense the rumbling of *something* in what Levi deems "a perpetual Babel" of "languages never heard before."[53] It is a confusion of tongues, as we recall from Rabbi Yaakov Culi's commentary, that produces "corpses."[54] In the case of Auschwitz, however, it produces "living corpses": it produces the Muselmann, who has been muted not merely through deprivation but through a fundamental assault on the word. He is unable to speak because words have been reduced to what Levi calls the "dreadful sound and fury signifying nothing"[55] that characterizes the camp.

The Italian version of this phrase from Levi's *The Drowned and the Saved* conveys more of this violence than does the English translation. "Sound," for example, is a translation of *fracasso,* from *fracassare,* meaning "to smash, shatter, crash"; and "signifying nothing" is *privo di significato,* or "destitute of meaning."[56] The memory of the silence of the Muselmann, the memory of languages never heard before, is the memory of a shattering, of sheer violence, and violence arises precisely where the word has collapsed. The Muselmann is he who has suffered the most radical violence that can be done to a man: he is the Jew whom the Nazi has fashioned into a nonman, signifying nothing. Because there is no word *from* him, there is no word *for* him. He is simply "there," a tear in the fabric of being, a blank that cannot be filled in. Hence there is no word for what is done to him, no word "to express this offense," as Levi says, no word for "the demolition of a man,"[57] for the demolition of a man *is* the demolition of the word. It is the demolition of what imparts meaning to a man, and it begins with the demolition of the Jew, for it is the Jew who affirms that *this* is a human being, infinitely dear, a *medaber* created in the Divine image, to whom every human being is a *fellow* human being.

It is the Jew, therefore, who affirms that the demolition of a man is the demolition of the word, beginning with the word that names the man—beginning with his name. The prelude to the anonymity of the Muselmann is the rendering anonymous of every human being who enters the antiworld. How? By replacing the name with a number that signifies the *anonymous* in the anonymous rumbling of the *Lager.* Indeed, in many memoirs the Nazi assault on the name is remembered with horror, as we recall from chapter 4. In Levi's memoir we read, "They will even take away our name, and if we want to keep it, we will have to find ourselves the strength to do so, to manage somehow so that behind the name something of us, of us as we were, still remains."[58] The tattoo is "your new name," he says.[59] Not just on the skin but *in the flesh,* the tattoo is now part of the man himself. It eclipses the wristwatch that once measured the minutes and hours of his life and thus turns him over to the timeless sameness of meaninglessness.

Recall from chapter 4 the teaching from Nachman of Breslov concerning what befalls a man when he dies.[60] As the man lies in his grave, says Rabbi Nachman, the Angel of Death comes to him to take him into the presence of the Holy One. But in order to rise from the grave and enter into the Divine Presence, the man must be able to answer a question: What is your name? For the name *is* the soul, says Rabbi Nachman.[61] The death of a man, in whom there abides a living soul, entails the posing of this question. But the Muselmann is denied even the question, for he is nameless; he is nameless because he is wordless. That is why his death is not death: the Angel of Death has nothing to ask him.

What does the erasure of the name have to do with the extinguishing of the Divine spark that both Levi and Fackenheim invoke? The substance of a person's name, his very *I,* derives from the Divine Being, from the Holy Name, from Him who alone can say, "I."[62] The Nazi's erasure of the Jew's name, then, is the Nazi's eclipse of the Divine "I." Similarly, inscribing the number on the body is part of emptying the body of its soul, which is the Divine image of the Holy Name. Indeed, Jewish tradition maintains that name and soul, name and person, are of a piece. In his commentary on Isaiah, for example, Abraham ibn Ezra asserts that the word *shem,* "name," is to be understood to mean "the person himself."[63] When the number takes over the name, not just the word but also the *being* attached to the word is assailed. And so, through the number, the Nazi makes the human being into an object that is all surface, devoid of any inner depth that would distinguish the human being as a *being.*[64] The number tattooed on the arm, therefore, is opposed to being: it is the cipher of indifferent nothingness that marks the Jew for his descent into the mute indifference of the Muselmann. Robbed of his name and marked with a number, the human being is robbed of what makes him a human *being*: the soul created in the Divine image.

Instead of the Divine image, we have the image of the destruction of the Divine image, the image of the Muselmann, who is the inescapable image of the Holocaust. Levi escaped the camp, but he did not escape the Muselmann, for the tattoo is the mark of the Muselmann: the Muselmann begins with a tattoo that eclipses his name. The tattoo, says Levi, means "you will never leave here."[65] Through the needle, Auschwitz invades the flesh; through the flesh, it enters his soul, working its way from his *nefesh* to his *neshamah.* Thus Levi, like many other memoir writers, dwells at length on the significance of the number in the antiworld. He notes, for example, that a prisoner would not be fed without first showing his number and repeating it in German;[66] thus the alien tongue further alienates the human being from his very being. The prisoner, showing the number in exchange for food, declares his namelessness and his nothingness: he is nothing more than an empty stomach wasting away on the meager ration. The eclipse of the name, then, is tied to the breakdown—to the slow starvation—of the body.

Once the assault on Hashem is undertaken through the assault on the name, meaning is torn from every name, from every word, and language itself is undermined. In Levi's memoir, a prominent symbol of the *Lager's* perversion of language is the Carbide Tower at Buna, the tower they called the *Babelturm,* or "Tower of Babel." Like the Tower of Babel, it represents not only the confusion of tongues but also the collapse of humanity. "Its bricks," says Levi, "were called *Ziegel, briques, cegli, kamenny, mattoni, téglak,* and they were cemented by hate."[67] As in the time of Babel, the tower's bricks were not bricks, and the men were not men. For, as we recall from chapter 2, "if a man fell [from the Tower] and died they paid no heed to him, but if a brick fell they sat down and wept, and said: Woe is us! When will another come in its stead?"[68] This is the confusion that leads to the question "What is a man?"

"If the Lagers had lasted longer," writes Levi, "a new, harsh language would have been born."[69] But it would have been a language with no room for the word *man,*[70] a language in which man is eclipsed by Muselmann, an antilanguage that tears human from human in the tearing of word from meaning, for if a human being is a *medaber,* a speaking being, then his or her being inheres in a relation to another being. Devoid of any story and emptied of every word, the Muselmann stands at an infinite distance from his fellow man. Indeed, he has no fellow man. And here we come to a critical insight: if the substance of a human being lies in the story he or she relates, then a human being is made of relation, so that with the murder of the soul comes the murder of relation. Since relation requires difference, the murder of relation comes with the collapse of difference into indifference. Indeed, if the Muselmann signifies anything, he signifies a radical, absolute indifference. Transforming difference into nonindifference, then, is a key to the movement from Muselmann to man, a movement that would restore the human-to-human relation that constitutes our humanity.

HUMAN BEING AND HUMAN RELATION

What has just been termed a transformation of "difference into nonindifference" is what Fackenheim refers to as a recovery from an illness.[71] The illness is the illness of indifference, both in the Muselmann and in those of us who are implicated by his image. Responding to that image, Fackenheim enjoins us to attend to the Voice that even from the silence of Auschwitz commands us to be other than indifferent. "The Voice of Auschwitz," he writes, "manifests a divine Presence which, as it were, is shorn of all except commanding Power. *This* Power, however, is inescapable."[72] The Voice of the Holy one always speaks in the imperative: where God is concerned, to speak is to command. The recovery from the illness of indifference, then, is a recovery of the sleepless gaze of the Holy One; and to be under that sleepless gaze is, as Levinas demonstrates, "to be the bearer of *another* subject—bearer and supporter—to be responsible for this other [human being]."[73] The Divine image that is "the other in me" stirs in the encounter with another human being, in such a way that I realize that *he* is the one who is "in me": thus human outcry is Divine commandment. As the story implicates us, so the word commands us; to attain the mending of the word is to recover the commandment that bids us to become the bearer of another subject, the one responsible for *this* human being.

Fackenheim offers an example of this mending of relation in his remarks on Pelagia Lewinska. In her memoir, Lewinska remembers that once she "grasped the motivating principle" of Auschwitz, she "felt under orders to live."[74] And Fackenheim asks, "Whose orders? Why did she wish to obey? And—this above all—where did she get the strength? We answer the last question by discovering that it is unanswerable. Once again 'willpower' and 'natural desire' are both inadequate. Once again we have touched an Ultimate."[75] Under orders to live, Lewinska was under orders to resist becoming a Muselmann, for the motivating principle of Auschwitz was more than the extermination of the Jew; it was the transformation of the Jew into a Muselmann. In that realm where the human being is reduced to a starved stomach, the "natural desire" is to fade into the empty indifference of the Muselmann, disconnected from everything and everyone. In the antiworld, to resist becoming a Muselmann means doing something "unnatural": it means living for the sake of another. To be under orders to live is to be commanded to live so that another might live, when slipping into a deadly indifference is the greatest temptation. Because she was commanded, Lewinska could not allow herself the luxury of dissipation. That she was somehow able to answer the commandment, as Fackenheim points out, brings us before an Ultimate. Which means: Lewinska brings us before the One who commands us to choose life, for the Infinite is manifest in the disturbance of the witness.

Commenting on the examples of Lewinska and others, Fackenheim asserts, "Our ecstatic thought must point to *their* resistance—the resistance in thought and the resistance in life—as *ontologically ultimate. Resistance in that extremity was a way of being. For our thought now, it is an ontological category.*"[76] What makes this resistance ontologically *ultimate* is that it was *commanded* by a Divine Voice, and not deduced from human ideals or a categorical imperative. Which means: resistance in that extremity was not only a way of being; it was a revelation of the Holy One, who is otherwise than being. And where the Holy One is revealed, there is ethical exigency. In order for post-Holocaust Jewish thought to determine a Jewish future and a Jewish identity, there must be a reentry into human relation. This *must* is an ethical *must* and rests on a Divine relation *already* there; it arises from the same Divine commandment that had *already* placed Lewinska under orders to live. As with the Good that chooses us before we choose between good and evil, the one who heeds the Voice draws us into the relation we must restore before we have restored it. Thus Lewinska, in the act of heeding the Voice, makes it heard so that through her example we hear a Voice that precedes her example. The Nazi, however, robbing the Jew of his story, erases everything that is *already* there; rendering the Jew mute, the Nazi renders the Jew deaf to the commandment. To restore the relation, then, is to bring the Jew back to the issue of restoring meaning to the word. For Jewish thought, this restoration means a restoration of Torah.

Thus the relation restored with the restoration of word and meaning is a relation both to God and to one's fellow human being, and the creation of the Muselmann constitutes an assault on both. Through those who resisted the living death of the Muselmann, the Jew receives the commandment to choose life and to live life as one of God's Chosen, and not as an ethnic accident defined either by the Nazis or by the ontological outlook that shapes speculative thought. Which means: Jewish thought must be *Jewish* in the ways proposed in chapter 2, for if the Jew is an ethnic accident and the Torah a cultural artifact, as postmodern thought would have it, then the Divine spark is mere metaphor. And if that is the case, then the only reality is the material reality of what is weighed, measured, and counted. But one whose reality is no more than material is locked into an impenetrable solitude and can have no relation to anything outside himself. And the most radical image of the "material man" is the Muselmann.

Levi warns, and Fackenheim demonstrates, that Western civilization—as shaped by Christian doctrine and Greek philosophy—would make the Jew into the object first of conversion, then of assimilation, and finally of annihilation. Similarly, Western civilization would view the Torah first as superseded, then as antiquated, and finally as a thing to be eliminated. Because there can be no Jews without Torah, the very existence of the Jew attests to the teachings of Torah, among which is the teaching concerning the absolute sanctity of every human life based on a *meta*physical reality. In his very existence, the Jew attests to the Divine image within the human being so that modernity's eradication of the Jew has been a removal of the Divine image from the human reality. Once God had been reduced to a concept or an ideal, it was not long before He was pronounced dead. Parallel to the erasure of the Divine spark from the human being has been the erasure of God from the world so that the only reality is a material reality and the only truth is power.

Thus, in Auschwitz, the Jew who had attested to the truth of the Divine image and the reality of God was reduced to raw material. As Fackenheim points out, "that the dead had been human when alive was a truth systematically rejected when their bodies were made into fertilizer and soap."[77] This comes about with a tearing of the material away from the spiritual, that is, with a rupture of the soul that emerges in the midst of human relation. It is a rupture that turns back on the soul, to produce in the Jew what Fackenheim calls "self-loathing."[78] This is a key contributor to the creation of a Muselmann. The purpose of imposing upon the Jew a "life" lived in the midst of filth is not to inflict the soul *with* illness but to transform the soul *into* illness through an increasingly radical isolation from the other human being.

Further, relation to another is always *for the sake of* another. If Levi tells his tale to seek an "interior liberation," as he states it,[79] it is a liberation attained by entering into a relation with another, with a reader, who now must answer for what he or she has encountered in the Muselmann. Levi does not open the wound of memory for the sake of self-gratification but in order to restore the human being to human relation through a dialogical engagement with another, for another, an engagement in which his outcry over the "demolition of a man" signifies the dearness of a man. While it is true that Levi rejected Judaism, his sense of what is holy within the human is all too Jewish. The essence of Jewish tradition lies in loving God with all your heart, all your soul, and all the "more" that you are, *b'kol me'odekha*. "All the more" commands the return to human relation; that is what takes us beyond the confines of ego in a movement upward: the movement toward the neighbor. God "confronts man with the demand to turn to his human neighbor, and in doing so, to turn back to God Himself," as Fackenheim states it; for "there is no humble walking before God unless it manifests itself in justice and mercy to the human neighbor."[80] A Nazi, however, perceives no neighbor other than the Aryan neighbor, who is not a neighbor but merely a "co-racialist." If there is a definitive link between idolatry and Auschwitz, as Fackenheim maintains,[81] it is because there is a definitive link between idolatry and the Nazi blindness to the neighbor.

To a Jew, whom the Talmud defines as anyone who repudiates idolatry (*Megillah* 13a), every human being is his or her neighbor, for every human being is a *ben adam*, a child of Adam. Therefore, a Jew is who he is to the extent that he expresses his love for God through a caring relation to his fellow human being: that is the tradition and is what makes the tradition sacred. The loss of the tradition is therefore inextricably linked to the onset of the illness of indifference so that the recovery from the illness is tied to a recovery of the tradition: mending the relation entails relating the tale that imparts to each human being his *storia*. The Jews may have been threatened with starvation, torture, and murder, but the real threat, the ontological illness, lay in being transformed from a caring man into the indifferent Muselmann.

The Nazis, regarding the being of the Jew as a disease, inflicted upon the Jew the disease of indifference toward all being. They induced in the Jew first a revulsion and then an indifference toward their own existence as Jews,[82] something that carries over into the post-Holocaust age. And yet, in Pelagia Lewinska and others like her, that collapse into a living death was resisted. "For all the resistance fighters inside and outside Nazi-occupied Europe, resistance was a doing," Fackenheim points out. "For Jews caught by the full force of the Nazi logic of destruction, resistance was a way of being."[83] And, as a way of being, resistance is a resistance to indifference, *for the sake of another.*

In his elaboration on Levi's question, Fackenheim himself engages in this resistance that is a way of *Jewish* being, and therein lies his greatness as a *Jewish* thinker. It is a thinking attained despite the nonbeing of the Muselmann that would seem to void all thought, for the Muselmann renders void the centuries of thought that shaped Western civilization. Recall the scene from *Sunrise over Hell* referred to in chapter 2: caressing the lifeless head of Marcel Safran, Harry Preleshnik "caressed the head of the Twentieth Century," and in the Muselmann "he saw the value of all humanity's teachings, ethics and beliefs."[84] Nothing in the speculative tradition, from Aristotle to Descartes, from Kant to Heidegger, can mend what was broken in the creation of the Muselmann. Only the Jewish tradition slated for annihilated can make the movement from Muselmann to man that would restore the Divine spark to humanity. "Though infinitely above the world and the humanity that is part of it," says Fackenheim of the God of Abraham, Isaac, and Jacob, "He creates man—him alone—in His very own image! The god of Aristotle does no such thing."[85] And the god of Aristotle is the preeminent god of the philosophers, the indifferent god of a humanity that inevitably succumbs to indifference.[86]

As we have seen, the Muselmann is much more—or much less—than a victim of starvation. In addition to the emaciation of his body, he suffers an emaciation of the soul. And yet, as an assault on the nonindifference that defines human relation, the assault on the soul is possible only for a being of flesh and blood, for the nonindifference that affirms the dearness of another is possible only among beings of flesh and blood. "Only a subject who eats," as Levinas says, "can be for-the-other,"[87] because the being "for-the-other" that characterizes nonindifference comes "not in elevated feelings" but "in a tearing away of bread from the mouth that tastes it, to give it to the other."[88] Bread is bread only when it is offered to another: a human being is not what he eats—he is what he offers another to eat.

The offering of bread to another person affirms the One in whose image that person is created, for He is the One of whom we say *hamotsi lechem min haarets,* the one "who brings forth bread from the earth"—bread to be offered to another. Therefore, in the Talmud, Rabbi Yochanan and Resh Lakish teach that since the destruction of the Temple, the table in our home, where we offer bread to another and prayers to God, takes the place of the Holy Altar (see *Chagigah* 27a). The act of offering bread to another therefore signifies a humanity created in the image of the Divine. Thus, as Levi demonstrates, bread, in the process of the Muselmann's creation, is made into something else. It is the "grey slab" of "bread-brot-Broid-chleb-pain-lechem-keynér" that in this realm is the inmates' "only money."[89] Bread is not bread when bread is currency; meaning has been torn from this word *bread,* and with the tearing of meaning from this word, human is torn from human. Hence the humanity is torn from the human being.

In the last chapter of his memoir, "The Story of Ten Days," Levi shows that when the meaning of the word *bread* is regained, human relation is regained, for the moment came during those ten days when one person offered bread to another so that bread was no longer currency—bread was bread. And when bread is once again bread, human beings are once again human beings. "It really meant that the Lager was dead," writes

Levi. "I believe that that moment can be dated as the beginning of the change by which we who had not died slowly changed from Häftlinge [a term used to refer to the camp inmate] to men again."[90] This tearing of bread from one's own mouth to offer it to another not only constitutes the restoration of bread, it is the restoration of the link between word and meaning, beginning with the restoration of the name.

Becoming a man again, Levi assumed his name again. Assuming a name again, he was summoned by name to come to the aid of other men, the sick who shouted his name "day and night with the accents of all the languages of Europe."[91] Whenever they heard him approaching the infirmary, "their cries redoubled; bony hands came out from under the blankets, grabbed hold of my clothes, touched me icily on the face."[92] Here, Levi discovers that to be a man—to have a story and a name, a word and a meaning—is to be responsible: subjectivity is responsibility. Therefore, to be a man is to be unable to hide, like Adam, who could not hide from Him who asked, "Where are you?" (Genesis 3:9)—and who repeated His question by asking Cain, "Where is your brother?" (Genesis 4:0). The Commanding Voice of Auschwitz is a voice that calls upon me by name and commands me to snatch the bread from my own mouth and offer it to another. In the concentrationary universe, the Commanding Voice was at times swallowed up by the silence of the Muselmann. After Auschwitz, it cries out from the image of the Muselmann, whose bony hands reach out from under the ashes and plead with us to be human beings.

THE MUSELMANN AND
POST-HOLOCAUST JEWISH THOUGHT

Primo Levi's question concerning what a human being is turns out to be a question concerning what bread is, what meaning is, what memory is. It is the one serious philosophical question that the Holocaust poses for Jewish thought, and Emil Fackenheim is one Jewish thinker who takes it seriously. Whereas others write about trauma and hermeneutics, justice and reconciliation, rescuers and bystanders, postmodern approaches and competing narratives, Fackenheim wrestles, like Jacob at Peniel, with the question of why the matter of the human being matters and what must be done. He wrestles with a dark angel to extract the blessing that is couched in the name of Israel. Like Jacob—and unlike Jacob—in his wrestling he kicks up dust; "not ordinary dust," as it is written in the Zohar, "but ashes, the residue of fire" (*Zohar* I, 179a). Which is to say: Fackenheim has the courage to confront what most of us evade, to confront the Holocaust in the Holocaust, to confront the *Jew* in the Holocaust *as* a Jew, and to confront it all as a Jewish thinker. Because the Jew bears witness to the sanctity of the human being, the Jew responds to Levi's question of the human being. This question concerning a unique singling out of the Jew concerns not just the extermination of the Jew—it concerns the transformation of the Jew into a Muselmann.

And so we are left with an either / or that defines the Holocaust and decides our future, not only as Jews but as human beings: either man or Muselmann. Fackenheim shows that only the teaching and tradition transmitted through the Jew targeted for this transformation can adequately respond to the question. And because the Jew is he who repudiates idolatry, Fackenheim demonstrates that the question is a question concerning idolatry:

> Before Nazism happened, we thought it could not happen. Now that it has happened, we resort to explanations that explain it away. We take it, in the style of Enlightenment liberalism, as a mere lapse into atavistic prejudice, superstition, or neurosis, ills that should not happen in this day and age and for which—soon if not now—there will be a cure. Or we take it, in neo-Lutheran style, as a mere case of national pride, lust for power or xenophobia, sins will always happen because we are all sinners. Possibly we take it as a mixture of the two. In any case we resist confronting it as a modern idolatry—one might say, as *the* modern idolatry, because, being unsurpassable, it reveals all that idolatry can be in the modern world.[93]

With their supposition that idolatry has been surpassed, neither Christianity nor Enlightenment philosophy can resolve the matter of the human being posed by the Shoah, for both, in their thinking, are contrary to the Jewish thought required for a post-Shoah movement from the Muselmann back to humanity.

Indeed, both Christianity and the philosophy of the Enlightenment have proved bankrupt in this regard. Christianity's contribution to the Holocaust lies not only in its anti-Semitic, supersessionist teachings; it is also rooted in the doctrine of inherited sin, according to which to be born is to be in a state of sin, and faith alone—and not deeds, no matter how righteous—can redeem us from sin (see Romans 3:28; Galatians 2:16). Redeeming us from our inherited sin, the Christian's redemptive faith rests upon the creed that Jesus paid the ultimate ransom not merely for the sin we have *committed* but for the sin that we *are.* The blood of Jesus redeems the believing Christian from judgment for the crime of being; those who, like the Jews, explicitly reject all faith in the Nazarene as their redeemer remain fundamentally sinful in their *essence,* their Divine spark dimmed by their unredeemed sin. Therefore, they are subject to the judgment of damnation.

As for the modern philosophy that stems from the Enlightenment, we saw in chapter 2 that it regards as suspect all talk concerning a Divine creation of the human being in the image of the Holy One. Having rid the world of the Commanding Voice of Mount Sinai, modern philosophy is deaf to the Commanding Voice of Auschwitz. Subsequently, it led to a postmodern outlook rooted in the thinking of the Nazi Martin Heidegger, which cannot escape the logical conclusion that nothing is true and that everything is permitted. Neither Christian doctrine—at least not without serious revision—nor postmodern thought can respond to the matter of the human being posed by the Shoah, because each has inherited ways of thinking that contributed to the making of the Muselmann. Certainly, neither Christian thought nor postmodern thought can be equated with Nazi thinking. But both play into its hands. Christianity does so by asserting that the Jew, like all who conscientiously reject Jesus of Nazareth, is unredeemed; postmodernism does so by maintaining that there are no absolutes other than the power struggles of class and culture, of race and gender.

The Holocaust, which occurred in the heart of Christendom and originated at the center of "enlightened" thought, was the occasion for the revelation with which Ka-tzetnik confronted the Rabbi of Shilev: "At last you must admit, Rabbi, that the God of the Diaspora himself is climbing into this truck [on His way to the gas chamber]—a Muselmann."[94]

Who loaded the God-turned-Muselmann into the truck bound for the ovens? Not lunatics, monsters, or madmen but people shaped by the sum of Christian doctrine and modern thought, people who attended churches and universities, who read their Gospels and listened to Mozart. The world, transforming the Jew into a Muselmann, purged itself of God and humanity. Indeed, it purged itself of the very notion of "world," for the image of the holy within the human is "a pillar of the Universe," as the Maggid of Dubno reminds us; once it is removed "from the Divine scheme of things, the equilibrium of the Divinely-built structure of the entire universe" ceases to exist.[95]

Neither the Christian nor the Kantian nor, least of all, the postmodernist has a credible reply to Ka-tzetnik, for none of them can fathom the notion of a pure soul, of the *neshamah tehorah,* that the Jew invokes every morning. Therefore, none of them can fathom Hillel's meaning when he teaches, "In a place where there are no men you must strive to be a man" (*Avot* 2:5). What Hillel teaches us to be is precisely the opposite of the Muselmann: a *neshamah tehorah,* which is the human being in whom the Divine spark burns, as attested to in the Jewish tradition. Therefore, *from the perspective of a future for Jewish thought and for the Jewish people,* only Judaism is adequate to respond to the matter of the human being, for only Judaism can affirm the absolute purity of the soul that is the Divine spark within the human being. Only Judaism can affirm the absolute link between the meaning of the word and the value of the human being. Only Judaism can affirm the absolute commandment to love the neighbor, who is every human being. And how shall the Jewish thinker join his thought to Judaism and accomplish this affirmation? Through the 614th Commandment, which commands the post-Holocaust *tikkun haolam,* or mending of the world. Let us consider, then, what the two premier post-Holocaust Jewish thinkers—Emil Fackenheim and Emmanuel Levinas—can teach us about a post-Holocaust *tikkun.*

7

Jewish Thought and a
Post-Holocaust *Tikkun Haolam*

Every *Mitzvah* aims to make a dwelling-place for God in the
world—to bring God to the light within the world, not above it.
A *Mitzvah* seeks to find God in the natural, not the supernatural.
—R. Menachem Mendel Schneerson, *Torah Studies*

A few years ago, I visited Emil Fackenheim at his home in Jerusalem, as
was my custom whenever I was in the Holy City. I was sitting on the
side of his good ear, listening to him discuss his engagement with the
Holocaust. Suddenly he fell silent. His lower lip began to tremble. Tears
rolled down his cheeks.

"I just realized what I've been trying to do for the last thirty-five years,"
he said, his voice hushed in desperation. "I've been trying to *undo* it. But
I can't . . . I can't!"

In these simple words, Fackenheim expressed the profound longing that
overwhelms so many students and scholars of the Holocaust: we want to
undo it. Failing that, we want to fix it. Indeed, we want to fix the world
itself, realizing as we do that Auschwitz is not some historical tragedy that
we can put behind us. This breaking of the body of Israel has left the
world itself broken. And there is no getting over it. Like the ashes of its
dead, Auschwitz is in us, and it will not leave us alone: it nags. The longing to fix it is a longing to mend not only the world but also the soul and

substance of who we are. And because our broken humanity begins with the Jews, we look to a term from the Jewish tradition: we look to a *tikkun haolam,* a mending of the world. Even where there is little concern for ways in which Hebrew might inform post-Holocaust thought, many turn to this Hebrew concept for the notion most needful.

With the Holocaust, however, there occurs a breach in thought and tradition that occludes our hearing and alters our understanding of this most needful notion. Prior to that breach, the mending of creation fell within categories that belonged to an intelligible world, where relationships among human beings were linked to a higher relation. Even in times of tragedy, there was still a general sense of high and low by which the tragic took on meaning. But with the Holocaust, tragedy itself is undermined: an antiworld inserts itself into the world, in an assault against every form of the meaning, truth, and sanctity that would distinguish human and Divine being. "Throughout the ages," Fackenheim points out, "pious Jews have died saying the *Shema Yisrael*—'Hear, O Israel, the Lord our God, the Lord is One' (Deuteronomy 6:4). The Nazi murder machine was systematically designed to stifle this *Shema Yisrael* on Jewish lips before it murdered Jews themselves."[1] Stifling the "Hear, O Israel," the antiworld threatens the hearing and the response most essential to *tikkun haolam.*

And yet the phrase *tikkun haolam* itself has been broken and abused by most who use it, both among Christians and among Jews. True, the words mean a "repair" or "mending of the world." But most thinkers use the term in a purely social and moral sense, without addressing what it means in its original contexts of Jewish teaching and tradition. More than invoking a moral order or a renewed social consciousness, in the Jewish tradition *tikkun haolam* refers to the process of making God, world, and humanity, and the relationships that bind them together, once again hale, whole, and holy. Rabbi Aryeh Kaplan describes it as the removal of "the barriers that prevent us from hearing God's voice."[2] Therefore, if it does not attend to the commanding Voice of Hashem—in prayer and in Torah study, as well as in good deeds—it is not *tikkun haolam.*

The phrase, moreover, has meanings and shades of meaning rooted in the talmudic and mystical traditions, which, even if rendered problematic by the Shoah, must nevertheless inform Jewish thought in the aftermath of Auschwitz if that thinking is indeed to be Jewish. Otherwise, we have no sense of what has changed or what to do about it. Further, if we are to open up the mystical teachings, we can do so only by first establishing some understanding of the talmudic teachings. "Chasidism and Kabbalah," Emmanuel Levinas cautions us, "are established in the Jewish soul only where that soul is full of talmudic science."[3] This should be kept in mind as we proceed in this chapter, as well as in the next chapter, where we shall go a bit deeper into Chasidic and mystical dimensions of Jewish thought.

In chapter 6, we saw that the Nazis' creation of the Muselmann entailed the undoing of creation itself. It is a return of creation to the *tohu* that is chaos, to an anticreation in which *everything* is possible because *everything* is permitted; the world is not merely broken—it hangs on the edge of the darkness and the deep overcome in the Divine act of creation. Recall the words of Resh Lakish: "God made a condition with the works of creation, saying: 'If Israel accepts My Torah, then it will be well; but if not, creation will revert to chaos'" (*Avodah Zarah* 3a). From a Jewish standpoint, then, *tikkun haolam* requires the restoration of distinctions outlined in the Torah and exemplified in the Jewish adherence to Torah. It entails the rebuilding of a world in which good is good and evil is evil—and Jewish thought is Jewish. The post-Holocaust *tikkun haolam,* in other words, seeks the mending not of a world gone wrong; what is sought, rather, is a restoration of the very idea of world as it is transmitted through Torah. The wound inflicted by Auschwitz cuts through God and humanity; it cuts through the very origin of word and world, through the very basis of all *tikkun.* With *this* wounding, mending itself is undermined. The post-Holocaust *tikkun haolam* thus seeks a *tikkun* of *tikkun* itself, a mending of the very notion of mending. That, in part, is why the Shoah creates a crisis for Jewish *thought,* and not just for Jewish history.

Two Jewish thinkers are known for their efforts to address the implications of this problem. We have already mentioned both of them: Emil Fackenheim and Emmanuel Levinas. Each in his own way explores various facets of a post-Holocaust *tikkun haolam.* Combining their insights with a consideration of the meaning of *tikkun haolam,* we may arrive at a deeper understanding of this issue so essential not only to post-Holocaust Jewish thought but also to the lives of Jews and non-Jews alike.

Levinas, for instance, writes, "To act for far-off things at the moment in which Hitlerism triumphed, in the deaf hours of this night without hours—independently of every evaluation of the 'forces in presence'— is, no doubt, the summit of nobility."[4] There, in the midst of the event, Levinas sees a kind of *tikkun haolam* already at work. Still, he does not go into the Jewish implications of the nobility he invokes, since he does not make explicit what that nobility means in the contexts of a Jewish understanding of *tikkun haolam*.

As for Fackenheim, he sees that among the things far off in the deaf hours of the Shoah was the very being of those who acted. "The German resistance, such as it was," he argues, "had to discover a true self to be respected. The Jewish resistance had to *recreate* Jewish selfhood and self-respect."[5] This recreation of selfhood—this repair of the soul as a Jewish soul—is central to a mending of the Jewish notion of *tikkun haolam* after Auschwitz. Here we "touch upon an Ultimate," to use Fackenheim's phrase,[6] because this mending entails drawing the "otherwise than being" into being. And it is a category not only for Jewish thought but also for our lives as Jews. Fackenheim explains: "*The* Tikkun *which for the post-Holocaust Jew is a moral necessity is a possibility because during the Holocaust itself a Jewish* Tikkun *was already actual.* This simple but enormous, nay, world-historical truth is the rock on which rests any authentic Jewish future, and any authentic future Jewish identity."[7] But if this *tikkun* is essential to a *Jewish* identity, it entails not only a moral necessity but also a sacred obligation to affirm the holiness of God and humanity.

In Fackenheim's terms, the post-Holocaust *tikkun* is composed of three elements: a recovery of Jewish tradition; a recovery in the sense of recuperation from illness; and a never-ending movement of mending.[8] Because Fackenheim employs the notion of *tikkun* more explicitly than does Levinas, our discussion will be organized according to these three dimensions of a post-Holocaust *tikkun* that Fackenheim has identified. And since Levinas has undertaken a *tikkun* of thinking that is distinctively Jewish, we shall find that his insights combine with Fackenheim's to open up a future for Jewish thought after Auschwitz. Before examining the idea of *tikkun haolam* as a recovery of Jewish tradition, however, we must first briefly consider what *tikkun haolam* means in the contexts of that tradition.

TIKKUN HAOLAM IN THE CONTEXTS
OF JEWISH TRADITION

In order to understand the teachings on *tikkun haolam* in the talmudic and mystical traditions, we should first consider the nuances of the phrase itself. It has already been noted that *tikkun haolam* is a "mending of the world," of the *olam*. Recall, then, the levels of meaning associated with the word *olam* that were discussed in chapter 4. Exceeding the limits of ontological "being," *olam* denotes world, universe, space, time, and eternity. A *tikkun haolam* is a mending not only of this ontological realm but also of eternity itself. It is a mending of the infinite. It is a mending of the very stuff of creation. *Olam* also signifies "humanity" and "community," and so *tikkun haolam* entails the mending not just of the world but also of what is *better* than the world; it entails the mending of the ethical, not as determined by human reason but as commanded by Divine love. *Tikkun haolam* is a mending of the bond with Hashem through a mending—that is, a renewed observance—of the *mitzvot*. It is a mending of the mission, the destiny, and the testimony established through the Covenant of the Commandments, not as though the Shoah had not happened but precisely because it did. Because it *did* happen, it brought about a rupture is history that has made manifest the truth of Leo Baeck's insight: "Through the unity of the ethical is realized the unity of history."[9] As a mending of ethical integrity, *tikkun haolam* is a mending of history, and therefore of time itself.

Note, too, that *olam* pertains to what is hidden, so that *tikkun haolam* is a mending of the hidden, a mending of the Invisible One, a mending of what invisibly sanctifies all there is, from beyond and from within all there is. It is a mending of the word and a mending of silence through the restoration of meaning to both. Here, we glimpse a special significance of the notion of *tikkun haolam* in the post-Holocaust era; for, as we have seen, in the time of the Shoah, words were swallowed up in the silence that André Neher describes as "the 'inert' silence," which "comes forward not as a temporary suspension of the Word but as a spokesman for the invincible Nothingness. Thus Silence replaces the Word because Nothingness takes the place of Being."[10] That is, it takes the place of *olam*. The aim of *tikkun haolam,* however, is not to fill the silence with words.

Rather, it is to fill the silence with sanctity. Only then can meaning be returned to words. Only then can poetry seek to make heard the voice hidden in the silence.

Bearing in mind what the Hebrew phrase tells us, we may now consider the meaning of *tikkun haolam* in its talmudic contexts. The tractate in which this notion is most thoroughly explored is *Gittin,* where the sages examine laws of divorce. The mending of the world is, in fact, much like the mending of a marriage, the marriage between God and humanity enacted at Mount Sinai, as it is written: "At Mount Sinai God went forth to meet them; like a bridegroom who goes forth to meet the bride, so the Holy One, blessed be He, went forth to meet them to give them the Torah" (*Pirke de Rabbi Eliezer* 41; see also *Shemot Rabbah* 41:6; *Tanchuma Ki Tisa* 16). Therefore, as we wrap the *tefillin* around our middle finger each morning, we say these words from Hosea 2:21–22: "I shall betroth myself to You forever; I shall betroth myself to You through righteousness and justice, through loving kindness and compassion; I shall betroth myself to You through faith. And you will know Hashem." How does one "know" Hashem? Through a betrothal to Him. Repeating these words that God spoke to the prophet, we enter into the "marriage" for which humanity was created.

As usual, the Talmud addresses concrete, pragmatic issues in its consideration of *tikkun haolam.* And, as usual, one may pursue many levels of meaning in the rabbis' rulings. Rabbi Yochanan, for example, says that *tikkun haolam* entails the prevention of childbirth out of wedlock, while Resh Lakish maintains that its aim is to prevent the desertion of wives (*Gittin* 33a). The question we must ask is not which view is correct, but rather what each view reveals about *tikkun haolam.* Bearing children within the framework of holy matrimony, for instance, is an expression of the holiness of the human being, something essential to *tikkun haolam.* The commandment to get married and have children is the first to appear in the Torah (see Genesis 1:28 and 2:24); it is a commandment to draw God's presence into the world in its purest form, and the Talmud associates this duty with *tikkun haolam* (see *Gittin* 41b). Just so, the Midrash states that the horror of the generation of Noah—the evil that brought on the destruction of the world—was that they tried to minimize the number of children they brought into the world (*Midrash Hagadol* 10:5).[11]

And in the *Shulchan Arukh* it is written, "Every man must marry a wife in order to beget children, and he who fails in this duty is as one who sheds blood, diminishes the image of God, and causes the Divine Presence to depart from Israel" (*Even Haezer* 1:1).[12] Anyone who has held in his or her arms a human being only five seconds old—anyone who has gazed into the Divine light in those eyes as they catch their first glimpse of this world—has an inkling of the truth of this Jewish teaching on the meaning of *tikkun haolam*. When the relation that brings a human life into the world is taken casually, human life is itself taken casually. And humanity is wounded to the quick.

Similarly, inasmuch as a wife is the vessel of holiness, devotion to one's wife amounts to a devotion to the holiness of human life. One sign of the open wound in need of mending, then, lies in how we regard the institution of marriage and how we treat the women of our society. Suddenly we have an eerie insight into the Nazis' calculated assault on the mothers of Israel. One recalls the decrees requiring Jewish women to have an abortion,[13] as well as Yitzhak Katznelson's lament over "the murderous German nation," whose "chief joy" was "to destroy women with child."[14] It was not only the Nazis' "chief joy"; it was central to their assault on Torah. Remember the ancient teaching that Torah had to be accepted by the women at Mount Sinai before the men could receive it, for the House of Jacob mentioned in Exodus 19:3 precedes the reference to the Children of Israel, and the House of Jacob refers to the women (see, for example, Rashi's commentary on Exodus 19:3; see also *Mekilta de-Rabbi Ishmael, Bachodesh* 2; also *Zohar* II, 79b). Only through the wives and mothers of Israel do we have Torah, and therefore a dwelling place in the world. Simply stated, the aim of *tikkun haolam* is to create a dwelling place in the world for every human being.[15] And dwelling happens only where wives are not deserted, only where there is devotion to mothers and motherhood.

In a similar vein, Hillel the Elder taught that *tikkun haolam* requires the protection of widows and orphans (see *Gittin* 34b and 51a), each of whom represents not only a pristine holiness in the world but also a holiness *without recourse* and thus placed in our care. The Torah enjoins us to be especially attentive to widows and orphans, as they are especially close to Hashem (see, for example, Exodus 22:20–21). Indeed, among the Hebrew expressions for God are *Dayan Almanot,* the "Protector of Widows," and *Avi Yetomim,* the "Father of Orphans" (as in Psalms 68:6, for example). Therefore, we must be very careful in our treatment of widows, orphans, and others who have nowhere to turn: it is essential to *tikkun haolam.*

Another person who, according to the Talmud, is without recourse is the slave. Here, the discourse on *tikkun haolam* pertains to the protection of freed slaves against any claims that their previous owners might have against them (see *Gittin* 40b). One sees yet another dimension of *tikkun haolam* in the elimination of what Levinas refers to as the appropriation of the other by the same, both ontologically and epistemologically. "My responsibility," he writes, "is the exceptional relationship in which the Same can be concerned by the Other without the Other being assimilated into the Same."[16] A claim made against a freed slave is a form of this assimilation of the "Other" by the "Same"; it is also a flight from responsibility. *Tikkun haolam,* then, requires the pursuit of my responsibility for the protection of my neighbor's freedom—not the other way around; in *tikkun haolam* there is no room for "my rights." It entails a way of thinking in which the ego is not "posed" but "deposed," as Levinas states it.[17] In a word, the mending of the open wound of the post-Holocaust world demands the Jewish thinking in which the holy displaces the ego.

Which brings us to three other aspects of *tikkun haolam* addressed in the Talmud: the refusal to pay an exorbitant ransom for someone who has been captured by the enemy (*Gittin* 45a); the refusal to pay exorbitant prices for Torah scrolls, *tefillin,* and *mezuzot* (*Gittin* 45a); and the refusal to sell portions of the Land of the Covenant to non-Jews (*Gittin* 47a). Each of these aspects is interwoven with the others: the Word of Torah sanctifies the human being and the Land; the Land signifies a dwelling place for the human being; and the human being is entrusted with the care of Torah and the Land. All three come together in the Shekhinah, that is, in the Divine Indwelling Presence. The term *Shekhinah* is a cognate of *shekhen,* which means "dwelling," and the presence of the Shekhinah in the world is precisely the presence of Torah and *mitzvot* in the world so that both God and humanity may dwell in the world together. Thus Yaakov Yosef of Polnoe teaches that *tikkun* is attained through the observance of the *mitzvot* because that observance is just what enables the Shekhinah to enter the world (see *Toledot Yaakov Yosef,* *Chukat* 8).

In the post-Holocaust world, these aspects of *tikkun haolam* arise in the contexts of the world's hostility toward Jewish teaching as it concerns the sanctity of the human being, the holiness of the Word, and the holiness of the Land. In the age of terror and terrorism, we understand only too well the threat to innocent lives when terrorists are able to demand any ransom for the people they kidnap. As for paying too much for Torah scrolls, *tefillin,* and *mezuzot,* these are all vessels of the Holy Word, and the Holy Word is not to be bought and sold; what is purchased is the effort and the skill that go into the creation of these objects. Wherever the Word has a price, the world is wounded. The Talmud also sees a wounding of the world whenever the Holy Land is sold out. Here, too, *tikkun haolam* is about attending to holiness in the world, for the Land is holy not merely because it is a haven for the Jews nor even because it is where the Temple stood. No, it is holy for the same reason the human being is holy: it has been sanctified by God's commandments. To be sure, the Maharal of Prague teaches that "God's Name is identified with the Land of Israel."[18] Inasmuch as *tikkun haolam* entails drawing the Holy Name into the world, it requires attending to the sanctity of the Land of Israel, not merely for the sake of the Jews but for the sake of the world and humanity.

The process of drawing the Holy Name into the world is where the talmudic thinking about *tikkun haolam* meets the mystical concept.[19] In the mystical tradition, *tikkun haolam* is the process of joining the first two letters of the Tetragrammaton *(yud-hey-vav-hey),* with the last two in a mending not only of the world but of worlds, above and below (see, for example, *Toledot Yaakov Yosef, Shelach* 10).[20] The first two letters, the *yud* and the *hey,* parallel the World of Emanation *(Olam Atsilut)* and the World of Creation *(Olam Beriah)*; this is where, at every instant, the Divine light undertakes the movement of creation from beyond creation.[21] The second two letters, the *vav* and the *hey,* parallel the World of Formation *(Olam Yetsirah)* and the World of Action *(Olam Asiyah)*; this is where our finite realm emerges from the Infinite One. Our task is to open up channels between the upper and lower worlds so that holiness may flow from the uppermost World of Emanation into our World of Action.

Because everything in this world has its parallel in the upper worlds, the "movement below," as it is written, "initiates the movement above" (see, for example, *Zohar* II, 31b; *Toledot Yaakov Yosef, Shelach* 7, 10)[22] so that we can bring about a *tikkun* of all the worlds through our actions in this world.[23] Indeed, *only* through our actions in this world can *tikkun haolam* transpire, since only in this world can we perform *mitzvot*. From the standpoint of Judaism, then, the mystical concern is the opposite of an otherworldly concern: God's kingdom is precisely in and of this world.

Central to the process of *tikkun haolam* is prayer, where prayer is broadly understood as ritual, study, and the performance of *mitzvot*. The Zohar addresses this matter in sections known as the *Idrot,* or "Convocations." They mainly consist of the *Idra Rabbah* (*Zohar* III, 127b–145a) and the *Idra Zuta* (*The Zohar* III, 287b–296b), which deal with the Divine "body" and the effluence of Divine light into the world.[24] The emanation of holiness from the upper worlds into this world passes through ten *sefirot,* or manifestations of the Divine light, as noted in chapter 5; the ten *sefirot* constitute the Divine "body." From above to below, the *sefirot* are *Keter* (Crown), *Chokhmah* (Wisdom, which is associated with the World of Emanation), *Binah* (Understanding, which is associated with the World of Creation), *Chesed* (Loving Kindness), *Gevurah* (Judgment), *Tiferet* (Beauty), *Netsach* (Victory), *Hod* (Praise), *Yesod* (Foundation; these last six are associated with the World of Formation), and *Malkhut* (Kingdom, which is associated with the World of Action).

The critical point of connection in this model is between *Yesod* and *Malkhut,* which are call *Zeir Anpin* and *Nukva,* or the Lower Male and the Lower Female, respectively. In the process of *tikkun haolam,* the marriage of these two is achieved so that the Shekhinah may assume her dwelling place in the *Malkhut* that is this realm. Therefore, the Talmud's interest in childbearing and in the treatment of wives, widows, and orphans—in a word, its fundamental concern with *marriage*—has its mystical meaning, as does the interest in the holiness of the Word and the holiness of the Land.[25] For the marriage of *Zeir Anpin* and *Nukva* is, among other things, the marriage of the Word and the Land: the Word is the seed, the Land is the womb, and the two combine to bring forth life. The sages involved in the talmudic discussion were well aware of these mystical meanings.

Isaac Luria, the renowned kabbalist of sixteenth-century Safed, developed further the concepts from the Zohar to identify four levels of *tikkun*: perfection of the soul through the observance of the *mitzvot*; the restoration of this world through deeds of loving kindness; the restoration of the upper worlds through prayer; and the subsequent restoration of the Holy Name.[26] These four levels of *tikkun* correspond to the four worlds, which in turn parallel the four sections of the morning prayers, demonstrating that prayer, in all its forms, is essential to *tikkun haolam*. Luria saw *tikkun haolam* as a means of rectifying the *shevirat hakelim,* or the "breaking of the vessels."[27] The *shevirat hakelim* is a necessary part of creation: just as a light bulb may burst if it cannot handle an electrical current, the Divine light is too much for any of the four worlds to endure. The "fallout" from this shattering process hides the Divine light and is the source of evil. Indeed, the greater the shattering, the greater the potential for evil, and there was no shattering greater than the shattering at Auschwitz. Just so, there has never been a greater need for *mitzvot*.

Through the *mitzvot* that connect God and humanity, we open up the flow of holiness through the *sefirot*. In keeping with Lurianic Kabbalah, Rabbi Schneur Zalman teaches that "all worlds, the exalted and the lowly, are dependent on the precise and meticulous performance of a single *mitzvah*."[28] According to Luria's view, as transmitted by his disciple Chayyim Vital, the consummation of the marriage of God and humanity—that is, of *tikkun haolam*—will be the coming of the Messiah (see *Ets Chayyim* 39:1).[29] Therefore, from a mystical standpoint, *tikkun haolam* can be attained only through the observance of the commandments of Torah, in the persistent anticipation of the coming of the Messiah, even though he may tarry. In a word, it can be attained only through *teshuvah*. That is why *tikkun haolam* must begin with the recovery of Jewish tradition, draw human beings into more loving relations, and continue in a never-ending fashion.

THE RECOVERY OF TRADITION

In chapter 4 we noted that the Hebrew word for "tradition" is *masoret*. Understood in terms of a *tikkun haolam, masoret* is a *mesirut*, a "devotion" or "dedication," to the teachings of the *sifrei kodesh* and to our fellow human beings. Therefore, the *tikkun* of tradition, which might otherwise seem rather abstract and nebulous, entails living a life of concrete, flesh-and-blood loving kindness toward our fellow human beings. And the *sifrei kodesh* of the tradition reveal the *why* of that relation. To speak of a *tikkun haolam* outside Jewish tradition is meaningless, since it is tradition, *masoret,* that defines the very notion.

More than a chronicle of the past or an accumulation of cultural habits, tradition consists of a sacred history and a history of the sacred. The memory that is the substance and sanctity of tradition is a memory of God that has God both as its subject and as its object. Just as our thinking transpires under the canopy of Divine thought, so is our memory of Hashem His remembrance of us. Indeed, the tenth-century sage Saadia Gaon identifies tradition as a form of revelation (see *Sefer Emunot Vedeot* 9:4). Inasmuch as tradition is a vehicle of revelation, it is a means of redemption. It takes hold of the past that has slipped behind us and places it before us. Tradition makes us contemporary, for example, with the events of the first Passover, which is the Jewish paradigm of redemption. Thus the Mishnah teaches, "In every generation a person is duty-bound to regard himself as if he has personally gone forth from Egypt" (*Pesachim* 10:5). From this passage we see that tradition, as the memory of God, is God's calling forth our memory of His remembrance of us. And His remembrance of us is called Torah. *Tikkun haolam,* then, begins with a *tikkun* of our own person through a personal devotion to Torah: *I* am part of the world that is in need of mending, and the memory of my emergence from Egypt is a memory of a summons to live according to the commandments of Torah.

This memory of a deliverance and a responsibility underlies the essence of the Jew and the *tikkun haolam* he or she seeks in the post-Holocaust era. A Jew today, says Fackenheim, "feels at one with Holocaust survivors if he is not himself a survivor. He too thinks of the blood of the children [slaughtered in Egypt]—and all talk about meaning in those grim four centuries is wiped from his lips. Instead, as he reads the Tanach itself, he has nothing but that bold, powerful, magnificently anthropomorphic phrase: 'And God remembered' [Exodus 2:24]. That and nothing else."[30] And yet that is everything; on that rests any *tikkun* of tradition, for in God's memory of His creature lies the key to His entry into creation.

And the entry of the Holy One into the world is the key to *tikkun haolam*. What, indeed, did God remember? The agonizing outcry of His children (see Exodus 3:7), who cry out once again. In that outcry, He cries out to us: "Return to Me, and I shall return" (yes, God Himself is in need of *teshuvah*; see Malachi 3:7).

Says Fackenheim, "God *cannot* enter the world He has created, lest in doing so He destroy it. Yet a Jew knows that God *has* entered into the world. He led Israel out of Egypt, He gave the Torah on Mount Sinai."[31] What is more, according to the tradition in search of *tikkun,* He gave the Oral Torah transmitted through Talmud, Midrash, and Kabbalah, all of which must come to bear if we are to attain the *tikkun* of tradition necessary to Jewish thought. To be sure, these are precisely the "Scriptures" that Levinas deems "the primary foundation of meaning."[32] The Midrash teaches that when the Israelites heard the word *Anokhi* at Mount Sinai, their souls left them; but the Torah that God gave them restored their souls (*Shemot Rabbah* 29:4), for the soul needs meaning as the body needs bread, and the Torah, in all its forms, is the foundation of meaning. "One understands this Midrash," Fackenheim asserts, "and one understands what Judaism is."[33] With the Shoah, the eclipse of the Divine utterance of *Anokhi* sucks forth our souls; but the same Torah may restore our souls in a *tikkun haolam.* Truthfully, which of the postmodern fashions and fads can mend the open wounds in the Jewish soul? Is there, in fact, a better source for the *tikkun* of tradition than the tradition itself? Is there any trace of the Divine Absolute among the postmodern antics of the academics?

If God has entered the world, as Jewish teaching maintains, then tradition, as sacred history, is the tale of God's presence *within* history. Levinas identifies sacred history precisely as the existence of God,[34] and that existence must be understood in terms of a *living presence.* Without the tradition that is sacred history, God remains the empty abstraction of philosophical speculation. That is why a *tikkun haolam* demands the *tikkun* of tradition: without the Divine Presence in history, there is no tradition and nothing to be mended. The teachings of the prophets and rabbis are central to a *tikkun haolam* because, Fackenheim asserts, "the God of the prophets and rabbis is a God capable of *presence.* Having created heaven and earth, He, as it were, *Himself* walks in the garden."[35] In this approach to God, however, we have a contradiction, as Fackenheim is well aware:

"The 'sole Power' present at the Red Sea and Mount Sinai manifests a *transcendent* God, for involvement would limit His Power; it manifests an *involved* God as well if only because it *is* a Presence."[36] The *tikkun* that is a recovery of tradition, then, does not resolve contradiction. A post-Holocaust *tikkun haolam* most especially does not eliminate this particular contradiction; rather, it restores a tension between the terms.

And it restores that tension by restoring the commandment that arises in revelation. "If the astonishment [at revelation] abides," Fackenheim explains, "it is because Divinity is *present in* the commandment. Because it is a *commanding* rather than a saving Presence, however, the abiding astonishment turns into deadly terror. . . . And the human astonishment, which is terror at a Presence at once Divine and commanding, turns into a second astonishment, which is *joy*, at a Grace which restores and exalts human freedom by its commanding Presence."[37] Yes, joy, steeped in wonder and awe: the two are interwoven, as it is written in the *Eliyyahu Rabbah*,[38] and there is no *tikkun haolam* without this joy. For joy "gives completeness to a commandment," Joseph Albo reminds us (*Sefer Ha-'Ikkarim* 3:33); it makes whole the connection between above and below. Remember the words of Moshe Leib of Sassov: "When someone asks the impossible of me, I know what I must do: I must dance!"[39] If the post-Holocaust *tikkun* of tradition seems impossible, then we must learn to dance. There, in the rejoicing dance of tradition, we may keep our footing on the shifting ground. There, in the rejoicing dance of tradition, we discover the human freedom restored by the commanding Presence. There, in the rejoicing dance of tradition, we may draw the Divine into the midst of human relation. To be sure, tradition is the tale of drawing the Divine into human relation; it is the tale of *tikkun haolam*.

Which means: the mending of tradition entails a *tikkun* of *tikkun*, whereby the mending of the world begins with the mending of what transpires *between* one human being and another. This *between* space is the portal through which the Divine enters the *olam* of creation. Recall, in this connection, Levinas's assertion "I can only go towards God by being ethically concerned by and for the other person."[40] The ethical, of course, is rooted in commandment; says Levinas, "What you perceive of God is a Divine verbal message (*devar elohim*), which is, more often than not, an order. It is commandment rather than narration which marks the first step towards human understanding."[41] The recovery of tradition after the Holocaust must begin not just with the retelling of its tale, as if to get the narrative straight. Rather, with *this* assault on tradition, the post-Holocaust *tikkun haolam* must begin with the commandment.

If the flesh and blood of the commandment lies in *gemilut chasadim,* in "acts of loving kindness," toward our fellow human beings, those actions rest upon the commandments of Torah, which we affirm through study and prayer. As it is written in the *Pirke Avot,* none of these pillars—*Torah, avodah,* and *gemilut chasadim,* that is, Torah study, prayer, and acts of loving kindness—can stand without the other two (see *Pirke Avot* 1:2).[42] Thus the turning toward the human being that *tikkun haolam* demands is a turning toward God, as Fackenheim insists: "There is no humble walking before God unless it manifests itself in justice and mercy to the human neighbor. And there can be only fragmentary justice and mercy unless they culminate in humility before God,"[43] which is a *mesirut,* a devotion to Torah, lived in Torah observance—that is what is incumbent upon the post-Holocaust Jewish thinker seeking a *tikkun haolam.*

A mending that draws us nigh unto the other, both human and Divine, the commandment points up a "proximity," to use Levinas's term, that is the opposite of alienation.[44] That a deep sense of alienation has cut through world Jewry since the Holocaust is evident. The underlying cause of that alienation, however, is not only God's apparent absence but also the human attempt to escape the commanding Voice. Levinas enables us to see how all of this is tied to the recovery of tradition when he writes, "The past signifies starting from an irrecusable responsibility, which devolves on the ego and precisely is significant to it as a commandment."[45] Through the commandment, we are contemporary with the past of tradition; indeed, the commandment that announces our "irrecusable responsibility" is what establishes the past *as* tradition. If *tikkun haolam* is a mending of the relation between the holy and the human, then it happens upon the transformation of the past into tradition through the commandments of Torah, *avodah,* and *gemilut chasadim.*

Fackenheim brings out the implications of this idea for a post-Holocaust *tikkun haolam* by explaining, "A Jew cannot take upon himself the age-old task of testifying to the Divine image without believing his own testimony. In our time, however, he cannot authentically believe in this testimony without exposing himself to the fact that the image of God was destroyed, *and* to the fact that the unsurpassable attempt to destroy it was successfully resisted, supremely so, by the survivor. *Hence the wish to bear witness turns into a commandment, the commandment to restore the Divine image to the limits of his power.*"[46] This, of course, is Fackenheim's 614th Commandment. What must be emphasized is that the Divine image can be restored only through a return, through a *teshuvah,* to the Torah that articulates that image, in all of its 613 commandments. After all, it is a *614th* Commandment, not just a new commandment. It must also be emphasized that, for Jewish thought, *teshuvah* is not a movement of faith, nor is action contingent upon belief; it is the other way around: belief is born of action, as indicated in the cry of the Israelites at Mount Sinai, *"Naasei venishma"*—"We will do, and we will hear" (Exodus 24:7). Indeed, what can it mean to authentically believe in the testimony without living according to what is commanded?

Fackenheim deems the commanding Word that arises from Auschwitz the 614th Commandment for two reasons. First, the breach in tradition creates a distance between the post-Holocaust Jew and the 613 Commandments of tradition. Second, the commanding Voice of Auschwitz issues a 614th Commandment because, far from belonging to a human realm of something like a categorical imperative, it implicates the human being in his or her relation to the Divine. Fackenheim develops this insight by saying, "The Nazi logic of destruction . . . is a *novum* in human history, the source of an unprecedented, abiding horror: but resistance to it on the part of the most radically exposed, too, is a *novum* in history, and it is the source of an unprecedented, abiding wonder. *To hear and obey the commanding Voice of Auschwitz is an 'ontological' possibility, here and now, because the hearing and obeying was already an 'ontic' reality, then and there.*"[47] This *novum* calls for a new commandment, a commandment to heed the commandments—therein lies the *tikkun* of *tikkun.*

What are we commanded to do? To restore the Divine image to the human being and thus to draw the transcendent back into the immanent. Fackenheim reminds us that the Divine image might be destroyed when he writes, "In manufacturing the *Muselmaenner*—walking corpses— the Auschwitz criminals destroyed the Divine image in their victims; and in doing what they did they destroyed it in themselves as well. In consequence a new necessity has arisen for the ethics of Judaism in our time. What has been broken must be mended. Even for a Jew who cannot believe in God it is necessary to *act as though* man were made in His image."[48] From a Jewish perspective, the image lies in the action. And what is the action by which I act as though I were created in His image? It is the embrace of the other person through deeds of loving kindness, Torah study, and prayer.

Note well: as though the human being were *created* in His image. In this phrase we discover that the recovery of tradition entails not only the *tikkun* of a time remembered but the mending of an immemorial past that proclaims my responsibility to and for the other person and thus lays claim to me prior to any action. For to be created is to be entrusted with a charge from a time prior to the beginning. And so, Levinas insists, "responsibility for my neighbor dates from before my freedom in an immemorial past, an unrepresentable past that was never present and is more ancient than consciousness of. . . ."[49] To be created in the Divine image is to be imprinted with the trace of this immemorial past that both precedes and permeates tradition. Creation is the opposite of chance occurrence or "natural" selection; it is the imposition of a responsibility that cannot be refused. The *tikkun* of tradition is a recovery of this responsibility that comes with being created so that the Creator may return to the midst of His creation. And the avenue of that return is a return to human relation. Here lies the connection between the recovery of tradition and the recovery from an illness. Which illness? The illness of indifference.

THE RECOVERY FROM INDIFFERENCE

The *tikkun* of indifference lies in a *tikkun* of the Word of Torah, beginning with the words that begin the Torah: "In the beginning God created. . . ." Everything that we are to understand about human being returns us to the idea that God *created*, and that He created the human being—a *single* human being, from whom all human beings derive—in His image. "Never was a more exalted view of man conceived than that of the Divine image, and never one more radically antiracist," argues Fackenheim. "It was therefore grimly logical—if to be sure uniquely horrifying—that the most radical racists of all time decreed a unique fate for the Jewish people."[50] Here one realizes the metaphysical depths of the Nazi assault on the Jews. It was launched not only against the men, women, and children among God's Chosen but against the first human being and therefore against every human being created in the image of the Creator. It was launched against the notion and the action of creation itself and therefore against the Covenant between Creator and creature. Covenant derives from Creation, *brit* from *bara*, as Nachmanides points out.[51] Israel is chosen for the Covenant not as a blessing for itself alone but so that "all the nations" (Genesis 18:18) may be blessed as human beings who bear the likeness of Divine being. The Covenant *is* that image and likeness so that whether the world shall endure or be destroyed is determined by the Covenant that sanctifies human and Divine relation.[52]

The Covenant that defines the human-to-Divine relation also defines the relation of human to human. And in both relations we have the being-for-the-other that opposes indifference. Levinas describes this relation when he says, "All my inwardness is invested in the form of a despite-me, for-another."[53] If the post-Holocaust *tikkun haolam* includes a mending of meaning, it begins with the significance we assume when we signify the infinite dearness of the other human being, a dearness rooted in what cannot be weighed, measured, counted, or observed. One must be careful, of course, not to confuse this "despite-me, for-another" with the self-disgust that Fackenheim describes, where self-disgust means precisely the obliteration of the "for-another." Fackenheim writes, "Excremental assault was *designed* to produce in the victim a 'self-disgust' to the point of wanting death or even committing suicide. And this—nothing less—was the essential goal."[54] Self-disgust is a form of the destruction of the Divine image that constitutes the soul, because it is opting for an absolute silence, for an end to all response and responsibility.

Here, too, we find that the Hebrew language can inform Jewish thought. In Hebrew the word for "responsibility" is *acharayut*; its root is *acher*, which means "other." The implication? If responsibility is subjectivity, as Levinas maintains,[55] then I am the "not-I"—the "other" (or *acher*)—of *acharayut*. When I fail in my responsibility—when, in an imitation of God, I declare, "I am I" (see Exodus 3:14)—then I become other than who I am, hence absent from my fellow human being. Absent from my fellow human being, I have no time, a point underscored by the verb *achar,* meaning "to be late," "to tarry," or "to lag behind." Only through the responsibility that defines me do I generate a presence before the other, where I have time because I am on time: I am present. "By taking upon himself the responsibility of others," as Levinas makes this point, "Israel would teach that the greatest intimacy of me to myself consists in being at every moment responsible for the others."[56] Israel would teach the substance of the Covenant that Israel signifies. And it is the opposite of the indifference with which the Nazis would infect the world and upon which they rely. Just as the responsibility that issues from the commanding Voice of Auschwitz has metaphysical dimensions, this indifference has an ontological aspect; here, too, *tikkun haolam* is a *tikkun* of being.

The ontological indifference characterizes what Levinas calls the "there is," a notion discussed in the previous chapter. The "there is," we recall, is the "impersonal, anonymous, yet inextinguishable 'consummation' of being, which murmurs in the depths of nothingness itself."[57] In our age, the rumbling of indifferent being is the roar of the flames that consumed the body of Israel. This evil does not lie "out there" in some cosmic beyond but creeps into the intimate space between my neighbor and me. There this "consummation" of being consumes the soul. The task of a post-Holocaust *tikkun haolam* is to negate this negation that begins with the distance of difference and transform it into the proximity of nonindifference. Says Levinas, "The difference in proximity between the one and the other, between me and a neighbor, turns into nonindifference, precisely into my responsibility. Non-indifference, humanity, the one-for-the-other is the very signifyingness of signification."[58] *Tikkun haolam* attains this "signifyingness of signification." The sign I become through giving is not locked into a system of signs, as postmodernists would have it; rather, it is the sign of the giving of signs, the sign of the very possibility of signification and significance.

Tikkun haolam, therefore, transcends the sign. Which means: this mending of the world transcends the world in a movement toward the other human being, through a caring for the widow, the orphan, and the stranger. In the human signification of one-for-the-other, *tikkun haolam* opens up an interaction with the Divine. It refuses the appropriation of the other by the Same, in an obedience to the commanding Voice that I encounter through the other. Allowing the other person this freedom,

I am free. "To be free," Levinas asserts, "is simply to do what nobody else can do in my place. To obey the Most High is to be free. But man is also the irruption of God within Being, or the bursting out of Being towards God; man is the fracture in Being which produces the act of giving, with hands which are full, in place of fighting and pillaging."[59] The "fracture in Being," in this case, is a fracture in the impersonal being of the "there is"; such a fracture is a mending of human and Divine being. Commanding us to seek a recovery from the illness of indifference, God announces our responsibility to and for the other person; through our obedience to His commandment, we participate in *tikkun haolam*. And we encounter that commandment in the face of the other person.

Zygmunt Bauman points out that for Levinas the face reveals "an authority without force."[60] Which means: the face is not part of the landscape of being, where power is the one reality and weakness the only sin. The face, rather, is otherwise than being, a break in being: it is where holiness emanates into an otherwise meaningless and indifferent realm. Says Levinas, "A face enters into our world from an absolutely foreign sphere, that is, precisely from an absolute."[61] A face is the incursion of the Absolute into a realm empty of absolutes. Looking at the Hebrew word for "face," *panim,* we note that its cognate *penim* means "inside" or "interior": as a breach of being from beyond being, the face is where *above* and *within* become synonyms. Nothing that meets the eye belongs to the face: the face is the exposure of the utterly interior without the loss of interiority's hiddenness. The face reveals the hidden *as* hidden. It is where the *tikkun haolam* as a *tikkun* of the hidden transpires. The word *panim,* moreover, is plural, suggesting that the face both reveals and veils the depth dimension of an *inner* being that is *distinct* from being. To paraphrase Levinas, the *in-* of the Infinite is "both *non-* and *within*,"[62] and the face is precisely a manifestation of what is "both *non-* and *within*." This is the height that "ordains being," as Levinas puts it,[63] and that opposes the postmodern impetus toward a leveling of everything into a sameness, without "hierarchy" or meaning.

Emerging from this metaphysical dimension of height, "the face is signification, and signification without context," says Levinas. "I mean that the Other, in the rectitude of his face, is not a character within a context. Ordinarily, . . . the meaning of something is in its relation to another thing. Here, to the contrary, the face is meaning all by itself."[64] "As *à-Dieu*," Levinas states it elsewhere, the face "is the latent birth of meaning,"[65] latent because it confronts the one who steps before the face with a responsibility to answer, "I am here for you." Postmodernism, insisting that meaning derives only from cultures, contexts, and systems of signs, is a muting of the responsive being-there-for-the-sake-of-another. Only from the standpoint of a meaning that transcends context can a *tikkun* of the illness of indifference take place.

In previous chapters, it has been pointed out that Jewish thought views the human being not as an animal but as a *medaber* and that language is not a natural phenomenon. Nor is it a human phenomenon. It is a Divine phenomenon, as evidenced by the face that refuses indifference. "The face speaks," says Levinas; "the face forbids us to kill."[66] *Because* the face speaks, it bespeaks not an infinite power but an infinite goodness "stronger than murder."[67] To speak—to give utterance to the word in a mending of word and meaning—is to forbid murder *absolutely*. And so we come to a crucial realization about *tikkun haolam*: the mending of God, world, and humanity can happen only with the restoration of the Divine and absolute prohibition against murder, as it is received from the tradition of Torah. It is the one antidote to the illness of indifference. If "the presence of the Other is a presence that teaches," as Levinas maintains,[68] it is because through the face we receive the commandment of Torah, which *is* the Teaching. To encounter the face is to encounter Torah; it is through the face that Torah enters this world. Through the face, Torah commands us to be there for the sake of another.

Torah, therefore, is indispensable to *tikkun haolam,* understood both as a *tikkun* of tradition and as a *tikkun* of indifference. One place where the two come together is in the daily ritual of putting on *tefillin* for our morning prayers. To be sure, in the mystical tradition, *tefillin* are called *chayim,* or "life."[69] Why? Because as we bind ourselves to the Word of God, we bind ourselves to the life of the other, both as God and as fellow human being. Recall the halakhic question noted in chapter 2: At what hour of the morning shall a Jew put on his *tefillin*? The answer: when it is light enough to recognize the face of the neighbor (*Kitsur Shulchan Arukh* 10:2). Beholding the face of our neighbor, we attain the betrothal to Hashem. In this thinking we have an illustration of Fackenheim's state-

ment that "the revealed morality of Judaism demands a three-term relationship, nothing less than a relationship involving man, his human neighbor, and God Himself."[70] Putting on *tefillin*, we affirm that there is no
Torah without the face, no face without the Torah. Putting on *tefillin*,
therefore, is no mere ritual; it is, in the words of Levinas, the confirmation of "the conception of God in which He is welcomed in the face-to-
face with the other, in the obligation towards the other."[71] This welcome,
this greeting, Levinas regards as the very meaning of Judaism.[72] By now
we can see that it is the very meaning of *tikkun haolam*.

Because the meaning of our humanity lies in this summons to greet
the other person, we find in the Torah three fundamental questions put
to each of us: "Where are you?" (Genesis 3:9); "Where is your brother?"
(Genesis 4:9); and "What have you done?" (Genesis 4:10). These three questions are variations of a single question that comes to us from the God
who is One. The oneness of the questions lies in the one response they
call for: *Hineni*—Here I am! Here I am before You, O Lord; here I am
for you, my brother; here I am, ready to act and to answer. "When in the
presence of the Other I say 'Here I am,'" Levinas insists, "this 'Here I am!'
is the place through which the Infinite enters into language."[73] It is the
place through which meaning enters into language; it is the place where
tikkun happens. When the Infinite enters into language, infinite possibility enters into life, enters precisely as nonindifference, for "the difference
between the Infinite and the finite," says Levinas, "is a non-indifference
of the Infinite to the finite, and is the secret of subjectivity."[74] Thus the
Infinite enters by way of an infinite responsibility to and for the other,
both as person and as God. With this appearance of the Infinite, difference
becomes nonindifference, and the portal to *tikkun haolam* opens up.

The link to the Infinite is the link mended in a *tikkun haolam*. The
mending happens when I answer the summons of my fellow human being
in an act of response and responsibility that announces the Infinite through
my one responsibility *more*. "This is not owing to such or such a guilt,"
Levinas explains, "but because I am responsible for a total responsibility, which answers for all the others and for all in the others."[75] Rashi
makes a similar observation: "All Israelites are held responsible for one
another."[76] In these words we have the seed of a post-Holocaust *tikkun*
that would mend the heart of human relation that has fallen so mortally

ill. Adding Levinas's notion of the *more* to Rashi's insight, we discover an infinite open-endedness in the *tikkun haolam* that is a being-for-the-other. Where *tikkun haolam* is concerned, there is always *more* to be done. Indeed, the debt increases in the measure that it is paid.

THE NEVER-ENDING NATURE OF *TIKKUN HAOLAM*

This brings us to the third aspect of recovery in the post-Holocaust *tikkun haolam*. To the extent that the *tikkun* of being-for-the-other inserts the Infinite into life, it opens up an infinite aspect of responsibility. "The more I answer," Levinas asserts, "the more I am responsible; the more I approach the neighbor with which I am encharged, the further away I am."[77] Through the approach to the neighbor, the human being draws nigh unto the Holy One. Drawing nigh unto the Holy One, we realize the infinity of God, and with that realization, our eyes behold the infinite distance between the human and the Divine. Hence the realization of the demand for a never-ending drawing nigh unto the other person, in an eternal movement toward the Infinite. As always, this approach is rooted in a hearing, where the commanding Voice is heard ever more deeply with every act of response.

Each instance of response adds depth to the capacity for response so that as soon as I answer with all I have, I have held something back, something *more* with which I may answer. For with each response I have already heard more: the tongue is the organ of hearing. And so I must answer again and ever again, launched ahead of myself in a continual effort to catch up. "Proximity," Levinas asserts, "is never close enough; as responsible, I am never finished with emptying myself of myself. There is infinite increase in this exhausting of oneself."[78] This exhausting of oneself—this purging the self of *self*—is a liberation from the illusion and delusion of self through a being-for-the-other. This breaking out of the shell of the ego is just what is essential to a mending of the world. It is a wounding of the self through which the human being is made whole, just as Abraham was made whole by circumcision (see *Nedarim* 31b). Indeed, circumcision, too, is essential to *tikkun haolam*. Through this sign of the Covenant by which Abram becomes Abraham, all the nations of the world find their blessing, not in Abraham, exactly, but in the *Covenant* of Abraham. Through Abraham's saying of "Here I am," the "I" of every human being overflows with a responsibility to and for the other that no identity can contain. Thus the principle of identity, of I = I—of I-for-myself—is broken in the *tikkun* that draws us nigh unto the other, broken by the insertion of the holy into the human, which heals the relation to both.

Opposite the Divine "I Am That I Am" or "I Shall Be Who I Shall Be" (Exodus 3:14), therefore, we have the human "I am that I am not." Instead of being equal to itself, the "I" becomes what it is *not yet*; it is defined not by a fixed position but by its movement in a commanded direction, which in turn is shaped by its mission as the one who bears one responsibility *more*. The post-Holocaust *tikkun haolam* does not mend a past but posits a future in which meaning unfolds. Thus the post-Holocaust *tikkun haolam* regains a messianic *yet-to-be* that is a mending of time itself. Said Nachman of Breslov, "You must know that time does not exist of itself, and that days are made only of good deeds. It is through men who perform good deeds [for the sake of others] that days are born, and so time is born."[79] Why? Because in order for a human being to be who he *is*, he must become *more* than he is, for the sake of another, and thus must be what he *is not yet*. Therefore, each good deed we do implicates us for the good deed we have not yet done. This *not yet* is the messianic time that belongs to the never-ending nature of *tikkun haolam*.

Drawing nigh in answer to the call, I realize that I have always been called and that I am eternally too late, like Jacob, who awoke from his dream and said, "God was in this place all along, and I did not know it" (Genesis 28:16). In this "too late," time and the other are knotted together, merging in the one task *more* that I must *yet* engage for the sake of the other. Time is made of this "more," of this *od* in Hebrew, because the responsibility for the sake of the other is forever to be met *once more*. Therefore, in the time of being there for the sake of another—in the time of our lives—we encounter a trace of "eternity," a point that becomes clear when we observe that *od* also means "yet" or "still" and that its cognate *ad* means "eternity." All of it comes together in the "testimony," or *ed*, offered to another for the sake of another. When we declare to another, "Here I am for you," we attest to the dearness of the human that derives from the Divine, and thus to the urgency of the time that contains—yes, *contains*—eternity.

The testimony in which time and eternity intersect is an instance of answering. What abides in the depths of this "answering," of this *aniyah,* becomes clear upon consideration of the verb *anah.* Meaning "to answer" or "to hearken" in the light of having heard something, *anah* signifies an answering that is a hearing, or a hearing in the midst of answering. Also meaning "to be humble," *anah* indicates a consciousness of the One before whom we stand and to whom we answer when we say, "Here I am for you," to our fellow human being. Because this answering is also a hearing or understanding, each time we answer we realize more profoundly that we are *yuad,* "assigned" or "destined," for one responsibility *more.* And so we come back to the *od,* to the "yet" and its cognate *ad,* meaning "eternity": in this answering that eternally summons yet another answer, we encounter the Eternal One. Our lives are made of that eternity, of the eternal "while" and "until" that constitute our lives as lives made of responsibility. That is the meaning of the psalmist's assertion "I shall sing praises unto my God *beodi,*" that is, "with all my being" (Psalms 146:2): with all my *od,* with all my time and eternity, all my response and responsibility. This *beodi* signifies the open-endedness of a life lived for the sake of another, a life that is never enough, and therefore a life in which eternity is continually at work. It opens up the open-endedness of *tikkun haolam.*

The Good that we seek in the yet-to-be of *tikkun haolam* is not only awaited—it *precedes* the wait that constitutes time and confounds identity, just as the name of the Messiah whom we await precedes creation (see *Pesachim* 54a). It is not our invention, not something we choose. The eternal incompleteness of *tikkun haolam,* rather, arises from the fact that the Good sought in the yet-to-be has *already* laid claim to us. My responsibility, therefore, consists of "this pre-original hold of the Good," as Levinas states it, "always older than any present, any beginning. This diachrony prevents the one from joining up with itself and identifying itself as a substance, contemporary with itself, like a transcendental ego."[80] The original temptation confronting the ego is to be this transcendental ego, that is, to be as god. But the true "transcendental ego" is the One who alone can say "I," the One who reveals Himself as "I" at Mount Sinai. The incompleteness of the self in relation to the other derives from the completeness of this "I," the Divine *Anokhi,* who summons the relation.

The Good, then, is neither something that suits me nor something that pleases the other. It is neither culturally determined nor a matter of opinion. Rather, it chooses and commands prior to all choosing, and that is what makes our choices matter. Further, although we are eternally *already* commanded, we are forever contemporary with the commandment. The commanding Voice never leaves off, and in this eternal aspect of the Voice we have the never-ending movement of the *tikkun haolam* that is a being-for-the-other. "The attachment to the Good," Levinas insists, "precedes the choosing of the Good,"[81] and that attachment is just what we have termed *tikkun*. Here we discover a striking aspect of *tikkun* itself: a post-Holocaust *tikkun haolam* calls us forth before we have had time to hear it. Our pursuit of it does not arise from any freedom we would claim; no, *tikkun* itself makes possible any freedom we may enjoy. The problem of a post-Holocaust *tikkun haolam,* therefore, may be post-Holocaust, but *tikkun* as such precedes the problem, thus making it a problem. Like the commanding Voice of Auschwitz, it speaks now because it was heard then, spoken in an immemorial *then* that precedes our beginnings and shapes our horizons.

An insight from André Neher comes to mind: "God suddenly vanishes to the rear; but there is no purpose in seeking Him in that rear, . . . for God is already waiting out there in front, on the horizon-edge of a Promise which only restores what it has taken, without ever being fulfilled. . . . For the man of the Exodus, encounters with the Word are inevitably 'missed appointments.'"[82] It is the missed appointment that determines the *never-ending* movement of being-for-the-other, and this makes *tikkun haolam* into a never-ending *movement.* This point has vital implications for the mending of a world defined by our relation to one another and by our relation to God. It implies, for example, that, in the words of Levinas, "time is the most profound relationship that man can have with God, precisely as a going towards God."[83] It implies further that, as Levinas says, "the other is the future. The very relationship with the other is the relationship with the future."[84] Humanity—Jewish and otherwise—has no future without the movement toward the other that is a going toward God. In its incomplete aspect, *tikkun haolam* lies in this *toward.* It lies in a future forever yet to be realized, and it issues from a past prior to all origins.

All of this is couched in the ancient watchword of Jewish life: *teshuvah.* It is the turning back that is a going toward. And it returns us, from the 614th Commandment to the very first commandment: have children. Indeed, as noted in the talmudic usage of the term *tikkun haolam,* the notion has a great deal to do with bearing children into the world. And, as we saw in chapter 5, Jewish children were the first to be targeted for extermination in the antiworld. Elie Wiesel's words once again come to mind: in the time of the Shoah, "children were old, and old men were as helpless as children."[85] The old men were humiliated. And the children grew old—as old as God. Remember the lines from Wiesel's *Ani Maamin*:

> These children
> Have taken your countenance,
> O God.[86]

In a post-Holocaust world, that countenance is the face that must be restored through a never-ending *tikkun haolam,* for the face of a child is where the assault on God and the wounding of creation takes place. And the Nazis knew it. Therefore, the children must be the first to be embraced in the mending of the world summoned by a post-Holocaust *tikkun haolam.*

It is not only the life of humanity that is at stake in a post-Holocaust *tikkun haolam* but the life of God as well; here, too, lies the infinite aspect of *tikkun's* open-endedness. Thus "for us to cease to be Jews (and to cease to bring up Jewish children)," says Fackenheim, "would be to abandon our millennial post as witnesses to the God of history."[87] Being Jews by bringing up Jewish children: can the post-Holocaust *tikkun haolam* be as simple as that? Well, yes: as simple and as profound. For this bearing Jewish children into the world as Jewish witnesses is just what returns us to our ancestors and their tradition. Thus the Commanding Voice of Auschwitz returns us to the Commanding Voice of Sinai. That *teshuvah* is the key to the recovery of tradition, the recovery from an illness, and the open-ended future. And it is the key to the future of the State of Israel, which Fackenheim regards as the embodiment of *tikkun haolam.*[88] We recall the words of Levinas, cited in chapter 4: "All men are on the verge of being in the situation of the State of Israel. The State of Israel is a category."[89] It is a category not only for Jewish thought but also for the *tikkun haolam* that would heal God, world, and humanity. For the Land of Israel is among the ten things called "living" (*Avot d'Rabbi Nathan* 34:11); it is alive inasmuch as Jewish children dwell in the land, and they can dwell in the land only as long as the State of Israel exists as a Jewish State.[90]

"The Land of Israel," says Rabbi Abraham Isaac Kook, "is not something external, not an external national asset, a means to an end of collective solidarity and the strengthening of the nation's existence, physical or even spiritual. The Land of Israel is an essential unit bound by the bond-of-life to the People, united by inner characteristics to its existence."[91] Therefore, says Neher, "is not the State of Israel, in its very existence, a meta-state? And surely the war launched against Israel on Yom Kippur, October 6, 1973, was not only horizontal. . . . Zion, which is only a fragment of Jerusalem and the Land of Israel, is a word one can neither play around with, nor play tricks with, nor beat around the bush with. It is the key word of the 'meta' of Jewish history. Through Zion, Zionism becomes bi-dimensional. The vertical is interlocked with the horizontal."[92] As we have seen, the mystics maintain that *tikkun haolam* is ultimately attained with the coming of the Messiah, and the coming of the Messiah is definitively tied to the restoration of the Land of Israel. Therefore, Zion and Zionism are essential features of *tikkun haolam,* particularly in the post-Holocaust era.

In the interlocking of the vertical and the horizontal signified by the Jewish return to Israel lies the mending of the world that is *tikkun haolam*. In it we see more profoundly the wherefore behind the argument that Jerusalem must become the "capital" of Jewish thought: it is because a Jewish Jerusalem is essential to *tikkun haolam*. We see why, in the words of Rabbi Adin Steinsaltz, "harm done to Jerusalem strikes at the light of the world."[93] And the Nazis of yesterday and today wish nothing more than to do harm to Jerusalem. As Rabbi Yochanan taught: "The Holy One, blessed be He, said: 'I will not enter the heavenly Jerusalem until I can enter the earthly Jerusalem'" (*Taanit* 5a). Creating an opening for just such an entry is the work of *tikkun haolam* in the post-Holocaust era.

8

Mystical Dimensions of
Post-Holocaust Jewish Thought

I do not fear the hidden; rather, I fear the hidden that is hidden.
—Baal Shem Tov, *Sefer Habesht*

In the last chapter, we encountered Emil Fackenheim's insistence that the possibilities for Jewish thought, here and now, are real because they were already a reality "then and there."[1] With regard to the possibilities for the mystical dimensions of Jewish thought that were voiced "then and there," Pesach Schindler notes that there are two major texts written by Chasidic rabbis who deal with the mystical aspects of the Shoah.[2]

One is the *Em Habanim Smechah (A Happy Mother of Children),* by Rabbi Yissachar Shlomo Teichtal of Budapest. Rabbi Teichtal was sent to Auschwitz in 1944, with the deportation of Hungarian Jewry; he died on a transport from Auschwitz to Bergen-Belsen on January 24, 1945. Written between January and December 1943 (when it was first published), the *Em Habanim Smechah* addresses four basic themes. The first theme is that in the Shoah the Jews were witnessing the birth pangs of the Messiah, which is a common Jewish reaction to catastrophe.[3] The second theme is related to the first: the actions of human beings can hasten the coming of the Messiah.[4] To some extent, however, Rabbi Teichtal's next two themes represent a break with many of his contemporaries. Here he upbraids the *golus Yid,* or the "Jew in exile," for failing to learn the lessons of the Diaspora and not returning to the Land of Israel when the Jews had a chance.[5] His third theme reflects his belief that, in part, the Jews' neglect of *Erets Yisrael* may have contributed to the Shoah,[6] since, in keeping with mystical teachings, he identifies the Holy Land with the Shekhinah herself.[7] Rabbi Teichtal's fourth theme is along similar lines: he blames the Chasidic and Orthodox rabbis for failing to lead the Jews back to Israel with the first signs of the Zionist movement, which most religious leaders opposed.[8] Thus, while Rabbi Teichtal's text addresses the relation between the horrors of the Diaspora and the Jewish return to the Land of Israel, it does not directly address the issues of *Machshavah Yehudit* that are of interest here.

The more profound Chasidic text for our concerns is the *Esh Kodesh (Sacred Fire)* of Rabbi Kalonymos Kalmish Shapira, Rebbe of the Warsaw Ghetto. Drawing heavily on talmudic, mystical, and Chasidic traditions, the *Esh Kodesh* consists of the combined diary and Torah commentary that the Rebbe recorded from September 14, 1939, to July 18, 1942. Written from the core of the catastrophe, this sage's response to the murder of the Jewish people was retrieved from the archival testimonies gathered by Emmanuel Ringelblum and the Oneg Shabbat Circle.[9] In it we see the development of a Jewish response to the Nazi evil, a response that takes Jewish thinking not farther away from the texts and teachings of the tradition, as is common among thinkers today, but deeper into them. As Rabbi Shapira brings the reader into the traditional texts, he does so by sounding the mystical depths of Jewish teaching.

Many thinkers today, reluctant to accommodate any mystical thinking at all, are reluctant as well to retain much of the very Torah that the Nazis set out to destroy. Even those thinkers who urge a return to Torah and tradition are often suspicious of Jewish mysticism. And yet mystical thinking is interwoven with mainstream Jewish practice, far more than most people realize. The concepts that shape the mystical tradition can be found throughout Torah, Talmud, and Midrash. They permeate the songs of the Psalms, the visions of the Prophets, and the tales of the sages. They shape our prayers and our observances, our customs and our practices. Just as in physics there is no piece of matter that does not harbor the mystery of quarks and antimatter, of superstrings and multiple dimensions, so is there in Judaism no teaching or text, no prayer or practice, that does not have its mystical meaning. And all of our sages have been quite aware of this.

What is the first thing an observant Jew does upon waking? He thanks God for returning his soul from the upper realms to this world—there we have mysticism. The *Ana Bekoach* that we say each morning is based on the mystical forty-two-letter Name of God, and the *Brikh Shmeh* that we recite when taking the Torah from the Holy Ark is straight from the Zohar. The order of the prayers; the Kaddish; the Kiddushah; the welcoming of the Sabbath Bride in the *Lekhah Dodi*; the counting of the *omer*, or grain offering, from Passover to Shavuot (the holiday in remembrance of the giving of the Torah); the laying of *tefillin*, with the four-branched letter *shin* worn on the head; wrapping ourselves in the *tallit*, with its four fringes of eight threads and five knots; placing the mezuzah precisely seven-tenths of the way up the doorpost—all of it is laden with Jewish mysticism.

Indeed, the great codifiers of Jewish laws concerning the practical day-to-day life of a Jew—from Ravad to Maimonides, from Joseph Caro to Schneur Zalman—were mystics. In order to be thoroughly versed in the *what* of the law, one had to be versed in the *why*; and you cannot get very far into the *why* without finding yourself awash in the mystical traditions. In Judaism there can be no discourse concerning the Divine spark and Divine image, the human soul and human holiness, or life's meaning and life's mission, without a prompt sounding of the depths of mystical insight. Therefore, if Jewish thought is to bring additional depth to its response to the Shoah, it must consider how Jewish mysticism might inform that response, just as it informs every other aspect of Jewish existence.

Steeped in the mystical traditions of Chasidism, the *Esh Kodesh* of Rabbi Shapira is a good place to turn for those mystical insights in the contexts of the Shoah. Indeed, Mendel Peikazh rightly describes Shapira as the most important Chasidic thinker involved in the event,[10] and the Chasidic tradition is where the mystical teachings are most alive today. But before exploring Rabbi Shapira's *Esh Kodesh* and its implications for Jewish thought, we should explain a few more concepts from Jewish mysticism. Since Chasidism is influenced primarily by the mystical teachings of Isaac Luria, the "Ari" of Safed, our emphasis will be on those teachings.[11] To be sure, if God has gone into hiding, then Kabbalah—

chakham hanistar, the "wisdom of what is hidden"—may be just was is needed to take post-Holocaust Jewish thought to new levels.

MYSTICAL CONCEPTS:
SOME POST-HOLOCAUST FUNDAMENTALS

Simply stated, Jewish mysticism is a means of delving deeper into the secrets of Torah and the of creation that transpires at every instant. Because the nature of creation is a chief concern of Jewish mysticism, one of the biblical texts of particular interest to the mystics is the account of creation in the first chapter of Genesis. The idea is not that reality consists of a chain of cause and effect set into motion by a First Cause or Unmoved Mover; rather, according to the Jewish mystical view, every quark and every galaxy *is* by virtue of God's continual speaking. The evening, for example, does not come because of laws of nature governing the rotation of the earth; evening comes through God's word, as we affirm each day in our prayers. Arising from a Divine utterance, every detail of creation has a Voice, what the Zohar calls "the supernal Voice from which all other voices proceed" (*Zohar* I, 210a). Which means: every detail of creation addresses us and has meaning.

For this reason, the Torah does not relate that Adam named the animals, for instance, as if he had dreamt up some sound of his own. No, it says *vayikra haAdam shemot,* "Adam read the names" of the animals (Genesis 3:20); that is, his wisdom was such that he could read the Divine word of which each creature was made. Recall, too, Adin Steinsaltz's commentary on the biblical verse "man lives not by bread alone, but by every utterance from the mouth of God does man live" (Deuteronomy 8:3). The verse does not suggest that we have a physical aspect and a spiritual aspect; it does not divide the human being into halves, as it is often misunderstood. Rather, says Rabbi Steinsaltz, it means that "man does not live only from the calories provided by bread, but from Divine energy. This is what the Torah calls the *'utterance from the mouth of the Lord.'* It makes the bread 'live' and forms its true essence. In other words, although superficially I am only eating matter, in fact I am ingesting language, because the raw material of bread is the Divine word."[12] Thus the physical is also metaphysical; the material is also spiritual. Every "item" or "thing," every "tool" or "utensil," is also a "vessel," as these various possibilities of meaning for the Hebrew word *kli* suggest. A vessel of what? Of the Divine word, by which all things exist and through which we are commanded.

The other biblical text that forms the basis for mystical thought is the first chapter of the Book of Ezekiel, where the prophet relates his vision of the *Merkavah*, or "Chariot." One key aspect of that vision is the *chashmal*, the "electrum," that the prophet saw amidst clouds of flame (Ezekiel 1:4). In modern Hebrew, *chashmal* translates as "electricity"; biblical scholars maintain that the word designates a brightly polished metal. At a deeper level, however, the sages of the Talmud teach that the word *chashmal* is made of the words *chash*—from *chashai*, meaning "silent"—and *mal*, which means "to speak" (see *Chagigah* 13b). The word *mal* is the root of *milah*, meaning "word" or "speech." What, then, did Ezekiel "see?" He saw a "speaking silence" at the heart of the Divine utterance, in the shift from the silence of the ineffable *alef* to the eloquence of the *beit* that begins the Torah. Which is to say: he saw the word that gives utterance to the world and thus confers meaning upon the world—silently. It is the *kol demamah dakah* that Elijah perceived, a phrase usually mistranslated as "a still small voice" but which means "the voice of a thin silence" or the "thin voice of silence" (see 1 Kings 19:11–12).

Recall, in this connection, an insight from Resh Lakish: "The Torah scroll that was given to Moses was made of a parchment of white fire, and was written upon with black fire and sealed with fire and was swathed with bands of fire" (*Devarim Rabbah* 3:12). The black fire is word. The white fire is silence. Each is aflame with meaning; each defines the other. As Levi Yitschak of Berditchev has taught, when God gave Moses the Torah, He gave not only the words but also the silence between and around the words.[13] Listening ever more intensely to the *chashmal,* to the speaking silence, that surrounds God's utterance, the mystic pursues the meaning hidden in this silence.

The mystical pursuit entails a process of moving upward and inward in order to attain an ever-greater proximity to God by attaining an ever-deeper understanding of His Torah. Indeed, Jewish tradition teaches that God and His Torah are one and the same (see, for example, *Pesikta Rabbati* 1:3–2:18).[14] Because the Torah is the blueprint for creation, it precedes creation (*Zohar* I, 5a); and since the Torah is made of Hebrew let-ters, the letters themselves precede creation—that is why Hebrew is the holy tongue. To be sure, Rabbi Shapira compares the holiness of Hebrew to the holiness of the Sabbath: just as the Sabbath imparts meaning and sanctity to the other days of the week, he maintains, so does the Hebrew language impart meaning and sanctity to the other languages of human-ity.[15] He bases this insight on a teaching from Rabbi Yochanan, who main-tains that when God created the heavens and the earth, His first utterance broke into seventy sparks; from those seventy sparks emerged the sev-enty languages of the world (*Shabbat* 88b). Further, the ancient mysti-cal text, the *Sefer Yetzirah,* teaches that creation unfolds through thirty-two paths, which consist of the twenty-two letters of the Hebrew alphabet and the ten *sefirot* identified in the previous chapter. (Thus, adopting an examination of some Hebrew words as a means of informing Jewish thought, this investigation has taken a mystical approach all along.)

According to Lurianic Kabbalah, as the Divine Utterance of Creation proceeds along the paths of the ten *sefirot,* God undergoes a *tsimtsum,* or "contraction," in order that the Infinite One may create this finite, material world without its being swallowed up by His infinity.[16] This process is rather like having the light and heat in the center of a star withdraw enough so that a candle could burn without being obliterated by the star; the light and heat are still there but much less intensely than in the rest of the star. As the worlds unfold from above to below, from within to without—from *Olam Atsilut* to *Olam Asiyah,* as discussed in the last chapter—the Holy One becomes more and more hidden, until in this world, the *Olam Asiyah,* or World of Action, He appears to be all but absent. To be sure, Rabbi Steinsaltz notes that "a world can exist only as a result of the concealment of its Creator."[17] Our task in this world is to reveal the Infinite One, who is both within and beyond the finite realm, precisely as the *Hidden* One. "God's concealment and God's essence," in fact, "are one," as Rabbi Steinsaltz has said.[18] We make the Hidden One manifest by opening up the flow of holiness along the channels of the ten *sefirot* through the performance of *mitzvot.* Opening the channels of holiness, we close the gap separating God and humanity by drawing into this realm the Divine Presence manifest in the Tetragrammaton.

It is written, "All that is formed and all that is spoken emanates from one Name" (*Sefer Yetzirah* 2:5). From a mystical standpoint, to live a life in accordance with the *mitzvot* is to draw the Name into creation and thus sustain creation through the observance of *mitzvot*. Rabbi Shapira explains this point by noting that the word *mitzvah* (spelled *mem-tzadee-vav-hey*) contains the four-letter Holy Name (spelled *yud-hey-vav-hey*), so that God, the *Infinite* One, is *in* the *mitzvah*. While the last two letters of the Name, *vav-hey*, are the same in both words, the first two are hidden in the first two letters, *mem-tsadi*, of *mitzvah*; for, when transformed according to the *At-Bash* method of kabbalistic interpretation, the *mem* and *tsadi* become *yud* and *heh*, the first two letters of the Name.[19] The *mitzvah*, therefore, is a portal through which the Holy One enters the world. As it is written, "The *mitzvah* is the candle and the Torah the light" (Proverbs 6:23), and both are manifestations of Hashem. "The mitzvah," as Rabbi Steinsaltz states it, "makes an incision into the veil of the hiddenness of God."[20] Without the *mitzvah*, He cannot enter the world. And when He cannot enter the world, evil flourishes.

According to Lurianic teaching, there is a "latent evil" or "darkness" in the finite world that results from the continual act of Divine creation, from "the breaking of the vessels" noted in the last chapter. But there is also a latent holiness. Therefore, we must release the Divine sparks by elevating the things of the world. The ink that is used to write a Torah scroll, for example, is elevated, and its Divine sparks are released; ink used to sign a deportation order is denigrated, and the sparks are more deeply hidden. Both deeds, moreover, create angels, for good or for ill, that go into the world either to release or to hide more Divine sparks. According to the Talmud, every word creates an angel (see *Avot* 4:11; *Chagigah* 41a). Deeds are like prayers because both create angels. As the Baal Shem Tov has stated it, "Of every good deed we do, a good angel is born. Of every bad deed, a bad angel is born."[21] And Isaac Luria's teacher, Rabbi Moses Cordovero, writes, "When a person transgresses, a destructive creature is created."[22] Mystically speaking, the post-Holocaust world is overrun with these "destructive creatures." They invade not only our words and deeds but also our thoughts and attitudes. This, too, is a reason why we must be careful to ask whether our post-Holocaust Jewish thought is in any way consistent with the thinking that led to the murder of European Jewry.

The potential for latent evil to become actual derives from what the Zohar refers to as the *Sitra Achra,* or the "Other Side" (see, for example, *Zohar* I, 14a–14b).[23] The *Sitra Achra* is not a blank or the mere absence of the good; made of the "residue" left by the Divine *tsimtsum* in the breaking of the vessels, it is rather like a force of gravity that weighs down the good and opposes it. It underlies whatever occludes the flow of holiness and life into the world. The *Sitra Achra,* however, does not exist independently of the Holy One; if it had no Divine spark, it could have no existence. Just as one must have gravity and friction in order to stand or walk, so must one have the *Sitra Achra* in order to have a *movement* of holiness. Therefore, in order to dwell on this side of holiness, there must be a *Sitra Achra,* the Other Side. There can be no "perfect" world, because such a world would be identical with God; creation itself self requires this Other Side. And only we can either strengthen it or weaken it.

Lurianic thinking about evil as both latent and essential is rooted in other teachings from the Zohar. Related to the teaching on the breaking of the vessels and the emergence of the *Sitra Achra,* for example, is the idea that the Divine contraction produces a kind of fallout called *kelipot,* or "shells" (*Zohar* I, 19b). Rabbi Cordovero compares the process to the digestion of food (*Pardes Rimonim* 25:1). As the body absorbs just so much nourishment and then produces waste, so does the physical world absorb just so much holiness and then produces "shells" or "fragments." Because the *kelipot* veil God's holiness, whether they become sources of evil depends on how human beings handle them. The evil of the *kelipot,* moreover, is sustained not so much by physical matter as by the ego that would equate the thinking "I" with being.[24] Thus for Rabbi Shapira, as Esther Farbstein points out, the end of exile requires the *tsimtsum* or withdrawal of the ego, in keeping with the mystical notion of *bitul hayesh,* or "annulment of the self."[25] Only through the human being's annulment of the ego can holiness be released into the world; only through human agency—through our thoughts, words, and deeds—can evil flourish.

How, then, might this mystical thinking about evil inform Jewish thinking about evil after the Shoah?

THE JEWISH THINKER'S ENGAGEMENT WITH EVIL

The Shoah drives to extremes the perennial question of why God does not intervene in the assault on His children. While the mystical teachings do not resolve the question, they can lead to innovative ways of handling it. The process of *tsimtsum* through which our world comes into being is simultaneously a process of Divine withdrawal and Divine incursion. It is the withdrawal of a manipulative power that would preclude all relation; it is the incursion of the absolute love, in the form of Divine commandment, which establishes relation. The establishment of relation requires that the Eternal One be "temporalized," as Hans Jonas expresses it.[26] God enters into a relation with humanity through an utterance that requires a response so that in the self-limitation of God, He is limited by *time.* Where there is world enough and time, there is room enough for evil.

If God were to determine everything, the *mitzvah,* and with it all of creation, would be meaningless. "Even if the course of life, down to its most minute detail, is in the hands of God," Rabbi Steinsaltz states it, "the *relation* to God is still in the hands of man."[27] Therefore, it is written in the Talmud, "everything is in the hands of heaven except the fear of heaven" (*Berakhot* 33b; *Megillah* 25a; *Niddah* 16b), yet everything—all of creation—depends on the fear of heaven, which is most profoundly manifest in our love for the other human being. This fear is not a fear of getting zapped; it is a fear of offending or doing harm, a fear of not doing or being enough for the sake of another. As Creator, God neither forces us to love nor prevents us from loving, but, through His commandment, He makes it matter *whether* we love. Simply stated, then, each of us is destined to love. As we fail to meet our destiny, the world grows ever darker, until evil takes over.

In the Yom Kippur liturgy, to take this point further, we invoke God as the One who knows who will die in their time and who will die before their time. Those who die in their time have fulfilled their mission and thus die according to the Divine will; those who die before their time die without having fulfilled their mission, either by murder or by some other means contrary to the Divine will. What, then, is Divine Providence? It is the assignment of a mission and a meaning to each life, and the authority by which it matters whether we die in our time or before our time. "Providence," or *hashgachah* in Hebrew, implies the "attention" and "care" (other meanings of *hashgachah*) of One who is concerned with human affairs. While God's care and ethical authority *over* the finite realm is infinite, His power *within* this world is not; if the world were flooded with God's infinite power, there would be no world. And where God is not ontologically all-powerful there is room for evil.

In Jewish thought, the application to the Holy One of such notions as omniscience, omnipotence, and other "omni"s is unintelligible. Looking at the mystical view of evil outlined above, one sees that the existence of evil is not a matter of God's deciding to intercede or not to intercede. Rather, in order for creation to flourish rather than collapse, God insists that *we* intercede. If creation implies Covenant, then creation implies a relationship between the Holy One and the one created in His image. And a relationship must be free of interference if it is to be a relationship; we cannot insist that God keep His Covenant and then complain when He does not manipulate our lives. Further, since God is not confined to the contexts and contingencies of being—that is, of space and time—it is unintelligible to speculate on what God might have done or might do, as is the habit of theodicy and theology. God is *Ehyeh Asher Ehyeh,* "I Am Who I Am" or "I Shall Be Who I Shall Be" (Exodus 3:14); God is what He does, and He will do what He will do. And His doing lies in the commandment that *we* do something, precisely in the light—or in the darkness—of the evil in the world.

And yet (in Jewish thought there is always an *and yet*) we must not be too quick to let God off the hook. After all, do we not pray to Him for healing? Do we not repeat three times each morning that God is "the King who answers on the day we call out to Him?" Is He not the Guardian of Israel, who neither sleeps nor slumbers? Does humanity not live in the Covenant of Noah and the Jewish people in the Covenant of Abraham? Do we not, therefore, have grounds for crying out to God, as He cried out to Adam (Genesis 3:9), "Where are you?"

Absolutely. That, too, is God's will. And His Presence is manifest in that outcry. Because we do indeed live in a Covenant with God, we must put to God the question that Abraham put to Him: Will the Judge of the world be unjust? (see Genesis 18:25.) Although, like Abraham, we declare that we are but dust and ashes, God wants us to press Him on the matter of justice—for the sake of the ashes. Therefore, His first conversation with Abraham after sealing the Covenant of Circumcision is an argument. It is the one instance in the Torah where we find God thinking to Himself: "Shall I hide from Abraham what I am about to do?" (Genesis 18:17.) He tells Abraham what He is about to do, because He wants to see whether Abraham understands the meaning of the Covenant, which is to argue with God—not because God will or will not do what He will do, but because it demonstrates *our* responsibility. Similarly, after rightly rebuking Job, God declares, "My servant Job has spoken rightly" (Job 42:7). God *likes* Job's concern over justice in the world. In the face of evil, our task is neither to justify God nor to get rid of God but to maintain the tension of a dialogue, even an argument, with God.[28] If God confronts Abraham or His servant Job with an excess of evil, it is because He wants to ensure the impossibility of their accepting it.

"The excess of evil by which it is a surplus in the world," says Emmanuel Levinas, "is also our impossibility of accepting it. The experience of evil would then be also our waiting on the good—the love of God."[29] What Levinas calls an "excess of evil" the mystics refer to as the *kelipot*; what he deems "the love of God" is the process of releasing the divine sparks hidden within the *kelipot*. Our task is not to bring light to darkness but to transform the darkness into light, as the Lubavitcher Rebbe has taught.[30] In Levinas's insight, moreover, we see how even evil might in some sense be in service to God, since it awakens the commanding Voice of the Good, which forbids us to murder: the prohibition against murder arises with the prospect of murder. The task of transforming darkness into light arises in the face of darkness. That is why the Commanding Voice is sobering. It lays bare a horror that strips "consciousness of its very 'subjectivity,'" says Levinas, "not in lulling it into unconsciousness, but in throwing it into an *impersonal vigilance, a participation*. . . . Horror is the dominant emotion, is in the destruction of categories which had hitherto been used to describe the feelings evoked by 'the sacred.'"[31] Only where there is a sense of the holy can there be a sense of horror. The Commanding Voice that disturbs our sleep awakens us not just to evil but to the *horror* of evil, and thus to the urgency of acting.

"The horror of the evil that aims at me becomes the horror over the evil in the other man," Levinas comments on this point. And yet in the encounter with evil there is "a breakthrough of the Good which is not a simple inversion of Evil, but an elevation. This Good does not please, but commands and prescribes."[32] Here, too, we see elements of the Jewish mystical tradition: the Good *breaches* evil so that in the face of idolatry God speaks the *Anokhi*. What is more, if the collision with evil is a confrontation with *the other human being*, then it is an encounter with the *monstrous*, as Levinas suggests: "In the appearing of evil, in its original phenomenality, in its *quality*, is announced a *modality*, a manner: not finding a place, the refusal of all accommodation with . . . , a counternature, a monstrosity, what is disturbing and foreign of itself."[33] Nothing in nature can be monstrous; it may be fearsome, but it is not monstrous. Only a human being, who comes into being from beyond being, can become utterly foreign to being, that is, monstrous. Only a human being can become a Nazi. And only a human being can seek reconciliation with a repentant Nazi in a mutual movement toward the transformation of horror and darkness into the light of holiness.

Because evil manifests itself in the monstrosity that a human being becomes, it manifests itself as a twisting and perverting of one created in the image of the Holy One. And it manifests itself most glaringly in the Nazi assault on the image of the Holy One in the *other* human being. According to the Midrash, this assault on the holy within the human has its paradigm in Cain, who wanted not simply to kill his brother but to return creation and its Creator to the void (see *Bereshit Rabbah* 1:11). Thus Cain was left a wanderer, cut off from human contact: he was marked so that no one should touch him, left to languish in the Land of Nod, literally the Land of "Wandering" (see Genesis 4:15–16). The lesson? The soul suffers what it inflicts.

One finds this to be the case with the Nazis as well: the assault on the Holy One takes place not only in the humiliation and brutalization of the Jew but also within the soul of the Nazi. Recall, for example, an incident that Ringelblum relates: "A police chief came to the apartment of a Jewish family, wanted to take some things away. The woman cried out that she was a widow with a child. The chief said he'd take nothing if she could guess which of his eyes was the artificial one. She guessed the left eye. She was asked how she knew. 'Because that one,' she answered,

'has a human look.'"[34] The evil perpetrated against another is an evil perpetrated against one's own soul because each soul is bound to the other
through its tie to the Holy One. Therefore, the monstrosity that per-
verts the soul of the perpetrator and afflicts the soul of the victim is
launched against the Holy One Himself. And so God *suffers*.

Absurd, this mystical notion that God can suffer, as when Isaiah declares,
"In all their suffering, He suffers" (Isaiah 63:9; see also *Shemot Rabbah*
2:5)? Nevertheless! If the claim that God can suffer in the collision with
evil is an absurdity, then the God of Abraham and the prophets is an
absurdity. And if that is the case, then the Divine prohibition against
murder is an absurdity. Therefore, if God's suffering is an absurdity, it is
an absurdity that we desperately need in the post-Holocaust age. Here,
in the infinite suffering of the Infinite One, we have the chief mystical
concern with God and evil as expressed in the Chasidic tradition, especially in the *Esh Kodesh* of Rabbi Shapira. Let us consider, then, how the
Rebbe of the Warsaw Ghetto may help us with the mystical dimensions
of post-Holocaust Jewish thought.

FIRE IN THE ASHES: THE *ESH KODESH*

Fackenheim relates the story of how the Chasidim of Buchenwald
would risk their lives to secretly put on *tefillin* when they prayed. What
made their prayers great, says Fackenheim, "was not their ability to explain
or understand what was happening, but precisely the insight that this
was impossible; not a classification on their part of the Holocaust with
other Jewish catastrophes, but the recognition of it as unclassifiable. Then
why did they obey the *mitzvah* of *tefillin*? . . . Once again we have touched
an Ultimate."[35] We touch upon a similar "Ultimate" in the Rebbe of the
Warsaw Ghetto. The difference? In the *Esh Kodesh* he provides us with
an unparalleled penetration of the "Ultimate." Here we not only touch
upon it—we are awash in it.

Born on May 16, 1889 (some sources say 1888), in Grodzisk, Poland,
Rabbi Kalonymos Kalmish Shapira was the Rebbe of Piaseczno before
attaining the status of Rebbe of the Warsaw Ghetto.[36] The youngest son
of the renowned Rabbi Elimelekh Shapira (author of the *Imre Elimelekh*),
Rabbi Shapira was a descendant of the Chasidic masters Elimelekh of

Lizhensk, the Maggid of Kozhnits, and the Holy Seer of Lublin. When the war broke out, in 1939, he resolved not to leave the Warsaw Ghetto, despite the opportunities he had to do so.[37] Instead, he stood fast as the spiritual leader of the Jews in the Ghetto, Chasidic and otherwise. The Rebbe was known for his courage as well as for his *Ahavat Yisrael,* his "love for the people of Israel."[38] Rabbi Shimon Huberband, a member of Ringelblum's Oneg Shabbat Circle, illustrates this point with a story of how Rabbi Shapira secretly led a group of Jews to the *mikveh,* the Jewish ritual bath, in the predawn darkness on Erev Yom Kippur 1940, so as to purify themselves for the holy day; because the Nazis had forbidden the use of the *mikveh,* Rabbi Shapira took this action at the risk of his life.[39] Why risk one's life simply to go into the *mikveh?* Because the *mikveh* is a fundamental symbol of the sanctity of life: without the *mikveh,* there is nothing to risk.

By the time the deportations of the summer of 1942 were under way, Rabbi Shapira had lost both parents, his wife, his son, and his daughter. He remained in the Warsaw Ghetto until just after the uprising of April 1943, when he was deported to labor camps at Budzyn, Plaszow, and Wielcka. His final destination was Trawniki, where on November 3, 1943, the Germans murdered him. But he left us his *Esh Kodesh,* the "sacred fire," retrieved from the ashes of death and destruction.[40]

In the *Esh Kodesh,* Farbstein points out, Rabbi Shapira addresses three general realms of the Nazi assault on the Jewish people: *olam, shanah,* and *nefesh.*[41] According to the mystical tradition, *olam,* or "world," is the realm of space, form, and substance, of God in the mode of *Hamakom,* or "the Place." *Shanah,* or "year," is the hidden world that is revealed through human relation; it is the dimension of time, where, in the words of Levinas, "the other [human being] is the future."[42] Here, we recall Abraham Joshua Heschel's insight that "time is the presence of God in the world of space."[43] *Nefesh,* or "soul," is where the life of the human being, with all its sanctity and meaning, unfolds in space and time. It is the manifestation of the metaphysical meaning in the physical human being, of the human being in the image and likeness of the Holy One. These are the general mystical concepts at work in the *Esh Kodesh.* These are the general dimensions of the Nazi assault on the Jewish people. These are the facets of the Nazi assault on creation.

We have seen the Nazis' transformation of world into antiworld. We have seen the Nazis' obliteration of time and memory in the obliteration of human relation. And we have seen the physical and metaphysical assault on the soul, manifest in the Muselmann. Writing from within the event, Rabbi Shapira could not see its full historical scope. But he saw far more than the historian can see. And as he saw more and more, he realized more and more profoundly the transcendent, metaphysical scope of the Shoah. He attained his probing vision of the event from within the event that André Neher describes afterward by saying, "Here on earth it is no longer a question of a man but of Job. Here on earth one no longer has the horizontal pattern of man hunted by man, but the vertical pattern of the Jew harassing God. Thus the enigma of time is electrified by the eternity of a question. There is no longer just the 'anti': the 'meta' plants itself within it, penetrating to its deepest roots."[44] And no one penetrates more deeply into the roots of the "meta" than Rabbi Shapira.

In the first entry of his diary, dated September 14–15, 1939, Rabbi Shapira wrote, "All the cries of the Jewish people heard in this period are a revelation of God's sovereignty and the acceptance of God's sovereignty upon us."[45] In his penultimate entry, dated July 7, 1942, he insists that the Germans are torturing the Jews "only as a consequence" of the Nazi hatred of Torah.[46] One sees in Rabbi Shapira's diary, then, a progression from the view that the suffering of the Jews resulted from their rejection of Divine authority to the view that the Jews were being targeted not for *their* rejection of God but as part of the *Nazi* assault on God. Perhaps he realized the truth of a midrashic teaching: "In the future Gog and Magog will say: 'How foolish of Haman! Did he not know that the Jews have a protector in heaven? We will first overcome their protector and then destroy them!'" (See *Midrash Shochar Tov* 2:4.)[47] Elsewhere it is written: "The enemies could not use their power against Your dwelling place in heaven, so they used it against Your dwelling place on earth" (*Midrash Tehillim* 3:74:3). And His dwelling place on earth is the Jewish people. Indeed, as Schindler points out, Rabbi Shapira sees that God's suffering and the suffering of the Children of Israel are of a piece.[48] The Jewish people, greater than the sum of individuals, embody the presence of God in the world; in the Zohar, we recall, the Community of Israel and the

Shekhinah are taken to be one and the same (see *Zohar* II, 98a).[49] And Rabbi Shapira was quite familiar with the Zohar.

It has been noted that room for evil opens up wherever the human "I" eclipses the Divine *Anokhi*; in modern times that eclipse takes place most fundamentally in philosophy, as Rabbi Shapira is quick to realize. Indeed, he sees in the ontological speculative tradition a manifestation of Amalek. Amalek "singles out Israel for attack," Fackenheim explains, "*because* Israel is singled out by God for a covenant, his aim being to destroy the covenant as he destroys Israel."[50] There is a teaching in the Midrash that breaks the name of Amalek down into *Am lak*, meaning a "people" who "lick" the blood of the Jews.[51] And the fifteenth-century sage Don Isaac Abrabanel teaches that the essence of Amalek is pure hatred; his aim is the extermination of the Jews.[52] Indeed, it is written that, like the Nazis, the Amalekites attacked the Israelites "from behind" (Deuteronomy 25:18) because that is where the children and the elderly were; like the Nazis, Amalek first targets the manifestations of the messianic hope, of Israel's past and future, of Israel's holiness and testimony.

Here it is worth citing again Rabbi Shapira's address to the Jews cited in chapter 3:

> Before Amalek came to fight with you, there were among you servile people who esteemed the very thinking championed by Amalek. You were impressed with the superficial culture in which Amalek takes such pride. As a result, your response to Jewish culture and the wisdom of Torah was chilly. You were sure that Amalek was very cultured, that his philosophy was quite as good as anything. To be sure, it had its ethics, and there is profit to be had from it in this world. What did God do? He brought you face to face with Amalek.[53]

This statement is based on the rabbi's insight into the phrase *asher karkha baderekh*, referring to how Amalek "encountered you on the road" (Deuteronomy 25:18). He notes that *karkha*, or "encountered," also means "chilled you," and that *baderekh*, "on the road," is also a euphemism for "thought": Amalek chilled Jewish thinking with the cold, detached deception of speculative thought. And so the Jews were confronted with the murderous character of totalizing, ontological thought, what had become the "common knowledge" that began with German Idealism and contributed to the Third Reich. Whether they were being punished for buying into this evil cloaked in the good, the Rebbe had yet to work out.

As late as February 7, 1942—but without invoking the wayward ways of the Jews—Rabbi Shapira continued to insist that the "purpose" of Jewish suffering was "to crush and remove 'common knowledge,' of which man [not just Jews] thinks that he knows, and upon which he relies."[54] What is this "common knowledge?" It is the ego-centered presumption that *my* freedom to do as I please lies in *my* self-legislating autonomy, that *my* authenticity lies in *my* resolve. Therefore, the Rebbe maintains, "the destruction and suffering are a Torah that God is teaching us."[55] What is the teaching? It is this: no appeal to natural order or to human society, no invocation of human reason or of human decency, can convey the authority of the *Divine* and therefore *absolute* prohibition against murder. Period.

In the process of creation, God withdraws His absolute power from this realm, yet through Torah He fills this realm with His absolute ethical authority. As soon as we refuse the revelation of "I am Hashem" (Exodus 20:2), we refuse that authority and with it the absolute commandment of "Thou shalt not murder" (Exodus 20:13), as determined by God, and not by culture or ego. According to the Midrash, "Thou shalt not murder" derives from "I am Hashem" (*Mekilta de-Rabbi Ishmael, Bachodesh* 5). The former is the first "commandment" in the relation between the human being and God, and the latter is the first commandment in the relation between human and human. As it is written in the Tosefta, "whoever sheds blood renounces the image and likeness of the Holy One" (*Yevamot* 8:4). Evil, then, is manifest as the refusal of the absolute, Divine commandment: "Thou shalt not murder." And the Nazis refused this commandment *absolutely*; this is precisely the *mitzvah* that they were out to obliterate in their assault on the One who says, "I am Hashem." But the righteous among the Jews cling to the Divine commandment and to the Divine authority of Torah; Torah is the reason the old and the innocent were singled out in the Nazis' singular assault on the Jews. How, then, should the Jews respond to their singular suffering?

RABBI SHAPIRA'S RESPONSE TO THE
SINGULARITY OF THE ASSAULT

In an entry dated December 15, 1941, Rabbi Shapira notes that there were some who cried out, "Why have You forsaken us? If we are being tortured in order to bring us closer to Torah and worship, then why, on the contrary, is the Torah and everything holy being destroyed?"[56] And from an earlier entry we read: "How is it possible to study the Torah when every head is stricken? Is it possible to be inflamed with passions of the heart when every heart is broken?"[57] But there is room for outcry: "If a Jew utters these words in a form of prayer or supplication, as an outpouring of his heart before God, it is a good thing."[58] And: "What can we do when they do not permit us to cry out, or even to congregate for prayer, and we are forced to pray in hidden places, and every Jewish heart must lament this alone? At least in the depths of his heart every Jew must shout to God about it."[59] If post-Holocaust Jewish thought is to learn from Rabbi Shapira's thinking, it too must shout to God, *in the name of the Covenant.* If Amalek sets out to destroy the Covenant, then our task is neither to reject it nor to blindly accept it but rather to affirm it through outcry. Just what that is like, Rabbi Shapira suggests on August 9, 1941, when he turns to a mystical teaching from the Talmud to raise his own outcry.

Noting the talmudic explanation that the Ten Martyrs of the Roman oppression died to atone for Joseph's brothers, who sold him into slavery (see Rashi's commentary on *Avodah Zarah* 11a),[60] he points out a difficulty: since Reuben argued against the rest for sake of Joseph's life (Genesis 37:21), there were only nine who required atonement. Who, then, was the tenth in that grisly minyan? In response to this question, the rabbi invokes the line from Torah that "the tenth shall be holy unto God" (Leviticus 27:32). From this passage he concludes that "Rabbi Akiba was the tenth martyr, sanctified for God, in the place of God, as it were. This is because when the brothers sold Joseph, they implicated God, including God in their quorum when they swore an oath not to reveal to Jacob what had occurred."[61] God Himself has a hand in this evil: God Himself was the tenth! Therefore God Himself—if one may say so—is in need of atonement so that His world may endure. And, like the Righteous Ones, only through our own righteousness can we make an atonement *of God Himself*: because the Jews live in a Covenant with Hashem, not only does He atone for us, but we—*you and I*—also atone for Him.

This turning of the table is realized through Rabbi Shapira's probing the depths of the mystical teachings. Unlike human sin, God's "sin" was not that He committed a transgression *in* the world; rather, His transgression came from *beyond* the world, in His creation *of* the world and in the *kelipot* necessary for that creation. Therefore, the Jews, as the single conduit of the Divine light unto the world, suffer in a singular fashion at the hands of those who would remove that light from the world. According to the Ari, when the Romans murdered the Ten Martyrs, the world "stood ready for destruction" (*Likutei Shas Berakhot* 61a),[62] and the Divine sparks released through the martyrs' Sanctification of the Name were enough to redeem the world from destruction. Just so, the Jews martyred in the Shoah—*martyred* because the Jewish people *represented* Torah in the world, despite their personal beliefs—had the terrible task of saving a world whose thinking had exiled God from the world.[63] On the basis of teachings from the Zohar (*Zohar* I, 88a), Rabbi Shapira views God's exile as an exile of the higher, thinking level of the soul, of the *neshamah*, which parallels the exile of the Shekhinah.[64]

In the mystical scheme of things, the *neshamah* is associated with the *sefirah* of Binah, or Understanding; with *Binah* rooted in *ben,* meaning "between," it is the key to the connection between the upper realms of what exceeds creation and creation itself. According to our prayers, the *neshamah* remains *tahor,* or "pure," within the human being; this purity is the very essence of the human being, as written in the Tosefta: "What is human in the human being is what is pure in purity; the human being lies in what is pure, and what is pure lies in the human being" (*Tohorot* 6:3). This purity is the object of the Nazis' *excremental* assault on the Jews. If this essence of the human's being human is just what the Nazis set out to destroy, it is precisely what post-Holocaust Jewish thought must preserve, a task that postmodern thought is incapable of undertaking. And if, as it is written in the Zohar, the *neshamah* finds its way into this realm only where the human being is devoted to righteousness (see *Zohar* I, 206a; II, 141b; III, 70b), then post-Holocaust Jewish thought must embody the righteousness of Torah—also a task that eludes postmodern thought.

Understanding the assault on the *neshamah* in Chasidic terms, Rabbi Shapira follows the mystical principle that what happens below has its analog in what happens above. Which means: the greater the evil *is* in this world, the greater the evil *will be* in this world—unless we can effect a change in the upper realms. Unless we do *teshuvah,* in other words, there will be no *teshuvah* of God, as it is written: "Return unto Me, and I shall return unto you" (Malachi 3:7; see also *Toledot Yaakov Yosef, Bo* 10). To be sure, it is a distinctively Jewish notion that redemption comes both to God and to humanity. When does God do *teshuvah?* "When," says Rabbi Shapira, "He repents of the evil He had rendered, God forbid, to His people Israel."[65] Thus in the Book of Isaiah God refers to His own salvation (Isaiah 56:1), as does the Midrash, in conjunction with the salvation and redemption of Israel. "The salvation of God," it teaches, "is identical with the salvation of Israel" (*Vayikra Rabbah* 9:3; see also *Bamidbar Rabbah* 2:2; *Shemot Rabbah* 15:12, 30:24; *Midrash Tehillim* 1:13:4).

In keeping with many sages before him, Rabbi Shapira maintains that "the *Akeida* [the Binding of Isaac] and all the murders of the Jews since are components of one event,"[66] namely, the redemption both of God and of humanity. "The murder of a Jew by idolaters," he says, "is in absolute antithesis to the *Akeida,*" and, as the antithesis of the *Akeida,* it is the dialectical consummation of the *Akeida,* both above and below.[67] The Nazi murder of the Jews is the antithesis of the *Akeida* because it undermines the God whose angel orders Abraham not to kill the child; instead, the Nazi murder of the Jews begins with the murder of the child. Dialectically, this sacrifice of the righteous, in Rabbi Shapira's terms, restores the God who stays the hand of Abraham for the sake of humanity, just as it sanctifies a humanity willing to endure anything for God. Thus the teaching from the sage Shimon bar Yochai in the *Sifre* on Deuteronomy (33:5): "When you are My witnesses," God cries out, "I am God; when you are not my witnesses, I am not God" (see also *Pesikta de-Rav Kahana* 12:6). As terrible as it may sound, Rabbi Shapira sees the Jews slaughtered by the Nazis as God's witnesses and therefore as God's saviors who live and die in a Sanctification of the Name.

This vision is grounded in the mystical tradition, where we speak of the sacrifice of the righteous not only in this realm but also in the upper chambers of the Holy One—for our sake and for His. "When the world becomes full of sin and is doomed to destruction," it is written in the Zohar, "woe to the righteous man who is found in it, for he is first made answerable for its sins" (*Zohar* I, 67b). In the time of the Shoah, Israel suffered not for their own sins but for the sins of humanity—of Christendom and Western civilization. Not only does the assault on the righteous include an assault on God, but in the upper realms the murder of the righteous leads to a protest against God. Rabbi Shapira invokes this mystical teaching as he turns to the Talmud, where it is written that in the firmament called *Zebul* stand the heavenly Jerusalem, the Temple, and the Altar. At the Altar, the angel Michael offers up to God the souls of the righteous. And, as he makes his offering, the angel puts the question to God: "How can You tolerate the suffering of Your children?" (See *Chagigah* 12b; *Menachot* 110a; *Zevachim* 62a.)[68] There are times when God needs our help and the help of the angels in order to be moved to answer us.

The Midrash relates, for instance, that when the Second Temple was destroyed, Rabbi Tsadok—who fasted and prayed forty years in an effort to divert the destruction (see *Gittin* 56a–56b; *Eichah Rabbah* 1:5)—entered the ruins and cried out, "My Father in Heaven, You destroyed Your city and burned Your Temple, and You are sitting in tranquility and quiet!" Then he had a vision of God saying a eulogy, with the angels around Him crying out, "Woe the faithful Jerusalem!" (See *Sefer Tanna debe Eliyahu Rabbah* 28.)[69] Here, too, through Rabbi Tsadok's vision, the angel Michael moves God to tears with his account of what is befalling God's children. In the course of his thinking about God and evil, Rabbi Shapira invokes this teaching about the angel Michael on October 5, 1940, and again a year later, on October 6, 1941. As always, it is not that he changes his mind about God but rather that his thinking goes to deeper, more mystical levels that may inform our own post-Holocaust thinking. More and more, his thinking assumes the aspect of prayer.

This is where, in the words of Levinas, "the suffering self prays on behalf of God's suffering, for the God who suffers both through man's transgression and through the suffering by which this transgression can be expiated."[70] The sacrifice of the righteous on high attains an opening of the channels of holiness that flow from above to below, from below to above, through the testimony of the righteous, so that humanity may return to God and God may return to humanity. *The sacrifice of the righteous is not a ransom—it is a testimony* that it brings us to *teshuvah*. This movement of return, then, is not a matter of suddenly acquiring faith; rather, it rests upon a return—to Torah, prayer, and deeds of loving kindness.

What that movement is like in the contexts of the Shoah, Rabbi Shapira explains in an entry dated January 20, 1940, where he relates an episode from the Talmud about Rabbi Yose. Like Rabbi Tsadok, Rabbi Yose once entered the ruins of Jerusalem after the destruction of the Temple in order to pray (see *Berakhot* 3a). As he prayed, he heard a "heavenly echo" that he had never heard before. The sage had not heard it before because the world's corruption had obstructed the echo. There are times, says Rabbi Shapira, when God can get through only as we stand and pray in the ruins that remain after the assault on God Himself.[71] Of course, the Romans did not set out to exterminate the Jews; they simply wanted to destroy Judaism, and they thought they could do so by exiling the Jews from their homeland and by killing them for teaching Torah. But that is just where they made their mistake: they did not realize, as the Nazis did—as Rabbi Shapira did—that the Jews and Judaism are of a piece. And what better way to inflict suffering upon the Holy One than to destroy Judaism through the torture and murder His children?

On November 30, 1940, Rabbi Shapira relates his first insight into God's suffering over the slaughter of Israel, when he cites the talmudic teaching that when even a single person suffers, the Shekhinah cries out, "O woe, My head! O woe, My arms!" (See *Sanhedrin* 46a; *Chagigah* 15b.) In the mystical contexts, the head is associated with *Binah* and the two arms with *Chesed* and *Gevurah*. Which means: as the Jews come under assault, the Understanding through which the Divine light enters the world is obscured, as are Divine Love and Divine Judgment. The Nazi assault on the Jews is so extreme that there is no understanding of what is taking place, no compassion for the Jews, and no judgment upon the Nazis: God's hands, as it were, are tied, and He goes into a swoon, something like the "madness of God" that Elie Wiesel invokes through his character Zalman.[72] If God goes mad, it is for the same reason that other fathers went mad when they witnessed the slaughter of their families.[73] He goes mad because His hands are tied. And we—not the Jews who prayed the Shema "at the very doors of the gas chambers"[74]—have tied them. We have tied them with our thoughts and our deeds, with our words and our silence. We have tied them with a philosophical outlook that casts aside Torah and the prohibition against murder. Thus eliminating the Commanding Voice of Torah, we are deaf to the Commanding Voice of Auschwitz, deaf to every "I" except the "I" of the ego.

More than a year later, on February 14, 1942, Rabbi Shapira returns to his concern with God's suffering by writing, "A Jew, tortured in his suffering, may think he is the only one in pain, as though his personal pain and the pain of all other Jews has no effect above, God forbid. But . . . we learn in the Talmud (*Chagigah* 15b; *Sanhedrin* 46a) in the name of R. Emir, . . . God, as it were, suffers with a Jew much more than that person himself feels it."[75] Whereas R. Yose "heard a Divine Voice like the cooing of a dove," the Rebbe goes on to say, we know from Jeremiah 25:30 that "God roars, howling over His city."[76] And His Holy City is His Shekhinah, which, in mystical terms, is the body of Israel. How does God roar? Through the cry of His people, through the screams of "Mama" that reverberated throughout the camps and ghettos and shattered the souls of the Jews, through screams that threatened to undermine the very fabric of creation.

This claim concerning the extremity of God's suffering comes from a man whose own suffering was extreme, a man who himself roared and screamed, but like a Chasid: silently.[77] Devoted to Jews and Judaism, the rabbi maintains that "possibly because God is infinite—and hence unknowable in the world—His pain at the suffering of the Jewish people is also infinite. . . . And so, the world continues to exist steadfast, it is not obliterated by God's pain and His voice at the suffering of His people and the destruction of His house, because God's pain never enters into the world."[78] It does not enter, Rabbi Shapira concludes, because God retreats to a place of concealment to weep. The Talmud, in fact, speaks of a special place that God has for weeping, the place "called *Mistarim* [meaning 'concealment'], in the inner chambers" (*Chagigah* 5b).[79] For God's pain cannot enter the world without destroying it. Thus the angel Metatron, who rules over this world (see *Sanhedrin* 94a; *Yevamot* 16b; *Shemot Rabbah* 17:4),[80] weeps in God's place (*Tanchuma Vaetchanan* 6). This weeping is the outcome not of Jewish sin but of the Nazi evil: God is driven into hiding, where He weeps in secret and roars in silence so that just enough of the Divine Presence abides to sustain Creation. Or does it?

OLAM SHOAH: THE CHALLENGE FOR JEWISH THOUGHT

Hannah Arendt once stated that totalitarianism had transformed not only categories of thought and human nature but also essence of reality itself.[81] About this she was right, but in ways that even she could not fathom. According to the mystical tradition, when God entered creation to reveal the Torah at Mount Sinai, it was not merely a matter of our receiving more information. No, the essence of all of creation was transformed. Once the *mitzvot* were manifest, the *Olam Asiyah,* the World of Action, attained a fullness, a *shlemut,* or "wholeness," that it had not previously known. With the sealing of the Covenant at Mount Sinai, creation approached a consummation that will reach completion with the messianic redemption.

If, however, God has withdrawn too deeply into the *Mistarim,* then creation may have undergone another transformation. Indeed, the great mystic of the eighteenth century, Moshe Chayim Luzzatto, teaches, "When either the Force of good or that of evil gains power, its qualities and effects influence all created things, both through their Roots and their Branches,"[82] that is, throughout the ten *sefirot.* Is it possible that this *tsimtsum,* this contraction of the Holy One in the Shoah, has resulted in the emergence of a new world, of an *Olam Shoah,* a World of Shoah? Rabbi Shapira's insights lead us to entertain such a notion, however horrific it may be. Indeed, his thinking not only informs post-Holocaust Jewish thought, it instills it with horror: with Rabbi Shapira, we experience the *shudder* of thought.

In the *Esh Kodesh,* the Rebbe writes in horror, writes *through* his horror: "It is a marvel how the world exists after so much screaming."[83] Theodor Adorno's fear comes to mind: "Everything," he writes, "has been destroyed without realizing it; humankind continues to vegetate, creeping along after events that even the survivors cannot really survive, on a rubbish heap that has made even reflection on one's own damaged state useless."[84] Can it be that, mystically speaking, the Holocaust resulted in the collapse of creation, and we did not even notice it? After all, the mystics teach that if the *ki tov*—the Divine assertion that "it is very good"—is removed from the world, then "the whole world is destroyed and *tov* [the good] is not to be found in the world."[85] This surely seems to be the case in the Shoah. Can it be, then, that we grope in the ashen darkness of a World of Shoah, and not in the World of Action where action is commanded by a viable God? Can it be, therefore, that the question posed by this event concerns not so much God and evil as it does world and evil?

Raising this question, we come to a realization: the question of theodicy is not the real question. It certainly is not a question intelligible for Jewish thought. No, the question is: How can such radical evil and the universe itself exist in the same space and time? For without God, not only is there infinite room for evil, there is also no room for a world—at least not for any world as humanity has long understood the term. In the previous chapter, we saw that the word *olam* means not only "world" but also "humanity" and "community." Has the darkness of the Shoah not rendered us blind to humanity and community? Indeed, the abyss of the *Olam Shoah* is the blindness itself. And so in the *Olam Shoah* we curl up in a "fortress," a *metsudah* that might pass for a home, only to discover that it is in fact nothing more than a *metsodah,* a comfortable "trap." Waiting for a message that does not come, we drift from diversion to diversion. We do not live: we merely hope to live. We do not dwell: we languish. We grow angry. And our being "angry," our being *zaum,* lies in our feeling as though we mean nothing, as though we were "trifling," another meaning of *zaum.* Indeed, we feel as though we were "cursed," which is still another meaning of *zaum,* cursed without anything higher to curse us.

The problem? Our eyes have grown so used to the darkness that we do not notice it is dark. It no longer occurs to us that *in truth* God creates humanity in His image and likeness and that *in truth* His Divine Presence, His Shekhinah, is precisely the human community. It is not postmodern to think in such terms. But it is Jewish. With the Holocaust, the problem that staggers the imagination often lies in the extreme forms of suffering and murder, in the zeros that signify the nothingness of such huge and incomprehensible numbers. But the problem that eludes the imagination in the aftermath of Auschwitz—the problem for Jewish thought—is this: we can no longer *imagine* that as we think, we stand before the Holy One, the Creator of heaven and earth, who continually puts to us the question "Where are you!?"—which is both a question and an outcry from One who is "the Witness, the Judge, and the Plaintiff."[86] That is why Jewish thought faces an unprecedented crisis. It is a matter not so much of acumen as of sheer imagination: if we are to emerge from the *Olam Shoah,* we have to muster the imagination—and the courage—to respond to the Holy One from the ruins of the *Olam Shoah.* But to do that, we must venture into the ruins—and pray, as Rabbi Yose did. In this case, however, the ruins are more than the ruins of a culture and a people—they are the ruins of thought.

Among the upheavals for thought after the Shoah is a reversal of Ivan Karamazov's famous assertion. Whereas Ivan rightly understood that if there is no God, then nothing is true and everything is permitted,[87] the Shoah has reversed the proposition: if nothing is true and everything is permitted, then there is no God—or rather there is no room for the weeping God to find His way back into creation.[88] And so we are left to the darkness over the face of the deep, to the *tohu-vavohu,* of the World of Shoah, which is the postmodern world, a world in which so few answer, "Here I am," because so few hear the Divine cry of "Where are you?" At best, we insist that God come out of hiding and answer us. Or we declare that there is no God and therefore no question: there are only value systems and systems of signs, only power struggles and culture wars—that is the *Olam Shoah*: it is the postmodern emptiness and intellectual game playing that characterize post-Holocaust thought. In the aftermath of Auschwitz, we are left with the intellectual "café" that Levinas describes as

> a place of casual social intercourse, without mutual responsibility. One goes in without needing to. One sits down without being tired. One drinks without being thirsty. . . . The café is not a place. It is a non-place for a non-society, for a society without solidarity, without tomorrow, without commitment, without common interests, a game society. The café, house of games, is the point through which the game penetrates life and dissolves it. Society, without yesterday or tomorrow, without responsibility, without seriousness—distraction, dissolution. . . . Here you are, each at your own little table with your cup or your glass. You relax completely to

the point of not being obligated to anyone or anything; and it is because it is possible to go and relax in a café that one tolerates the horrors and injustices of a world without a soul. The world as a game from which everyone can pull out and exist only for himself, a place of forgetfulness— of forgetfulness of the other—that is the café.[89]

And that is the *Olam Shoah.* In the *Olam Shoah,* the academic enclaves and intellectual circles have been transformed into so many cafés, where we clamor after the anesthesia of philosophical oblivion.

And yet an opening to the *Olam Asiyah,* to the world in which a homeless humanity may yet find a dwelling place, remains: the God who has turned away reveals a trace of Himself in the outcry of figures like the Rebbe of the Warsaw Ghetto. For God reveals himself in the disturbance of His witness, even—or precisely—in the witness who cries out over His absence. While the silence that Rabbi Shapira collided with was "total," as Nehemia Polen correctly points out, "he refused to accept the silence as definitive. He felt certain that a new revelation would yet emerge in some unspecified way from the catastrophe."[90] And that revelation lay in the phenomenon of Rabbi Shapira himself: he *was* the revelation, he and others like him. Hence, says Polen, "his teaching and writing were acts of spiritual transcendence, a renewed affirmation of the ancient verities of God, Israel, and Torah, but under circumstances so extreme, so astonishing, that the affirmation bespeaks a *novum,* an emergent utterance yielding awe and wonder: in short, a revelation."[91] If an *Olam Shoah* has indeed unfolded, there remains an avenue of return to the *Olam Asiyah,* a return not to how it used to be but to how it is meant to be.

How, then, according to Jewish mysticism, can Jewish thought effect a return to the Divine Presence so that His Presence may itself return? There are three ways.

First, it may help to consider some of Rabbi Shapira's thoughts on Jewish thought. He views Jewish thought, for example, not as a conceptual system but as a means of drawing nigh unto the Holy One; it is characterized not by the stasis of categories but by the dynamic of a "delight" in God and a love for the people of Israel.[92] In this connection, he introduces the notion of *machshavah gufanit,* a "thinking with the body"— that is where Jewish thought must begin: with the body, and not with the brain.[93] Only with the body can we experience and express the *hit-lahavut,* or "enthusiasm," of delighting in God and loving our fellow humans beings; only with the body can we *serve,* which is the whole point of Jewish thought.[94] What prepares the body for Jewish thought? According to Rabbi Shapira, it is the performance of *mitzvot.*[95] Perhaps the most crucial requirement for Jewish thought in the *Olam Shoah* is this: no matter how remote or unreal the Holy One may seem, Jewish thinking must proceed in the conviction that we think and act in His presence.[96] Because He is more interested in our deeds than in our thoughts, we must think *with* our deeds, and not merely with our intellect. As thoughts influence deeds, so do deeds influence thoughts. Therefore, Jewish thought requires Jewish deed. And it is Jewish mysticism that determines the link between the two. If we are to think our way from *Olam Shoah* into *Olam Asiyah,* then we must pursue and sustain the three pillars upon which the creation stands, as it is written in the Mishnah: Torah, prayer, and acts of loving kindness (*Pirke Avot* 1:2). That is where we make the movement below that initiates the movement above.

Second, if we are to turn God's tears of sadness into tears of joy and draw Him out of the *Mistarim,* we must continue to challenge and question God; we must continue to disturb His sleep, even as He disturbs ours—*in the name of Torah.* As it is written in the Talmud, God likes to be defeated by His children (*Bava Metzia* 59b; *Pesachim* 119a).

Third, we must fill our days with joy and thanksgiving, since, according to Chasidic teaching, the gates to the upper realms are unlocked only through joy.[97] Joy in what? Not, certainly, in suffering, but in the truth that suffering *matters,* absolutely and from on high. As Schindler correctly notes, Rabbi Shapira sees God's hiddenness as a hiddenness in suffering.[98] Therefore, although this can in no way justify suffering, in human suffering there is a revelation of the Holy One, who suffers as well, as long as we are disturbed by the suffering and not indifferent toward it. Only if suffering matters can we move from the *Olam Shoah* to the *Olam Asiyah,* and from there to the upper realms that constitute the depth dimension of our lives. Only then can we regain the *absolute* authority of the prohibition against murder.

The abyss of the *Olam Shoah,* made of the Nazi assault on the Divine prohibition against murder, is made of murder. It feeds on murder. It insists on murder. It glorifies murder. It transforms murder into a martyrdom that is horrifically unlike the martyrdom of the Ten Martyrs. Whereas the Jewish tradition sees martyrdom, or Kiddush Hashem, in terms of a choice to die rather than commit murder (see *Pesachim* 25a–25b; *Sanhedrin* 74a; *Ketuvot* 19a), "martyrdom" in the *Olam Shoah* is a dying precisely *in order to* commit murder. And instead of asserting that this is wrong, we sigh and say, "Well, that's how they define martyrdom"—as if a word can mean anything at all. To be sure, in the radical exile that is *Olam Shoah,* words have come to mean anything, everything, and nothing.

In chapter 4 we noted that a key to the return from exile is a return of meaning to the word. We also noted that *galah,* "to be exiled," is a cognate of the noun *gilui,* meaning "revelation." And we pointed out that the difference between *galah* and *geulah,* between "exile" and "redemption," is the insertion of the letter *alef* into the word. What does the *alef,* the silent letter, signify? Meaning. The presence of the *alef* of the Divine *Anokhi* is just what is veiled in the proliferation of the *kelipot* of the Shoah. Even in our exile in the *Olam Shoah,* then, we have the seeds of revelation and redemption. Which means: our exile in the *Olam Shoah* is not something we endure "for our sins." Rather, it harbors a mission to which we are summoned. In Jewish terms, that mission is to hasten the coming of the Messiah, for the Messianic Kingdom has its foundation not in the upper, unearthly realms but precisely in the *Olam Asiyah* that is *this* world.

9

Though the Messiah May Tarry

When the talmudic sage Rabbi Yehoshua ben Levi asked Elijah
when the Messiah would come, the prophet directed him to a
leper at the gates of Rome, saying, "Ask him yourself." And so
Rabbi Yehoshua asked the Messiah, "When will you come?"
And the Messiah answered, "Today"—that is, "Today, if you
heed the Voice of Hashem."—Talmud Bavli, *Sanhedrin* 98a

The Talmud teaches that the name of the Messiah is among the seven
things that preceded Creation (*Pesachim* 54a).[1] The Zohar teaches that
"the 'spirit of God which hovered over the face of the deep' (Genesis 1:2)
is the spirit of the Messiah" (*Zohar* I, 240a). Therefore, like the Torah
itself, the Messiah precedes the beginning; like the Torah itself, the Messiah determines the meaning of all that is from beyond all that is; like
the Torah itself, the Messiah is essential to all of creation. If Jewish thought
cannot establish a place for the Messiah in the post-Shoah world, then
the world will languish in the shadows of Auschwitz, just as the Messiah
languishes at the gates of Rome.[2] And the Jews will be reduced to no
more than a vanishing ethnic group, despite the establishment of the State
of Israel.[3] No spirit will hover over the face of the deep, and we shall be
left with the deep alone.

Among the Thirteen Principles of Faith outlined by Maimonides, the twelfth is an affirmation of *Ani maamin beemunah shlemah beviat haMashiach; veaf al pi sheyimanmeah, im kol zeh achakeh lo bekol yom sheyavo*: "I believe with complete faith in the coming of the Messiah; even if he may tarry, no matter what, I shall await his coming every day." That is, I believe despite the evidence of the eyes. I believe no matter how foolish the belief. And not only shall I "await" his coming, but I shall "expect" it, which is another meaning of *achakeh,* as if he might come at any instant, with the performance of *this* very *mitzvah*—even and especially in a post-Shoah world. To be sure, the refrain of this *Ani maamin* has been set to music and is sung at many Yom Hashoah observances. It is also the title of Elie Wiesel's *Ani Maamin: A Song Lost and Found Again*; unless a song of the Messiah can be found, we shall be lost.

Like any affirmation of faith, *Ani maamin beemunah shlemah beviat haMashiach* affirms something both literal and symbolic. It has meaning on all the levels of meaning that belong to Jewish thinking: *pshat,* which is the literal sense; *remez,* which is the allegorical level; *drash,* the homiletical or moral meaning; and *sod,* the inexhaustible mystical meaning. The wait for the Messiah is a wait for something real, on all levels, no matter how long it may take; otherwise, the wait itself is unreal and pointless, no matter how persistent it may be. Just as Jewish thinking is rooted in the Jewish faith that something real transpired at Mount Sinai, so does it live in a movement toward something real that will transpire in a messianic age. But what, exactly, will transpire?

Martin Buber maintains that it will come with the realization of "the true community" so that the Messiah is he who makes it possible for God and humanity to dwell in the world, throughout the world; Buber might even say that the Messiah *is* that dwelling. The "longing for God," he writes, "is the longing to prepare a place for Him in the true community; its consciousness of Israel is the consciousness that out of it the true community will emerge; its wait for the Messiah is the wait for the true community."[4] Recalling that the Hebrew word for "community," *edah,* also means "testimony," we see that "the true community" lies in "the true testimony," a testimony to the truth of the holiness of the human being created in the image and likeness of the Holy One. For Jewish consciousness, the longing for God is not a longing to enter His kingdom; rather, it is a longing to enable Him to enter *this* kingdom. The flesh-and-blood reality of *this* world is what makes both the wait for the Messiah and the advent of the Messiah something as concrete as human community.

As Buber explains, two things are required for the creation of a true community: each member of the community must live in a relation to a transcendent center, and each must live in a relation to the other that is expressive of the higher relation.[5] The failed utopian movements of history have shown that neither the vertical nor the horizontal relation can stand on its own; each requires the other, and only the Messiah can open up both. Emil Fackenheim has rightly asserted that "the 'brotherhood of man,' unless it is part of a messianic hope, is a romantic illusion."[6] For Jewish thought, "the brotherhood of man" is no illusion. Therefore, Jewish thought—*Machshavah Yehudit*—is messianic to the core. That is why a Jew strives to think and act in such a way as to hasten the coming of the Messiah, *bimherah beyameinu,* "speedily in our days." Which is to say: we expect the Messiah to show himself *now.*

The messianic age, therefore, is always upon us: the Messiah lives in every generation, in a variety of disguises. According to the passage from the Talmud cited above, the Messiah told Rabbi Yehoshua that he would come today, if we should heed the Voice of Hashem. But what would heeding the Voice of Hashem amount to? It would at least entail coming to the aid of the leper or the beggar, the widow, the orphan, and the stranger. The Messiah, whom we keep in exile as long as we keep ourselves from Torah, is often disguised as a beggar or a leper—often as a child or as an old man—that is, as one who is in need of others. From figures such as these we receive the Messiah's plea to heed the Voice of Hashem. Jewish thinking heeds that plea. The major obstacle to Jewish thought, what renders us deaf to the plea couched in the outcry of our neighbor, is our complacent, egocentric indifference toward other human beings. Our own exile, an exile from one another, then, is tied to the exile of the Messiah.

In the previous chapter, we considered how the mystical tradition, particularly in the context of Rabbi Shapira's Chasidic outlook, informs Jewish thought. Here, we see that Chasidism, more than informing our way of thinking, is a key to the advent of the Messiah. Indeed, Chasidism is about the advent of the Messiah. It is written, for instance, that when the Baal Shem Tov ascended to the upper worlds and demanded to know when the Messiah would come, the Messiah himself told the Besht, "When your teachings will spread and be revealed throughout the world."[7] Why do Lubavitch Chasidim rejoice in every *mitzvah* performed rather than lament the one not performed? Because the next *mitzvah* may be the one that puts us over the top so that the Messiah may be revealed, for a *mitzvah* is a connection to God, a portal through which the light of holiness illuminates the world. Once that light is bright enough, the Messiah will be manifest. Not only shall we see the path to him, he will be able to see his way toward us. From a Chasidic point of view, this is the meaning of the teaching "The *mitzvah* is the lamp and the Torah the light" (Proverbs 6:23). The time of the Shoah is a time of the extinguishing of that light. In the post-Shoah period, we are summoned to become lamplighters.

It is no accident that images of night and darkness are often used to invoke the time of the Shoah.[8] Because the Chasidic testimony is about bringing the light of Torah into the world, no other testimony in Jewish life came more radically under the Nazi assault. And no other testimony has flourished more successfully, in more places throughout the world, than the Chasidic testimony. Jews of all persuasions turn to the tales of the Chasidim for learning, precisely because the soul of Judaism lives in those tales. Very few speeches from Jewish pulpits begin with the words, "We have a tale from the Reform masters. . . ." But many open by saying, "There is an old Chasidic tale. . . ." It is not for nothing that the most prominent voice to emerge from the Holocaust is the voice of the Chasid Elie Wiesel; it is not for nothing that so many are drawn to him in their reaction to the Shoah. This seeking after a voice from the ashes is part of the messianic longing. And sustaining that longing is aim of Chasidism.

But who, according to Jewish teaching, is the one we long for?

JEWISH TEACHINGS ON THE AWAITED ONE

There are perhaps no views in Jewish tradition more confused and conflicting than the views on the Messiah.[9] A few things, however, are clear. The one whom the Jews await is not the son of God, any more than any other human being is a child of the Holy One.[10] He is neither the incarnation of God nor part of a triune divinity; the Midrash, in fact, speaks of his mortal death, saying that when the Messiah dies, the World to Come will be ushered in (see *Tanchuma Ekev* 7). Further, he is not born of a virgin, who in turn requires an immaculate conception. Indeed, from a Jewish perspective, the conception of any human being can be "immaculate," since in marriage the sexual union that produces a child is itself holy, as is the one born from that union. Hence the dual meaning of *kiddushin*: it translates both as "holiness" and as "marriage." And because we do not inherit Adam's sin, we are born innocent and untainted, as we affirm each morning in our prayers: *neshamah shenatata biy tehorah hiy,* "the soul You have placed within me is pure."

According to Jewish teaching, children are not in need of redemption—they are the source of redemption, as the Vilna Gaon maintains.[11] In the Midrash, Rabbi Assi teaches that children begin their study of Torah with the Book of Leviticus because "children are pure, and the sacrifices are pure; so let the pure come and engage in the study of the pure" (*Vayikra Rabbah* 7:3). The one whom we await, then, is not one whose blood will cleanse us of our *inherently* sinful being; rather, he will return us, body and soul, to the inherently holy *relation* to God and to one another. This may be one reason why the Midrash calls the Messiah the Son of Perets (*Bereshit Rabbah* 12:6), the child born to Judah and Tamar (see Genesis 38:29): the name Perets means "breach" or "opening," and the Messiah is he who creates the most complete opening for holiness to flow into this realm.

Jesus' statement "My kingdom is not of this world" (John 18:36) is alien to Jewish thinking about the Anointed One. Jewishly speaking, the Messiah's kingdom is *in* this world and *of* this world: *this* world, the *Olam Asiyah,* as Adin Steinsaltz points out, "is the most perfect form of the Revelation of God. It is said, 'The existence of the material is the substance of the Divine.' In other words, the highest values are found within matter, in the material world."[12] Therefore, the Messiah comes not to deliver us *from* the world but to draw Torah *into* the world, so transparently that the word of the Holy One will become part of every human heart (Jeremiah 31:33), and justice and righteousness will reign throughout this world (Isaiah 9:6). Swords will be beaten into plowshares, and "nation will not lift up sword against nation" (Micah 4:3). The Jewish wait for the Messiah is a wait for and a preparation of such a world.

With regard to other prophecies of the Messiah, in the famous disputation at Barcelona held in 1263 Nachmanides pointed out that "you will never find in any book of Jewish tradition—neither the Talmud nor the Hagadoth—that the Messiah son of David will be killed, that he will be handed over into the hands of his enemies, or that he will be buried with the wicked."[13] Most prevalent of all the prophecies as yet unfulfilled is that the Jews will be returned from their exile. Various prophets invoke various signs of the coming of the Messiah, but almost all of them invoke this one: the ingathering of the Jews, and the end of the exile.[14] In the Midrash, in fact, we have the teaching that in the time of the Messiah the nations of the world will assist in the return of the Jews to the Holy Land (*Shir Hashirim Rabbah* 4:8:2).

Beyond that, the teachings are less clear and often more mysterious. In the Talmud, for example, it is written, "Know that there exists on high a substance called 'body' [*guf*] in which are found all the souls destined for life. The son of David will not come before all the souls which are in the *guf* have completed their descent to the earth" (*Yevamot* 63b; *Avodah Zarah* 5a; *Niddah* 13b; see also *Zohar* I, 119a). This mystical tradition underscores the connection between the upper worlds and this world. Because the most crucial point of connection for channeling holiness into this world is between the *sefirot* of *Yesod* and *Malkhut,* the Messiah is mystically associated with *Yesod,* which is the Foundation of all creation.[15] This mystical view associates the completeness of creation with the coming of the Messiah; it also articulates a connection between each soul and all of creation—between each soul and the Messiah himself. On the day of his coming, "Hashem will be One and His Name will be One" (Zechariah 14:9). Which is to say: in the Tetragrammaton, the upper letters *yud-hey* and the lower letters *vav-hey* will be joined so that the holiness of the Holy One will be manifest throughout the world. Thinking and doing will be one; teaching and practice will be one; love of God and love of neighbor will be one.

Of course, Jewish tradition has many other teachings concerning the Messiah. The Midrash, for example, says that Gog and Magog will launch three wars against the Messiah in the winter month of Tevet. Messiah ben Joseph will fight those wars; in some accounts, he will be killed and then followed by Messiah ben David, who will usher in the everlasting age of peace.[16] In addition to Gog and Magog, the archenemy of the Messiah is sometimes called Armillus, who is spawned from Satan's mating with a stone statue in Rome. Forty days after the spawning of Armillus, Messiah ben David will rise up to build the Temple in Jerusalem and defeat the offspring of Satan.[17] That Armillus is the offspring of Satan's mating with a stone is indicative of the Messiah's defeat of the view that what is real is what can be weighed, measured, and counted, and that power, therefore, is all that matters. Further, along the lines of what we saw in the last chapter—namely, that the Torah is black fire on white fire (*Devarim Rabbah* 3:12)—it is said that the Messiah will reveal the meaning of the blanks between the words and in the margins of the Torah, the meaning of the white fire.[18] Perhaps he will also reveal the meaning of other flames.

He is the one who will voice the ineffable to bring about the ultimate *tikkun haolam*. He is the one whose coming post-Holocaust Jewish thought must labor to bring about—even though he may tarry. Which means: Jewish thought, especially in the post-Holocaust era, must be steeped in faith.

FAITH AS WAITING, WAITING AS DOING

Jewish thinking about "faith," about *emunah*, entails much more than matters of belief or the acceptance of a doctrine. It is not reducible to the "assent of the understanding to what is believed" that Thomas Aquinas defines as faith,[19] nor to the passion that Kierkegaard defines as faith.[20] In addition to "faith," *emunah* means "conscientiousness," "honesty," and "trust." In the Talmud, for example, a person who does not keep his word is called a *mechusar amanah*, literally, "one who is lacking in honesty" or "one who is lacking in faith" (see, for example, *Bava Metzia* 49a); each amounts to the other. The mystical tradition defines "faith" as *devekut*, that is, as a clinging to God that lies in a devotion to one's fellow human being (see, for example, *Tolodot Yaakov Yosef, Yitro* 6). From the standpoint of Jewish thought, there is no question of "faith or deeds"; each is a manifestation of the other. Faith, then, implies a certain character, a certain condition of the soul, which in turn implies living in a loving relation with other people, and not just with God. Just as thought is an emanation of the God who "thinks" us, so is faith an emanation of the God who commands us. God is not the object of belief; rather, He is the subject who summons honesty.

Looking at other dimensions of *emunah,* we note that the cognate verb *aman* means "to foster" or "to bring up"; *neeman* is "to be educated" as well as "to be found true" or "trustworthy," and the adjective *amun* means both "faithful" and "educated." Fackenheim, understanding these shades of meaning of *emunah,* describes faith as a "listening openness while yet no voice is heard."[21] Rabbi Steinsaltz states it in even stronger terms: "Faith is, then, not a matter of simple believing but of that special quality which goes beyond the mind, which is of wisdom—that is to say, it is an experience directly connected with the Divine and not with knowing this or that about Him."[22] In a word, faith is not the opposite of disbelief; indeed, Abraham Joshua Heschel points out that in biblical Hebrew there is no word for "doubt."[23] Rather, faith is the opposite of folly, the complete reversal of our deadly isolation within the illusory ego.

Thus Heschel writes, "Faith is the beginning of the end of egocentricity. 'To have faith is *to disregard self-regard,*' said the Kotzker. It involves the realization that, confined to our ego, we are in another man's house. Our home is where the self lives in fellowship with Him Who is all and Who includes us. 'I believe in God' does not mean that *I* accept the fact of *His* existence. It does not signify that *I* come first, then *God,* as the syntax of the sentence implies. The opposite is true. Because God exists, I am able to believe."[24] Which means: I do not "believe" in God, as someone might believe in the tooth fairy. Rather, God "believes" in me—and through me. Truth happens through me. Torah enters the world through me, as an *event.* For the wisdom that is faith unfolds through action. It is an action that unites the Divine Name into One, as it is written in the Zohar: "The essence of the mystery of faith is to know that this is a complete Name. This knowledge that Y-H-V-H is one with *Elokim* is indeed the synthesis of the whole Torah, both the Written and the Oral, for 'Torah' stands for both, the former being symbolic of Y-H-V-H and the latter of *Elokim*" (*Zohar* II, 161b). In other words, faith means imparting flesh and blood to our teaching of Torah through deeds of Torah. Faith is an unfolding, an overflowing of sanctity into the world, from within the world.

Having faith, then, is not a matter of affirming, "I believe in God," as Emmanuel Levinas correctly points out, but of declaring, "Here am I, Your servant, ready to serve,"[25] ready to enter a service that is the opposite of servitude. Stated differently, to have faith is to know one's name, in which is inscribed the meaning and the mission of a life. It is to live in a "covenant," which is a meaning of the cognate *amanah*, and to live in a covenant is to live not just with a particular belief—which may wax and wane—but according to the *mitzvot*, through which we enter into a partnership with God to create a world where the Messiah may become manifest. Understood in terms of covenant, faith becomes an issue for God as well. In the psalms, for example, we declare that God accomplishes His works *beemunah*, "through faith" (Psalms 33:4), and that He judges the nations *beemunato*, "in His faith" or, as it is often translated, "in His truth" (Psalms 96:13). Each morning upon waking, we affirm in the *Modeh Ani* God's "great faith" in us for returning us to life and sending us on the day's mission: it is truth that returns us to life, and, as Nachman of Breslov has said, "the only way to attain faith is through truth."[26] Jewishly understood, faith entails truth, relation, understanding, partnership, readiness, judgment, and more.

This is why "faith," as Heschel puts it, "is the achievement of the ages, an effort accumulated over centuries."[27] In biblical language, Heschel points out, "the religious man is not called a 'believer,' as he is for example in Islam *(mu'min)*, but *yare hashem*,"[28] that is, one who has attained a profound awe of God—an awe steeped in wisdom[29]—through study, prayer, and actions. Chief among these actions, according to the Chasidic master Nachman of Breslov, is having children. "The Hebrew word for 'faith,'" he notes, "is *emunah*. Turn the letters into number, and the *gematria* is *banim*—'children.'"[30] Where there is faith, there are children. For where there are children, there is a future we await and an action we perform.

With these dimensions of faith in mind, Rabbi Abraham Isaac Kook offers additional insights into the nature of faith as a waiting and a doing. "Faith and love," he writes, "are always interconnected when both shine in the soul with perfection, and when the light of one of them is complete, through it, the other is aroused and emerges from the depths of the spirit. . . . The Torah is the love, and the *mitzvot*, the faith."[31] Jewishly speaking, love lies in learning, and faith lies in doing, that is, in a way of life expressive of love and learning through the observance of the *mitzvot.* To believe, then, with perfect faith in the coming of the Messiah is to take up the stance that Rav Kook describes: it means living according to the *mitzvot,* loving our fellow human beings, and striving for a deeper understanding of Torah. Just how urgent that striving can be, we discover in the aftermath of the Shoah. Rav Kook, however, did not live to witness the singular horrors of the Shoah. Although his teachings can certainly add to our post-Holocaust Jewish thinking, faith in the coming of the Messiah, in its post-Holocaust contexts, must be understood from additional perspectives.

In the Talmud, Rabbi Yochanan says that the Son of David will come in a generation that is either altogether righteous or altogether evil (*Sanhedrin* 98a); Yehuda Hanasi maintains that he will come in a time of catastrophe (*Sanhedrin* 97a). And Jews find it difficult to picture a catastrophe greater than the Shoah. Shall we then abandon our faith in the coming of the Messiah, since he has tarried too long? Shall we jettison the trust and the covenant, the learning and the integrity, that make faith what it is? Eliezer Berkovits has a good response to this question: "In the presence of the holy faith of the crematoria, the ready faith of those who were not there is vulgarity. But the disbelief of the sophisticated intellectual in the midst of an affluent society—in the light of the holy disbelief of the crematoria—is obscenity."[32] Jewishly speaking, disbelief can be holy because, as we have seen, faith is not reducible to belief. It can be holy when, insisting on the truth of what Jewish tradition places in our care, it insists on a certain fidelity on the part of the One who summons us to *emunah.* Here, holy disbelief is not no much an absence of faith as it is the presence of outrage in the midst of faith.

After Auschwitz, then, the wait for the Messiah is an impatient wait, an outraged wait, a wait made not only of doing but also of questioning. That is where we encounter God: in the question, in the *shelah,* at the center of which is *el,* or "God"—God is alive in the question. A question concerning what? Not the truth of Torah. No, it is a question put to the God of the Covenant precisely in the name of Torah; it is a confrontation with the One who—if one dares to speak such words—seems to have abandoned His Torah. Remaining in the Covenant, we remain within the relation, and we have good reason for our outcry; abandoning the Covenant, we have no grounds for complaining, which, outside the Covenant, amounts to little more than pretentious whining. If we abandon the Torah—if we abandon the wait—then the outrage and the question become sheer vanity, as does everything else. If we abandon the Torah, the outrage and the question amount to no more than the self-serving, indignant, intellectual arrogance so common in academic circles. Only when we adhere to Torah does God adhere to Torah. And only when we adhere to Torah are we in a position to argue with God, as the Torah commands us to do.[33]

A teaching from Torah is pertinent here. It concerns the discovery of the body of a murder victim "lying in the field" (Deuteronomy 21:1) and whose murderer is unknown. In such a case, the elders of the nearest Jewish community must come out and say to God, "Our hands have not shed this blood. . . . Suffer not innocent blood to remain in the midst of Your people Israel" (Deuteronomy 21:7–8). That is, the hands with which we perform the *mitzvot* of Torah have not brought this about—how, then, God, can You stand silently by? Similarly, Jewish law states that if we find someone who has been murdered, with his body and clothing bloodied, and there is no prospect of identifying the murderer, then we must bury that person just as we found him (*Kitsur Shulchan Arukh* 197:9). The point? To put the question and the outrage in God's face, as if to say, "Behold what has become of Your creation! What are You going to do about it?" Of course, the vast majority of the Jews' murderers in the Shoah were never identified.

The code also states that "benevolent people who in their lifetime fed the poor at their table should be interred in a coffin made out of the boards of that table" (*Kitsur Shulchan Arukh* 199:1). Why? To demonstrate to God, even in death, our commanded, covenantal care for the most vulnerable of our fellow human beings, for the Messiah himself is surely among them. And there is no shortage of the poor whom we might have at our table. Therefore, the souls of the righteous may rise, stand on their tables made into their coffins, and cry to God, "When will You seat the poor at *Your* table?" This question and this care are the basis of the waiting for the Messiah that is also a doing.

To "believe" *beemunah shlemah*, in "complete faith," is to draw both the question and the care into our thoughts, words, and deeds—into what the mystical tradition describes as God's *levushim,* or "clothing." That is how the Invisible One is made manifest, which in turn makes manifest the one whom we await. This *shlemah,* this "completeness" or "wholeness" of faith, is the *shalom,* the "peace," that we seek in the Messiah. It is not a state of contentment, which may characterize a state of blissful indifference. Rather, it is about maintaining the tension of the longing and the intensity of the care. It is about a certain strife of the spirit, a certain post-Shoah wounding, without which we are not whole. For in the *afterward* of the Shoah, we bear a new wound as the sign of the Covenant, without which there is no peace. It is an open wound.

MESSIANIC DIMENSIONS
OF COVENANTAL JEWISH THOUGHT

We have seen that a cognate of *emunah,* the word *amanah,* means "covenant." Living in faith, the human being expresses the covenantal relation to God through a care for the other human being, as when Abraham rushed out to greet the three strangers approaching his tent (see Genesis 18:2)—his first action after sealing the Covenant of Circumcision. Thus the tradition teaches that Abraham was an innkeeper who would seek out travelers to whom he could offer a *place* at his table and thereby draw the *presence* of the Holy One into the world (see *Sotah* 10b; see also *Bereshit Rabbah* 48:7). And his second action? It was to enter into an argument with God (Genesis 18:25). With the first Jew, then, we see two basic dimensions of covenantal Jewish thought in the post-Holocaust era: care and outrage.

For Jewish thinking rooted in Judaism, however, "covenant" is not just *brit*: it is *brit milah,* which means both a "covenant of circumcision" and a "covenant of the word."[34] On the basis of this association between circumcision and word, the Chasidic master Rabbi Mordechai Yosef of Isbitza teaches that the *brit* of the foreskin and the *brit* of the tongue (cf. *Sefer Yetzirah* 1:3) are one and the same.[35] Both demand truth, which in turn makes both a matter of faith. In Hebrew, the difference between *milah* as "word" and *milah* as "circumcision" is the insertion of the letter *yud* into the latter. In mystical terms, this *yud* is the *chashmal,* the "speaking silence," discussed in the last chapter. It is the "word within the word," which is the word as covenant and covenant as meaning: to enter into the Covenant is to enter into meaning. For the insertion of *yud* into the word—the insertion of the letter with a numerical value of ten—signifies the addition of ten to the word, which is the revelation of the Ten Utterances, without which there is no meaning.

This revelation of meaning transforms the word, the *milah*, into a sign of the Covenant, making it a *brit milah*. Revelation makes silence speak, and when silence speaks, covenant happens. Hence it is written in the Tosefta that circumcision weighs as much as the deeds of creation (see *Nedarim* 2:5): as Covenant—as *brit milah*—circumcision is a sign of the word of creation: *brit* points to *bara*.[36] Rabbi Chayim ben Attar compares circumcision to the Sabbath that gives meaning to all of creation: just as the Sabbath is called a "sign" (Exodus 31:13), so is circumcision called a "sign" (Genesis 17:1).[37] Like the Sabbath, circumcision is a sign of Torah and of the Holy One Himself, as Nachman of Breslov teaches: God, Torah, and *Brit Milah* are of a piece.[38]

If Abraham was not whole until he was circumcised, as it is written in the Talmud (*Nedarim* 31b), it is because he was not whole until he entered into a relation with the speaking silence, a relation manifest in care and outrage. And if Fackenheim is right about the 614th Commandment, then even in the abysmal silence of Auschwitz there is a *chashmal,* a speaking silence, that summons us to the covenantal relation of *brit milah.* Therefore, to be *mul,* or "circumcised," is also to be "facing" or "confronting" another, both human and Divine. To be circumcised is to be accountable for another, for the sake of another, even for the sake of the one whom we might oppose, both human and Divine. This accountability means the rectification of the link between word and meaning, drawing the *yud* into the word. In that linkage the Messiah abides. Earlier we noted that in the mystical tradition, the Messiah is associated with *Yesod*; here we remind ourselves that, according to the Baal Shem Tov, *Yesod* is associated with *brit milah* (see, for example, *Toledot Yaakov Yosef, Kedushim* 8). Thus everything we have said about *brit milah* applies also to the Messiah: the belief in the coming of the Messiah with *complete* faith lies in the wholeness attained in the Covenant of Circumcision.

That wholeness, moreover, is tied to the fullness of consciousness that

Rabbi Yitzchak Ginsburgh refers to when he says, "In order to bring the *Mashiach* into one's full consciousness, each of us must strive to purify and make potent our faculty of speech in Torah, prayer, and the communication of love between us."[39] What this means in terms of the wait for the Messiah, Rabbi Ginsburgh states quite clearly: "Every living creature possesses a spark of *Mashiach,* a spark entrusted with the power to fulfill its mission, to bring redemption to its 'portion' on earth."[40] What makes the wait for the Messiah interminable, therefore, is not just that *he* tarries. It is that *we* tarry, especially in the modern and postmodern era, in the post-Shoah era, when so many of us throw up our hands and declare that we cannot go on as if it were business as usual—with the implication that the Jewish testimony slated for annihilation is now meaningless.

It is true that the "business" of Jewish thought is no longer "as usual." But if we are to transform the darkness of Auschwitz into light, rather than throw up our hands, we must roll up our sleeves and mend the piece of creation entrusted to our care. Here, Fackenheim realizes, faith means viewing history as a "dialectic of the doing of man and the doing of God," in such a way that the messianic wait is not just our waiting for the Messiah—it is his waiting for us: in Fackenheim's words, he is "waiting for man to perfect the world" or "waiting for him to ruin it."[41] If each of us possesses a messianic spark, it ignites a fire that can either save or destroy. That each living creature possesses a spark of the Messiah has other ramifications. It means, for example, that the *other* human being bears a trace of the Messiah; indeed, tradition teaches that the other person may *be* the Messiah. Here we have an enlargement upon the point made earlier about the many disguises of the Messiah, namely, that the Messiah might be *anyone.* A tale will illustrate the import of this teaching.

There was once a Rosh Yeshivah, the head of a religious school, whose students treated each other with terrible rudeness, despite the teachings of the *sifrei kodesh* that they studied. He tried everything to solve the problem, but everything failed. Finally, the Rosh Yeshivah consulted a rabbi known for his wisdom. After listening to the Rosh Yeshivah's story, the sage told him, "I cannot tell you exactly what to do, but it occurs to me that one of your students may be the Messiah."

The Rosh Yeshivah returned to the school and declared to his students, "One of you may be the Messiah."

After that they treated each other with great courtesy.

In a similar vein, the Talmud teaches that two times are destined for the coming of the Messiah: now and the appointed time (*Sanhedrin* 98a). This teaching is based on the words of the prophet Isaiah: "I Hashem will hasten it in its time" (Isaiah 60:22); that is, I will either hasten it to make it now, or it will be in its appointed time. *Now,* if we perform the task for which we were created. *Now,* if we treat others, especially those who are most defenseless, with the loving kindness we would show the Messiah himself. *Now,* says the Midrash, if for just one Sabbath every Jew were to observe the Sabbath (*Shemot Rabbah* 25:12; *Midrash Tehillim* 4:95:2).[42] In short, now *is* the appointed time: it is the time ushering in time, through the realization of our responsibility for one another. Thus it is written that the Messiah is called the "Head of Days" (1 Enoch 48:2). Without the wait for the Messiah, there is nothing to hasten and no time appointed. Waiting for the Messiah, though he may tarry, is just the opposite of the languishing that characterizes so much of our intellectual game playing, which is no more than a means of marking time by killing time.

In keeping with this view of the relation between time and the Messiah, Levinas notes that for Judaism "salvation does not stand as an end to History, or act as its conclusion. It remains *at every moment* possible."[43] And since in each of us there is a spark of the Messiah, "in concrete terms this means that each person acts as though he were the Messiah. Messianism is therefore not the certainty of the coming of a man who stops History. It is my power to bear the suffering of all. It is the moment when I recognize this power and my universal responsibility."[44] So what about the literal meaning of the Messiah, the scion of David, whose coming we pray for three times a day? According to Levinas, it is all too literal, more literal than we care to think: *I* am the one who must take upon myself the messianic task and testimony—literally. *I* am the one who must observe just one Sabbath—literally. *I* am the one whose bears responsibility for creation and humanity—literally. Precisely because the other may be the Messiah, I must be for the other what the Messiah is for me.

For a Jew, this responsibility includes mending the piece of world that he or she is summoned to mend through the Covenant of Torah. Which means: even though the Messiah may tarry, we must not tarry. We must study, even though we do not understand; we must pray, even though we hear no reply; we must treat our fellow human being with kindness, even though we see no point or profit. Even though—or especially because—there can be no resolution. Here we come to a most crucial realization: the Messiah is precisely the one who tarries, precisely the one who is *hidden,* as Buber states it.[45] He will come at two times, either now or at the appointed time, which is always future, always *not yet,* because what we do now is never *enough.* Hence the ancient association between the Messiah and a child (Isaiah 11:6, for instance): the child is one whose completeness is *yet* to be realized, the one who recedes even as we approach him.

"The line of the horizon vanishes as one approaches it," in the words of André Neher, "but the Jew knows that even if the horizon vanishes, in its vanishing it turns toward a vertical position. The point of turning towards the vertical is the 'maybe' of the Messiah."[46] And the turning toward the vertical is a turning toward the certainty of the Covenant that chooses me, inescapably, for this "maybe." This "maybe" that constitutes the future derives from the "certainty" that constitutes the past. As Levinas states it, this covenantal past that is central to covenantal Jewish thought "signifies starting from an irrecusable responsibility, which devolves on the ego and precisely is significant to it as a commandment."[47] A commandment to do what? To wait. Not to serve by waiting but to wait by serving. For the irrecusable responsibility not only devolves on the ego—it dissolves the ego, to reveal the spark of the Messiah that abides in every soul. Once again we find that, mystically speaking, the ego is the *kelipah,* the shell, that hides the Divine spark; only now we see that it also hides the "maybe" and the "certainty" of the future and the past. Now we see that it is the primary obstacle to the coming of the Messiah, both within us and beyond us.

To open this closed door of the ego, which renders us blind to everything except our illusory self, is to open the wound of the wait. And the wait is infinite.

THE OPEN WOUND OF THE INFINITE WAIT

The open wound of Jewish thought is not just a wounding that has arisen from within the community of Jewish thinkers. Far more than that, it is a wounding that the Jewish people have suffered from without. It is a wounding that we continue to suffer, from the remnants of the Christian hatred of the Jew to the current liberal intellectual hatred of the Jew to the ongoing Arab Muslim hatred of the Jew. Situating this Jew hatred in the context of the Jewish wait for the Messiah, we discover at last the true essence of anti-Semitism: it is an antimessianism. It is a terror at the open wound of the infinite wait, and it breeds terrorism. The "wandering" Jew turns out to be the waiting Jew and therefore the hated Jew, for the Jew's wait unsettles those who would have things settled by declaring the redemption to be accomplished and the conundrum solved. Rooted in a longing for resolution, anti-Semitism is a longing to be relieved of the endless waiting and the endless doing, of the infinite responsibility that devolves on the ego.

That's it: the anti-Semite hates the Jew because the very presence of the Jew robs him of his ego. It robs him of his ego because it signifies the infinite responsibility that makes the wait for the messianic redemption infinite. In a word, it robs him of his ego because it disturbs his sleep. The presence of the Jew forces him into an "awakening," as Levinas puts it, that is "a demand that no obedience equals."[48] Thus the presence of the Jew is a constant reminder that we are forever in debt and that redemption is always yet to be. There is no settling the accounts: no payment will do, because payment is always due. And so among the anti-Semites it is a truism that the Jews control the banks and ledgers of the world.

In the ontological tradition, anti-Semitism shows itself in the philosophical impetus toward the last line in the syllogism, toward a truth that is rational, resolved, and self-legislated. In religious traditions that preach personal salvation through a specific belief in a specific doctrine, and not a never-ending responsibility to and for the other human being, anti-Semitism arises when the fixed formulas and ready answers of the creed are challenged by the prospect that the creed is not enough. For this reason, what Franz Rosenzweig says of Christianity may also be said of Islam: "The existence of the Jew constantly subjects Christianity to the idea that it is not attaining the goal, the truth."[49] The hatred of the Jews is the oldest hatred because the challenge from the Jews is the oldest challenge to the personal autonomy and the personal salvation that would curl up in the comfort of looking out for Number One: for Christianity, as for Islam, salvation is about *me*. And my ego insists that everyone be like *me* in his or her belief.

Resting upon a final solution, both the religious and the ideological forms of anti-Semitism would have the last word, settle the matter of redemption, and slip into the egocentric sleep of salvation—all for the sake of the egocentric self. In an appropriation of the other by the Same, both the religious and the ideological anti-Semite would either assimilate or annihilate the Jew, whose *very existence* disturbs their sleep with the insistence that the wait for the Messiah is an interminable service to the other person, which allows no sleep, and that salvation is a communal, not a personal, matter. There is no closure for the open wound of this infinite wait. Jewish thought, especially after the Shoah, thinks from within that open wound.

This open wound is the opposite of the concern for personal salvation; it is the concern for a communal salvation, as when God tells Moses, "I shall destroy them and make a great people of you" (Exodus 32:10), and Moses answers, "If You do that, then erase my name from Your Book" (Exodus 32:32). This community of salvation includes "all the nations of the earth," for whose sake God enters into the Covenant with Abraham (Genesis 12:3) and for whose sake sacrifices were brought to the Temple during Sukkot—not so that the nations should become Jews but so that the peoples of the world might treat each other with righteousness and loving kindness (see *Sukkah* 55b). For Judaism, contrary to certain forms of Christianity, Islam, and left-wing postmodern ideology, there is no dividing the world into the damned and the saved on the basis of belief. This point is made most perfectly in the story of Jonah. For most Christians and Muslims, to bring the people of Nineveh to God would mean converting them to Christianity or Islam; for the Jew Jonah, it does not mean converting them to Judaism; it means leading them to realize that their treatment of one another is an expression of their relation to God, the Creator of heaven and earth, without whom life has no meaning. And so the Jew waits, not for the world to adopt a certain creed but for the world to take on a certain character.

How long shall we wait? According to a commentary on Isaiah 63:4 in *Pesikta Rabbati* 1:7,[50] we have another 365,000 years of waiting. Which is to say: the wait is infinite. In the endlessness of the wait—in the tarry-

ing of the Messiah—we encounter the One known in the mystical tradition as the *Ein Sof,* the "Infinite One" or "the One without End." Jews
do not pronounce the Holy Name, because to utter the Name would be
to determine the end. Thus, said Rabbi Samuel ben Nachman, in the
name of Rabbi Yonatan, "Cursed be the bones of those who calculate
the end. For they would say, since the predetermined time has come, and
yet the Messiah has not come, he will never come. Nevertheless, wait for
him" (*Sanhedrin* 97b). In that *nevertheless* lies the *Ein Sof* not only of the
wait but of the one whom we await. Here, too, in this talmudic passage,
for "wait" we have the verb *chikah,* which also means "to expect": even
if he will never come, *expect* him. Therefore, do not calculate the "end"—
hasten it. Indeed, in the Talmud it is written that there will be no Messiah for Israel, because those days have already passed, in the time of
Hezekiah (*Sanhedrin* 99a); the point is not to put an end to the wait and
the expectation but to underscore its infinite duration. Just so, it is written in the *Sifre* on Deuteronomy 3:23, "Says the Torah: whether You
redeem us or not, whether You heal us or not, we shall seek to know You."
Our task is not to know God, . . . or rather it *is* to know God in the mode
of "not knowing" that constitutes the open wound of the infinite wait.
In our morning prayers, then, we are enjoined to seek God's face, even
though we can never behold God's face. That seeking *is* God's face.

Much like Rabbi Samuel ben Nachman, Rav maintains that all the
dates for the ultimate redemption have passed (*Sanhedrin* 97b). Once
again, however, the teaching is not that we should leave off with waiting; rather, it is that now only *we* can bring the Messiah, for only *we* can
wait infinitely, through the continual effort to meet an infinite responsibility to and for the other person. Only we can wait, and not God,
because only we operate within the narrow confines of time. "The await-
ing of the Messiah," says Levinas, "is the duration of time itself—waiting
for God—but here the waiting no longer attests to the absence of Godot,
who will never come, but rather to a relationship with that which is not
able to enter the present, since the present is too small to contain the
Infinite."[51] Perhaps better: time is the tarrying of the Messiah; that the
Messiah tarries is what gives meaning to life, for the dimension of meaning is the dimension of time.

The Messiah, therefore, does not end history—the Messiah *is* history, inasmuch as the meaning of the Messiah lies in the wait for the Messiah. That wait is constitutive of time because it is the opposite of killing time or marking time: it is time as the drawing nigh unto the Holy One that Levinas describes when he says, "Time is the most profound relationship that man can have with God, precisely as a going towards God. . . . 'Going towards God' is meaningless unless seen in terms of my primary going towards the other person. I can only go towards God by being ethically concerned by and for the other person."[52] And, in keeping with Rav's teaching cited above, only *I* can go toward God, by getting rid of the "I" of the ego. Because "all the dates for the ultimate redemption have passed," I cannot wait: I have to *move now*. That is, my waiting must consist of this movement that is an urgent "going towards God," toward the One who both recedes and draws near as I approach, who is *in* the approach itself. Here, we discover a deeper meaning to the insight from Levinas cited in chapter 7: "Proximity is never close enough; as responsible, I am never finished with emptying myself of myself. There is infinite increase in this exhausting of oneself."[53] What we seek in the proximity that is never close enough is the Messiah himself. The "infinite increase" characterizes the infinite wait. And "this exhausting of oneself" is the open wound.

THE MEANING OF THE MESSIAH
FOR POST-HOLOCAUST JEWISH THOUGHT

The coming of the Messiah is the advent of dwelling in the world. What does Jewish thought make possible that, for the Jew, other modes of thought cannot make possible? Dwelling in the world. And, for the Jew, dwelling in the world means dwelling in Jerusalem, as Fackenheim insists: "*The messianic hope died during the Holocaust. The post-Holocaust State of Israel has resurrected it.*"[54] This is the meaning of Israel's "unofficial" national anthem *Hatikvah*, "The Hope." Significantly, *tikvah* means not only "hope" but also "cord" or "thread." The messianic hope revived through the Jewish return to Jerusalem is a messianic tie to history, to God, and to humanity. It is a return to a living link both to the sacred tradition and to the messianic future. Hence the talmudic teaching: "Three are called by the Name of the Holy One, blessed be He, and they are the righteous, the Messiah, and Jerusalem" (*Bava Batra* 75b). What was said in chapter 3 about the return to Jerusalem as the philosophical center for Jewish thought may also be said about making the Messiah a philosophical center for Jewish thought. Because the Messiah signifies the Jewish return to the Jewish home, he signifies the advent of dwelling in the world. That dwelling, and not merely abstract understanding, is the whole aim of post-Holocaust Jewish thought.

Recalling the phrase we have used for "Jewish thought," *Machshavah Yehudit,* we recall that the root of the word for "Jewish," *Yehudit,* is *hodah,* which means "to give thanks." Gratitude, then, is essential to the dwelling that Jewish thought would bring about. It is essential to the coming of the Messiah. Therefore, it is essential to wait not with impatience and frustration but with anticipation and gratitude—gratitude not only for the advent of the Messiah but for the wait itself. Steeped in gratitude, the wait for the Messiah is itself messianic. Inasmuch as Jewish thought assumes certain aspects of prayer, it assumes certain aspects of thanksgiving. To be sure, Rabbi Yochanan taught in the name of Rabbi Menachem the Galilean that in the messianic age all prayers will cease except the prayers of thanksgiving (*Midrash Tehillim* 2:56:4). The thanksgiving born of post-Holocaust Jewish thought is not a gratitude for what has befallen us or for what we have received. Rather, it is a gratitude for having been commanded, and thus entrusted with a mission, no matter how impossible the mission may seem. It is a gratitude for the outrage and the care of our open wounds. It is a gratitude for the meaning of the Messiah and for the strife of the spirit that the long wait entails.

Because the strife of the spirit—the outrage and care of the open wound—is something for which the Jewish thinker is grateful, it is something in which he or she can rejoice. Madness? Perhaps. From the postmodern standpoint, Jewish thought must indeed seem like madness. But remember the parable from the Baal Shem: "Once, in a house, there was a wedding festival. The musicians sat in a corner and played upon their instruments, the guests danced to the music, and were merry, and the house was filled with joy. But a deaf man passed outside the house; he looked in through the window and saw the people whirling about the room, leaping, and throwing about their arms. 'See how they fling themselves about!' he cried. 'It is a house filled with madmen!' For he could not hear the music to which they danced."[55] To be sure, the waiting for the Messiah that assumes the form of doing is often compared to the preparations for a wedding festival. As part of the preparation for the advent of the Messiah, Jewish thought must appear very strange indeed to those who do not hear the Voice of revelation that summons such thought. And in the post-Holocaust world, a dance of joy and thanksgiving must appear to be as impossible as it is absurd.

And so we return to Moshe Leib of Sassov: "When someone asks the impossible of me, I know what I must do: I must dance!"[56] Indeed, the head of the messianic line, King David himself, teaches the importance of the dance when he dances before the ark (2 Samuel 6:16). And Moshe Leib of Sassov teaches that the dance is most crucial when gravity most weighs us down, when we are wounded. That is when our joy can take on substance. And joy is essential to the advent of the Messiah. Rabbi Ginsburgh notes, in this connection, that the Hebrew word *Mashiach* "can be understood as a permutation of the word *yismach,* meaning 'he will rejoice,' or of the word *yesamach,* meaning 'he will make others rejoice.'"[57] And long before Rabbi Ginsburgh, Maimonides taught that "the highest peaks of faith, truth, and devotion are reached only through joy."[58] Those peaks represent the Messiah. In the joy that Maimonides invokes lies the meaning of the Messiah for post-Holocaust Jewish thought. Post-Holocaust Jewish thought, then, would be an answering that is a crying out of the word *yes.* Yes to what? Yes to the Divine pronunciation that creation is good, worthwhile, and meaningful. Yes to the truth, so that those who seek the truth must speak the truth. Yes to the interminable wait for the Messiah, though he may tarry.

Here, too, the holy tongue opens our eyes to some crucial interconnections. In Hebrew, *ken,* the word for "yes," also means "sincere," "honest," and "truthful," as in the word *kenut.* Related words include *nakhon,* which is "correct" or "true"; *kinah,* a verb meaning "to name"; *mukhan,* which means "ready" or "prepared"; and *kavanah,* meaning "intention" or "purpose." All of these meanings underlie Rosenzweig's comments on the primal significance of *ken* when he says, "Such is the power of the Yea that it adheres everywhere, that it contains unlimited possibilities of reality. It is the arch-word of language, one of those which first make possible, not sentences, but any kind of sentence-forming words at all. . . . It is the silent accompaniment of all parts of a sentence, the confirmation, the 'sic!' the 'Amen' behind every word."[59] Meaning is not only in the word; the word is in meaning. Says David Aboulesia, the Messiah seeker in Wiesel's *The Testament,* "The story of the Messiah is the story of a quest, of a name in search of being"[60]—or perhaps a name in search of meaning. The word—*every* word—contains the cry of meaning that is ready, *mukhan,* to burst forth: the word uttered with *kenut* and *kavanah,* with honesty and intensity, is *pregnant* with meaning. Or better: it is the word *about* to be uttered that forever seeks to join with meaning.

In this readiness to burst forth, in this intensity that is about to give birth, we have the messianic essence of post-Holocaust Jewish thought. To seek the truth is precisely to seek the Messiah and the Name of the Messiah, the name that preceded the beginning. For truth, *emet,* is never nameless: it is a *who,* not a *what,* a living presence and not a dead datum. Containing the beginning, the middle, and the end of all the Hebrew letters, *emet* contains all utterance and every name. It bespeaks the Holy Name without naming the Name. And it sustains the wait without the coming. Here, "waiting for Him becomes waiting with Him, sharing in the coming," as Heschel states it.[61] Here, "waiting for Him" becomes a mode of thinking from the depths of an open wound inflicted upon God and humanity alike.

10

Conclusion

No Closure

On the occasion of Jacob's wrestling with the Angel,
Rabbi Shimon said: "This dust was not ordinary dust, but ashes,
the residue of fire."—*Zohar* I, 170a

Nearly two thousand years ago, our sages of the Talmud raised the question of why both Jeremiah and Daniel tampered with the original text of Moses' invocation of the Lord's attributes: *Hael hagadol, hagibor, vehanora,* "God, the Great, the Mighty, and the Awesome" (Deuteronomy 10:17). Having witnessed the destruction of the First Temple, Jeremiah cried out to God, "O great and mighty God" (Jeremiah 32:18) and left out "awesome." Having witnessed the enslavement of the Jewish people after the destruction, Daniel cried out to God, "O great and awesome God" (Daniel 9:4) and left out "mighty." The sages asked, "How could Jeremiah and Daniel tamper with the text received through Moses?" Rabbi Eliezer explained that since they had experienced such horrific events and knew that God insists upon truth, they would not ascribe to God false attributes. That is to say, since they could not address God with all the praises of His mercy and kindness in view of what they had seen, they skipped these attributes because in those cases these attributes were hidden. Thus, says Rabbi Eliezer, there is no reason not to be honest with the God who demands honesty (see *Yoma* 69).[1] But in order to be honest *with* God, we must remain in a relation *to* God. While the biblical prophets and the talmudic sages had the courage to sustain that covenantal relation, it has eluded many of us in the post-Holocaust era. Thus left with nothing to say to Hashem, we are left only with the echoes of our empty outcry.

One way in which the relation to the Holy One has eluded us lies in our turning either to theodicy or away from theodicy in our response to the Shoah. Theodicy has no place in Jewish thought, in either a positive or a negative sense. It is not that theodicy is right or wrong from a Jewish standpoint; it is simply unintelligible. For Jewish thought, the question "Where was God?" is not a question concerning His absence or presence, His intervention or lack of intervention. It is a question concerning the Nazis' radical assault on the *relation* to God, for the living God abides in the lived relation. Here one may recall the assembly of prisoners forced to witness the hanging of a child in Elie Wiesel's *Night*. There the young Eliezer hears a Jew next to him asking, "Where is God? Where is He now?" And from within his soul comes the terrifying reply: "Where is He? Here He is—He is hanging here on these gallows."² He is not absent—He is assailed. And He commands even as He is assailed, from within the very core of the assault.

Theodicy's question is a question concerning the lack of Divine intervention, a question rooted in the assumption that God is manifest not in holiness, goodness, truth, or meaning but rather in power. Jewishly speaking, God neither intervenes nor fails to intervene—He *sanctifies* through His holiness. Theologies of intervention that try to explain why God did not manipulate the situation at hand rest on assumptions tainted by ontological thinking, which is a power-based thinking, not a holiness-based thinking. One can speak of providence, yes. One can speak of a destiny to which God summons us, over against a fate to which "the gods" doom us. But this providence and this destiny, this form of Divine "intervention," lies not in the stopping of evil but rather in the determination of evil *as* evil. God does not stop the Holocaust; He simply makes it matter that *humanity* did not stop it. At least not soon enough.

Unable to escape the assumptions of theodicy, many modern and postmodern thinkers insist that there is no judgment and no judge. Judgment, they maintain, is a projection of our own psychological agenda, and when it is applied to the Holocaust, they rightly understand, it falls apart. All we have left, then, is the agenda, which is a system of signs and illusions, of cultural convention and class envy, of racial tension and gendered power struggles—everything except the acknowledgment of an assault on a transcendent holiness that, *precisely because of the assault,* holds us accountable for how we shall respond. We live in a generation of which the Midrash declares, "Woe unto the generation whose judges are judged!" (See *Ruth Rabbah,* Proem 7:5.) In the post-Holocaust era, postmodern and "post-postmodern" philosophers are nothing if not the self-styled judges of God. And yet even as they judge, they—we—bring ourselves under a judgment. If, as Rabbi Joseph Soloveitchik says, "there is a past that persists in its existence, that does not vanish and disappear but remains firm in its place,"[3] we cannot engage in the postmodern luxury of the resolution, abrogation, or delegation of responsibility for the Holocaust to sociocultural, political, economic, social, psychological, or other academically sanctioned aberrations that would explain away the event.

No, try as we may to escape anything Jewish about our thinking, the truth of the Midrash remains: "Since the Torah is called *fiery law,* said Rabbi Yochanan, he who is about to engage it is standing within fire" (*Pesika de-Rab Kahana,* supplement 1). But it is a truth with a difference: now we realize that, since the Torah is called *fiery law,* we, who must engage the Torah so that the Jewish people and God's presence will not perish from the earth, now stand within the very flames that tried to consume the Torah in the Shoah. And so we read, with a difference, another teaching from the Torah (Leviticus 6:1–6):

The Lord spoke to Moses, saying: Command Aaron and his sons, saying:
This is the Torah of the burnt offering: The burnt offering shall remain in the place on the altar all through the night, until morning, and the fire of the altar shall be kept burning. And the priest shall don his linen raiment and his linen breeches and clothe his flesh, and he shall remove the ashes that the fire has made in consuming the offering upon the altar and place them beside the altar. Then he shall remove his garments and don other garments and carry the ashes outside to camp to a place of purity. The fire of the altar shall be kept burning; it must not go out. And the priest shall burn wood upon it every morning and arrange upon it the

burnt offering and there burn the fat of the peace offerings. Fire shall be kept burning upon the altar always: it must not go out.

Do we dare regard the flames of Birkenau as an altar fire? If that is possible, then we are faced with the task of illuminating our thinking with those flames. If it is impossible, then those flames mean nothing to the Jewish people as Jews. If it is impossible, then those ashes are neither pure nor holy; if it is impossible, then there is nothing to keep burning, neither faith nor Torah, neither prayer nor deeds of loving kindness.

For if we cannot incorporate this teaching from the Torah into our response to the Shoah, then we have no response as Jews. We have only our despair and our desperation, only our sophistication and our abnegation, only our pretense and our nonsense. To turn to Torah as Jewish thinkers is not to succumb to Irving Greenberg's facile phrase that "no statement, theological or otherwise, should be made that would not be credible in the presence of the burning children."[4] Indeed, Greenberg suggests no such thing. It does mean, however, that we must take seriously the words of those who turned to Torah even as the flames of the Shoah raged around them. And it is no voluntary matter. David Weiss Halivni provides a perfect illustration of this point. Commenting on his experiences in the camps, he recalls a *bletl,* or a page of Torah or Talmud, that prisoners might have come across, which had been torn from one of the holy volumes, used to wrap a sandwich, and then tossed. The *bletl,* he explains, "became a visible symbol of a connection between the camp and the activities of Jews throughout history."[5] It is from just such an ashen *bletl* that Jewish thought must arise if it is to emerge from the shadows of Auschwitz.

The Jewish ashes that rained upon the earth and now flow in our blood summon us to this Jewish thought. It is a thinking that takes in hand a *magrefa* as it proceeds one faltering step at a time. Noting the dual meaning of *magrefa,* Rabbi Shapira explains that it was a shovel used to remove ashes from the Temple altar, but it was also a trumpet that resounded with loud music.[6] "The purpose of all the music" made with the *magrefa,* says Rabbi Shapira, was not to soothe or to assuage; no, it "was to raise a clamor on high."[7] Just so, he adds, the ashes of the dead create a stir on high: "When someone is looking at the ashes, it intensifies the Divine pain and increases God's compassion to the point where R. Jose could hear what he was unable to hear before—the weeping of God."[8] The ego-centered thinking of postmodern thought turns away from the ashes to gaze only upon the illusory image in the mirror. Like those who mourn, we must cover that mirror and attend to the weeping of God and the pleading of the dead, who cry out to us in their outcry to God. Our thinking must be steeped in that weeping and that pleading, even as it is steeped in joy and thanksgiving. The instrument that we use to attend to the ashes must also be the instrument with which we now make music and thus create a stir on high so that here below we might be stirred. Thus stirred, we think from a wound that refuses closure.

Coming to an end, therefore, we come to no conclusion. Rather, we return to a question, to the *shelah,* with the *el* of Hashem that abides in its midst. Yet here, too, in this ending that is a beginning, we embrace the teachings of the sages, as Adin Steinsaltz reminds us: "One of the great talmudic commentators, the Maharsha, often ended his commentaries with the word *vedok,* 'continue to examine the matter.' This exhortation is an explicit admission that the subject has not been exhausted and that there is still room for additions and arguments on the question."[9] And so I say: *Vedok!*

NOTES

I INTRODUCTION

1. *Nachmanides, Commentary on the Torah,* vol. 1, 398.

2. *Mekilta de-Rabbi Ishmael, Bachodesh* 2.

3. See Moshe Weissman ed., *The Midrash Says,* vol. 4, 423.

4. As Heschel has noted, "the Bible knows neither the dichotomy of body and soul nor the trichotomy of body, soul, spirit, nor [even] the trichotomy within the soul"; see Abraham Joshua Heschel, *The Prophets,* vol. 2, 37.

5. The Baal Shem transmitted this teaching to his disciple Yaakov Yosef of Polnoe, who relates it in the introduction to his *Toledot Yaakov Yosef al Ha Torah,* 19. See also Schneur Zalman, *Likutei Amarim Tanya,* 589.

6. Yitzhak Katznelson, *Vittel Diary,* 202–3.

7. See Herman Kruk, *The Last Days of the Jerusalem of Lithuania,* 311.

8. Ignaz Maybaum, *The Face of God after Auschwitz,* 25–26, cited in Steven T. Katz, *Post-Holocaust Dialogues,* 156–57.

9. See Maybaum, *The Face of God after Auschwitz,* 32.

10. Fackenheim has correctly noted that the scapegoat theory loses its plausibility "when public incitement [is] turned in[to] top-secret action. And plausibility becomes sheer absurdity when at length the 'big' question comes into view"; see Emil L. Fackenheim, *Jewish Philosophers and Jewish Philosophy,* 149.

11. See Oskar Rosenfeld, *In the Beginning Was the Ghetto,* 134.

12. Said Rosenberg, "This heroic attitude [of National Socialism], to begin

with, departs from the *single* but *completely* decisive avowal, *namely from the avowal that blood and character, race and soul are merely different designations for the same entity*"; see Alfred Rosenberg, *Race and Race History and Other Essays,* 131–32 (quoted in Max Weinreich, *Hitler's Professors,* 26; Rosenberg's emphasis).

13. Rosenberg, *Race and Race History,* 181. This thinking that is in the soul is precisely what makes the Jew a *pathological* threat to the German *Volk.* Thus, for example, in 1935 the journal of the Association of German Physicians stated, "The comparison between Jews and the tuberculosis bacilli is a telling one. Almost all people harbour TB bacilli, almost all nations on earth harbour the Jews—a chronic infection, which it is difficult to cure. Just as the human body does not absorb the TB germs into its general organism, so a natural, homogeneous society cannot absorb the Jews into its organic association" (quoted in H. H. Ben-Sasson, ed., *A History of the Jewish People,* 1019).

14. Cited in Fackenheim, *Jewish Philosophers and Jewish Philosophy,* 122.

15. Reported in *Die Zeit,* Dec. 29, 1989; see Theodore Kisiel, "Heidegger's Apology," 12.

16. Yehuda Bauer, *A History of the Holocaust,* 99.

17. Commentary on Numbers 31:3 in Rashi, *Commentary on the Torah.*

18. See Louis I. Newman, *The Hasidic Anthology,* 147; see also *Zohar* III, 73a. Yitzhak Katznelson makes the same point; see Katznelson, *Vittel Diary,* 122. And recall what Kalmanovitch wrote in his diary from the Vilna Ghetto: "A war is being waged against the Jew. But this war is not merely directed against one link in the triad [of Israel, Torah, and God] but against the entire one: against the Torah and God, against the moral law and Creator of the universe." See Zelig Kalmanovitch, "A Diary of the Nazi Ghetto in Vilna," 52.

19. Katz, *Post-Holocaust Dialogues,* 142.

20. Arthur A. Cohen, *The Tremendum,* 100–101.

21. Michael L. Morgan, *A Holocaust Reader,* 160–61.

22. See Adin Steinsaltz, *Beggars and Prayers,* xx–xxi.

23. See H. J. Zimmels, *The Echo of the Nazi Holocaust in Rabbinic Literature,* 339.

24. Ibid., 64.

25. Ibid., 214.

26. See Katz, *Post-Holocaust Dialogues,* 144.

27. See Michael L. Morgan, *Beyond Auschwitz,* 12, 22. Equally enamored of the Nazi Heidegger is Funkenstein, who insists that no human life has tran-

scendent meaning or value and that the Holocaust therefore poses no particular problem for Jewish religious thought; see Amos Funkenstein, "Theological Interpretations of the Holocaust."

28. Immanuel Kant, *The Conflict of the Faculties*, 95.

29. From the *Freiberger Studentenzeitung*, Nov. 3, 1933, cited in Guenther Neske and Emil Kettering, eds., *Martin Heidegger and National Socialism*, 45.

30. Richard L. Rubenstein, *After Auschwitz*, 145.

31. Michael L. Morgan, *Interim Judaism*, 32.

32. See Rubenstein, *After Auschwitz*, 68, 119.

33. See Katz, *Post-Holocaust Dialogues*, 148; see also Rubenstein, *After Auschwitz*, 135 ff. Katz, in fact, correctly describes Rubenstein's paganism as a form of idolatry; see Katz, *Post-Holocaust Dialogues*, 197–98.

34. Rubenstein, *After Auschwitz*, 198. See also Zachary Braiterman, *(God) after Auschwitz*, 99 ff.

35. Adin Steinsaltz, *The Strife of the Spirit*, 192–93.

36. See especially Yvonne Karow, *Deutsches Opfer*, 49, 76. See also Margaret Brearley, "Fire and Ashes," 7–33.

37. See Morgan, *Beyond Auschwitz*, 101. Significantly, Alfred Rosenberg described Nietzsche as "the greatest figure of the German and European intellectual world of his day"; see Rosenberg, *Race and Race History*, 145.

38. Maybaum, *The Face of God after Auschwitz*, 66–67.

39. Katz, *Post-Holocaust Dialogues*, 162.

40. Maybaum, *The Face of God after Auschwitz*, 32.

41. See ibid., 68.

42. Cohen, *The Tremendum*, 81.

43. Ibid., 46.

44. Ibid., 94.

45. Irving Greenberg, "Cloud of Smoke, Pillar of Fire," 23.

46. Elie Wiesel, *Ani Maamin*, 57.

47. Sara Nomberg-Przytyk, *Auschwitz*, 81.

48. Greenberg, "Cloud of Smoke, Pillar of Fire," 27.

49. Ibid., 25. Actually, Greenberg's recommendation is an ancient one. In the *Eliyyahu Rabbah*, for example, it is written, "[True, He will redeem Israel, but in the meantime Israel must do justice and save the oppressed.] And so, kindred of David, why are you sitting still?" See *Tanna debe Eliyyahu*, 83.

50. Irving Greenberg, "Voluntary Covenant," 17. For an excellent discus-

sion of Greenberg, see Morgan, *Beyond Auschwitz*, 121–40. It is also worth noting that Greenberg is not original in this view of a "voluntary covenant." In a reaction to the tribulations of Spanish Jewry, the fourteenth-century rabbi Kanah ibn Gedor declared that the God of Israel "has sold them and exiled them and they have gone among other nations. Now there can certainly be no mouth or tongue to declare that they are bound by the commandments of their Lord . . . and this being the case they are no longer bound to His service . . . as God is true and there is no injustice in Him, He should not judge them at all. . . . Incest is permissible, as are forbidden foods. And the whole of the Covenant is now a matter of willing acceptance, and we are not bound by it or subject to any obligations or punishment" (quoted in Ben-Sasson, ed., *A History of the Jewish People*, 614).

51. Irving Greenberg, *The Jewish Way*, 252 (emphasis added).

52. Emmanuel Levinas, *Nine Talmudic Readings*, 135.

53. Lustig states it more eloquently than I: "These ashes would be indestructible and immutable, they would not burn up into nothingness because they themselves were remnants of fire. . . . No one living would ever be able to escape them; these ashes would be contained in the milk that will be drunk by babies yet unborn and in the breasts their mothers offer them. . . . These ashes will be contained in the breath and expression of every one of us and the next time anybody asks what the air he breathes is made of, he will have to think about these ashes; they will be contained in books which haven't been written and will be found in the remotest regions of the earth where no human foot has ever trod; no one will be able to get rid of them, for they will be the fond, nagging ashes of the dead who died in innocence"; see Arnŏst Lustig, *A Prayer for Katerina Horovitzova*, 50–51.

54. "Let him who wants fervor," said the Maggid of Mezeritch, "not seek it on the mountain peaks. Rather let him stoop and search among the ashes." See Elie Wiesel, *Souls on Fire*, 71. But what if the ashes themselves form a mountain?

55. Eliezer Berkovits, *Faith after the Holocaust*, 78.

56. Ibid., 90.

57. Ibid., 68.

58. In that passage Isaiah cries out, "Truly You are a God that hides Yourself, O God of Israel, the Savior."

59. Berkovits, *Faith after the Holocaust*, 107. Jonas makes a similar point by invoking the mystical notion of *tsimtsum,* which is the contraction or with-

drawal of God from Creation, so that this finite human realm may exist without being swallowed up by the Infinite; see Hans Jonas, *Mortality and Morality*, 136–42. Cf. David Birnbaum, *God and Evil*, 164–65; see also Cohen, *The Tremendum*, 86–95.

60. Zachary Braiterman correctly points out that the sacred texts of the Jewish tradition are full of teachings that are opposed to theodicy; see Braiterman, *(God) after Auschwitz*, 58, 102; see also Josh Cohen, *Interrupting Auschwitz*, 10.

61. Elie Wiesel tells the story of how the inmates of Auschwitz secretly gathered in a barracks one day to put God on trial for having failed to abide by the Covenant in the matter of the murder of so many millions of His children. Just as they found Him guilty, one prisoner said, "We must stop now: it is time for Minchah" (the afternoon prayers). That is the tension Berkovits is talking about.

62. Berkovits, *Faith after the Holocaust*, 69.

63. See Emil L. Fackenheim, *God's Presence in History*, 6.

64. Recall, for example, the assertion of a Nazi officer as he watched a synagogue full of Jews go up in flames: "The Jewish God is burnt to ashes." See Judith Dribben, *And Some Shall Live*, 24.

65. For an excellent essay on Levinas's response to the Holocaust, see Leonard Grob, "Some Fundamental Doubts about Posing the Question of Theodicy in the Post-Holocaust World," 189–214.

66. Maurice Blanchot, "Our Clandestine Companion," 50.

67. Levinas, *Nine Talmudic Readings*, 41, Levinas echoes the thought of the thirteenth-century mystic Abraham Abulafia: "God's intention in giving the Torah is that we reach this purpose, that our souls be alive in His Torah. For this is the reason for our existence and the intention for which we were created" (quoted in Moshe Idel, *Language, Torah, and Hermeneutics in Abraham Abulafia*, 37).

68. See Emmanuel Levinas, *Ethics and Infinity*, 105.

69. Emmanuel Levinas, "Reflections on the Philosophy of Hitlerism," 63 (quoted in Cohen, *Interrupting Auschwitz*, 5–6).

70. Emmanuel Levinas, "Useless Suffering," 163. This view, of course, calls to mind Fackenheim's 614th Commandment, discussed below.

71. Emmanuel Levinas, *Totality and Infinity*, 46–47.

72. Emmanuel Levinas, *Collected Philosophical Papers*, 52.

73. See, for example, Emil L. Fackenheim, *The Jewish Return into History*, 19–24. Morgan correctly points out that what makes Fackenheim a *Jewish* thinker

is that he takes the source of the 614th Commandment to be the Divine; see Morgan, *Beyond Auschwitz*, 168.

74. See Michael Wyschogrod, "Faith and the Holocaust," 168.

75. Fackenheim, *The Jewish Return into History*, 246. As Elie Wiesel states it, "At Auschwitz, not only man died, but also the idea of man"; see Elie Wiesel, *Legends of Our Time*, 230. Therefore, says Fackenheim, with the Holocaust, "philosophers must face a *novum* within a question as old as Socrates: what does it mean to be human?"; see Fackenheim, *Jewish Philosophers and Jewish Philosophy*, 133. Even Arendt, although for different reasons, recognizes this dimension of the Holocaust *as* Holocaust: the Nazis' attempt "to make the entire Jewish people disappear from the face of the earth," she says, was "a crime not against 'fellow-nations'" but "against the very nature of mankind"; see Hannah Arendt, *Eichmann in Jerusalem*, 268.

76. Emil L. Fackenheim, *To Mend the World*, 100. See also Emil L. Fackenheim, *What Is Judaism?*, 180.

77. Emil L. Fackenheim, *Encounters between Judaism and Modern Philosophy*, 190–91.

78. Ibid., 194.

79. See Emil L. Fackenheim, *Quest for Past and Future*, 134.

80. See Fackenheim, *To Mend the World*, 310.

81. Fackenheim, *Quest for Past and Future*, 18.

82. Morgan, *Beyond Auschwitz*, 56.

83. Fackenheim, *To Mend the World*, xix.

84. Fackenheim, *Jewish Philosophers and Jewish Philosophy*, 186.

85. One may recall Greenberg's insistence upon a "troubled theism"; see Greenberg, "Cloud of Smoke, Pillar of Fire," 33. But, as Morgan rightly points out, all authentic Jewish thinking about God is troubled; see Morgan, *Beyond Auschwitz*, 131.

86. See Alice L. Eckhardt and A. Roy Eckhardt, *Long Night's Journey into Day*, 136–43.

87. Franklin H. Littell, *The Crucifixion of the Jews*, 65.

88. Fackenheim, *Jewish Philosophers and Jewish Philosophy*, 107–8.

89. See Maimonides, *Moreh Nevuchim* 1:69. (This work has been translated as *The Guide for the Perplexed*.)

90. Plato, *Euthyphro*, 10e.

91. For a good discussion of Kant's views in this regard, particularly as related in his *Religion within the Limits of Reason Alone,* see Allen W. Wood, "Rational Theology, Moral Faith, and Religion."

92. Some scholars try to distinguish between Maimonides and Judah Halevi, or between Maimonides and Nachmanides, by labeling the former a rationalist and the latter a mystic. But this is a false distinction. Maimonides opens part III of *The Guide for the Perplexed,* for example, by saying, "We have stated several times that it is our primary object in this treatise to expound, as far as possible, the Biblical account of the Creation (*Ma'aseh bereshit*) and the description of the Divine Chariot (*Ma'aseh mercabah*) in a manner adapted to the training of those for whom this work is written"; see Maimonides, *The Guide for the Perplexed,* 251. These two topics, of course, form the basis of Jewish mysticism, and no Aristotelian rationalist would take them seriously, as Maimonides does.

93. See Levinas, *Ethics and Infinity,* 120.

94. See René Descartes, *Meditations on First Philosophy,* 26–27, 29–30.

95. See Don Isaac Abrabanel, *Abrabanel on 'Pirke Avot,'* 217.

96. See, for example, *Shushan Sodot,* 27. The Chasidic master Rabbi Shlomo of Ludmir taught that the "essence" of teshuvah is thought; see Milton Aron, *Ideas and Ideals of Hassidism,* 131.

97. Joseph Soloveitchik, "Kol Dodi Dofek," 55–56.

98. See, for example, Rabbi Chayim ben Attar, *Or Hachayim,* on Numbers 16:1.

99. Franz Rosenzweig, *On Jewish Learning,* 39.

100. See, for example, Zalman, *Likutei Amarim Tanya,* 13–21.

101. Sacks makes a good point when he notes that "the fissures that mark modern Jewish thought have their origins in the nineteenth century, not the twentieth"; see Jonathan Sacks, *Crisis and Covenant,* 248. Still, I think the Holocaust has made those fissures into wounds that refuse closure.

102. Yehudah Leib Alter, *The Language of Truth,* 10.

103. Jewish mysticism teaches that there are five levels of the soul; the other two are *chayah* ("life force") and *yechidah* ("oneness"), both of which remain in realms that are beyond this world (see, for example, *Bereshit Rabbah* 14:9; *Sefer Yetzirah* 1:14; *Zohar* II, 94b). For a detailed explanation, see Gershom G. Scholem, *On the Mystical Shape of the Godhead,* 301–31. See also David Patterson, *Hebrew Language and Jewish Thought,* esp. chap. 6.

2 THE BANKRUPTCY OF MODERN AND POSTMODERN THOUGHT

1. See Louis I. Newman, ed., *The Hasidic Anthology*, 257.

2. Yaakov Yosef of Polnoe, *Toledot Yaakov Yosef, Emor* 11. For a good account of the Chasidic view on how an "original thought" finds its way into consciousness in this "awakening," see also Rabbi Yosef Yitzchak Schneersohn, *Four Worlds*, 34–36.

3. *The Bahir* 87.

4. Aryeh Kaplan, commentary, *The Bahir,* 150. The mystics, in fact, teach that each level of the soul has its own mode of thought: as thinking ascends "up" the soul, thinking is transformed.

5. Emmanuel Levinas, *Otherwise than Being, or Beyond Essence,* 69.

6. Adin Steinsaltz, *The Sustaining Utterance,* 32.

7. See Solomon ibn Gabirol, *Selected Religious Poems,* 104.

8. Joseph Albo, a sage of the fourteenth and fifteenth centuries, makes a definitive connection between prayer and thought, saying that prayer derives from *sechel,* which is "intellect" or "intelligence"; see Joseph Albo, *Sefer Ha-'Ikkarim* 4:17).

9. Cf. Adin Steinsaltz, *Simple Words,* 166.

10. Chofetz Chaim, *Ahavath Chesed,* 92.

11. Abraham Joshua Heschel, *God in Search of Man,* 160. A similar teaching can be found in Albo, *Sefer Ha-'Ikkarim* 4:43.

12. Abraham Joshua Heschel, *The Prophets,* vol. 2, 267.

13. See Martin Buber, *The Legend of the Baal Shem,* 27. Thus, before Jews pray the highest of the prayers, the Amidah, they recite the verse from Psalms 51:17: *Adonai sfatai tiftach, ufi yagid tehilatekha,* "O Lord, open my lips, and I shall sing Your praise."

14. Emmanuel Levinas, *Collected Philosophical Papers,* 162; see also Emmanuel Levinas, *Of God Who Comes to Mind,* 66. The awakening Levinas refers to brings to mind a line from the *Lekhah Dodi,* a hymn he knew quite well, since Jews throughout the world sing it each week to welcome the Sabbath: "Arouse yourself, arouse yourself, for your light has come; arise, shine. Awake, awake, utter a song; the glory of the Lord is revealed upon you."

15. See Dovid Kirschenbaum, ed., *Fun di Chasidishe Ostros,* 134; see also Victor Cohen, ed., *The Soul of the Torah,* 69.

16. See Nachmanides, *Igeret HaRamban,* 40.

17. Recall, in this connection, an insight from Rabbi Steinsaltz: "We are living in an age of psychological values. Everything is measured by the effect on one's subjective thoughts and feelings. Does it inspire one? Does it depress one? And the spiritual life has also become dominated by the same shallow measure." See Adin Steinsaltz, *The Long Shorter Way,* 239.

18. Martin Buber, *I and Thou,* 158.

19. See Elie Wiesel, *Somewhere a Master,* 110.

20. See Elie Wiesel, *Sages and Dreamers,* 360; see also Elie Wiesel, *Souls on Fire,* 46.

21. To his credit, Søren Kierkegaard recognizes the paralyzing nature of thought when he tries to "think" Abraham: "When I have to think about Abraham I am virtually annihilated. I am all the time aware of that monstrous paradox that is the content of Abraham's life, I am constantly repulsed, and my thought, for all its passion, is unable to enter into it, cannot come one hairbreadth further. I strain every muscle to catch sight of it, but the same instant I become paralyzed." See Søren Kierkegaard, *Fear and Trembling,* 62–63. As central as Abraham is for Kierkegaard, he is irrelevant to the postmodernist.

22. Related in Elimelekh of Lizensk, *Noam Elimelekh,* 72; see also Cohen, *The Soul of the Torah,* 100.

23. In a letter to Johann Caspar dated Apr. 28, 1775, Kant refers to prayer as "the so-called worshipful supplications which have perennially constituted the religious delusion"; see Ernst Cassirer, *Kant's Life and Thought,* 377.

24. Abraham Joshua Heschel, *Man's Quest for God,* 12.

25. See René Descartes, *Meditations on First Philosophy,* 19.

26. This is the theme, for example, of the Fifth Ennead of Plotinus; see Plotinus, *The Enneads,* 347–439.

27. See Descartes, *Meditations on First Philosophy,* 30–31.

28. Heschel, *God in Search of Man,* 16.

29. See, for example, Aristotle, *Eudemian Ethics,* VII, 1244b. See also Heschel, *The Prophets,* 12ff.

30. Bachya ibn Paquda, *Chovot Halevavot* 9:5.

31. Compare this to Plato's statement that thinking is a dialogue of the mind with itself; see Plato, *Sophist,* 263e.

32. Heschel, *Man's Quest for God,* 69.

33. Commentary on Exodus 30:13 in Chayim ben Attar, *Or Hachayim.*

34. Adin Steinsaltz, *Teshuvah,* 28. Elsewhere the Rabbi writes, "The mitz-

vah makes an incision into the veil of the hiddenness of God"; see Steinsaltz, *The Long Shorter Way,* 164.

35. Just to note that such thinking about thought is not peculiar to Jewish thinking, one may recall Karl Jaspers's statement that "in thinking, something which is not this thought itself awakens"; see Karl Jaspers, *Truth and Symbol,* 47. Still, from a Jewish point of view, the "something which is not this thought" is the agent who does the awakening.

36. Levinas, *Collected Philosophical Papers,* 134–35.

37. Quoted by Thomas J. J. Altizer, *Mircea Eliade and the Dialectic of the Sacred,* 26; see also Eliezer Berkovits, *Faith after the Holocaust,* 53.

38. Alfred Rosenberg, *Race and Race History and Other Essays,* 98.

39. Franz Rosenzweig, *Understanding the Sick and the Healthy,* 81–82.

40. Samson Raphael Hirsch, *The Nineteen Letters on Judaism,* 120–21.

41. Emmanuel Levinas, *Totality and Infinity,* 77.

42. Abraham Joshua Heschel, *Man Is Not Alone,* 153.

43. See Martin Heidegger, *Sein und Zeit,* 118.

44. Emmanuel Levinas, *Outside the Subject,* 47.

45. Emmanuel Levinas, *Difficult Freedom,* 159.

46. Levinas, *Of God Who Comes to Mind,* xv.

47. See Emmanuel Levinas, *Ethics and Infinity,* 86.

48. Cf. Levinas, *Of God Who Comes to Mind,* 160–61.

49. Levinas, *Outside the Subject,* 30.

50. See Nahum Glatzer's introduction to Rosenzweig, *Understanding the Sick and the Healthy,* 24.

51. Franz Rosenzweig, *Franz Rosenzweig's "The New Thinking,"* 96.

52. Baal HaTurim, *Commentary on the Torah: Bereshis* (that is, on Genesis 11:1); cf. *Zohar* I, 75a.

53. *Zohar* II, 124a; see also Ovadiah Sforno, *Commentary on the Torah* (that is, on Genesis 11:4).

54. The word *nevelah* is from the verb *naval,* which means "to wither," "to perish," or "to be destroyed." The noun *naval* refers to one who is base and vile; it can also refer to one who is godless, an "unbeliever."

55. Yaakov Culi, *The Torah Anthology,* 420.

56. Ka-tzetnik 135633, *Sunrise over Hell,* 111.

57. See Gillian Rose, *Mourning Becomes the Law,* 21, cited in Josh Cohen, *Interrupting Auschwitz,* 48.

58. Joseph Conrad, *Heart of Darkness,* 111; T. S. Eliot, *The Waste Land and Other Poems.*

59. Buber, *I and Thou,* 121–22.

60. See Franz Rosenzweig, *The Star of Redemption,* 4. Schopenhauer, of course, is famous for offering this recommendation; see Arthur Schopenhauer, *Parerga and Paralipomena,* vol. 2, 306–11. And Dostoyevsky's character Kirilov understood it very well: "God is indispensable and therefore must exist. . . . But I know there is no God and can't be. . . . Can't you really see that that alone is a sufficient reason to shoot oneself?" See F. M. Dostoyevsky, *The Possessed,* 634. See also Søren Kierkegaard, *Concluding Unscientific Postscript,* 273; Leo Tolstoy, *Confession,* 27–55.

61. Albert Camus, *The Myth of Sisyphus,* 3.

62. The Talmud, in fact, sees the denial of God and God's commandment as a form of madness; see *Sotah* 3a.

63. For a good discussion of this point, see Elie Wiesel, *Messengers of God,* 60–62.

64. In the Talmud it is written that the heart cannot contain the ego and the Shekhinah, God's Indwelling Presence, at the same time, as the two are antithetical (*Pesachim* 66b); hence the ego-based thinking of modern and postmodern thought is antithetical to *Machshavah Yehudit* (see also Moshe Weissman, ed., *The Midrash Says,* vol. 3, 93). In contrast to the modern cogito, the "I think," we have the Jewish notion of *bitul hayesh,* the "annulment of the self," to produce a " 'vessel' for truth to enter," as Rabbi Yitzchak Ginsburgh puts it; see Yitzchak Ginsburgh, *The Alef-Beit,* 72. See also Louis Jacobs, *Hasidic Prayer,* 21.

65. Levinas, *Collected Philosophical Papers,* 138.

66. Michel Foucault, *Madness and Civilization,* 281.

67. Hannah Arendt, *The Origins of Totalitarianism,* 459.

68. Levinas, *Totality and Infinity,* 46.

69. Plato, *Republic,* 338c.

70. Levinas, *Collected Philosophical Papers,* 52.

71. See Theodore Kisiel, "Heidegger's Apology," 34.

72. Quoted in Victor Farías, *Heidegger and Nazism,* 219.

73. Martin Heidegger, "The Self-Assertion of the German University," 13.

74. Ibid., 12.

75. For a good discussion of Kant's antireligious and anti-Semitic stance, see Michael Mack, *German Idealism and the Jew,* 23–41.

76. Introduction to Paul Gruyer, ed., *The Cambridge Companion to Kant*, 3.

77. Quoted in Frederick C. Beiser, "Kant's Intellectual Development: 1746–1781," 39.

78. Immanuel Kant, *The Critique of Practical Reason*, 101.

79. For a good discussion of Hegel's anti-Semitism, see Mack, *German Idealism and the Jew*, 60–62.

80. For a good discussion of this point, see Edith Wyschogrod, *Spirit in Ashes*, 69–72.

81. Emil L. Fackenheim, *Encounters between Judaism and Modern Philosophy*, 190–91.

82. G. W. F. Hegel, *The Phenomenology of Spirit*, 18–19.

83. See Ludwig Feuerbach, *The Essence of Christianity*, 12–13.

84. Fackenheim, *Encounters between Judaism and Modern Philosophy*, 144–45.

85. Joseph Soloveitchik, *The Halakhic Mind*, 78.

86. This is the meaning of Nietzsche's statement that "in man creature and creator are united"; see Friedrich Nietzsche, *Beyond Good and Evil*, 154.

87. Fackenheim, *Encounters between Judaism and Modern Philosophy*, 191.

88. See Friedrich Nietzsche, *The Gay Science*, sec. 125, where Nietzsche's most famous pronouncement on the death of God appears.

89. Wyschogrod, *Spirit in Ashes*, 146.

90. Cf. Gayatri Chakravorty Spivak's introduction to Jacques Derrida, *Of Grammatology*, lxxvii.

91. Martin Heidegger, *Nietzsche*, vol. 1, 18.

92. Heidegger, *Sein und Zeit*, 322.

93. Hans Jonas, "Heidegger's Resoluteness and Resolve," 202–3.

94. Martin Heidegger, *Vom Wesen des Grundes*, 38.

95. Jacques Taminiaux, *Heidegger and the Project of Fundamental Ontology*, xxi.

96. Martin Heidegger, *Kant and the Problem of Metaphysics*, 245.

97. See John D. Caputo, "Heidegger's Scandal," 265–81.

98. Wyschogrod, *Spirit in Ashes*, 166.

99. Buber, *I and Thou*, 63.

100. Buber, *I and Thou*, 57.

101. Heschel, *Man Is Not Alone*, 47.

102. Levinas, *Of God Who Comes to Mind*, 12.

103. Primo Levi, *Survival in Auschwitz,* 98.

104. Adin Steinsaltz with Josy Eisenberg, *The Seven Lights,* 121.

105. Jonathan Sacks, *Crisis and Covenant,* 268–69.

106. Berel Lang, *Act and Idea in the Nazi Genocide,* 185.

107. Ibid., 184–85.

108. Jean-François Lyotard, *Heidegger and "the jews,"* 22.

109. Ibid., 23. While Lyotard is generally regarded as a postmodernist, this insight demonstrates his integrity as a thinker.

110. Emil L. Fackenheim, "Jewish Existence and the Living God," 260.

111. Ibid., 261.

112. Sacks, *Crisis and Covenant,* 242.

113. While Rabbi Simlai teaches that the 365 commandments correspond to the 365 days of the year, and not to parts of the body (*Makkot* 23b), we also have the tradition that of the 613 commandments, 248 correspond to the 248 bones of the body, and 365 to the 365 sinews of the body (see, for example, *Makkot* 24a; *Zohar* II, 165b; *Tikkunei Hazohar* 70:131a; Chayyim Vital's *Shaarei Kedushah,* part 1, gate 1; the commentary on Deuteronomy 20:11 in the *Or Hachayim; Keter Shem Tov* 53; and Yaakov Yosef of Polnoe in *Toledot Yaakov Yosef, Shemini* 2). The 248 positive commandments, says the Zohar, correspond to the 248 "upper organs," whereas the 365 negative commandments correspond to the 365 "lower organs" (see *Zohar* II, 165b). With regard to the soul, just as the Torah is made of black fire on white fire (*Tanchuma Bereshit* 1; *Devarim Rabbah* 3:12; *Shir Hashirim Rabbah* 5:11:6; *Zohar* II, 226b), so does the soul originate "in fire, being an emanation from the Divine Throne" (*Zohar* II, 211b). Therefore, each day in our prayers, we ask God: *veten chelkenu beToratekha,* "grant us our portion in Your Torah" (from the *Pirke Avot* 5:20)—a portion *in* Your Torah, not *of* Your Torah, which means—as Chayim ben Attar teaches in *Or Hachayim,* in his commentary on Numbers 16:1—that "the very letters in the written Torah represent the various souls God has planted in His people." Similarly, Levi Yitschak of Berditchev taught that every Jewish soul is like a letter that goes into the making of Torah, each one a syllable in God's utterance; see Harry M. Rabinowicz, *Hasidism,* 61.

114. Henri Crétella, "Self-Destruction," 159.

115. See Max Weinreich, *Hitler's Professors,* 78. This is added evidence of the claim made in the introductory chapter to the present volume: that the Nazis viewed the Jews not just as a racial or ethnic threat but also as a cosmic threat.

116. See Emil L. Fackenheim, "The Holocaust and the State of Israel," 132.

117. Here it will be asked: What about the anti-Semitism that permeates the Arab Muslim world; surely Islam is just as antithetical to the Western ontological project as Judaism is? The answer, I think, is that the Arab Muslims associate Jews themselves with Western ontological thinking. Thus, like their allies among postmodernist thinkers, they wrongly cast Zionism in terms of colonialism and imperialism; they falsely label the Jewish State an "apartheid state," and they are the largest publishers and distributors of *The Protocols of the Elders of Zion,* which is intended to show that the Jews are interested only in absorbing the Other into the Same. But this is a topic that far exceeds the parameters of the present volume.

118. Levinas, *Difficult Freedom,* 262. Is this not precisely what becomes of "the Good that glorifies Being" in postmodern thought? In postmodern thought, is this Good not "brought to unreality?" Does it not "shrivel up in the deepest recesses of a subjectivity?"

119. Ibid., 153.

120. See Levi, *Survival in Auschwitz,* 82.

121. Ibid., 88.

122. Fackenheim, *Encounters between Judaism and Modern Philosophy,* 147.

123. Ibid., 187.

124. Fania Fénelon, *Playing for Time,* ix.

125. Bertha Ferderber-Salz, *And the Sun Kept Shining,* 15.

126. Charlotte Delbo, *None of Us Will Return,* 126.

127. Michael L. Morgan, *Beyond Auschwitz,* 6.

128. Quoted in Morgan, *Beyond Auschwitz,* 159.

129. Eugene Borowitz, *Choices in Modern Jewish Thought,* 281–82.

130. Emil L. Fackenheim, *Quest for Past and Future,* 138.

131. Ibid., 139.

132. Fackenheim, *Encounters between Judaism and Modern Philosophy,* 193.

133. The other two sins outlined in the Talmud's definition of *Kiddush Hashem* are murder and adultery, both of which spring from idolatry; see *Pesachim* 25a–25b; *Sanhedrin* 74a; *Ketuvot* 19a.

134. See H. J. Zimmels, *The Echo of the Nazi Holocaust in Rabbinic Literature,* 64.

135. Abraham Joshua Heschel, *I Asked for Wonder,* 45.

136. André Neher, *The Prophetic Existence,* 338–39.

137. Fackenheim, *Quest for Past and Future,* 6.

138. The other six are Torah, the Garden of Eden, Gehinnom, the Throne of Glory, the Temple, and the name of the Messiah.

139. Quoted in Newman, ed., *The Hasidic Anthology,* 147.

140. For a detailed discussion of how and why God and the *mitzvah* are one, see Kalonymos Kalmish Shapira, *Sacred Fire,* 61. See also the commentary on Leviticus 18:4 in Rabbi Chayim ben Attar, *Or Hachayim.*

141. Joseph Gikatilla, *Sha'are Orah,* 301.

142. See Newman, ed., *The Hasidic Anthology,* 382.

143. Emmanuel Levinas, "L'actualité de Maimonides," *Traces* (Fall 1982), 97, quoted by Annette Aronowicz in the introduction to Emmanuel Levinas, *Nine Talmudic Readings,* xii.

144. See Newman, ed., *The Hasidic Anthology,* 123.

145. Elie Wiesel, *From the Kingdom of Memory,* 20.

146. Commentary on Exodus 34:18 in Chayim ben Attar, *Or Hachayim.*

147. Nehemia Polen, *The Holy Fire,* 20.

148. Heschel, *God in Search of Man,* 17.

149. From *Gevurot Hashem* 46, cited in Pinhas H. Peli, *The Jewish Sabbath,* 11–12. See also Avraham Yaakov Finkel, *Kabbalah,* 152.

150. Benjamin Blech, *More Secrets of Hebrew Words,* 7.

151. André Neher, *They Made Their Souls Anew,* 33.

3 ETHICAL MONOTHEISM AND JEWISH THOUGHT

1. Adin Steinsaltz with Josey Eisenberg, *The Seven Lights,* 87; see also Yaakov Yosef of Polnoe, *Toledot Yaakov Yosef, Bo* 10.

2. See Martin Buber, *Tales of the Hasidim,* 149.

3. Leo Baeck, *The Essence of Judaism,* 63.

4. Ibid., 129–30 (emphasis added).

5. "We keep the commandments," says Rabbi Nachman of Breslov, "because they were decreed by God and not for any logical or moral reasons. A Jew may be called Godly, but never merely 'ethical'"; see Nathan of Nemirov, *Rabbi Nachman's Wisdom,* 243.

6. See Samuel Sandmel, *Philo's Place in Judaism,* 139ff.

7. Edmund Husserl, *Phenomenology and the Crisis of Philosophy,* 110.

8. Emil L. Fackenheim, *Quest for Past and Future,* 178.

9. Nothing illustrates this point better than the Hungarian film *Sunshine.* See also Zsuzsanna Ozsváth's excellent study of the Hungarian poet Miklós Radnóti, *In the Footsteps of Orpheus.*

10. Neher makes a crucial point related to this matter: "When a Jew questions himself about his identity, he feels himself questioned by the desert, assailed by a series of questions left by the biblical desert in the collective memory of the Jewish people"; see André Neher, *They Made Their Souls Anew,* 83.

11. Samson Raphael Hirsch, *The Nineteen Letters on Judaism,* 110. The religious Zionist Isaac Breuer, who lived later than Hirsch, saw clearly what lay behind the Europeans' "emancipation" of the Jews: "Their [the Jews'] bodies are covered with the scars your hand [has] inflicted and now you are disgusted by these scars. Your disgust is your Jewish question—such as you understand it. In order to solve it you have offered emancipation to the Jews like some wretched scrap of charity—there you are, take it and disappear! And when they failed to do your pleasure immediately, then you did not waste any time in turning their scars into crimes, and you would have liked best to have taken back your charity because of their insolent ingratitude." See Isaac Breuer, *Concepts of Judaism,* 306. Breuer wrote these lines before many European countries did in fact take back their charity, first through anti-Semitic legislation and then through mass extermination.

12. Adin Steinsaltz, *On Being Free,* 22.

13. Steinsaltz with Eisenberg, *The Seven Lights,* 126.

14. Emil L. Fackenheim, *Encounters between Judaism and Modern Philosophy,* 107. Elsewhere Fackenheim points out that the Maccabees introduced two firsts to Jewish history: "They, as it were, invented martyrdom, the witnessing of God unto death. Also, theirs was the first war in history in defense of a faith." See Emil L. Fackenheim, *What Is Judaism?,* 67.

15. Michael Wyschogrod, *The Body of Faith,* 181; see also Jonathan Sacks, *Crisis and Covenant,* 133.

16. See Emmanuel Levinas, *In the Time of the Nations,* 64; see also Josh Cohen, *Interrupting Auschwitz,* 98–99.

17. Emmanuel Levinas, *Difficult Freedom,* 153.

18. Levinas, *In the Time of the Nations,* 59.

19. For a valuable insight into Leopold Zunz, see Luitpold Wallach, *Liberty and Letters*; see also Peter Wagner, *Wir werden frei sein.* Of course, among the most famous Jews who converted to Christianity was Heinrich Heine, who

embraced the German Enlightenment only to realize that "the German revolution will not be milder and gentler because it was preceded by Kant's *Critique*, by Fichte's transcendental idealism, and even by the philosophy of nature. These doctrines have developed revolutionary forces that wait only for the day when they can erupt and fill the world with terror and admiration. There will be Kantians forthcoming who will hear nothing of piety in the visible world, and with sword and axe will mercilessly churn the soil of our European life, to exterminate the very last roots of the past. Armed Fichteans will enter the lists, whose fanaticism of will can be curbed neither by fear nor by self-interest. . . . But the most terrible of all would be natural philosophers . . . , [who] can call up the demoniac energies of ancient Germanic pantheism. . . . A play will be performed in Germany that will make the French Revolution seem like a harmless idyll in comparison." See Heinrich Heine, *Words of Prose*, 51–53.

20. See Leopold Zunz, *Die gottesdienstlichen Vorträge der Juden*; Leopold Zunz, *Die Literaturgeschichte der synagogalen Poesie*.

21. Also worth noting in this connection is Moritz Steinschneider (1816–1907), the nineteenth century's greatest bibliographer of Judaica; see Moritz Steinschneider, *Bibliographische Handbuch über die theoretische und praktische Literatur für hebräische Sprachkunde*.

22. For a good study of Nachman Krochmal, see Jay Michael Harris, *Nachman Krochmal*. See also Maimonides, *The Guide for the Perplexed*.

23. See Salomon Formstecher, *Die Religion des Geistes*; Samuel Hirsch, *Die Religionsphilosophie der Juden*.

24. For works that provide good explanations of this development of Jewish thought, see Joseph Blau, *Modern Varieties of Judaism*; Jacob Agus, *Modern Philosophies of Judaism*; and Nathan Rotenstreich, *Jewish Philosophy in Modern Times*.

25. See, for example, Immanuel Kant, *The Critique of Practical Reason*, 101.

26. See Immanuel Kant, *Grounding for the Metaphysics of Morals*, 30–32.

27. Responding to the Voice of God at Mount Sinai, the Israelites cried out, "We will do, and we will hear" (Exodus 24:7), to affirm their devotion to Torah. Emmanuel Levinas correctly points out that such an outcry "cannot be assimilated to the categorical imperative, where a universal suddenly finds itself in a position to direct the will; it derives, rather, from the love of one's neighbor, a love without eros, lacking self-indulgence, which is, in this sense, a love that is obeyed"; see Emmanuel Levinas, "Revelation in the Jewish Tradition," 206.

28. Immanuel Kant, *The Critique of Pure Reason,* 745–46.

29. Kant, *The Critique of Practical Reason,* 107.

30. See Moritz Lazarus, *The Ethics of Judaism,* vol. 2, 56–57. Paul Lawrence Rose has shown that Kant, in *Religion within the Limits of Reason Alone,* denies that Judaism is even a religion; rather, he says, it is nothing more than a "national community." Therefore, Kant says, Judaism lacks the "inner moral imperative that constitutes freedom" and that is the basis of any "true" religion. See Paul Lawrence Rose, *German Question/Jewish Question,* 93–94.

31. Sacks, *Crisis and Covenant,* 262; see also Kant, *Religion within the Limits of Reason Alone,* 116ff.

32. Immanuel Kant, *The Conflict of the Faculties,* 95.

33. Lazarus, *The Ethics of Judaism,* vol. 1, 112.

34. For example, see ibid., vol. 2, 123.

35. Abraham Joshua Heschel, *Man's Quest for God,* 76.

36. See, for example, Emmanuel Levinas, *Ethics and Infinity,* 105.

37. In fact, the word *tsedek* is repeated: "Justice, justice shall you seek." The second "justice," or *tsedek,* says Nachmanides, "is that which frightens the righteous"; see Nachmanides, *Commentary on the Torah,* vol. 2, 196. If so, perhaps it is the justice that even the righteous fall short of: even the righteous have a task *yet to be* performed. They, too, have to show up on the Day of Atonement.

38. See, for example, Lazarus, *The Ethics of Judaism,* vol. 2, 52.

39. Emmanuel Levinas, *Otherwise Than Being, or Beyond Essence,* 11.

40. See Emil L. Fackenheim, "Jewish Existence and the Living God," 255–56.

41. Fackenheim, *Quest for Past and Future,* 14.

42. Cited in the introduction to Hermann Cohen, *Reason and Hope,* 17.

43. Ibid.

44. Ibid., 122. Of course, from the perspective of Jewish thought, God is neither a concept nor a hypothesis, as Fackenheim has shown; see Fackenheim, *Encounters between Judaism and Modern Philosophy,* 15. See also Emil L. Fackenheim, *God's Presence in History,* 40.

45. See, for example, Cohen, *Reason and Hope,* 94–98. Here it is worth noting Buber's opposing view that "for Judaism, God is not a Kantian idea but an elementally present spiritual reality—neither something conceived by pure reason nor something postulated by practical reason, but emanating from the immediacy of existence as such, which religious man steadfastly confronts and non-

religious man evades"; see Martin Buber, *On Judaism,* 109. Therefore, says Buber, "the meaning of the act of decision in Judaism is falsified if it is viewed merely as an ethical act" (Buber, *On Judaism,* 83).

46. Cohen, *Reason and Hope,* 96.

47. Ibid., 141–42. Cohen's accent on justice, rather than on freedom, is a Jewish feature of his thinking, one that distinguishes him from a strict Kantian in the tradition of German Idealism.

48. See Maimonides, *Moreh Nevuchim* 1:54.

49. See ibid., 2:39.

50. See, for example, ibid., 1:33.

51. Hermann Cohen, *Religion of Reason out of the Sources of Judaism,* 208.

52. Ibid., 187. This position is in sharp contrast to that of an earlier Jewish rationalist, Gersonides, who in the fourteenth century wrote, "Adherence to reason is not permitted if it contradicts religious faith"; see Gersonides, *The Wars of the Lord,* vol. 1, 226.

53. Cohen, *Religion of Reason out of the Sources of Judaism,* 237.

54. Ibid., 324.

55. Ibid., 157. Here we may contrast Cohen's notion of "rest" with the Jewish notion of *menuchah,* which is not merely "rest" but "peace" and "repose," a condition of wholeness attained not in having a "day off" but in the embrace of the Holy One.

56. Ibid., 259.

57. Says Maimonides, "God commanded us to abstain from work on the Sabbath, and to rest, for two purposes, namely, (1) That we might conform to the true theory, that of the Creation, which at once and clearly leads to the theory of the existence of God. (2) That we might remember how kind God has been in freeing us from the burden of the Egyptians"; see Maimonides, *Moreh Nevuchim* 2:31.

58. Abraham Joshua Heschel, *The Sabbath,* 89.

59. Cohen, *Religion of Reason out of the Sources of Judaism,* 371.

60. See, for example, R. Solomon Ganzfried, comp., *Kitsur Shulchan Arukh* 29:3.

61. Abraham Joshua Heschel, *Man Is Not Alone,* 194.

62. See Franz Rosenzweig, *Franz Rosenzweig's "The New Thinking,"* 86.

63. For an exposition of the primacy of speech over thought in Judaism, see Shalom Dov Ber Schneersohn, *Yom Tov Shel Rosh Hashanah 5659: Discourse One.*

64. See Franz Rosenzweig, *Understanding the Sick and the Healthy*, 91–92.

65. Ibid., 71.

66. Ibid., 72.

67. Emmanuel Levinas, *Outside the Subject*, 35.

68. Emmanuel Levinas, *Of God Who Comes to Mind*, 56.

69. See Levinas, *Ethics and Infinity*, 109.

70. Levinas, *Of God Who Comes to Mind*, 148.

71. Levinas, *Difficult Freedom*, 17.

72. Levinas, *Outside the Subject*, 57.

73. God is not love, says Levinas; rather, God is the *commandment* to love. See Emmanuel Levinas, "The Paradox of Morality," 176–77.

74. See, for example, Emmanuel Levinas, *Collected Philosophical Papers*, 59.

75. See, for example, Levinas, *Of God Who Comes to Mind*, 71.

76. See, for example, Levinas, *Ethics and Infinity*, 99.

77. Recall Levinas's assertion that "the meaning of being, the meaning of creation, is to realize the Torah" in Emmanuel Levinas, *Nine Talmudic Readings*, 41.

78. See, for example, Levinas, "Ethics and Spirit," in *Difficult Freedom*, 3–10.

79. Levinas, *Ethics and Infinity*, 86.

80. Levinas, *Outside the Subject*, 148.

81. Levinas, "Revelation in the Jewish Tradition," 204.

82. Levinas, *Difficult Freedom*, 173.

83. See Emmanuel Levinas, "Bad Conscience and the Inexorable," 40. Note the implication that, if Levinas is right, there is no inauthenticity more inauthentic than Heidegger's *Sein zum Tod,* or "being-toward-death," which is a being toward *my* death and an indifference toward the death of the other.

84. Kalonymos Kalmish Shapira, *Sacred Fire,* 56. For more about Amalek, see chap. 8, this volume.

85. Joseph Soloveitchik, *The Halakhic Mind,* 51.

86. Ibid., 53.

87. Cohen, *Religion of Reason out of the Sources of Judaism,* 160.

88. See Emil L. Fackenheim, *Hermann Cohen—After Fifty Years,* 20.

89. Fackenheim, *God's Presence in History,* 83.

90. Note here the teaching of the great sixteenth-century mystic Rabbi Shabtai Sheftl Horowitz: "There is no essential difference between the soul of man and the blessed Creator, except for the fact that the Creator is the totality of

existence, the all-embracing Infinite Light, and the soul is a particle of that great Light" (introduction to the *Shefa Tal*); see Avraham Yaakov Finkel, *Kabbalah*, 158.

91. Jean-François Lyotard, *Heidegger and "the jews,"* 23.

92. See Cohen, *Interrupting Auschwitz*, xvii.

93. Zachary Braiterman, *(God) after Auschwitz*, 166.

94. Levinas, *Otherwise Than Being, or Beyond Essence*, 169–70.

95. Braiterman, *(God) after Auschwitz*, 166.

96. See Finkel, *Kabbalah*, 315.

97. See Matityahu Glazerson, *Building Blocks of the Soul*, 175.

98. Adin Steinsaltz, *The Strife of the Spirit*, 214–15.

99. See Elie Wiesel, *Ani Maamin*, 27.

100. The Kotel, or Western Wall, immediately comes to mind in this connection. Drawing both Jewish and non-Jewish worshipers from all over the world, its cracks and crevices are filled with prayers written on scraps of paper in all the languages of the world. Indeed, the Western Wall is not a wall—it is a portal.

101. Says Neher, "Zion, which is only a fragment of Jerusalem and the Land of Israel, is a word one can neither play around with, nor play tricks with, nor beat around the bush with. It is the key word of the 'meta' of Jewish history. Through Zion, Zionism becomes bi-dimensional. The vertical is interlocked with the horizontal." See André Neher, *They Made Their Souls Anew*, 58.

102. Adin Steinsaltz, *The Long Shorter Way*, 28.

103. The seven other things distinguished by the word *living* are the righteous, the Garden of Eden, a tree, the Land of Israel, loving kindness, the wise, and water.

4 THE HOLOCAUST AND THE HOLY TONGUE

1. Primo Levi, *Survival in Auschwitz*, 26.

2. Sara Nomberg-Przytyk, *Auschwitz*, 72.

3. Ka-tzetnik 135633, *House of Dolls*, 125.

4. Matityahu Glazerson, *Building Blocks of the Soul*, 63–64.

5. Adin Steinsaltz, *Simple Words*, 18.

6. Emmanuel Levinas, *Ethics and Infinity*, 87–88.

7. Ibid., 86.

8. See ibid.

9. Emmanuel Levinas, *Nine Talmudic Readings,* 46.

10. Cf. Emil L. Fackenheim, *Quest for Past and Future,* 43.

11. See Avraham Moshe Rabinowitz, *Chachimah Birmizah,* 282; see also Victor Cohen, ed., *The Soul of the Torah,* 216.

12. Primo Levi, *The Drowned and the Saved,* 93–94.

13. Yehudah Leib Alter, *The Language of Truth,* 16.

14. Michael L. Munk, *The Wisdom in the Hebrew Alphabet,* 222. See also *Sefer Yetzirah* 1:1.

15. The Chasidic master Rabbi Yehudah Leib Alter makes the point that "all seventy languages flow forth from the holy tongue"; see Alter, *The Language of Truth,* 62.

16. This teaching is discussed in Nachmanides, *Commentary on the Torah,* vol. 2, 543. For similar teachings of the Baal Shem Tov on Betsalel, see Yaakov Yosef of Polnoe, *Toledot Yaakov Yosef, Pekudei* 4; see also *Keter Shem Tov,* 319.

17. Louis Jacobs, *Hasidic Prayer,* 76.

18. Kaplan attests to the Nazi assault on prayer in the entry he recorded in his diary on the eve of Tisha B'Av 1940: "Public prayer in these dangerous times is a forbidden act. Anyone caught in this crime is doomed to severe punishment. If you will, it is even sabotage, and anyone engaging in sabotage is subject to execution." See Chaim A. Kaplan, *The Warsaw Diary of Chaim A. Kaplan,* 179.

19. Recall, too, that, according to the Talmud, when Pharaoh tested Joseph on the seventy languages of the world, Hebrew was not among those languages; thus Joseph knew one language more than the Pharaoh: he knew the holy tongue (see *Sotah* 36b).

20. Alter, *The Language of Truth,* 106.

21. Yitzchak Ginsburgh, *The Alef-Beit,* 2–3.

22. Adin Steinsaltz, *The Sustaining Utterance,* 32.

23. Abraham Isaac Kook, *Orot,* 93.

24. Primo Levi, *The Reawakening,* 33.

25. Ibid., 128.

26. Primo Levi, *La tregua,* 250.

27. Elie Wiesel relates a story that comes to mind in this connection. It is about "the Great Fall" suffered by Rabbi Yaakov Yitzchak, the Holy Seer of Lublin. In the midst of a Simchat Torah celebration, the Seer left his Chasidim

and retired to his study on the second floor of the synagogue. After some time had passed, the Chasidim went to check on their master. But he was nowhere to be found: he had simply disappeared. After they searched the streets of the city, they finally discovered him lying in an alley. They rushed to him and heard a repeated whisper coming from his lips: "And the abyss calls for another abyss, the abyss. . . . " And Wiesel asks: Can it be "that in a sudden flash of fear the Seer had a glimpse of the distant future when night would descend upon the Jewish people and particularly upon its most compassionate and generous children—those of the Hasidic community? . . . Lublin, during the darkest hours, became a center for torment and death. Lublin, an ingathering place for condemned Jews, led to nearby Belzec. Lublin meant Majdanek. Lublin meant the great fall not of one man, nor of one people, but of mankind." See Elie Wiesel, *Somewhere a Master*, 117, 137–38. See also Shlomo Yosef Zevin, *A Treasury of Chasidic Tales on the Torah*, 98.

28. Elie Wiesel once asked a friend what he thought of Auschwitz. His friend answered, "I found it a spectacle of terrifying beauty." See Elie Wiesel, *Legends of Our Time*, 216.

29. Charlotte Delbo, *None of Us Will Return*, 6.

30. Elie Wiesel, *Night*, 105.

31. See Levi, *Survival in Auschwitz*, 98.

32. André Neher, *The Prophetic Existence*, 277.

33. Ibid., 142.

34. George Lucius Salton, *The 23rd Psalm*, 218.

35. Leo Baeck, *The Essence of Judaism*, 234.

36. Fackenheim, *Quest for Past and Future*, 84.

37. Ibid., 89. Recall, too, this insight from Abraham Joshua Heschel: "To the modern historian, history is not the understanding of events, but rather the understanding of man's experience of events. What concerns the prophet is the human event as a divine experience." See Abraham Joshua Heschel, *The Prophets*, vol. 1, 172.

38. See *Zohar* I, 22b.

39. Franklin Littell raises a key question in this connection: "On what basis do we affirm that the Exodus, Sinai, the return from the first exile, . . . the destruction of the Temple, . . . the Holocaust, . . . a restored Israel, and a united Jerusalem . . . [are] more important to our view of history than, say, the Battle of

Waterloo or Custer's Last Stand?" See Franklin Littell, *The Crucifixion of the Jews,* 10.

40. Elijah Benamozegh, *Israel and Humanity,* 124.

41. Abraham Joshua Heschel, *Israel,* 129–30.

42. Heschel, *The Prophets,* vol. 1, 198.

43. Elie Wiesel, *From the Kingdom of Memory,* 239.

44. According to a talmudic legend, the Messiah is disguised as a leper and waits at the gates of Rome to see whether humanity has merited redemption; see *Sanhedrin* 98a. See also Adolph Jellinek, ed., *Sefer Zerubavel,* vol. 2, 54–55; Raphael Patai, *The Messiah Texts,* 110–11.

45. For an extended dialogue on what this *after* might mean, see David Patterson and John K. Roth, eds., *After-Words.* In chap. 9 of this volume, we shall discuss at length the place of the Messiah in post-Holocaust Jewish thought.

46. See Dovid Kirschenbaum, ed., *Fun di Chasidishe Ostros,* 120; see also Cohen, ed., *The Soul of the Torah,* 58.

47. Heschel, *The Prophets,* 172.

48. Eliezer Berkovits, *Faith after the Holocaust,* 64.

49. Emmanuel Levinas, "Zionisms," 271.

50. Levinas, *Nine Talmudic Readings,* 190–91. These words become more and more prophetic as more and more countries suffer from the sort of terrorist attacks that Israel has endured for decades.

51. Ka-tzetnik 135633, *Shivitti,* xi.

52. Recall, in this connection, Jean Améry's astute observation: "It was not the case that the intellectual . . . had now become unintellectual or incapable of thinking. On the contrary, only rarely did thinking grant itself a respite. But it nullified itself when at almost every step it ran into its uncrossable borders. The axes of its traditional frames of reference then shattered." See Jean Améry, *At the Mind's Limits,* 19. Recall, too, the observations of Primo Levi and Simon Wiesenthal. "We had an incorrigible tendency," says Levi, "to see a symbol and a sign in every event"; see Levi, *Survival in Auschwitz,* 77. And Wiesenthal: "At that time we were ready to see symbols in everything"; see Simon Wiesenthal, *The Sunflower,* 40.

53. Nachman of Breslov, *Advice,* 301.

54. Wiesel, *Night,* 39.

55. Alexander Donat, *The Holocaust Kingdom,* 168.

56. Moshe Sandberg, *My Longest Year,* 55.

57. André Neher, *The Exile of the Word*, 37.

58. See Saadia Gaon, *The Book of Belief and Opinions*, 255–56. See also Talmud tractate *Avodah Zarah*, 20b.

59. Says Nachman of Breslov, "All a person's deeds are inscribed in his soul. That is why after death a person is asked if he remembers his name." See Nachman of Breslov, *Tikkun*, 102. See also Rabbi Nathan of Nemirov, *Rabbi Nachman's Wisdom*, 148.

60. Cf. Emmanuel Levinas, *Difficult Freedom*, 17.

61. Edmond Jabès, *A Foreigner Carrying in the Crook of His Arm a Tiny Book*, 67.

62. Wiesel, *Night*, 15.

63. Livia E. Bitton-Jackson, *Elli*, 38.

64. Recall here Franz Rosenzweig's notion of the "speaking thinker," discussed in chap. 3.

65. See, for example, Chayyim Vital, *Shaarei Kedushah*, part 1, gate 2.

66. See also Shalom Dov Ber Schneersohn, *Yom Tov Shel Rosh Hashanah 5659: Discourse One*, 36.

67. See *Zohar* I, 8a. The Talmud identifies Dumah as the angel who is in charge of all the souls; see *Sanhedrin* 94a.

68. Kalonymos Kalmish Shapira, *Sacred Fire*, 22.

69. Ibid., 23.

70. Josef Bor, *The Terezín Requiem*, 41–42.

71. See Josef Bor, *Terezínské rekviem*, 27.

72. George Topas, *The Iron Furnace*, 114.

73. Wieslaw Kielar, *Anus Mundi*, 158.

74. Nathan Shapell, *Witness to the Truth*, 81–82.

75. Meir ibn Gabbai, *Sod ha-Shabbat*, 55.

76. Neher, *The Exile of the Word*, 10.

77. See Franz Rosenzweig, *Understanding the Sick and the Healthy*, 65–66.

78. Josh Cohen, *Interrupting Auschwitz*, 108.

79. Emmanuel Levinas, *Collected Philosophical Papers*, 136.

80. Shapira, *Sacred Fire*, 291. See also Judah Halevi, *Kuzari* (*Kitav al khazari* 1:91).

81. See Nachmanides, *Commentary on the Torah*, vol. 1, 112.

82. Fania Fénelon, *Playing for Time*, ix.

83. Alter, *The Language of Truth*, 86.

84. Elie Wiesel, *The Gates of the Forest*, 197.

85. Benjamin Blech, *More Secrets of Hebrew Words*, 213. In his commentary on Exodus 20:2, Rashi says that all of the words of the Revelation at Mount Sinai were given in this single utterance.

86. Levinas, *Difficult Freedom*, 12.

5 THE *SIFREI KODESH* AND THE HOLOCAUST

1. Elie Wiesel, *Against Silence: The Voice and Vision of Elie Wiesel*, vol. 1, 239.

2. Emil L. Fackenheim, *To Mend the World* , 18.

3. Emil L. Fackenheim, *What Is Judaism?*, 60.

4. Franz Rosenzweig, *On Jewish Learning*, 81.

5. Emmanuel Levinas, *New Talmudic Readings*, 75–76.

6. Emmanuel Levinas, *Difficult Freedom*, 220.

7. See, for example, Abraham ibn Ezra, *The Secret of the Torah*, 64–65.

8. Menachem M. Schneerson *Torah Studies*, 74.

9. Ibid., 74–75. The same applies if you wish to know the One who remained silent and reverted the world to nothingness.

10. Yitzchak Abohav, *Menoras Hamaor*, 246.

11. Elie Wiesel, *Legends of Our Time*, 230.

12. Recall Alfred Rosenberg's insistence on the definitive relation between the essence of the Jew and the Talmud, regardless of the stated beliefs of any particular Jew; see Alfred Rosenberg, *Race and Race History and Other Essays*, 181.

13. *Sefer Yetzirah*, 16.

14. Recall passages such as the one from Dribben's memoir, where a Nazi beholds a synagogue in flames and declares, "The Jewish God is burnt to ashes!"; see Judith Dribben, *And Some Shall Live*, 24.

15. Recall, in this connection, Fackenheim's astute observation: "The conjunction of birth and crime is a *novum* in history"; see Emil L. Fackenheim, *The Jewish Bible after the Holocaust*, 87.

16. Emmanuel Levinas, *Nine Talmudic Readings*, 183.

17. See, for example, Martin Heidegger, *Sein und Zeit*, 251.

18. Yitzchak Ginsburgh, *The Alef-Beit*, 46.

19. It should be noted that "seeing to the affairs of the house" entails a responsibility for four of the most sacred realms of Jewish life: adherence to the laws

of *kashrut,* the mitzvah of *challah,* the observance of the laws of family purity, and ushering in the Sabbath—all of which are in the care of women.

20. See also the commentary on Exodus 19:3 in Rashi, *Commentary on the Torah.*

21. Joseph Gikatilla, *Sha'are Orah,* 204.

22. This noun appears, for example, in the verse *Moshivi akeret habayit em-habanim smechah,* "He makes a barren woman to dwell in her house, as a joyful mother of children" (Psalms 113:9).

23. For this reason, the Maharal of Prague declared, "Woman is the consummation of man's existence, for through her, man becomes complete. When a man has his own woman [a bride], his existence is essential, not casual. When he has an illicit relationship with a woman, however—when the lust strikes him—his very existence is casual. Thus 'He who has illicit relations with a woman lacks a heart.' The Torah, too, completes man; it is often compared to a woman [see, for example, *Kiddushin* 30b] because, like woman, it makes man complete." See Yehuda Loeve, *Nesivos Olam,* 106.

24. Aryeh Kaplan, commentary, *The Bahir,* 127–28.

25. Primo Levi, *Survival in Auschwitz,* 42.

26. Ginsburgh, *The Alef-Beit,* 88.

27. Schneur Zalman, *Likutei Amarim Tanya,* 593.

28. The verse adds: "And you shall be comforted in Jerusalem"—yet another key to making Jerusalem the center of Jewish thought, for Jewish thought must be guided by this love if it is truly to be Jewish.

29. Ginsburgh, *The Alef-Beit,* 45.

30. If, as it is written, the Messiah is the *avi-ad,* the "Everlasting Father" (Isaiah 9:6), it is because he is the Everlasting Teacher, the one whose teaching is so powerful, so compelling, that it will be inscribed in the heart of every human being (cf. Jeremiah 24:7); but that Everlasting Father has yet to come.

31. Nachman of Breslov, *The Aleph-Bet Book,* 219–20.

32. Maimonides, *The Guide for the Perplexed,* 74.

33. Gersonides, *The Wars of the Lord,* vol. 1, 157.

34. Matityahu Glazerson, *Building Blocks of the Soul,* 253.

35. Moshe Chayim Luzzatto, *The Path of the Just,* 147–49.

36. Wiesel, *Legends of Our Time,* 18.

37. Among the earliest texts to address the ten *sefirot* is the *Sefer Yetzirah* (1:4).

38. See Kaplan, commentary, *The Bahir,* 145.

39. Charlotte Delbo, *None of Us Will Return,* 6.

40. Jean Améry, *At the Mind's Limits,* 19.

41. Emmanuel Levinas, *Collected Philosophical Papers,* 112.

42. Kaplan, commentary, *The Bahir,* 92.

43. Says Elie Wiesel, "It was as though the Nazi killers knew precisely what children represent to us. According to our tradition, the entire world subsists thanks to them." I would make just one slight change to his insightful remark: it was not "as though." See Elie Wiesel, *A Jew Today,* 178–79.

44. Israel Gutman, introduction to Adam Czerniakow, *The Warsaw Ghetto Diary of Adam Czerniakow,* 70.

45. Elie Wiesel, *Night,* 62.

46. Elie Wiesel, *Ani Maamin,* 27.

47. Cited in Nehemia Polen, *The Holy Fire,* 102. In the Zohar it is written: "For they who are the friends of the Shekhinah and are near to Her are regarded as Her face" (*Zohar* II, 163b).

48. Elik Rivosh, "From the Notebook of the Sculptor Elik Rivosh (Riga)," 397.

49. See David Patterson, *In Dialogue and Dilemma with Elie Wiesel,* 21.

50. See Ka-tzetnik 135633, *House of Dolls,* 44.

51. "She was six years old," Wiesel relates of a little girl who embodies the ontological condition of all these children, "a pale, shy and nervous child. Did she know what was happening around her? How much did she understand of the events? She saw the killers kill, she saw them kill—how did she translate these visions in her child's mind? One morning she asked her mother to hug her. Then she came to place a kiss on her father's forehead. And she said, 'I think that I shall die today.' And after a sigh, a long sigh: 'I think I am glad.'" See Wiesel, *A Jew Today,* 128. The child who is glad to die has been robbed of her life before that life has been extinguished.

52. See Emil L. Fackenheim, *The Jewish Return into History,* 246.

53. Elie Wiesel, *The Oath,* 132.

54. Vilna Gaon, *Even Sheleimah,* 45.

55. Benno Heinemann, *The Maggid of Dubno and His Parables,* 200–201.

56. James E. Young, "Interpreting Literary Testimony," 414. To Young's credit, what he says is at least intelligible. There are others who, in order to hide the fact that they have nothing to say, resort to a calculated obfuscation. Commenting on the distinction between absence and loss in "texts," for instance, LaCapra explains, "Absence applies transhistorically to absolute foundations; loss applies to historical phenomena. The conflation of absence and loss induces

either a metametaphysical etherealization, even obfuscation, of historical problems or a historicist, reductive localization of transhistorical, recurrently displaced problems—or perhaps a confusingly hybridized, extremely labile discourse that seems to derive critical analyses of historical phenomena directly from the deconstruction of metaphysics and metametaphysical, at times freely associative (or disseminatory), glosses of specific historical dynamics." See Dominick LaCapra, *Writing History, Writing Trauma,* 195.

57. Herman Kruk, "Diary of the Vilna Ghetto," 20.

58. Avraham Tory, *Surviving the Holocaust,* 114.

59. Emmanuel Ringelblum, *Notes from the Warsaw Ghetto,* 230.

60. Yitzhak Katznelson, *Vittel Diary,* 109.

61. Sara Zyskind, *Stolen Years,* 11.

62. Ibid., 44.

63. Isabella Leitner, *Fragments of Isabella,* 32.

64. Zyskind, *Stolen Years,* 100–101.

65. Gerda Weissmann Klein, *All But My Life,* 20.

66. Ibid., 8.

67. Leon Wells, *The Death Brigade,* 103.

68. Livia E. Bitton-Jackson, *Elli,* 3–4.

69. Aryeh Klonicki-Klonymus, *The Diary of Adam's Father,* 24.

70. Hanna Levy-Hass, *Vielleicht war das alles erst der Anfang,* 15 (my translation).

71. Hersh Wasser, "Daily Entries of Hersh Wasser," 223.

72. Wiesel, *A Jew Today,* 81.

73. Simon Wiesenthal, *The Sunflower,* 47.

74. Wells, *The Death Brigade,* 107.

75. Alexander Donat, *The Holocaust Kingdom,* 94.

76. See Emil L. Fackenheim, *God's Presence in History,* 84.

6 THE MUSELMANN AND THE MATTER OF THE HUMAN BEING

1. Albo points out that, according to Jewish tradition, our souls were brought into being on the first day of creation, with the utterance "Let there be light"; see Joseph Albo, *Sefer Ha-'Ikkarim,* vol. 4, 30. See also *Shushan Sodot,* 6.

2. Leon Poliakov, *The Harvest of Hate,* 222.

3. Rudolf Vrba with Alan Bestic, *I Cannot Forgive,* 91.

4. See, for example, *Makkot* 24a; *Zohar* II, 165b; Chayyim Vital, *Shaarei Kedushah,* part 1, gate 1; commentary on Deuteronomy 20:11 in Chayim ben Attar, *Or Hachayim*; *Keter Shem Tov* 53).

5. In the words of the eleventh-century sage Bachya ibn Paquda, "Life and Death are brethren, dwelling together closely to one another, inseparable, holding fast to the two ends of a tottering bridge over which all the world's creatures pass. Life is at its entrance; Death is at its exit. Life builds, Death breaks up. Life sows, Death reaps. Life unites, Death divides. Life strings together, Death scatters what has been strung together." See the Admonition in Bachya ibn Paquda, *Chovot Halevavot,* vol. 2, 389.

6. Abraham Joshua Heschel, *Man's Quest for God,* 76.

7. Emil L. Fackenheim, *The Jewish Return into History,* 246.

8. See Primo Levi, *Se questo è un uomo.* An earlier translation rendered the title literally; see Primo Levi, *If This Is a Man.*

9. Emil L. Fackenheim, *God's Presence in History,* 86.

10. Primo Levi, *Survival in Auschwitz,* 90.

11. I am quite aware that Levi rejected God. "I'd like to be [a believer], but I don't succeed," he told Ferdinando Camon. "There is Auschwitz, and so there cannot be God. I don't find a solution to this dilemma. I keep looking, but I don't find it." See Ferdinando Camon, *Conversations with Primo Levi,* 68. But I take Levi at his word: he would like to believe. And he keeps looking. Therefore, he is moved by a religious impulse. Further, given his extreme sensitivity to the Nazis' assault on language, I assume that Levi is very careful with his words so that he is serious when he refers to the Divine spark. Finally, I believe that religious thinkers can learn from Levi and from the implications of his thought, whether he is himself religious or not.

12. Levi, *Survival in Auschwitz,* 90.

13. Emil L. Fackenheim, *To Mend the World,* 100.

14. Levi, *Survival in Auschwitz,* 88.

15. Fackenheim, *To Mend the World,* 100.

16. Fackenheim, *The Jewish Return into History,* 246.

17. Levi, *Survival in Auschwitz,* 90.

18. Levi, *Se questo è un uomo,* 82.

19. Elie Wiesel, *Evil and Exile,* 155.

20. Primo Levi, *The Drowned and the Saved,* 31.

21. See Primo Levi, *The Reawakening,* 128.

22. Emmanuel Levinas, *Outside the Subject*, 87.

23. Franz Rosenzweig, *The Star of Redemption*, 224.

24. Emmanuel Levinas, *Existence and Existents*, 35.

25. Abraham ibn Ezra, *The Commentary of Ibn Ezra on Isaiah*, 287.

26. Emmanuel Levinas, *Nine Talmudic Readings*, 135.

27. Abraham Joshua Heschel, *The Sabbath*, 100.

28. Emmanuel Levinas, "Dialogue with Emmanuel Levinas," 18.

29. Levi, *Survival in Auschwitz*, 66.

30. Fackenheim, *To Mend the World*, 18.

31. Levinas, *Nine Talmudic Readings*, 41.

32. Fackenheim, *God's Presence in History*, 84.

33. Emil L. Fackenheim, *Encounters between Judaism and Modern Philosophy*, 167.

34. Fackenheim, *The Jewish Return into History*, 251.

35. Ibid., 247.

36. Emil L. Fackenheim, *The Jewish Bible after the Holocaust*, 67.

37. Miklós Nyiszli, *Auschwitz*, 151.

38. Fackenheim, *The Jewish Return into History*, 265.

39. Ibid., 269.

40. Fackenheim, *God's Presence in History*, 73.

41. Elie Wiesel, *Night*, 5.

42. Levi, *Survival in Auschwitz*, 90.

43. Ibid.

44. Ibid., 19.

45. Ibid., 74.

46. Wiesel, *Night*, 50.

47. Emmanuel Levinas, *Totality and Infinity*, 75.

48. Fackenheim, *To Mend the World*, 135.

49. Levinas, *Existence and Existents*, 57–58.

50. Emmanuel Levinas, *Time and the Other*, 46.

51. Emmanuel Levinas, *Ethics and Infinity*, 52.

52. Levinas, *Existence and Existents*, 61.

53. Levi, *Survival in Auschwitz*, 38. Significantly, *babel* is a cognate of *mabul*, the Hebrew word for "flood," the flood by which creation was undone.

54. Yaakov Culi, *The Torah Anthology*, vol. 1, 420. Recall the discussion of the Tower of Babel in chap. 2, this volume.

55. Levi, *The Drowned and the Saved,* 93–94.

56. See Primo Levi, *I sommersi e I salvati,* 72.

57. Levi, *Survival in Auschwitz,* 26.

58. Ibid., 27.

59. Levi, *The Drowned and the Saved,* 119.

60. See Nathan of Nemirov, *Rabbi Nachman's Wisdom,* 148.

61. See Nachman of Breslov, *Tikkun,* 102.

62. See, for example, Elie Wiesel, *Somewhere a Master,* 39.

63. Abraham ibn Ezra, *The Commentary of Ibn Ezra on Isaiah,* 73.

64. In Levi's memoir, one sees this process of transforming the person into a thing under way from the beginning, for when the Jews were counted for transport to Auschwitz, the Nazi officer asked, "*Wieviel Stück?*—How many 'pieces'?" See Levi, *Survival in Auschwitz,* 16.

65. Levi, *The Drowned and the Saved,* 119. And recall a line from Olga Lengyel's memoir: "I was number '25,403.' I still have it on my right arm and shall carry it with me to the grave." See Olga Lengyel, *Five Chimneys,* 116.

66. Levi, *Survival in Auschwitz,* 27–28.

67. Ibid., 72–73.

68. *Pirke de Rabbi Eliezer* 24.

69. Ibid., 123.

70. Here is it interesting to note that the word *Mensch,* or "man," was under assault in Nazi Germany in literal ways. In 1935, for example, the Guild of National Socialist Attorneys proposed that the word *Mensch* be removed from the legal code, since it created "confusion."

71. See, for example, Fackenheim, *To Mend the World,* 310.

72. Fackenheim, *God's Presence in History,* 88.

73. Levinas, *Nine Talmudic Readings,* 168.

74. Pelagia Lewinska, *Twenty Months at Auschwitz,* 150.

75. Fackenheim, *To Mend the World,* 218.

76. Ibid., 248.

77. Fackenheim, *The Jewish Return into History,* 89.

78. See Fackenheim, *To Mend the World,* 209; see also the discussion of this point in chap. 7, this volume.

79. Levi, *Survival in Auschwitz,* 9.

80. Fackenheim, *Encounters between Judaism and Modern Philosophy,* 49.

81. Fackenheim, *To Mend the World,* 71.

82. Recall, for example, this passage from Yitzhak Katznelson's diary: "Instead of loathing and despising those foulest dregs of humanity, the accursed German nation, we have begun to hate ourselves"; see Yitzhak Katznelson, *Vittel Diary* 94.

83. Fackenheim, *To Mend the World*, 223–24.

84. Ka-tzetnik 135633, *Sunrise over Hell*, 111.

85. Emil L. Fackenheim, *What Is Judaism?*, 109.

86. It is no accident that by 1940 nearly half the so-called philosophers of Germany were card-carrying Nazis. Among them were not only Martin Heidegger but also Kantian Idealists such as Bruno Bauch, Max Wundt, Hans Heyse, and Nicolai Hartmann; the noted Hegelian Theodor Haerung; and those, such as Alfred Bäumler and Ernst Krieck, who turned to Nietzsche for their inspiration. It is also worth noting that Aristotle is among Hannah Arendt's chief influences.

87. Emmanuel Levinas, *Otherwise Than Being, or Beyond Essence*, 74.

88. Ibid., 64.

89. Levi, *Survival in Auschwitz*, 39.

90. Ibid., 160.

91. Ibid., 166.

92. Levi, *The Reawakening*, 72.

93. Fackenheim, *Encounters between Judaism and Modern Philosophy*, 192–93.

94. Ka-tzetnik 135633, *Shivitti*, 7.

95. Bruno Heinemann, *The Maggid of Dubno and His Parables*, 174.

7 JEWISH THOUGHT AND A POST-HOLOCAUST *TIKKUN HAOLAM*

1. Emil L. Fackenheim, *God's Presence in History*, 74.

2. Aryeh Kaplan, *Inner Space*, 170.

3. Emmanuel Levinas, *Difficult Freedom*, 6.

4. Emmanuel Levinas, *Collected Philosophical Papers*, 93.

5. Emil L. Fackenheim, *To Mend the World*, 222.

6. Ibid., 218–23.

7. Ibid., 300.

8. Ibid., 310.

9. Leo Baeck, *The Essence of Judaism*, 236.

10. André Neher, *The Exile of the Word*, 63.

11. See Moshe Weissman ed., *The Midrash Says,* vol. 1, 83.

12. See also Maimonides, *The Commandments,* vol. 1, 228.

13. See, for example, Emmanuel Ringelblum, *Notes from the Warsaw Ghetto,* 230.

14. Yitzhak Katznelson, *Vittel Diary,* 109.

15. Recall the discussion of women and the feminine in chap. 5 of this volume.

16. Emmanuel Levinas, *Of God Who Comes to Mind,* 13.

17. Emmanuel Levinas, *Ethics and Infinity,* 52.

18. Yehuda Loeve, *Maharal of Prague,* 322.

19. In any discussion of the mystical view of creation, it is important to keep in mind that we are speaking about the ineffable, and that we therefore use the language of metaphor.

20. Says the Chofetz Chaim, "A man must remember that each and every time he sins, he negatively affects the Heavenly realms. It is impossible to imagine how terrible is the effect of his sins on those upper realms." See Chofetz Chaim, *Let There Be Light,* 24. Recall, too, the teaching from the Maggid of Mezeritch: "Know that everything above is due to you. It is your life of holiness that creates holiness in Heaven." See Louis I. Newman, ed., *The Hasidic Anthology,* 170.

21. Many texts identify a fifth "world," *Adam Kadmon,* or the "Primal Adam," but it is so far beyond the other four that it is sometimes not counted among the worlds.

22. See also Schneur Zalman, *Likutei Amarim Tanya,* 405.

23. This is the meaning of Jacob's dream, in which he saw angels ascending and descending a ladder reaching to the upper realms (see Genesis 28:12). The ascending angels are mentioned first because they are the angels we create so that they may do the work of mending the upper worlds; the descending angels then bring holiness back into the lower worlds (see *Bereshit Rabbah* 68:12; see also *Toledot Yaakov Yosef, Chayei Sarah* 3 and *Shelach* 10).

24. See, for example, Pinchas Giller, *The Zohar: The Sacred Text of the Kabbalah,* 89–90.

25. Recall, in this connection, the point made in chap. 5 of this volume, namely, that *kidushin,* "marriage," also means "holiness."

26. See *The Zohar* II, 215b; see also Isaiah Tishby, "Prayer and Devotion in the Zohar," 362.

27. See Gershom Scholem, *Major Trends in Jewish Mysticism,* 265.

28. Zalman, *Likutei Amarim Tanya,* 621.

29. Ibid., 274.

30. Emil L. Fackenheim, *What Is Judaism?*, 85.

31. Ibid., 285.

32. See Emmanuel Levinas, *New Talmudic Readings*, 69–70.

33. Ibid., 135.

34. See Emmanuel Levinas, "Dialogue with Emmanuel Levinas," 19.

35. Fackenheim, *God's Presence in History*, 40.

36. Ibid., 17.

37. Ibid., 15–16.

38. See *Tanna debe Eliyyahu*, 69.

39. See Elie Wiesel, *Somewhere a Master*, 110.

40. Levinas, "Dialogue with Emmanuel Levinas," 23.

41. Emmanuel Levinas, "Revelation in the Jewish Tradition," 204.

42. Recall, in this connection, Fackenheim's point that "traditional Torah and what the moderns with vast equivocation call 'Torah' differ radically in that the former is, in principle, absolute instruction, whereas the latter is merely the random confirmation of the values to which the pupil subscribes to begin with"; see Emil L. Fackenheim, *Quest for Past and Future*, 57.

43. Emil L. Fackenheim, *Encounters between Judaism and Modern Philosophy*, 49.

44. Emmanuel Levinas, *Otherwise Than Being, or Beyond Essence*, 87.

45. Emmanuel Levinas, *Time and the Other*, 113.

46. Emil L. Fackenheim, *The Jewish Return into History*, 251.

47. Fackenheim, *To Mend the World*, 25.

48. Fackenheim, *What Is Judaism?*, 180 (emphasis added).

49. Emmanuel Levinas, "Ethics as First Philosophy," 84.

50. Fackenheim, *What Is Judaism?*, 109.

51. Nachmanides, *Commentary on the Torah*, vol. 1, 112.

52. See ibid., vol. 3, 36.

53. Levinas, *Otherwise Than Being, or Beyond Essence*, 11.

54. Fackenheim, *To Mend the World*, 209.

55. See, for example, Levinas, *Ethics and Infinity*, 97.

56. Emmanuel Levinas, *Nine Talmudic Readings*, 85.

57. Emmanuel Levinas, *Existence and Existents*, 57–58.

58. Levinas, *Otherwise Than Being, or Beyond Essence*, 166.

59. Levinas, "Revelation in the Jewish Tradition," 202.

60. Zygmunt Bauman, *Modernity and the Holocaust*, 214.

61. Levinas, *Collected Philosophical Papers*, 96.

62. Levinas, *Of God Who Comes to Mind*, 63.

63. Levinas, *Collected Philosophical Papers*, 100.

64. Levinas, *Ethics and Infinity*, 86–87.

65. Levinas, *Of God Who Comes to Mind*, 168.

66. Levinas, *Ethics and Infinity*, 86; see also Levinas, *Collected Philosophical Papers*, 43.

67. Levinas, *Otherwise Than Being, or Beyond Essence*, 99.

68. Emmanuel Levinas, *Outside the Subject*, 148.

69. Chayyim Vital, *Kabbalah of Creation*, 142.

70. Fackenheim, *Quest for Past and Future*, 222.

71. Levinas, "Revelation in the Jewish Tradition," 204.

72. Levinas, *Difficult Freedom*, 173.

73. Levinas, *Ethics and Infinity*, 106.

74. Levinas, *Collected Philosophical Papers*, 162.

75. Levinas, *Ethics and Infinity*, 98–99.

76. Commentary on Leviticus 26:37. in Rashi, *Commentary on the Torah*.

77. Levinas, *Otherwise Than Being, or Beyond Essence*, 93.

78. Levinas, *Collected Philosophical Papers*, 169.

79. Quoted in Meyer Levin, ed., *Hassidic Stories*, 344.

80. Levinas, *Otherwise Than Being, or Beyond Essence*, 57.

81. Levinas, *Nine Talmudic Readings*, 135.

82. Neher, *The Exile of the Word*, 123.

83. Levinas, "Dialogue with Emmanuel Levinas" 23.

84. Levinas, *Time and the Other*, 77.

85. See David Patterson, *In Dialogue and Dilemma with Elie Wiesel*, 21.

86. Elie Wiesel, *Ani Maamin*, 57.

87. Fackenheim, *God's Presence in History*, 71.

88. See Fackenheim, *To Mend the World*, 312.

89. Levinas, *Nine Talmudic Readings*, 190–91.

90. The nine other things called "living" are the Holy One, Torah, the righteous, the Garden of Eden, a tree, Jerusalem, loving kindness, the wise, and water.

91. Abraham Isaac Kook, *Orot*, 89.

92. André Neher, *They Made Their Souls Anew*, 58.

93. Adin Steinsaltz, *The Strife of the Spirit*, 214–15.

8 MYSTICAL DIMENSIONS OF POST-HOLOCAUST
JEWISH THOUGHT

1. Emil L. Fackenheim, *To Mend the World*, 25.

2. Pesach Schindler, *Hasidic Responses to the Holocaust in the Light of Hasidic Thought*, 6–8.

3. See Yissachar Shlomo Teichtal, *Em Habanim Smechah*, 22–23.

4. Ibid., 141–43.

5. Ibid., 245.

6. Ibid., 20.

7. Ibid., 13.

8. Ibid., 16.

9. The term *Oneg Shabbat* literally means "delight in the Sabbath." It was the name adopted by the group of Jewish men and women whom Ringelblum enlisted to keep diaries and other records of the Nazis' activities in Poland.

10. Mendel Peikazh, *Hateudah Hachasidut Hasefrotit Haachronah al Admat Polin*, 8.

11. For a detailed explanation of Lurianic Kabbalah, see Gershom G. Scholem, *Major Trends in Jewish Mysticism*, 244–86.

12. Adin Steinsaltz with Josy Eisenberg, *The Seven Lights*, 147.

13. Quoted in Elie Wiesel, *Against Silence*, vol. 2, 82. The Shoah has added a new fire to the fire of Torah as well as to the *chashmal* of Torah. Now we have a new silence, a post-Shoah silence, as well as a newly nuanced word for Jewish thought.

14. For an example of Chasidic teaching on this point, see Schneur Zalman, *Likutei Amarim Tanya*, 15.

15. See Kalonymos Kalmish Shapira, *Sacred Fire*, 46–47.

16. See Jacob Immanuel Schochet, *Mystical Concepts in Chassidism*, 49–59.

17. Adin Steinsaltz, *The Thirteen-Petalled Rose*, 21.

18. Adin Steinsaltz, *The Long Shorter Way*, 140.

19. See Shapira, *Sacred Fire*, 61. The *At-Bash* transformation is a means of interpretation whereby the first letter of the alphabet is interchanged with the last letter, the second letter with the penultimate letter, and so on.

20. Steinsaltz, *The Long Shorter Way*, 164.

21. Quoted in Meyer Levin, ed., *Hassidic Stories*, 47.

22. Moses Cordovero, *The Palm Tree of Devorah*, 6.

23. See also Gershom Scholem, *On the Mystical Shape of the Godhead*, 73–87; see also Zalman, *Likutei Amarim Tanya*, 23–25.

24. The ego, says the Chasidic master Yechiel Mikhal of Zlotchov, comprises the distance between the soul and the Eternal One; see Martin Buber, *Tales of the Hasidim*, 149.

25. Esther Farbstein, *Beseter Raam*, 436–37. See also Kalonymos Kalmish Shapira, *Tsav Veziruz*, 10–11.

26. Hans Jonas, *Mortality and Morality*, 137.

27. Adin Steinsaltz, *The Strife of the Spirit*, 30 (emphasis added).

28. Levinas makes the very important point that "the Word of the Living God" lies not in fixed formulas and ready answers but rather in "opposing theses"; see Emmanuel Levinas, *Difficult Freedom*, 116.

29. Emmanuel Levinas, *Collected Philosophical Papers*, 183.

30. Menachem Mendel Schneerson, *Torah Studies*, 4. Rabbi Shapira also espouses this teaching, but he adds that this transformation is impossible "when we are suffering"; see Shapira, *Sacred Fire*, 99–100.

31. Emmanuel Levinas, *Existence and Existents*, 60.

32. Levinas, *Collected Philosophical Papers*, 185.

33. Ibid., 180.

34. Emmanuel Ringelblum, *Notes from the Warsaw Ghetto*, 84.

35. Fackenheim, *To Mend the World*, 219.

36. A Rebbe is a *tsadik*, one who is holy and without sin, a being in a category of his own.

37. See Meilech Neustadt, ed., *Churban Vemarad shel Yehudi Varshah*, 431.

38. See ibid., 55–59. This is one thing that Rabbi Shapira had in common with Rabbi Teichtal in their responses to the Shoah; indeed, love of the people of Israel is a defining feature of a mystical, Chasidic outlook.

39. See Shimon Huberband, *Kiddush Hashem*, 199–201.

40. Rabbi Shapira's other works include *Chovot Talmudim* (translated as *A Student's Obligation*), *Chovot Haavrakhim* (*Young Men's Obligations*), and *Bnei Machshavah Tovah* (*The Offspring of Good Thinking*); see Yitschak Alfasi, *Hachasidut*, 102.

41. Farbstein, *Beseter Raam*, 445. For Rabbi Shapira, Farbstein correctly observes, the mending of world, year, and soul that will reveal the Divine light comes about through the mystical teachings, revelations, and way of life embodied in Chasidism; see Farbstein, *Beseter Raam*, 442. World, year, and soul corre-

spond to *sefer, sefar,* and *sipur,* respectively, discussed in chap. 5, this volume. For a good explanation of the interconnections, see Aryeh Kaplan, commentary, *Sefer Yetzirah,* 19–21; see also the discussion found in Judah Halevi, *The Kuzari* 4:25.

42. Emmanuel Levinas, *Time and the Other,* 77.

43. Abraham Joshua Heschel, *The Sabbath,* 100.

44. André Neher, *They Made Their Souls Anew,* 49–50.

45. Shapira, *Sacred Fire,* 5.

46. Ibid., 334.

47. See also Moshe Weissman, ed., *The Midrash Says,* vol. 1, 268.

48. Schindler, *Hasidic Responses to the Holocaust in the Light of Hasidic Thought,* 35.

49. See also Gershom Scholem, *Kabbalah,* 31, 111.

50. Emil L. Fackenheim, *What Is Judaism?,* 178.

51. See Weissman, *The Midrash Says,* vol. 2, 158.

52. Quoted in Weissman, *The Midrash Says,* vol. 5, 281.

53. Shapira, *Sacred Fire,* 56. In this translation, the word *ethics* might be granting the "wisdom" of Amalek more than its due; in the original text, the term is *midot tovot,* which means "good qualities"; see Kalonymos Kalmish Shapira, *Esh Kodesh,* 24.

54. Shapira, *Sacred Fire,* 284. The phrase "common knowledge" is a translation of *daat anoshi,* "human knowledge"; see Shapira, *Esh Kodesh,* 158.

55. Shapira, *Sacred Fire,* 186.

56. Ibid., 250.

57. Ibid., 100.

58. Ibid., 251. To be sure, in the Zohar it is written: "There is an anger that is blessed on high and below and it is called *barukh*—'blessed'" (*Zohar* I, 184a).

59. Shapira, *Esh Kodesh,* 124.

60. Cf. Rashi's commentary on Numbers 20:2: "Why is the section narrating the death of Miriam placed immediately after the section treating of the red cow? To suggest to you the following comparison: What is the purpose of the sacrifices? They effect atonement. So, too, does the death of the righteous effect atonement." See Rashi, *Commentary on the Torah,* vol. 4, 95b.

61. Shapira, *Sacred Fire,* 202. Note also the teaching from Isaac Luria that Jewish history unfolds according to four stages of *tikkun haolam,* corresponding to the four worlds and to the four letters of the Divine Name: the episode of Joseph and his brothers; the Ten Martyrs in the time of Rabbi Akiva; the emer-

gence of Rabbi Shimon bar Yochai and his circle, which produced the Zohar; and the appearance of the Lurianic Kabbalah. See Chayyim Vital, *Sefer Hachazonot*, 210–29. See also Lawrence Fine, "The Art of Metoposcopy," 331.

62. Quoted in Shapira, *Sacred Fire*, 224.

63. In this connection, Peikazh notes a parallel between Rabbi Shapira's view of the exile of the Holy One and the view expressed in Judah Halevi, *Kuzari* 4:23; see Peikazh, *Hateudah Hachasidut Hasefrotit Haachronah al Admat Polin*, 39.

64. Rabbi Shapira's understanding of exile has its precedents in the teachings of Rabbi Yaakov Yosef of Polnoe; see Yaakov Yosef of Polnoe, *Toledot Yaakov Yosef*, Vayigash 6.

65. Shapira, *Sacred Fire*, 10.

66. Ibid., 140. Contrary to most commentaries, which explain that Sarah died of shock when she discovered where Abraham was taking Isaac, Rabbi Shapira offers a mystical view more in keeping with the contexts of the Shoah. She died not of shock, he says, but in protest: her soul ascended to the upper realms "to show God that a Jew should not be expected to suffer" such anguish (ibid., 14).

67. Ibid.

68. The Midrash identifies the angel who makes these offerings as Metatron (see *Bamidbar Rabbah* 12:12).

69. Shulamis Frieman, *Who's Who in the Talmud*, 322.

70. Emmanuel Levinas, "Prayer without Demand," 234.

71. Shapira, *Sacred Fire*, 36.

72. See Elie Wiesel, *Zalman, or the Madness of God*. Recall, too, the character Menachem, who wonders whether God has gone mad, whether God might be madness itself. "Who knows?" he says. "And if, after all, He were? That would explain so much." See Elie Wiesel, *The Town beyond the Wall*, 148.

73. Perhaps God is rather like the fictional scholar who knows ten languages, yet "only three words ever break from Professor Raphael's mouth: the names of his wife and two children"; see Ka-tzetnik 135633, *Atrocity*, 136.

74. Eliezer Berkovits, *Faith after the Holocaust*, 69.

75. Shapira, *Sacred Fire*, 286–87.

76. Ibid.

77. Cf. Elie Wiesel, *Souls on Fire*, 235.

78. Shapira, *Sacred Fire*, 287–88.

79. According to the Midrash, this hiding place is the realm of darkness,

from which God drew the plague of darkness, the darkness in which "a man could not see his brother" (Exodus 10:23); that is the darkness that makes God weep (see *Midrash Tehillim* 1:18:16).

80. See also Scholem, *Kabbalah,* 377–81. The Talmud identifies him as the one referred to in Exodus 23:21, where it is written, "Hearken unto his voice; do not rebel against him, . . . for My Name is in him" (*Sanhedrin* 38b).

81. Hannah Arendt, *The Origins of Totalitarianism,* 438, 458; for a good discussion, see Michael L. Morgan, *Beyond Auschwitz,* 15–16.

82. Moshe Chayim Luzzatto, *The Way of God,* 85.

83. Shapira, *Sacred Fire,* 328.

84. Theodor W. Adorno, *Aesthetic Theory,* 153; see also Josh Cohen, *Interrupting Auschwitz,* 65.

85. Joseph Gikatilla, *Sha'are Orah,* 87.

86. Ovadiah Sforno, *Commentary on 'Pirke Avos,'* 115.

87. See F. M. Dostoyevsky, *The Brothers Karamazov,* 588–89.

88. Cf. Wiesel, *Against Silence,* vol. 1, 371.

89. Emmanuel Levinas, *Nine Talmudic Readings,* 111–12.

90. Nehemia Polen, *The Holy Fire,* 145.

91. Ibid., 145–46.

92. See Kalonymos Kalmish Shapira, *Benei Machshavah Tovah,* 7.

93. See ibid., 11, 17. Here, we must keep in mind that, from the standpoint of Jewish mysticism, the body is not distinct from the soul; rather, it is an extension and manifestation of the soul.

94. See ibid., 20, 56.

95. Ibid., 14.

96. See ibid., 41.

97. See, for example, Schneur Zalman, *Torah Or,* 20b, 46c, 61d, 64c.

98. Schindler, *Hasidic Responses to the Holocaust in the Light of Hasidic Thought,* 25.

9 THOUGH THE MESSIAH MAY TARRY

1. The six other things that preceded the Creation are Torah, Teshuvah, Gan Eden, Gehenna, Throne of Glory, and the Temple. As for the name of the Messiah, one Midrash identifies several names: Shiloh, Chaninah, Yinnon, Nehirah, and David (*Eichah Rabbah* 1:16:51). According to the Midrash on Proverbs,

"Rabbi Huna said: The Messiah has been given seven names, and these are: Yinnon, Our Righteousness, Shoot, Comforter, David, Shiloh, and Elijah"; see *Midrash on Proverbs,* 89–90.

2. Since Rome is a symbol of the Church and Christendom, one cannot but see the Messiah languishing at the gates of the Church after having been expelled by a Christendom that would rid itself of the Jews: ridding itself of the Jews, Christendom rids itself of the Messiah.

3. It is in this sense that we should understand Emmanuel Levinas's assertion that the State of Israel "will be religious or it will not be at all"; see Emmanuel Levinas, *Difficult Freedom,* 219.

4. Martin Buber, *On Judaism,* 110–11.

5. Martin Buber, *I and Thou,* 94.

6. Emil L. Fackenheim, *What Is Judaism?,* 170.

7. Related in a letter from the Baal Shem to his brother-in-law in Abraham Kahana, ed., *Sefer Hachasidut,* 73–74.

8. In addition to the most famous of Holocaust memoirs, Elie Wiesel's *Night,* we have Arnŏst Lustig's *Night and Hope* and *Darkness Casts No Shadow,* Edgar Hilsenrath's *Night,* Eugene Heimler's *Night of the Mist,* Edwin Silberstang's *Nightmare of the Dark,* Zvi Barlev's *Would God It Weren't Night,* Eva Brewster's *Vanished in Darkness,* Sidney Iwens' *How Dark the Heavens,* and numerous other examples.

9. The best anthology of Jewish teachings on the Messiah is Raphael Patai, *The Messiah Texts.*

10. Among the sages to make this point is the fourteenth-century scholar Hasdai Crescas, who lists ten principles crucial to the Christian understanding of the Christ and antithetical to a Jewish understanding of the Messiah: inherited sin, redemption from inherited sin, a triune god, incarnation of the divine in the human, virgin birth, transubstantiation, baptism by the Holy Spirit, the identification of Jesus as Messiah, the giving of a "new Torah," and the casting out of demons; see Hasdai Crescas, *The Refutation of Christian Principles,* 2.

11. Vilna Gaon, *Even Sheleimah,* 45.

12. Adin Steinsaltz with Josy Eisenberg, *The Seven Lights,* 229.

13. Nachmanides, *Writings and Discourses,* vol. 2, 667. Said Nachmanides, "Upon the Messiah will fall the task of gathering the banished of Israel and the dispersed ones of Judah—twelve tribes—but the Nazarene gathered no one. . . . The Messiah will have to build the Temple in Jerusalem, but the Nazarene neither

built nor destroyed it" (ibid., vol. 2, 685). For these reasons, Abraham Abulafia points out that the numerical value of *Yeshu,* or "Jesus," is 316, which is the value of *elohei nekhar,* or "alien god"; see Moshe Idel, *Studies in Ecstatic Kabbalah,* 54.

14. For example, Isaiah 11:11–12; Jeremiah 23:3, 29:14, 32:44, 33:7; Ezekiel 39:25; Joel 4:1; Zephaniah 3:20; and Zechariah 10:8–10.

15. See, for example, Chayyim Vital, *Kabbalah of Creation,* 42.

16. See commentary on Talmud tractate *Sotah* 51 in Rashi, *Commentary on the Torah*; commentary on Leviticus 14:9 in Chayim ben Attar, *Or Hachayim*; Patai, *The Messiah Texts,* 153.

17. *Midrash Aseret Hashevatim,* in Judah David Eisenstein, ed., *Otsar Midrashim,* 466.

18. See Patai, *The Messiah Texts,* 257.

19. See Thomas Aquinas, *On Faith,* 39.

20. See Søren Kierkegaard, *Fear and Trembling,* 95. Kierkegaard, of course, also defines faith in terms of "believing on the strength of the absurd" (ibid., 65) as well as in terms of the paradox that "interiority is higher than exteriority" and that "the single individual is higher than the universal" (ibid., 97).

21. Emil L. Fackenheim, *Encounters between Judaism and Modern Philosophy* 27.

22. Adin Steinsaltz, *The Long Shorter Way,* 118.

23. Abraham Joshua Heschel, *God in Search of Man,* 98.

24. Abraham Joshua Heschel, *A Passion for Truth,* 189–90.

25. Emmanuel Levinas, *Of God Who Comes to Mind,* 75.

26. Nachman of Breslov, *Advice,* 7.

27. Abraham Joshua Heschel, *Man Is Not Alone,* 161.

28. Heschel, *God in Search of Man,* 77.

29. In *The Book of Faith and Reliance,* the medieval mystic Jacob ben Sheshet of Gerona writes, "Faith is Wisdom and Wisdom is Faith"; quoted in Joseph Dan, ed., *The Early Kabbalah,* 116.

30. Quoted in Nathan of Nemirov, *Rabbi Nachman's Wisdom,* 137.

31. Abraham Isaac Kook, *Orot,* 174.

32. Eliezer Berkovits, *Faith after the Holocaust,* 5.

33. This commandment is implicit in Abraham's assertion "I take it upon myself to speak to my Lord" (Genesis 18:27).

34. While some may regard circumcision as a form of antiquated, savage brutality, Levinas correctly notes that it is just the opposite: it is "a limitation

of life's savage vitality" that opens life "to otherness and the other"; see Emmanuel Levinas, *New Talmudic Readings,* 60.

35. See Mordechai Yosef of Isbitza, *Mei HaShiloach,* 83; see also Aryeh Kaplan's commentary in *Sefer Yetzirah,* 32ff.

36. Recall the discussion of this point in chap. 4, this volume, in the section titled "The Wound of the Bleeding Word."

37. See commentary on Leviticus 19:3 in Chayim ben Attar, *Or Hachayim.*

38. See Nachman of Breslov, *Tikkun,* 8–10; see also *Zohar* III, 73b.

39. Yitzchak Ginsburgh, *The Alef-Beit,* 20.

40. Ibid., 7. This teaching is based on a teaching from the Baal Shem Tov; see, for example, Nachum of Chernobyl, *Meor Einaim,* vol. 2, 599, 692.

41. Emil L. Fackenheim, *Quest for Past and Future,* 90.

42. For this reason, we say the "Elijah prayer" during the Havdalah service that closes the Sabbath: "Every Saturday night, Elijah enters Paradise, where he sits under the Tree of Life and records the merits of the Israelites who observed the Sabbath" (*Kitsur Shulchan Arukh* 96:12). Why Elijah? Because it is he who determines whether we have merited the manifestation of the Messiah.

43. Levinas, *Difficult Freedom,* 84.

44. Ibid., 90.

45. See Martin Buber, *The Origin and Meaning of Hasidism,* 109.

46. André Neher, *They Made Their Souls Anew,* 61–62.

47. Emmanuel Levinas, *Time and the Other,* 113.

48. Levinas, *Of God Who Comes to Mind,* 59.

49. Franz Rosenzweig, *The Star of Redemption,* 413.

50. The *Pesikta Rabbati* was compiled in the ninth century.

51. Emmanuel Levinas, "Revelation in the Jewish Tradition," 203.

52. Emmanuel Levinas, "Dialogue with Emmanuel Levinas," 23.

53. Emmanuel Levinas, *Collected Philosophical Papers,* 169.

54. Fackenheim, *What Is Judaism?,* 268–69.

55. From Meyer Levin, ed., *Hassidic Stories,* 86.

56. See Elie Wiesel, *Somewhere a Master,* 110.

57. Yitzchak Ginsburgh, *Rectifying the State of Israel,* 123.

58. Maimonides, *The Commandments,* vol. 1, 286.

59. Rosenzweig, *The Star of Redemption,* 27.

60. Elie Wiesel, *The Testament,* 160.

61. Abraham Joshua Heschel, *Israel,* 96.

10 CONCLUSION

1. See Murray J. Kohn, *Is the Holocaust Vanishing?*, 99.
2. Elie Wiesel, *Night*, 62.
3. Joseph Soloveitchik, *Halakhic Man*, 117.
4. Irving Greenberg, "Cloud of Smoke, Pillar of Fire," 23.
5. David Weiss Halivni, *The Book and the Sword*, 69.
6. See Rashi's commentary on Arakhin 10b in Rashi, *Commentary on the Torah*.
7. Kalonymos Kalmish Shapira, *Sacred Fire*, 263–64.
8. Ibid.
9. Adin Steinsaltz, *The Essential Talmud*, 273.

BIBLIOGRAPHY

Abohav, Yitzchak. *Menoras Hamaor: The Light of Contentment.* Trans. Y. Y. Reinman. Lakewood, N.J.: Torascript, 1982.

Abrabanel, Don Isaac. *Abrabanel on 'Pirke Avot.'* Trans. Avraham Chill. New York: Sepher-Hermon, 1991.

Abraham ibn Ezra. *The Commentary of Ibn Ezra on Isaiah.* Trans. Michael Friedlander. New York: Feldheim, 1943.

———. *The Secret of the Torah.* Trans. H. Norman Strickman. Northvale, N.J.: Aronson, 1995.

Adorno, Theodor W. *Aesthetic Theory.* Trans. R. Hullot-Kentor. Minneapolis: University of Minnesota Press, 1997.

Agus, Jacob. *Modern Philosophies of Judaism.* New York: Behrman House, 1941.

Albo, Joseph. *Sefer Ha-'Ikkarim: Book of Principles.* 5 vols. Trans. Isaac Husik. Philadelphia: Jewish Publication Society, 1946.

Alfasi, Yitschak. *Hachasidut.* Petach-Tikvah: Sifrit Meivrit, 1977.

Alter, Yehudah Leib. *The Language of Truth: The Torah Commentary of the Sefat Emet.* Trans. Arthur Green. Philadelphia: Jewish Publication Society, 1998.

Altizer, Thomas J. J. *Mircea Eliade and the Dialectic of the Sacred.* Philadelphia: Westminster Press, 1963.

Améry, Jean. *At the Mind's Limits.* Trans. Sidney Rosenfeld and Stella P. Rosenfeld. Bloomington: Indiana University Press, 1980.

Aquinas, Thomas. *On Faith.* Trans. Mark D. Jordan. Notre Dame, Ind.: University of Notre Dame Press, 1990.

Arendt, Hannah. *Eichmann in Jerusalem: A Report on the Banality of Evil.* New York: Viking Press, 1964.

———. *The Origins of Totalitarianism.* New York: Harcourt Brace & Company, 1979.

Aristotle. *Eudemian Ethics.* Trans. M. Woods. Oxford: Oxford University Press, 1992.

Aron, Milton. *Ideas and Ideals of Hassidism.* Secaucus, N.J.: Citadel, 1969.

Baal HaTurim. *Commentary on the Torah: Bereshis.* Trans. Avie Gold. Brooklyn, N.Y.: Mesorah, 1999.

Bachya ibn Paquda. *Chovot Halevavot: Duties of the Heart.* 2 vols. Trans. Moses Hyamson. New York: Feldheim, 1970.

Baeck, Leo. *The Essence of Judaism.* Rev. ed. Trans. Victor Grubenwieser and Leonard Pearl. New York: Schocken Books, 1948.

The Bahir. Trans. and commentary Aryeh Kaplan. York Beach, Me.: Samuel Weiser, 1979.

Barlev, Zvi. *Would God It Weren't Night: The Ordeal of a Jewish Boy from Cracow through Auschwitz, Mauthausen, and Gusen.* Trans. Michael Sherbourne. New York: Vantage, 1991.

Bauer, Yehuda. *A History of the Holocaust.* Rev. ed. New York: Franklin Watts, 2001.

Bauman, Zygmunt. *Modernity and the Holocaust.* Cambridge: Polity, 1989.

Beiser, Frederick C. "Kant's Intellectual Development: 1746–1781." In Paul Gruyer, ed., *The Cambridge Companion to Kant.* Cambridge: Cambridge University Press, 1992.

Benamozegh, Elijah. *Israel and Humanity.* Trans. Maxwell Levine. New York: Paulist Press, 1994.

Ben-Sasson, H. H., ed. *A History of the Jewish People.* Cambridge, Mass.: Harvard University Press, 1976.

Berkovits, Eliezer. *Faith after the Holocaust.* New York: KTAV, 1973.

Bernasconi, Robert, and Wood, David, eds. *The Provocation of Levinas: Rethinking the Other.* London: Routledge and Kegan Paul, 1988.

Birnbaum, David. *God and Evil.* Hoboken, N.J.: KTAV, 1989.

Bitton-Jackson, Livia E. *Elli: Coming of Age in the Holocaust.* New York: Times Books, 1980.

Blanchot, Maurice. "Our Clandestine Companion." In Richard A. Cohen, ed., *Face to Face with Levinas.* Albany, N.Y.: SUNY Press, 1986.

Blau, Joseph. *Modern Varieties of Judaism.* New York: Columbia University Press, 1964.

Blech, Benjamin. *More Secrets of Hebrew Words.* Northvale, N.J.: Aronson, 1993.

Bor, Josef. *The Terezín Requiem.* Trans. Edith Pargeter. New York: Avon, 1963.

———. *Terezínské rekviem.* Prague: M Československý spisovatel, 1963.

Borowitz, Eugene. *Choices in Modern Jewish Thought.* New York: Behrman House, 1983.

Braiterman, Zachary. *(God) after Auschwitz.* Princeton, N.J.: Princeton University Press, 1998.

Brearley, Margaret. "Fire and Ashes: The 'Tempter-God,' Evil, and the Shoah." In John K. Roth and David Patterson, eds., *Fire in the Ashes: God, Evil, and the Holocaust.* Seattle: University of Washington Press, 2005.

Breuer, Isaac. *Concepts of Judaism.* Ed. Jacob S. Levinger. Jerusalem: Israel Universities Press, 1974.

Brewster, Eva. *Vanished in Darkness: An Auschwitz Memoir.* Edmonton: NeWest Press, 1986.

Buber, Martin. *Eclipse of God: Studies in the Relation between Religion and Philosophy.* Trans. Maurice Friedman et al. Atlantic Highlands, N.J.: Humanities Press International, 1988.

———. *I and Thou.* Trans. Walter Kaufmann. New York: Charles Scribner's Sons, 1970.

———. *The Legend of the Baal Shem.* Trans. Maurice Friedman. New York: Schocken Books, 1969.

———. *On Judaism.* Ed. Nahum N. Glatzer. Trans. Eva Jospe. New York: Schocken Books, 1967.

———. *The Origin and Meaning of Hasidism.* Ed. and trans. Maurice Friedman. New York: Horizon Press, 1960.

———. *Tales of the Hasidim: The Early Masters.* Trans. O. Marx. New York: Schocken Books, 1947.

Camon, Ferdinando. *Conversations with Primo Levi.* Trans. John Sheply. Marlboro, Vt. Marlboro Press, 1989.

Camus, Albert. *The Myth of Sisyphus.* Trans. Justin O'Brien. New York: Random House, 1955.

Caputo, John D. "Heidegger's Scandal: Thinking and the Essence of the Victim."

Bibliography

In Tom Rockmore and Joseph Margolis, eds., *The Heidegger Case: On Philosophy and Politics*. Philadelphia: Temple University Press, 1992.

Cassirer, Ernst. *Kant's Life and Thought*. Trans. James Haden. New Haven, Conn.: Yale University Press, 1981.

Chayim ben Attar. *Or Hachayim*. 5 vols. Trans. Eliyahu Munk. Jerusalem: Munk, 1995.

Chofetz Chaim. *Ahavath Chesed*. Trans. Leonard Oschry. Jerusalem: Feldheim, 1976.

————. *Let There Be Light*. Trans. Raphael Blumberg. Jerusalem: Feldheim, 1992.

Cohen, Arthur A., ed. *Arguments and Doctrines: A Reader of Jewish Thinking in the Aftermath of the Holocaust*. New York: Harper and Row, 1970.

————. *The Tremendum: A Theological Interpretation of the Holocaust*. New York: Crossroad, 1981.

Cohen, Hermann. *Reason and Hope: Selections from the Jewish Writings of Hermann Cohen*. Trans. Eva Jospe. Cincinnati: Hebrew Union College Press, 1993.

————. *Religion of Reason out of the Sources of Judaism*. Trans. Simon Kaplan. Atlanta: Scholars Press, 1995.

Cohen, Josh. *Interrupting Auschwitz*. New York: Continuum, 2003.

Cohen, Richard A., ed. *Face to Face with Levinas*. Albany, N.Y.: SUNY Press, 1986.

Cohen, Victor, ed. *The Soul of the Torah: Insights of the Chasidic Masters on the Weekly Torah Portions*. Northvale, N.J.: Jason Aronson, 2000.

Cohn-Sherbok, Dan. *Holocaust Theology: A Reader*. New York: NYU Press, 2002.

Conrad, Joseph. *Heart of Darkness*. New York: Penguin Books, 1983.

Cordovero, Moses. *The Palm Tree of Devorah*. Trans. Moshe Miller. Southfield, Mich.: Targum, 1993.

————. *Pardes Rimmonim*. Jerusalem: Y. Chasid, 1998.

Crescas, Hasdai. *The Refutation of Christian Principles*. Trans. Daniel J. Lasker. Albany, N.Y.: SUNY Press, 1992.

Crétella, Henri. "Self-Destruction." In Alan Milchman and Alan Rosenberg, eds., *Martin Heidegger and the Holocaust*. Atlantic Highlands, N.J.: Humanities Press, 1996.

Culi, Yaakov. *The Torah Anthology: MeAm Lo'ez*. Vol. 1. Trans. Aryeh Kaplan. New York: Moznaim, 1977.

Czerniakow, Adam. *The Warsaw Ghetto Diary of Adam Czerniakow*. Ed. Raul Hilberg, Stanislaw Staron, and Joseph Kermisz. Trans. Stanislaw Staron et al. New York: Stein and Day, 1979.

Bibliography

Dan, Joseph, ed. *The Early Kabbalah.* Trans. Ronald C. Kiener. New York: Paulist Press, 1986.

Delbo, Charlotte. *None of Us Will Return.* Trans. John Githens. Boston: Beacon Press, 1968.

Derrida, Jacques. *Of Grammatology.* Trans. Gayatri Chakravorty Spivak. Baltimore: Johns Hopkins University Press, 1976.

Descartes, René. *Meditations on First Philosophy.* 3rd ed. Trans. D. A. Cress. Indianapolis, Ind.: Hackett, 1993.

Donat, Alexander. *The Holocaust Kingdom.* New York: Holocaust Library, 1978.

Dostoyevsky, F. M. *The Brothers Karamazov.* Trans. Constance Garnett. New York: New American Library, 1957.

————. *The Possessed.* Trans. Andrew R. MacAndrew. New York: New American Library, 1962.

Dribben, Judith. *And Some Shall Live.* Jerusalem: Keter Books, 1969.

Eckhardt, Alice L., and Eckhardt, A. Roy. *Long Night's Journey into Day: A Revised Retrospective on the Holocaust.* Detroit: Wayne State University Press, 1988.

Ehrenburg, Ilya, and Grossman, Vasily, eds. *The Complete Black Book of Russian Jewry.* Trans. David Patterson. New Brunswick, N.J.: Transaction Publishers, 2002.

Eisenstein, Judah David, ed. *Otsar Midrashim.* New York: J. D. Eisenstein, 1915.

Elimelekh of Lizensk. *Noam Elimelekh.* Jerusalem: Mekhon Sod Yesharim, 1997.

Eliot, T. S. *The Waste Land and Other Poems.* New York: Harcourt Brace Jovanovich, 1962.

Fackenheim, Emil L. *Encounters between Judaism and Modern Philosophy.* New York: Basic Books, 1973.

————. *God's Presence in History: Jewish Affirmations and Philosophical Reflections.* New York: Harper & Row, 1970.

————. *Hermann Cohen—After Fifty Years.* Leo Baeck Memorial Lecture 12. New York: Leo Baeck Institute, 1969.

————. "The Holocaust and the State of Israel." In Michael L. Morgan, ed. *A Holocaust Reader: Responses to the Nazi Extermination.* New York: Oxford University Press, 2001.

————. *The Jewish Bible after the Holocaust.* Bloomington: Indiana University Press, 1990.

————. "Jewish Existence and the Living God: The Religious Duty of Survival." In Arthur A. Cohen, ed., *Arguments and Doctrines: A Reader of Jew-*

ish Thinking in the Aftermath of the Holocaust. New York: Harper & Row, 1970.

———. *Jewish Philosophers and Jewish Philosophy.* Ed. Michael L. Morgan. Bloomington: Indiana University Press, 1996.

———. *The Jewish Return into History.* New York: Schocken Books, 1978.

———. *Quest for Past and Future: Essays in Jewish Theology.* Bloomington: Indiana University Press, 1968.

———. *To Mend the World: Foundations of Post-Holocaust Jewish Thought.* Bloomington: Indiana University Press, 1994.

———. *What Is Judaism?* New York: Macmillan, 1987.

Farbstein, Esther. *Beseter Raam: Halakhah, Hagot, Veminhagiut Beyomai Hashoah.* Jerusalem: Mosad Harav Kook, 2002.

Farías, Victor. *Heidegger and Nazism.* Trans. Paul Burrell. Philadelphia: Temple University Press, 1989.

Fénelon, Fania. *Playing for Time.* Trans. Judith Landry. New York: Atheneum, 1977.

Ferderber-Salz, Bertha. *And the Sun Kept Shining.* New York: Holocaust Library, 1980.

Feuerbach, Ludwig. *The Essence of Christianity.* Trans. George Eliot. New York: Harper & Row, 1957.

Fine, Lawrence. "The Art of Metoposcopy." In Lawrence Fine, ed., *Essential Papers on Kabbalah.* New York: NYU Press, 1995.

———, ed. *Essential Papers on Kabbalah.* New York: NYU Press, 1995.

Finkel, Avraham Yaakov. *Kabbalah: Selections from Classic Kabbalistic Works from Raziel HaMalach to the Present Day.* Southfield, Mich.: Targum Press, 2002.

Fleischner, Eva, ed. *Auschwitz: Beginning of a New Era? Reflections on the Holocaust.* New York: KTAV, 1977.

Formstecher, Salomon. *Die Religion des Geistes.* New York: Arno Press, 1980.

Foucault, Michel. *Madness and Civilization.* Trans. Richard Howard. New York: Pantheon Books, 1965.

Friedman, H., Simon, Maurice, et al., eds. and trans. *Midrash Rabbah.* 10 vols. London: Soncino, 1961.

Frieman, Shulamis. *Who's Who in the Talmud.* Northvale, N.J.: Jason Aronson, 1995.

Funkenstein, Amos. "Theological Interpretations of the Holocaust." In Michael L. Morgan, ed., *A Holocaust Reader: Responses to the Nazi Extermination*. New York: Oxford University Press, 2001.

Ganzfried, R. Solomon, comp. *Kitsur Shulchan Arukh—Code of Jewish Law*. 4 vols. Rev. ed. Trans. Hyman E. Goldin. New York: Hebrew Publishing Co., 1961.

Gersonides. *The Wars of the Lord*. 2 vols. Trans. Seymour Feldman. Philadelphia: Jewish Publication Society, 1984.

Gikatilla, Joseph. *Sha'are Orah: Gates of Light*. Trans. Avi Weinstein. San Francisco: HarperCollins, 1994.

Giller, Pinchas. *The Zohar: The Sacred Text of the Kabbalah*. Oxford: Oxford University Press, 2001.

Ginsburgh, Yitzchak. *The Alef-Beit: Jewish Thought Revealed through the Hebrew Letters*. Northvale, N.J.: Jason Aronson, 1991.

———. *Rectifying the State of Israel: A Political Platform Based on Kabbalah*. Jerusalem: Linda Pinsky Publications, 2003.

Glazerson, Matityahu. *Building Blocks of the Soul: Studies in the Letters and Words of the Hebrew Language*. Northvale, N.J.: Jason Aronson, 1997.

Greenberg, Irving. "Cloud of Smoke, Pillar of Fire: Judaism, Christianity, and Modernity after the Holocaust." In Eva Fleischner, ed., *Auschwitz: Beginning of a New Era? Reflections on the Holocaust*. New York: KTAV, 1977.

———. *The Jewish Way: Living the Holidays*. New York: Simon & Schuster, 1988.

———. "Voluntary Covenant." In *Perspectives*. New York: National Jewish Resource Center, 1982.

Grob, Leonard. "Some Fundamental Doubts about Posing the Question of Theodicy in the Post-Holocaust World." In John K. Roth and David Patterson, eds., *Fire in the Ashes: God, Evil, and the Holocaust*. Seattle: University of Washington Press, 2005.

Gruyer, Paul, ed. *The Cambridge Companion to Kant*. Cambridge: Cambridge University Press, 1992.

Halevi, Judah. *The Kuzari*. Trans. Henry Slonimsky. New York: Schocken Books, 1963.

Halivni, David Weiss. *The Book and the Sword*. Boulder, Colo.: Westview Press, 1996.

Hand, Sean, ed. *The Levinas Reader.* Oxford: Basil Blackwell, 1989.

Harris, Jay Michael. *Nachman Krochmal: Guiding the Perplexed.* New York: NYU Press, 1991.

Hegel, G. W. F. *The Phenomenology of Spirit.* Trans. A. V. Miller. Oxford: Oxford University Press, 1979.

Heidegger, Martin. *Kant and the Problem of Metaphysics.* Trans. J. S. Churchill. Bloomington: Indiana University Press, 1962.

————. *Nietzsche.* 2 vols. Trans. D. Krell. San Francisco: Harper & Row, 1979.

————. *Sein und Zeit.* Tübingen: Max Niemeyer, 1963.

————. "The Self-Assertion of the German University." In Guenther Neske and Emil Kettering, eds., *Martin Heidegger and National Socialism.* Trans. Lisa Harries. New York: Paragon, 1990.

————. *Vom Wesen des Grundes.* 5th ed. Frankfurt: Klostermann, 1965.

Heimler, Eugene. *Night of the Mist.* Trans. Andre Ungar. New York: Vanguard, 1958.

Heine, Heinrich. *Words of Prose.* Trans. E. B. Ashton. New York: L. B. Fischer, 1943.

Heinemann, Bruno. *The Maggid of Dubno and His Parables.* New York: Feldheim, 1967.

Heschel, Abraham Joshua. *God in Search of Man.* New York: Farrar, Straus and Giroux, 1955.

————. *I Asked for Wonder.* Ed. Samuel H. Dresner. New York: Crossroad, 1983.

————. *Israel: An Echo of Eternity.* New York: Farrar, Straus and Giroux, 1969.

————. *Man Is Not Alone.* New York: Farrar, Straus and Giroux 1951.

————. *Man's Quest for God: Studies in Prayer and Symbolism.* New York: Charles Scribner's Sons, 1954.

————. *A Passion for Truth.* New York: Farrar, Straus and Giroux, 1973.

————. *The Prophets.* 2 vols. New York: Harper & Row, 1962.

————. *The Sabbath: Its Meaning for Modern Man.* New York: Farrar, Straus and Giroux, 1981.

Hilsenrath, Edgar. *Night.* Trans. Michael Ruloff. New York: Doubleday, 1966.

Hirsch, Samson Raphael. *The Nineteen Letters on Judaism.* Ed. Jacob Breuer. Trans. Bernard Drachman. Jerusalem: Feldheim, 1969.

Hirsch, Samuel. *Die Religionsphilosophie der Juden.* New York: Arno Press, 1980.

Horowitz, Shabtai Sheftl. *Sefer Shefa Tal.* Jerusalem, 1970 (publisher unknown).

Huberband, Shimon. *Kiddush Hashem: Jewish Religious and Cultural Life in Poland during the Holocaust.* Ed. Jeffrey S. Gurock and Robert S. Hirt. Trans. David E. Fishman. Hoboken, N.J.: KTAV and Yeshiva University Press, 1987.

Husserl, Edmund. *Phenomenology and the Crisis of Philosophy.* Trans. Quentin Lauer. New York: Harper & Row, 1965.

Idel, Moshe. *Language, Torah, and Hermeneutics in Abraham Abulafia.* Albany, N.Y.: SUNY Press, 1989.

———. *Studies in Ecstatic Kabbalah.* Albany, N.Y.: SUNY Press, 1988.

Iwens, Sidney. *How Dark the Heavens: 1,400 Days in the Grip of Nazi Terror.* New York: Shengold, 1990.

Jabès, Edmond. *A Foreigner Carrying in the Crook of His Arm a Tiny Book.* Trans. Rosemary Waldrop. Hanover, N.H.: Wesleyan University Press, 1993.

Jacobs, Louis. *Hasidic Prayer.* New York: Schocken Books, 1972.

Jaspers, Karl. *Truth and Symbol.* Trans. Jean T. Wilde, William Kluback, and William Kimmel. New Haven, Conn.: College and University Press, 1959.

Jellinek, Adolph, ed. *Sefer Zerubavel.* 6 vols. Jerusalem: Bamberger & Wahrmann, 1938.

Jonas, Hans. "Heidegger's Resoluteness and Resolve." In Guenther Neske and Emil Kettering, eds. *Martin Heidegger and National Socialism.* Trans. Lisa Harries. New York: Paragon, 1990.

———. *Mortality and Morality: A Search for the Good after Auschwitz.* Ed. Lawrence Vogel. Evanston, Ill.: Northwestern University Press, 1996.

Kahana, Abraham, ed. *Sefer Hachasidut.* Warsaw, 1922 (publisher unknown).

Kalmanovitch, Zelig. "A Diary of the Nazi Ghetto in Vilna." Ed. and trans. Koppel S. Pinson. *YIVO Annual of Jewish Social Sciences* 8 (1953), 9–81.

Kant, Immanuel. *The Conflict of the Faculties.* Trans. Mary J. Gregor. New York: Abaris, 1979.

———. *The Critique of Practical Reason.* Trans. Lewis White Beck. New York: Macmillan, 1985.

———. *The Critique of Pure Reason.* Trans. Werner S. Pluhar. Indianapolis, Ind.: Hackett, 1996.

———. *Grounding for the Metaphysics of Morals.* Trans. James W. Ellington. Indianapolis, Ind.: Hackett, 1981.

———. *Religion within the Limits of Reason Alone.* Trans. Theodore M. Greene and Hoyt H. Hudson. New York: Harper & Brothers, 1960.

Kaplan, Aryeh. *Inner Space.* Brooklyn, N.Y.: Moznaim, 1990.

Kaplan, Chaim A. *The Warsaw Diary of Chaim A. Kaplan.* Trans. and ed. Abraham I. Katsh. New York: Collier, 1973.

Karow, Yvonne. *Deutsches Opfer: Kultische Selbstausloschung auf den Reichsparteitagen der NSDAP.* Berlin: Akademie Verlag, 1997.

Katz, Steven T. *Interpreters of Judaism in the Late Twentieth Century.* Washington, D.C.: B'nai B'rith Books, 1993.

———. *Post-Holocaust Dialogues: Critical Studies in Modern Jewish Thought.* New York: NYU Press, 1983.

Ka-tzetnik 135633. *Atrocity.* Trans. Nina De-Nur. New York: Kensington, 1977.

———. *House of Dolls.* Trans. Moshe M. Kohn. New York: Pyramid, 1958.

———. *Shivitti: A Vision.* Trans. Eliyah De-Nur and Lisa Herman. New York: Harper & Row, 1989.

———. *Sunrise over Hell.* Trans. Nina De-Nur. London: W. H. Allen, 1977.

Katznelson, Yitzhak. *Vittel Diary.* Trans. Myer Cohn. 2nd ed. Tel-Aviv: Hakibbutz Hameuchad, 1972.

Keter Shem Tov. Brooklyn, N.Y.: Kehot, 1972.

Kielar, Wieslaw. *Anus Mundi: 1,500 Days in Auschwitz / Birkenau.* Trans. Susanne Flatauer. New York: Times Books, 1980.

Kierkegaard, Søren. *Concluding Unscientific Postscript.* Trans. David Swenson and Walter Lowrie. Princeton, N.J.: Princeton University Press, 1941.

———. *Fear and Trembling.* Trans. Alastair Hannay. New York: Penguin Books, 1985.

Kirschenbaum, Dovid, ed. *Fun di Chasidishe Ostros.* New York: Pardes Publishers, 1948.

Kisiel, Theodore. "Heidegger's Apology: Biography and Philosophy and Ideology." In Tom Rockmore and Joseph Margolis, eds., *The Heidegger Case: On Philosophy and Politics.* Philadelphia: Temple University Press, 1992.

Klein, Gerda Weissmann. *All But My Life.* New York: Hill and Wang, 1957.

Klonicki-Klonymus, Aryeh. *The Diary of Adam's Father.* Trans. Avner Tomaschiff. Tel-Aviv: Hakibbutz Hameuchad, 1973.

Kohn, Murray J. *Is the Holocaust Vanishing? A Survivor's Reflections on the Academic Waning of Memory and Jewish Identity in the Post-Auschwitz Era.* Ed. David Patterson. Lanham, Md.: University Press of America, 2005.

Kook, Abraham Isaac. *Orot.* Trans. Bezalel Naor. Northvale, N.J.: Jason Aronson, 1993.

Kruk, Herman. "Diary of the Vilna Ghetto." Trans. Shlomo Noble. *YIVO Annual of Jewish Social Science* 13 (1965), 9–78.

———. *The Last Days of the Jerusalem of Lithuania: Chronicles from the Vilna Ghetto and the Camps, 1939–1944.* Ed. Benjamin Harshav. Trans. Barbara Harshav. New Haven, Conn.: Yale University Press, 2002.

LaCapra, Dominick. *Writing History, Writing Trauma.* Baltimore: Johns Hopkins University Press, 2001.

Lang, Berel. *Act and Idea in the Nazi Genocide.* Syracuse, N.Y.: Syracuse University Press, 2003.

Lazarus, Moritz. *The Ethics of Judaism.* 2 vols. Trans. Henrietta Szold. Philadelphia: Jewish Publication Society, 1901.

Leitner, Isabella. *Fragments of Isabella.* Ed. Irving Leitner. New York: Thomas Crowell, 1978.

Lengyel, Olga. *Five Chimneys.* London: Granada, 1972.

Levi, Primo. *The Drowned and the Saved.* Trans. Raymond Rosenthal. New York: Vintage Books, 1988.

———. *If This Is a Man, and The Truce.* Trans. Stuart Woolf. Harmondsworth and New York: Penguin, 1979.

———. *I sommersi e I salvati.* Torino: Einaudi, 1986.

———. *La tregua.* Torino: Einaudi, 1989.

———. *The Reawakening.* Trans. Stuart Woolf. Boston: Little, Brown, 1965.

———. *Se questo è un uomo.* Torino: Einaudi, 1989.

———. *Survival in Auschwitz: The Nazi Assault on Humanity.* Trans. Stuart Woolf. New York: Simon & Schuster, 1996.

Levin, Meyer, ed. *Hassidic Stories.* Tel-Aviv: Greenfield, 1975.

Levinas, Emmanuel. "Bad Conscience and the Inexorable." In Richard A. Cohen, ed., *Face to Face with Levinas.* Albany, N.Y.: SUNY Press, 1986.

———. *Collected Philosophical Papers.* Trans. Alphonso Lingis. Dordrecht: Martinus Nijhoff, 1987.

———. "Dialogue with Emmanuel Levinas (with Richard Kearney)." In Richard A. Cohen, ed., *Face to Face with Levinas.* Albany, N.Y.: SUNY Press, 1986.

———. *Difficult Freedom: Essays on Judaism.* Trans. Sean Hand. Baltimore: Johns Hopkins University Press, 1990.

———. *Ethics and Infinity.* Trans. Richard A. Cohen. Pittsburgh: Duquesne University Press, 1985.

———. "Ethics as First Philosophy." Trans. Sean Hand and Michael Temple. In Sean Hand, ed. *The Levinas Reader.* Oxford: Basil Blackwell, 1989.

———. *Existence and Existents.* Trans. Alphonso Lingis. The Hague: Martinus Nijhoff, 1978.

———. *In the Time of the Nations.* Trans. M. B. Smith. London: Athlone Press, 1994.

———. *New Talmudic Readings.* Trans. Richard A. Cohen. Pittsburgh: Duquesne University Press, 1999.

———. *Nine Talmudic Readings.* Trans. Annette Aronowicz. Bloomington: Indiana University Press, 1990.

———. *Of God Who Comes to Mind.* Trans. Bettina Bergo. Stanford, Calif.: Stanford University Press, 1998.

———. *Otherwise than Being, or Beyond Essence.* Trans. Alphonso Lingis. The Hague: Martinus Nijhoff, 1981.

———. *Outside the Subject.* Trans. Michael B. Smith. Stanford, Calif.: Stanford University Press, 1994.

———. "The Paradox of Morality." In Robert Bernasconi and David Wood, eds., *The Provocation of Levinas: Rethinking the Other.* London: Routledge and Kegan Paul, 1988.

———. "Prayer without Demand." Trans. Sarah Richmond. In Sean Hand, ed. *The Levinas Reader.* Oxford: Basil Blackwell, 1989.

———. "Reflections on the Philosophy of Hitlerism." Trans. Sean Hand. *Critical Inquiry* 17 (1990), 62–71.

———. "Revelation in the Jewish Tradition." Trans. Sarah Richmond. In Sean Hand, ed., *The Levinas Reader.* Oxford: Basil Blackwell, 1989.

———. *Time and the Other.* Trans. Richard A. Cohen. Pittsburgh: Duquesne University Press, 1987.

———. *Totality and Infinity.* Trans. Alphonso Lingis. Pittsburgh: Duquesne University Press, 1969.

———. "Useless Suffering." Trans. Richard A. Cohen. In Robert Bernasconi and David Wood, eds., *The Provocation of Levinas: Rethinking the Other.* London: Routledge and Kegan Paul, 1988.

———. "Zionisms." Trans. Roland Lack. In Sean Hand, ed., *The Levinas Reader.* Oxford: Basil Blackwell, 1989.

Levy-Hass, Hanna. *Vielleicht war das alles erst der Anfang: Tagebuch aus dem KZ Bergen Belsen, 1944–1945.* Ed. Eike Geisel. Berlin: Rotbuch, 1969.

Bibliography

Lewinska, Pelagia. *Twenty Months at Auschwitz*. Trans. A. Teichner. New York: Lyle Stuart, 1968.

Littell, Franklin. *The Crucifixion of the Jews: The Failure of Christians to Understand the Jewish Experience*. Macon, Ga.: Mercer University Press, 1986.

Loeve, Yehuda. *Maharal of Prague: Pirke Avos*. Ed. and trans. R. Tuvia Basser. Brooklyn, N.Y.: Mesorah, 1997.

———. *Nesivos Olam: Nesiv Hatorah*. Trans. Eliakim Willner. Brooklyn, N.Y.: Mesorah, 1994.

Lustig, Arnŏst. *Darkness Casts No Shadow*. Trans. Jeanne Němcová. New York: Avon, 1978.

———. *Night and Hope*. Trans. George Theiner. New York: Avon, 1976.

———. *A Prayer for Katerina Horovitzova*. Trans. Jeanne Němcová. New York: Harper & Row, 1973.

Luzzatto, Moshe Chayim. *The Path of the Just*. 3rd ed. Trans. Shraga Silverstein. New York: Feldheim, 1990.

———. *The Way of God*. 4th ed. Trans. Aryeh Kaplan. New York: Feldheim, 1988.

Lyotard, Jean-François. *Heidegger and "the jews."* Trans. Andreas Michel and Mark S. Roberts. Minneapolis: University of Minnesota Press, 1990.

Mack, Michael. *German Idealism and the Jew: The Inner Anti-Semitism of Philosophy and German Jewish Responses*. Chicago: University of Chicago Press, 2003.

Maimon, Y. L., ed. *Sefer Habesht*. Jerusalem: Mosad Harav Kook, 1960.

Maimonides. *The Commandments*. 2 vols. Trans. Charles B. Chavel. New York: Soncino, 1967.

———. *The Guide for the Perplexed (Moreh Nevuchim)*. Trans. M. Friedlaender. New York: Dover, 1956.

Maybaum, Ignaz. *The Face of God after Auschwitz*. Amsterdam: Polak and Van Genep, 1965.

Maza, Bernard. *With Fury Poured Out: A Torah Perspective on the Holocaust*. Hoboken, N.J.: KTAV, 1986.

Meir ibn Gabbai. *Sod ha-Shabbat*. Trans. Elliot K. Ginsburg. Albany, N.Y.: SUNY Press, 1989.

Mekilta de-Rabbi Ishmael. 3 vols. Trans. Jacob Z. Lauterbach. Philadelphia: Jewish Publication Society, 1961.

Midrash Agadah. Jerusalem: Mekhon Haketov, 1996.

Midrash Hagadol al Chamishah Chumshe Torah: Sefer Bereshit. Jerusalem, 1947.

Midrash on Proverbs. Trans. Burton L. Visotzky. New Haven, Conn.: Yale University Press, 1992.

Midrash on Psalms (Midrash Tehillim). 2 vols. Trans. William G. Braude. New Haven, Conn.: Yale University Press, 1959.

Midrash Tanchuma. 2 vols. Jerusalem: Eshkol, 1935.

Milchman, Alan, and Rosenberg, Alan, eds. *Martin Heidegger and the Holocaust.* Atlantic Highlands, N.J.: Humanities Press, 1996.

Mordechai Yosef of Isbitza. *Mei HaShiloach.* Ed. and trans. Betsalel Philip Edwards. Northvale, N.J.: Jason Aronson, 2001.

Morgan, Michael L. *Beyond Auschwitz: Post-Holocaust Jewish Thought in America.* New York: Oxford University Press, 2001.

———, ed. *A Holocaust Reader: Responses to the Nazi Extermination.* New York: Oxford University Press, 2001.

———. *Interim Judaism: Jewish Thought in a Century of Crisis.* Bloomington: Indiana University Press, 2001.

Munk, Michael L. *The Wisdom in the Hebrew Alphabet: The Sacred Letters as a Guide to Jewish Deed and Thought.* Brooklyn, N.Y.: Mesorah, 1983.

Nachman of Breslov. *Advice.* Trans. Avraham Greenbaum. Brooklyn, N.Y.: Breslov Research Institute, 1983.

———. *The Aleph-Bet Book.* Trans. M. Myhoff. Jerusalem: Breslov Research Institute, 1986.

———. *Tikkun.* Trans. Avraham Greenbaum. Jerusalem: Breslov Research Institute, 1984.

Nachum of Chernobyl. *Meor Einaim.* 2 vols. New York: Mekhon Meor Hatorah, 1998.

Nachmanides. *Commentary on the Torah.* 5 vols. Trans. Charles B. Chavel. New York: Shilo, 1971.

———. *Igeret HaRamban: A Letter for the Ages.* Ed. and trans. Avrohom Chaim Feuer. Brooklyn, N.Y.: Mesorah, 1989.

———. *Writings and Discourses.* 2 vols. Trans. Charles B. Chavel. New York: Shilo, 1978.

Nathan of Nemirov. *Rabbi Nachman's Wisdom: Shevachay HaRan and Sichos HaRan.* Ed. Aryeh Rosenfeld. Trans. Aryeh Kaplan. New York: A. Kaplan, 1973.

Neher, André. *The Exile of the Word: From the Silence of the Bible to the Silence of Auschwitz.* Trans. David Maisel. Philadelphia: Jewish Publication Society, 1981.

———. *The Prophetic Existence.* Trans. William Wolf. New York: A. S. Barnes, 1969.

———. *They Made Their Souls Anew.* Trans. David Maisel. Albany, N.Y.: SUNY Press, 1990.

Neske, Guenther, and Kettering, Emil, eds. *Martin Heidegger and National Socialism.* Trans. Lisa Harries. New York: Paragon, 1990.

Neustadt, Meilech, ed. *Churban Vemarad shel Yehudi Varshah.* Tel-Aviv: Executive Committee of the General Federation of Jewish Labor in Palestine, 1946.

Newman, Louis I., ed. *The Hasidic Anthology.* New York: Schocken Books, 1963.

Nietzsche, Friedrich. *Beyond Good and Evil.* Trans. Walter Kaufmann. New York: Vintage Books, 1966.

———. *The Gay Science.* Trans. Walter Kaufmann. New York: Vintage Books, 1974.

Nomberg-Przytyk, Sara. *Auschwitz: True Tales from a Grotesque Land.* Trans. Roslyn Hirsch. Chapel Hill: University of North Carolina Press, 1985.

Nyiszli, Miklós. *Auschwitz: A Doctor's Eyewitness Account.* Trans. Tibere Kremer and Richard Seaver. New York: Fawcett Crest, 1960.

Oshry, Ephraim. *Responsa from the Holocaust.* Trans. Y. Leiman. Brooklyn, N.Y.: Judaica Press, 2001.

Ozsváth, Zsuzsanna. *In the Footsteps of Orpheus: The Life and Times of Miklós Radnóti.* Bloomington: Indiana University Press, 2001.

Patai, Raphael. *The Messiah Texts.* New York: Avon, 1979.

Patterson, David. *Hebrew Language and Jewish Thought.* London: Routledge-Curzon, 2005.

———. *In Dialogue and Dilemma with Elie Wiesel.* Wakefield, N.H.: Longwood Academic, 1991.

———, and Roth, John K., eds. *After-Words: Post-Holocaust Struggles with Forgiveness, Reconciliation, Justice.* Seattle: University of Washington Press, 2004.

Peikazh, Mendel. *Hateudah Hachasidut Hasefrotit Haachronah al Admat Polin: Divrei Harabi MePiaseczno Begeto Varsha.* Jerusalem: Yad Vashem, 1979.

Peli, Pinhas H. *The Jewish Sabbath: A Renewed Encounter.* New York: Schocken Books, 1988.

Pesikta de-Rab Kahana. Trans. William G. Braude and Israel J. Kapstein. Philadelphia: Jewish Publication Society, 1975.

Pesikta Rabbati. Trans. W. G. Braude. 2 vols. New Haven, Conn.: Yale University Press, 1968.

Pirke de Rabbi Eliezer. Trans. Gerald Friedlander. New York: Hermon Press, 1970.

Plato. *Euthyphro.* Trans. Lane Cooper. In Edith Hamilton and Huntington Cairns, eds., *The Collected Dialogues of Plato.* Princeton, N.J.: Princeton University Press 1969.

———. *Republic.* Trans. Paul Shorey. In Edith Hamilton and Huntington Cairns, eds., *The Collected Dialogues of Plato.* Princeton, N.J.: Princeton University Press 1969.

———. *Sophist.* Trans. F. M. Kornford. In Edith Hamilton and Huntington Cairns, eds., *The Collected Dialogues of Plato.* Princeton, N.J.: Princeton University Press, 1969.

Plotinus. *The Enneads.* Ed. John Dillon. Trans. Stephen MacKenna. New York: Penguin Books, 1991.

Polen, Nehemia. *The Holy Fire: The Teachings of Rabbi Kalonymus Kalman Shapira.* Northvale, N.J.: Jason Aronson, 1999.

Poliakov, Leon. *The Harvest of Hate.* Syracuse, N.Y.: Syracuse University Press, 1954.

Rabinowicz, Harry M. *Hasidism: The Movement and Its Masters.* Northvale, N.J.: Jason Aronson, 1988.

Rabinowitz, Avraham Moshe. *Chachimah Birmizah.* Brooklyn, N.Y., 1994 (publisher unknown).

Rashi. *Commentary on the Torah.* 5 vols. Trans. M. Rosenbaum and N. M. Silbermann. Jerusalem: The Silbermann Family, 1972.

Ringelblum, Emmanuel. *Notes from the Warsaw Ghetto.* Ed. and trans. Jacob Sloan. New York: Schocken Books, 1974.

Rivosh, Elik. "From the Notebook of the Sculptor Elik Rivosh (Riga)." Trans. David Patterson. In Ilya Ehrenburg and Vasily Grossman, eds. *The Complete Black Book of Russian Jewry.* New Brunswick, N.J.: Transaction Publishers, 2002.

Rockmore, Tom, and Margolis, Joseph, eds. *The Heidegger Case: On Philosophy and Politics.* Philadelphia: Temple University Press, 1992.

Rose, Gillian. *Mourning Becomes the Law: Philosophy and Representation.* Cambridge: Cambridge University Press, 1996.

Rose, Paul Lawrence. *German Question / Jewish Question: Revolutionary Antisemitism from Kant to Wagner.* Princeton, N.J.: Princeton University Press, 1990.

Bibliography

Rosenbaum, Irving J. *The Holocaust and Halakhah.* New York: KTAV, 1976.

Rosenberg, Alan, and Myers, Gerald E., eds. *Echoes from the Holocaust: Philosophical Reflections on a Dark Time.* Philadelphia: Temple University Press, 1988.

Rosenberg, Alfred. *Race and Race History and Other Essays.* Ed. Robert Pais. New York: Harper & Row, 1974.

Rosenberg, Bernhard H., and Heuman, Fred, eds. *Theological and Halakhic Reflections on the Holocaust.* Hoboken, N.J.: KTAV, 1992.

Rosenfeld, Alvin. *A Double Dying: Reflections on Holocaust Literature.* Bloomington: Indiana University Press, 1980.

Rosenfeld, Oskar. *In the Beginning Was the Ghetto: 890 Days in Łódź.* Ed. Hanno Loewy. Trans. Brigitte Goldstein. Evanston, Ill.: Northwestern University Press, 2002.

Rosenzweig, Franz. *Franz Rosenzweig's "The New Thinking."* Ed and trans. Alan Udoff and Barbara E. Galli. Syracuse, N.Y.: Syracuse University Press, 1999.

———. *On Jewish Learning.* Ed. and trans. Nahum N. Glatzer. New York: Schocken Books, 1955.

———. *The Star of Redemption.* Trans. William W. Hallo. Boston: Beacon Press, 1972.

———. *Understanding the Sick and the Healthy: A View of World, Man, and God.* Trans. Nahum Glatzer. Cambridge, Mass.: Harvard University Press, 1999.

Rotenstreich, Nathan. *Jewish Philosophy in Modern Times.* New York: Holt, Rinehart and Winston, 1968.

Roth, John K., and Patterson, David, eds. *Fire in the Ashes: God, Evil, and the Holocaust.* Seattle: University of Washington Press, 2005.

Rubenstein, Richard L. *After Auschwitz.* Indianapolis, Ind.: Bobbs-Merrill, 1966.

Saadia Gaon. *The Book of Belief and Opinions (Sefer Emunot Vedeot).* Trans. Samuel Rosenblatt. New Haven, Conn.: Yale University Press, 1976.

Sacks, Jonathan. *Crisis and Covenant: Jewish Thought after the Holocaust.* Manchester: Manchester University Press, 1992.

Salton, George Lucius. *The 23rd Psalm: A Holocaust Memoir.* Madison: University of Wisconsin Press, 2002.

Sandberg, Moshe. *My Longest Year.* Trans. S. C. Hyman. Jerusalem: Yad Vashem, 1968.

Sandmel, Samuel. *Philo's Place in Judaism.* New York: KTAV, 1971.

Schindler, Pesach. *Hasidic Responses to the Holocaust in the Light of Hasidic Thought.* Hoboken, N.J.: KTAV, 1990.

Schneerson, Menachem M. *Torah Studies*. Adapted by Jonathan Sacks. 2nd ed. London: Lubavitch Foundation, 1986.

Schneersohn, Shalom Dov Ber. *Yom Tov Shel Rosh Hashanah 5659: Discourse One*. Trans. Yosef B. Marcus and Moshe Miller. Brooklyn, N.Y.: Kehot, 2000.

Schneersohn, Yosef Yitzchak. *Four Worlds*. Trans. Yosef B. Marcus. Brooklyn, N.Y.: Kehot, 2003.

Schochet, Jacob Immanuel. *Mystical Concepts in Chassidism*. Rev. ed. Brooklyn, N.Y.: Kehot, 1988.

Scholem, Gershom G. *Kabbalah*. New York: New American Library, 1974.

———. *Major Trends in Jewish Mysticism*. New York: Schocken Books, 1961.

———. *On the Mystical Shape of the Godhead: Basic Concepts in the Kabbalah*. Trans. Joachim Neugrischel. New York: Schocken Books, 1991.

Schopenhauer, Arthur. *Parerga and Paralipomena: Short Philosophical Essays*. 2 vols. Ed. E. F. J. Payne. Oxford: Oxford Press, 2001.

Sefer Yetzirah: The Book of Creation. Trans. and commentary Aryeh Kaplan. York Beach, Me.: Samuel Weiser, 1990.

Sforno, Ovadiah. *Commentary on 'Pirke Avos.'* Trans. and notes Raphael Pelcovitz. Brooklyn, N.Y.: Mesorah, 1996.

———. *Commentary on the Torah*. 2 vols. Trans. Raphael Pelcovitz. Brooklyn, N.Y.: Mesorah, 1987–1989.

Shapell, Nathan. *Witness to the Truth*. New York: David McKay, 1974.

Shapira, Kalonymos Kalmish. *Benei Machshavah Tovah*. Tel-Aviv: Vaad Chasidei Piaseczno, 1973.

———. *Esh Kodesh*. Jerusalem: Vaad Chasidei Pisetsenah, 1997.

———. *Sacred Fire: Torah from the Years of Fury, 1939–1942*. Ed. Deborah Miller. Trans. J. Hershy Worch. Northvale, N.J.: Jason Aronson, 2000.

———. *A Student's Obligation*. Trans. Micha Odenheimer. Northvale, N.J.: Jason Aronson, 1991.

———. *Tsav Veziruz*. In *Hakashrat Haavrakhim, Mavo Hashaarim, Tsav Veziruz*. Ed. Moshe Yerachmiel. Jerusalem: Vaad Chasidei Piaseczno, 1962.

Shushan Sodot. Petach-Tikvah: Or Hagenuz, 1995.

Sifre on Deuteronomy. New York: Jewish Theological Seminary, 1993.

Silberstang, Edwin. *Nightmare of the Dark*. New York: Knopf, 1967.

Solomon ibn Gabirol. *Selected Religious Poems*. Ed. I. Davidson. Trans. Israel Zangwill. Philadelphia: Jewish Publication Society, 1952.

Soloveitchik, Joseph. *Halakhic Man.* Trans. Lawrence Kaplan. Philadelphia: Jewish Publication Society, 1983.

———. *The Halakhic Mind: An Essay on Jewish Tradition and Modern Thought.* New York: Free Press, 1986.

———. "Kol Dodi Dofek: The Voice of My Beloved Knocketh." In Bernhard H. Rosenberg and Fred Heuman, eds., *Theological and Halakhic Reflections on the Holocaust.* Hoboken, N.J.: KTAV, 1992.

Steinsaltz, Adin. *Beggars and Prayers.* Trans. Yehuda Hanegbi et al. New York: Basic Books, 1985.

———. *The Essential Talmud.* Trans. Chaya Galai. New York: Basic Books, 1976.

———. *The Long Shorter Way: Discourses on Chasidic Thought.* Trans. Yehuda Hanegbi. Northvale, N.J.: Jason Aronson, 1988.

———. *On Being Free.* Northvale, N.J.: Jason Aronson, 1995.

———. *Simple Words: Thinking about What Really Matters in Life.* Ed. Elana Schachter and Ditsa Shabtai. New York: Simon & Schuster, 1999.

———. *The Strife of the Spirit.* Northvale, N.J.: Jason Aronson, 1988.

———. *The Sustaining Utterance: Discourses on Chasidic Thought.* Ed. and trans. Yehuda Hanegbi. Northvale, N.J.: Jason Aronson, 1989.

———. *Teshuvah: A Guide for the Newly Observant Jew.* New York: Free Press, 1987.

———. *The Thirteen-Petalled Rose: A Discourse on the Essence of Jewish Existence and Belief.* Trans. Yehuda Hanegbi. New York: Basic Books, 1980.

———, with Eisenberg, Josy. *The Seven Lights: On the Major Jewish Festivals.* Northvale, N.J.: Jason Aronson, 2000.

Steinschneider, Moritz. *Bibliographische Handbuch über die theoretische und praktische Literatur für hebräische Sprachkunde.* New York: Hildscheim, 1976.

Taminiaux, Jacques. *Heidegger and the Project of Fundamental Ontology.* Ed. and trans. Michael Gendre. Albany, N.Y.: SUNY Press, 1991.

Tanna debe Eliyyahu: The Lore of the School of Elijah. Trans. William G. Braude and Israel J. Kapstein. Philadelphia: Jewish Publication Society, 1981.

Teichtal, Yissachar Shlomo. *Em Habanim Smechah.* Jerusalem: Hotset Makhon "Pri Haarets," 1983.

Tikkunei Hazohar. 3 vols. Jerusalem: A. Blum Sefarim Geshaft, 1993.

Tishby, Isaiah. "Prayer and Devotion in the Zohar." In Lawrence Fine, ed. *Essential Papers on Kabbalah.* New York: NYU Press, 1995.

Tolstoy, Leo. *Confession.* Trans. David Patterson. New York: Norton, 1983.

Topas, George. *The Iron Furnace.* Lexington: University Press of Kentucky, 1990.

Tory, Avraham. *Surviving the Holocaust: The Kovno Ghetto Diary.* Ed. Martin Gilbert. Trans. Jerzy Michalowicz. Cambridge, Mass.: Harvard University Press, 1990.

Tosefta. Jerusalem: Wahrmann, 1970.

Vilna Gaon. *Even Sheleimah.* Trans. Yaakov Singer and Chaim Dovid Ackerman. Southfield, Mich.: Targum Press, 1992.

Vital, Chayyim. *Kabbalah of Creation: Isaac Luria's Early Mysticism (Shaar HaKlalim).* Trans. and commentary Eliahu Klein. Northvale, N.J.: Jason Aronson, 2000.

———. *Sefer Hachazonot.* Jerusalem: Hamakhon Lehotset Sifrei Raboteinu, 2000.

———. *Shaarei Kedushah.* Jerusalem: Eshkol, 2000.

———. *The Tree of Life (Ets Chayyim).* Trans. D. W. Menzi and Z. Padeh. Northvale, N.J.: Aronson, 1999.

Vrba, Rudolf, with Bestic, Alan. *I Cannot Forgive.* Vancouver: Regent College Publishing, 1997.

Wagner, Peter. *Wir werden frei sein: Leopold Zunz, 1794–1886.* Detmold: Gesellschaft für Christlich-Jüdische Zuzammenarbeit, 1994.

Wallach, Luitpold. *Liberty and Letters: The Thought of Leopold Zunz.* London: East and West Library, 1959.

Wasser, Hersh. "Daily Entries of Hersh Wasser." Trans. Joseph Kermish. *Yad Vashem Studies* 15 (1983), 201–82.

Weinreich, Max. *Hitler's Professors: The Part of Scholarship in Germany's Crimes against the Jewish People.* New Haven, Conn.: Yale University Press, 1999.

Weissman, Moshe, ed. *The Midrash Says.* 5 vols. Brooklyn, N.Y.: Bnay Yakov Publications, 1980.

Wells, Leon. *The Death Brigade.* New York: Holocaust Library, 1978.

Wiesel, Elie. *Against Silence: The Voice and Vision of Elie Wiesel.* 3 vols. Ed. Irving Abrahamson. New York: Holocaust Library, 1985.

———. *Ani Maamin: A Song Lost and Found Again.* Trans. Marion Wiesel. New York: Random House, 1973.

———. *Evil and Exile.* Trans. Jon Rothschild. Notre Dame, Ind.: University of Notre Dame Press, 1990.

———. *From the Kingdom of Memory: Reminiscences.* New York: Summit Books, 1990.

―――. *The Gates of the Forest.* Trans. Frances Frenaye. New York: Holt, Rinehart and Winston, 1966.

―――. *A Jew Today.* Trans. Marion Wiesel. New York: Random House, 1978.

―――. *Legends of Our Time.* New York: Avon, 1968.

―――. *Messengers of God.* Trans. Marion Wiesel. New York: Random House, 1976.

―――. *Night.* Trans. Stella Rodway. New York: Bantam, 1982.

―――. *The Oath.* New York: Avon, 1973.

―――. *One Generation After.* Trans. Lily Edelman and Elie Wiesel. New York: Pocket Books, 1970.

―――. *Sages and Dreamers.* Trans. Marion Wiesel. New York: Summit Books, 1991.

―――. *Somewhere a Master: Further Hasidic Portraits and Legends.* Trans. Marion Wiesel. New York: Summit Books, 1982.

―――. *Souls on Fire: Portraits and Legends of Hasidic Masters.* Trans. Marion Wiesel. New York: Vintage Books, 1973.

―――. *The Testament.* Trans. Marion Wiesel. New York: Summit Books, 1981.

―――. *The Town beyond the Wall.* Trans. Stephen Becker. New York: Avon, 1964.

―――. *Zalman, or The Madness of God.* Adapted for the stage by Marion Wiesel. New York: Random House, 1974.

Wiesenthal, Simon. *The Sunflower.* Trans. H. A. Piehler. New York: Schocken Books, 1976.

Wood, Allen W. "Rational Theology, Moral Faith, and Religion." In Paul Gruyer, ed., *The Cambridge Companion to Kant.* Cambridge: Cambridge University Press, 1992.

Wyschogrod, Edith. *Spirit in Ashes: Hegel, Heidegger, and Man-Made Death.* New Haven, Conn.: Yale University Press, 1985.

Wyschogrod, Michael. *The Body of Faith: Judaism as Corporeal Election.* Minneapolis: Seabury Press, 1983.

―――. "Faith and the Holocaust." In Michael L. Morgan, ed., *A Holocaust Reader: Responses to the Nazi Extermination.* New York: Oxford University Press, 2001.

Yaakov Yosef of Polnoe. *Toledot Yaakov Yosef al HaTorah.* Jerusalem: Agudat Beit Vialipoly, 1944.

Yalkut Shimoni al Hatorah. 5 vols. Jerusalem, 1968 (publisher unknown).

Young, James E. "Interpreting Literary Testimony: A Preface to Rereading Holocaust Diaries and Memoirs." *New Literary History* 18 (1987), 403–23.

Zalman, Schneur. *Likutei Amarim Tanya.* Trans. Nissan Mindel et al. Brooklyn, N.Y.: Kehot, 1981.

———. *Torah Or.* New York: Otser Hachasidim, 1973.

Zaloshinsky, Gavriel, ed. *Orchot Tzadikim.* Trans. Shraga Silverstein. Jerusalem: Feldheim, 1995.

Zevin, Shlomo Yosef. *A Treasury of Chassidic Tales on the Torah.* Trans. Uri Kaploun. New York: Mesorah, 1980.

Zimmels, H. J. *The Echo of the Nazi Holocaust in Rabbinic Literature.* New York: KTAV, 1977.

The Zohar. 5 vols. Trans. Harry Sperling and Maurice Simon. London: Soncino, 1984.

Zunz, Leopold. *Die gottesdienstlichen Vorträge der Juden.* Piscataway, N.J.: Gorgias Press, 2003.

———. *Die Literaturgeschichte der synagogalen Poesie.* Berlin: Hildscheim, 1966.

Zyskind, Sara. *Stolen Years.* Trans. Margarit Inbar. Minneapolis: Lerner, 1981.

INDEX

Abba Isi ben Yochanan, 89
Abohav, Yitzchak, 121
Abrabanel Don Isaac, 25, 216
Abraham, 126, 134, 220, 241, 267*n21*,
   298*n66*, 301*n33*; chosen for the
   sake of all nations, 84; and the
   Covenant, 195–96, 210–11, 242
Abraham ibn Ezra, 152, 161
Abulafia, Abraham, 263*n67*, 301*n13*
Adam, 37, 53, 88, 166, 169, 204, 234
Adorno, Theodor, 224
Agadah, 121, 151
Agus, Jacob, 275*n24*
Akeida, 220
Akiva, 10, 55, 56–57, 297–98*n61*
Albo, Joseph, 146, 186, 266*n8*, 287*n1*
Alienation, 42–43, 65, 187
Alter, Yehudah Leib, 31, 93, 114, 280*n15*
Amalek, 82, 216, 218, 297*n53*
Améry, Jean, 133, 282*n52*
Ammi, 15
Amos, 20
Angel of Death, 103–4, 161

Antiochus Epiphanes, 66
Anti-Semitism, 10, 21, 56, 67; philo-
   sophical, 50–55, 246–47; and
   Arab Muslims, 272*n117*
Antiworld, 108–13, 136, 164, 215
Aquinas, Thomas, 236
Arendt, Hannah, 9–10, 24, 45, 224,
   264*n75*, 291*n86*
Ari, the. *See* Luria, Yitzchak
Aristotle, 10, 22, 37, 74, 167–68, 291*n86*
Armillus, 236
Assi, 234
Athens, 90
Auschwitz, 18, 20, 81, 89–90, 112–13,
   140, 173–74, 256; and modern
   thought, 42, 49–50, 83; and Jeru-
   salem, 87, 154; and Midrash, 156;
   essence of, 93, 102–4, 106, 160,
   164, 281*n28*; and Torah, 155; and
   tikkun haolam, 175
Authenticity, 18, 48, 83, 217, 278*n83*
Autonomy, 17–18, 69–77, 79, 217,
   246. *See also* Freedom

Avimelekh, 61
Avnimus, 142

Baal HaTurim, 41
Baal Shem Tov, 33, 207, 250–51, 259*n5*,
   280*n16*; on the Shekhinah, 4; on
   the word, 93, 94, 94–95, 119; on
   the Messiah, 232–33, 242
Babel, 41, 49, 57, 159–60, 162
Bachya ibn Paquda, 23, 33, 38, 64,
   131–32, 288*n5*
Baeck, Leo, 64, 99, 177
Barlev, Zvi, 300*n8*
Barukh, 36
Bauch, Bruno, 291*n86*
Bauer, Bruno, 47
Bauer, Yehuda, 5
Bauman, Zygmunt, 192
Bäumler, Alfred, 291*n86*
Belzec, 281*n27*
Benamozegh, Elijah, 100
Bergen-Belsen, 141
Berkovits, Eliezer, 8, 9, 12, 15–16, 24,
   101, 239
Beruriah, 116
Betsalel, 94, 280*n16*
Binding of Isaac. *See Akeida*
Birkenau, 158, 256
Bitton-Jackson, Livia, 105, 141
Blanchot, Maurice, 16
Blau, Joseph, 275*n24*
Blech, Benjamin, 61, 115
Body, the, 145, 227–28, 271*n113*; and
   the soul, 161, 162, 299*n93*
Book, the, 119–21
Bor, Josef, 107
Borowitz, Eugene, 56
Braiterman, Zachery, 9, 86, 263*n60*
Bread, 168–69

Breaking of the vessels, 183, 207, 208
Brearley, Margaret, 261*n36*
Breuer, Isaac, 274*n11*
Brewster, Eva, 300*n8*
Buber, Martin, 8, 35, 42–43, 49, 231,
   245, 276–77*n45*
Budzyn, 214

Cain, 24, 44, 169, 212
Camon, Ferdinando, 288*n11*
Camus, Albert, 43, 58
Caputo, John, 49
Cargas, Harry James, 21
Caro, Joseph, 203
Caspar, Johann, 267*n23*
Chananiah ben Teradyon, 116
Chariot, the, 205
Chasidism, 203–4, 213, 232–33,
   296*n38*, 296*n41*
Chayim ben Attar, 38, 60, 61, 242,
   271*n113*, 273*n140*
Child, the, 99, 220, 234; Nazi assault
   on, 98, 133–38, 141–42, 199, 254,
   286*n43*, 286*n51*; and the Messiah,
   245
Chofetz Chaim, 34, 292*n20*
Chosenness, 10, 26, 39, 84, 147, 153
Christianity, 12, 50, 51, 74, 165, 170–
   72, 246–47, 300*n2*
Circumcision, 195–96, 211, 241, 242,
   301–2*n34*
Clermont de Tonnerre, 51
Cohen, Arthur, 6, 8, 9, 11–12
Cohen, Hermann, 73–77, 79, 80,
   83, 85
Cohen, Josh, 85–86, 111
Cohn-Sherbok, Dan, 8
Commandment, 75, 101, 271*n113*,
   273*n5*; as a connection to God,

38–39, 58–59, 70, 163, 164–65, 233, 209, 273*n140*; and the face of the other human being, 80–81; and *tikkun haolam*, 177, 186–87, 192; and the Messiah, 238
Conrad, Joseph, 42
Copernicus, 40
Cordovero, Moses, 207, 208
Covenant, 10, 103, 195–96 238, 241–42, 247, 262*n50*; in post-Holocaust Jewish thought, 14–15, 112; Nazi assault on, 52, 98–99, 190, 218; and memory, 59–60; and questioning God, 210–11, 239–40; at Mount Sinai, 224
Crétella, Henri, 53
Crescas, Hasdai, 300*n10*
Crusades, 3, 16
Culi, Yaakov, 41, 159–60
Czerniakow, Adam, 134–35

Dance, 36, 186, 251
Daniel, 253
David, 61, 106, 251
Death, 10, 146–50, 153, 155; in Jewish thought, 40, 81, 288*n5*; in modern philosophy, 40, 278*n83*; no longer death, 151, 156
Delbo, Charlotte, 55, 59, 97, 113, 132
Descartes, René, 36, 37, 167
Destiny, 25–26, 254
Devekut, 236
Divine image, 132, 148, 160, 165, 187–89; Nazi assault on, 18–19, 149, 157–58, 161–63, 189–90. *See also* God; the Holy
Divine Presence. *See* Shekhinah
Divine Providence, 74, 209–10
Donat, Alexander, 103, 142

Dostoyevsky, F. M., 269*n60*
Dovid Chernobler, 35, 36
Dribben, Judith, 284*n14*
Dwelling, 124, 126, 127–28, 179, 180, 231, 249–50

Eckhardt, A. Roy, 21
Eckhardt, Alice L., 21
Ego, 63, 115, 166, 223, 237, 296*n24*; as the center of thought, 44, 47, 257; and anti-Semitism, 51, 54, 246–47; annulment of, 59, 195, 208, 245, 249, 269*n64*
Egypt, 61, 65–66, 76, 112, 151, 184
Eliezer, 253
Elijah, 128, 205, 302*n42*
Elimelekh of Lizhensk, 213–14
Eliot, T. S., 42
Elisha, 128
Elisha ben Avuya, 64
Enlightenment, 12, 42, 51–52, 66, 170–71, 275*n19*
Eternity, 196–97
Ethics, 67, 69–75, 86, 164; and Judaism, 17, 79–80, 110–11; and ontological thought, 48–49; and *tikkun haolam*, 186–87
Evil, 16, 31, 44–45, 48, 147, 216, 217, 220, 254; and Jewish thought, 25–26, 55, 209–13; in Jewish mysticism, 183, 207–8, 218–19
Exile, 63, 112–13, 128, 201–2, 208, 219, 232; and revelation, 114–15, 229
Existentialism, 43, 48
Ezekiel, 130, 155–56, 205

Face, the, 92–95, 192–94
Fackenheim, Emil L., xi, 8, 9, 116–17, 169, 173, 201, 284*n15*; on National

Fackenheim, Emil L. *(continued)*
Socialism, 16, 53, 54, 137, 259*n10*;
as a Jewish thinker, 18–21, 24, 89,
167, 170; and the 614th Commandment, 19, 20, 84–85, 143,
155, 163, 172, 187–88, 199, 242;
on the Nazi assault on the human
being, x, 166, 190, 264*n5*; on
modern philosophy, 46–47, 52, 57,
58, 165, 293*n42*; on anti-Semitism,
56; on liberal Judaism, 64–65, 66,
73, 83, 99; on the Maccabees, 66,
274*n14*; on the Muselmann, 148,
149, 150, 158, 159, 161, 188–89; on
the biblical text, 154, 155–56; on
midrashic madness, 156; on recovery from an illness, 163–64, 176;
on the Ultimate, 163–64, 176, 213;
on God, 166, 167–68, 184, 185–86,
187, 276*n44*; on Jewish resistance,
167, 176; on the Nazi assault on
prayer, 174; on *tikkun haolam*,
175–76, 199; on Judaism, 185, 193–
94; on Amalek, 216; on the messianic hope, 232; on faith, 237,
243; on the Messiah, 243
Faith, 13–14, 230–31, 236–41; and
the Tetragrammaton, 237; as
covenant, 238; and love, 238–39
Farbstein, Esther, 208, 214
Father, the, 128–33, 140–41
Fénelon, Fania, 55, 112
Ferderber-Salz, Bertha, 55
Feuerbach, Ludwig, 47
Fichte, Johann Gottlieb, 19, 275*n19*
Fine, Lawrence, 298*n61*
Formstecher, Solomon, 69
Foucault, Michel, 44
Freedom, 49, 53, 191–92, 198; as

autonomy, 17–18, 39, 40, 47, 48,
83, 217
Freud, Sigmund, 10, 55
Funkenstein, Amos, 260–61*n27*
Future, the, 198

Gans, Eduard, 68
Gehinnom, 106
German Idealism, 81, 277*n47*; and
National Socialism, 19, 46, 217;
and liberal Judaism, 64, 69, 74, 85
Gersonides, 23, 129, 277*n52*
Gikatilla, Joseph, 59, 126
Ginsburgh, Yitzchak, 95, 125, 126–
27, 243, 251, 269*n64*
Glazerson, Matityahu, 92, 129
God, 154, 185–86, 198, 220, 238,
240–41, 254–55, 298*n72*; loss of,
12–13, 31, 225–26; Nazi assault on,
16, 87, 109, 124, 133, 137, 144–45,
162, 260*n18*, 263*n64*, 284*n14*; and
philosophy, 23, 39–40, 46–47, 52,
64, 276*n44*; and thought, 33, 34–
38, 39, 236–37; as *Hamakom*, 49,
214; argument with, 59–60, 239–
40; and ethical monotheism, 66,
70, 73–74, 78, 83; as the Invisible
One, 111–12, 177; as Supernal
Mother, 99, 124–25; and *tikkun
haolam*, 184–85, 199; oneness with
Torah, 205, 242; in Jewish mysticism, 206–7; and evil, 209–12,
218–19, 221; suffering of, 213, 215,
222, 223, 228, 256–57. *See also*
Divine image; the Holy
Goethe, Johann Wolfgang, 121
Gog and Magog, 215, 235–36
Good, the, 14–15, 39, 72, 74, 130,
146–47, 153, 197–98

Gratitude, 59, 250, 251
Greek philosophy. *See* Western
 philosophy
Greenberg, Irving, 8, 9, 12–15, 24,
 256, 264*n85*
Grob, Leonard, 263*n65*
Gruyer, Paul, 46
Gutman, Israel, 134

Haerung, Theodor, 291*n86*
Halevi, Judah, 72, 119–20, 265*n92*,
 297*n41*
Halivni, David Weiss, 256
Haman, 156, 215
Harris, Jay Michael, 275*n22*
Hartmann, Nicolai, 291*n86*
Hatikvah, 249
Heart, 126
Hebrew alphabet, 93, 95
Hegel, Georg Wilhelm Friedrich, 19,
 36, 46–47, 50, 79
Heidegger, Martin, 36, 48, 50, 79,
 167, 291*n86*; as a Nazi, 5, 10, 45–
 46, 171; as an ontological thinker,
 17–18, 83; on death, 40, 278*n83*
Heimler, Eugene, 300*n8*
Heine, Heinrich, 68, 274*n19*
Heschel, Abraham Joshua, xi, 37,
 76, 259*n4*; on God, 34–35, 36, 39–
 40; on commandment, 38, 71; on
 ontological philosophy, 58, 60–
 61, 77; on history, 100, 101, 281*n37*;
 on prayer, 148; on time, 154, 214;
 on faith, 237, 238
Heuman, Fred, 8
Heyse, Hans, 291*n86*
Hezekiah, 248
Hillel, 172
Hillel the Elder, 179

Hilsenrath, Edgar, 300*n8*
Hirsch, Samson Raphael, 39, 65
Hirsch, Samuel, 69
History, Hebrew understanding of,
 97–102; and the Messiah, 244,
 248–49
Hitler, Adolf, 4–5, 11, 19, 43
Holy, the, 17, 22–23, 61, 71, 121–23,
 196; Nazi assault on, 155, 212, 255.
 See also Divine image; God
Holy Name. *See* Tetragrammaton
Holy Seer of Lublin, 214, 280–81*n27*
Horowitz, Shabtai Sheftl, 278–79*n90*
Huberband, Shimon, 214
Human being, the, 23, 53, 78–79, 88,
 89, 122, 157, 168–69; Nazi assault
 on, 19, 93, 105, 121, 138, 143, 160,
 219; in Jewish thought, 32–33, 34;
 relation to the other, 39–40, 77–
 78, 146–47, 186–87, 190, 196–97;
 ethical concern for, 48–49, 80, 249
Huna, 300*n1*
Hunger, 158
Husserl, Edmund, 64

Idolatry, 19, 54, 57, 60, 65, 166, 170,
 212, 261*n33*
Immemorial, the, 153, 189, 198
Indifference, 166–68; recovery from,
 189–95
Infinite, the, 192, 194, 195
Ingathering, the, 235
Isaac, 126, 134, 220
Isaac Meir of Ger, 115
Isaiah, 134, 213, 244, 262*n58*
Islam, 246–47
Israel, State of, 101–2, 147, 199–200,
 272*n117*
Iwens, Sidney, 300*n8*

Jabès, Edmond, 104, 111
Jacob, 104, 117, 124, 126, 134, 170,
    196, 292*n23*
Jaspers, Karl, 268*n35*
Jeremiah, 253
Jerusalem, 101, 114, 154, 222, 249–
    50, 285*n28*; as a center of thought,
    86–90; heavenly, 87, 200, 221
Jesus, 171, 234, 301*n13*
Job, 211, 215
Jonah, 247
Jonas, Hans, 8, 48, 262–63*n59*
Joseph, 106, 218, 280*n19*
Joy. *See* Rejoicing
Judah, 234
Judaism, 17, 22, 81, 185, 241,
    277–78*n63*; and post-Shoah
    Jewish thought, 10–11, 172; and
    philosophy, 19, 50–51, 57, 77,
    85–86, 276*n30*; teachings of, 25,
    59; Nazi assault on, 53, 222; and
    ethical monotheism, 66, 71–76,
    82, 83–84; and ethics, 79–80;
    and mysticism, 202–3
Justice, 71–72, 99–100, 276*n37*, 277*n47*

Kalmanovitch, Zelig, 260*n18*
Kanah ibn Gedor, 262*n50*
Kant, Immanuel, 36, 40, 79, 80, 121,
    167, 275*n19*; on Judaism, 10, 50,
    276*n30*; and National Socialism,
    17; on God, 23, 46; and ethical
    monotheism, 69–72; on prayer,
    267*n21*
Kaplan, Aryeh, 33, 124, 126, 174,
    297*n41*
Kaplan, Chaim A., 280*n18*
Karow, Yvonne, 10
Katz, Steven, 6, 8–9, 11, 24, 261*n33*

Ka-tzetnik 135633, 42, 91, 102, 167,
    171–72
Katznelson, Yitzhak, 4, 139–40, 179,
    260*n18*, 291*n82*
Kelipot, 208, 211, 219, 245
Kiddush Hashem, 57–58, 70, 77, 81,
    155, 220, 229, 272*n133*
Kielar, Wieslaw, 107
Kierkegaard, Søren, 43, 236, 267*n21*,
    301*n20*
Klein, Gerda, 140–41
Klonicki-Klonymus, Aryeh, 141
Kook, Abraham Isaac, 95, 200,
    238–39
Koretzer Rebbe, 6, 58
Kotzker Rebbe, 237
Kovno Ghetto, 139
Krieck, Ernst, 291*n86*
Krochmal, Nachman, 68–69, 275*n22*
Kruk, Herman, 4, 139

LaCapra, Dominick, 286–87*n56*
Lang, Berel, 51
Language, 160, 194. *See also* Word, the
Lazarus, Moritz, 69–72, 76, 85
Leitner, Isabella, 140, 152
Lengyel, Olga, 290*n65*
Levi, Primo, 22, 154, 159, 161 165,
    166, 170, 282*n52*, 288*n11*; on the
    Muselmann, x, 149, 150, 157, 162;
    on the essence of Auschwitz, 50,
    54, 93, 126, 158, 160, 168–69; on
    the Nazi assault on the human
    being, 91, 148, 160, 290*n64*; on
    the aftermath of Auschwitz, 96;
    on the Nazi assault on memory,
    151; on language, 159–60, 162;
    on the Nazi assault on the name,
    160–61, 169

Levi Yitzchak of Berditchev, 36, 205, 271*n113*

Levinas, Emmanuel, xi, 24, 59, 99, 152, 172, 175, 226–27; on the Good, 14, 72, 111, 153, 197–98, 212; as a Jewish thinker, 16–18, 24; on the other human being, 33, 39, 158, 163, 168, 186–87, 193; on thought, 35, 40; on evil, 44, 211–12; on modern philosophy, 45, 67, 79–82, 83, 85; on God, 49–50, 154, 221; on anti-Semitism, 54, 246; on the word, 86, 133; on the face, 92, 192–93; on the Book, 93, 118, 185, 296*n28*; on time, 151–52, 198, 214, 248, 249; on Torah, 154–55, 278*n77*; on the "there is," 159, 191; and *tikkun haolam*, 175–76; on responsibility, 180, 189, 190–91, 194, 195, 244, 245, 249; on freedom, 192; on the Infinite, 192, 194; on Judaism, 194; on the State of Israel, 199, 300*n3*; on faith, 238; on love, 275*n27*

Levy-Hass, Hanna, 141

Lewinska, Pelagia, 163–64

Liberal Judaism, 64–65, 66, 73, 80; and the State of Israel, 101–2, 115

Liberation, 112, 166

Littell, Franklin, 21, 281–82*n39*

Łódž Ghetto, 139

Loeve, Yehuda, 61, 181, 285*n23*

Logos, 37

Love, 80, 83, 124–25, 126–27, 128, 209, 238–39, 278*n73*

Lubavitcher Rebbe. *See* Schneerson, Menachem Mendel

Lublin, 281*n27*

Luria, Yitzchak, 126, 183, 203, 207, 219, 297–98*n61*

Lustig, Arnŏst, 262*n53*, 300*n8*

Luther, Martin, 121

Luzzatto, Moshe Chayim, 131, 224

Lyotard, François, 51–52, 85

Maccabees, 66, 274*n14*

Mack, Michael, 269*n75*, 270*n79*

Madness, 44, 61–62, 222, 269*n62*; of God, 298*n72*

Maggid of Dubno, 137–38, 172

Maggid of Koshnits, 214

Maggid of Mezeritch, 262*n54*, 292*n20*

Maharal of Prague. *See* Loeve, Yehuda

Maharsha, 257

Maimonides, 74, 105, 129, 230–31, 251, 277*n57*; his engagement with mysticism, x, 68–69, 75, 203, 265*n92*; philosophical influence on, 22, 23

Majdanek, 15, 281*n27*

Manemann, Juergen, 21

Mao Tse-tung, 43

Marriage, 97–98, 123, 178, 234, 292*n25*

Martyrdom. *See* Kiddush Hashem

Marx, Karl, 21, 55

Maybaum, Ignaz, 4–5, 8, 9, 11, 12, 24, 85

Maza, Bernard, 8

Meir, 147

Meir ibn Gabbai, 108

Menachem Mendel Rimanover, 101

Menachem the Galilean, 250

Memory, 59–60, 129–30, 151–53, 169; of God, 184

Messiah, 151, 201, 229, 243, 285*n30*, 300*n10*, 302*n42*; in ethical monotheism, 74; and the Name of the

Messiah *(continued)*
Holy One, 87; exile of, 100–101, 232, 282*n44*; and the child, 134, 137; Jewish teachings on, 183, 200, 233–36, 300–301*n13*; name of the, 197, 230, 252, 299–300*n1*; the wait for, 230–32; in Jewish thought, 241–45, 249–52; and history, 244, 248–49
Messiah ben David, 235–36, 239
Messiah ben Joseph, 235–36
Metatron, 223, 298*n68*, 299*n80*
Meyers, Gerald E., 8
Micah, 128
Michael, the Angel, 221
Midrashic madness, 156
Mikhal of Zlotchov, 63, 296*n24*
Mikveh, 214
Miriam, 297*n60*
Mistarim, 223, 224, 228, 298–99*n79*
Mitzvah. See Commandment
Modern philosophy, 19, 171–72.
See also Ontology; Western philosophy
Mordechai Yosef of Isbitza, 241
Morgan, Michael, 6, 8, 9, 20, 55, 261–62*n50*, 263–64*n73*, 264*n85*
Moses, 10, 22, 38, 110, 247, 253, 255; and Written Torah, 36, 94, 120, 205; and the Song at the Sea, 67; and Oral Torah, 75
Moshe Leib of Sassov, 36, 186, 251
Mother, the, 123–28, 139–40
Mount Sinai, 99, 134, 178, 179, 188, 197, 275*n27*; in Jewish thought, 14–15, 20, 231; and modern philosophy, 73, 79, 171; and the Covenant, 112, 224
Mozart, Wolfgang Amadeus, 172

Munk, Michael, 93
Munk, Salomon, 68
Murder, Divine prohibition against, 21, 22, 24, 43, 211, 213, 228; Nazi assault on, 18, 19, 217, 228–29; and the human face, 40, 83, 92–93, 193
Murder camp, 18–19, 137
Muselmann, x–xi, 19, 20, 42, 175; and post-Holocaust Jewish thought, 169–72

Nachman of Breslov, 32–33, 128, 242, 273*n5*; on *teshuvah*, 59; on importance of the name, 103, 161, 283*n59*; on time, 196; on faith, 238
Nachmanides, 3, 35, 112, 190, 235, 265*n92*, 276*n37*, 280*n16*, 300–301*n13*
Name, Nazi assault on the, 160–62, 169
Narcissus, 49
National Socialism, 17, 19, 53, 122, 137, 290*n70*
Neher, André, 58, 62, 97–98, 198, 215, 245, 274*n10*; on silence, 103, 108, 177; on Zionism, 200, 279*n101*
Nietzsche, Friedrich, 11, 47, 48, 50, 82, 261*n37*, 270*n86*
Nissenbaum, Yitzhak, 7, 58
Noah, 178
Nomberg-Przytyk, Sara, 13, 91

Olam Asiyah. See World of Action
Olam Atsilut. See World of Emanation
Olam Beriah. See World of Creation
Olam Shoah, 224–29
Olam Yetsirah. See World of Formation

Onkelos, 105

Ontology, 23, 32, 64, 79, 246, 254; Heideggerian, 17–18; and the Shoah, 22, 216–17; egocentrism of 36–37, 39–40; the horror of, 42–50. *See also* Modern philosophy; Western philosophy

Oral Torah, 185

Oshry, Ephraim, 7

Otto, Rudolph, 12

Oz, Amos, 20

Ozsváth, Zsuzsanna, 274*n9*

Passover, 184

Patai, Raphael, 300*n9*

Peikazh, Mendel, 203, 298*n63*

Perets, 234

Pharaoh, 280*n19*

Philo, 64

Plaszow, 214

Plato, 23, 45, 267*n31*

Plotinus, 267*n26*

Polen, Nehemia, 60, 227

Poliakov, Leon, 145

Pollefeyt, Didier, 21

Postmodernism, 59, 82, 142–43, 192–93, 255; and Jewish thought, 85–86, 219; its view of texts, 118, 138–39, 165; and the Shoah, 171–72, 226; egocentric nature of, 257, 272*n118*

Prayer, 13, 76–77, 154, 182; and thought, 34, 35, 36–37, 88, 250; Nazi assault on, 147, 280*n18*

Rachel, 126

Rashi, x, 5–6, 127, 179, 194–95, 284*n85*, 297*n60*

Rav, 248, 249

Ravad, 203

Reason, 46–47, 64, 67, 69–76, 79, 81, 90

Rebecca, 126

Redemption, 115, 133–38, 142, 220, 234, 246, 248; and tradition, 184

Reform Judaism. *See* Liberal Judaism

Rejoicing, 38, 81, 84, 186, 251

Relation, 120–21, 150–51, 163–69, 186–87, 209

Resh Lakish, 57, 135, 168, 175, 178, 205

Responsibility, 38, 81, 84, 101, 180, 187, 244–45, 246; as subjectivity, 169, 190–91, 196–97; and the immemorial, 189; and the Infinite, 194, 195

Resurrection, the, 21

Reuben, 218

Revelation, 18, 19, 20, 75, 186, 241; and exile, 113–15; and the father, 128–33; and tradition, 184

Riga Ghetto, 136

Ringelblum Emmanuel, 139, 202, 212–13, 214

Rivosh, Elik, 136

Rodin, Auguste, 36

Rose, Gillian, 42

Rose, Paul Lawrence, 276*n30*

Rosenberg, Alan, 8

Rosenberg, Alfred, 5, 39, 259–60*n12*, 261*n37*, 284*n12*

Rosenberg, Bernard H., 8

Rosenfeld, Oskar, 5

Rosenzweig, Franz, 28, 80, 81, 85, 118, 251–52; on modern philosophy, 39, 40, 43, 79, 109; on the "new thinking," 77–78; on Christianity, 246

Rotenstreich, Nathan, 275*n24*
Roth, John K., 21
Rubenstein, Richard, 8, 9–10, 12, 16, 24, 85

Saadia Gaon, 23, 184
Sabbath, 60–61, 76, 86, 129–30, 206, 242, 243, 266*n14*, 277*n57*, 302*n42*
Sacks, Jonathan, 50–51, 52, 70, 265*n101*
Sacred history, 154, 184, 185
Salton, George, 98
Sanctification of the Name. *See* Kiddush Hashem
Sandberg, Moshe, 103
Sarah, 126, 298*n66*
Sartre, Jean-Paul, 10
Schelling, Friedrich Wilhelm Joseph, 19
Schindler, Pesach, 201, 215, 228
Schneersohn, Shalom Dov Ber, 277–78*n63*
Schneersohn, Yosef Yitzchak, 266*n2*
Schneerson, Menachem Mendel, 21, 55, 121, 211
Scholem, Gershom G., 285*n11*
Schopenhauer, Arthur, 50, 269*n60*
Sefirot, Ten, 131, 182, 183, 206, 224, 235, 285*n37*
Self. *See* Ego
Seraphim, Peter Heinz, 53
Sforno, Ovadiah, 41
Shapell, Nathan, 107
Shapira, Elimelekh, 213
Shapira, Kalonymos Kalmish, 112, 202–3, 207, 227–28, 256–57, 273*n140*, 298*n66*; his response to the Shoah, 82, 106, 218–24, 227; on the holy tongue, 206; his *Esh Kodesh*, 213–17

Shekhinah, 4, 35, 114, 180–81, 182, 222, 269*n64*, 286*n47*; and the Sabbath, 86–87; and the feminine, 126; exile of, 135, 219; and the Holy Land, 202, 223; and the Community of Israel, 215–16
Shimon bar Yochai, 119, 220, 298*n61*
Shimon ben Gamaliel, 130–31
Shlomo of Ludmir, 265*n96*
Shmuel ben Nachman, 15, 87, 248
Shmuel Hakaton, 89
Shpole Zeide, 36
Silberstang, Edwin, 300*n8*
Silence, 105–8, 157–59, 177–78, 227, 241, 242, 295*n13*; and Divine utterance, 111, 205
Simlai, 271*n113*
Sin, 171
Sitra Achra, 208
Social justice, 74–75, 76
Socrates, 36, 264*n75*
Solomon ibn Gabirol, 34
Soloveitchik, Joseph, 25, 47, 82, 255
Sosnowiec Ghetto, 107
Soul, the, 4, 31, 85, 149, 161, 172, 185, 278–79*n90*, 283*n59*; origin of, 33–34, 117, 271*n113*; and the holy tongue, 92, 95; the Nazi assault on, 94, 103, 116, 144–45, 162–63, 168, 212–13, 219–20; and the body, 161, 162, 299*n93*; levels of, 265*n103*, 266*n4*
Stalin, Joseph, 43
Steinsaltz, Adin, 6–7, 33, 50, 204, 209, 234, 257, 267*n17*; on Judaism, 10; on the soul, 33, 92; on exile, 63, 65–66; on Jerusalem, 87, 200; on Torah, 88–89; on

God, 206; on the *mitzvah*, 207, 267–68*n34*; on faith, 237
Steinschneider, Moritz, 275*n21*
Story, 150–51, 153, 157, 169
Streicher, Julius, 5
Suicide, 43–44
Sukkot, 247
Supernal Mother, 99–100

Tabernacle, Holy, 94
Talmud, 75–76
Tamar, 234
Taminiaux, Jacques, 48
Teichtal, Yissacher Shlomo, 201–2
Temple, the, 87, 89, 92, 135, 168, 247, 253, 300*n13*
Ten Martyrs, the, 218, 219, 229, 297–98*n61*
Teshuvah, 25, 58–59, 63, 95, 101, 188, 199, 220
Tetragrammaton, 181, 182, 206–7, 235; and faith, 237
Theodicy, 15, 24, 25, 210, 225, 254
"There is," the, 159–60, 191, 192
Theresienstadt, 10
Thirteen Principles of Faith, 230–31
Thought, Jewish thinking about, 33–42
Tillich, Paul, 10
Time, 100, 134, 150–56, 196, 198, 248–49
Toledano, J. M., 7
Tolstoy, Leo, 43
Topas, George, 107
Torah, ix-x, 14, 25, 87, 111, 149, 217, 240, 255; teaching concerning the human being, 5, 34, 90, 105, 122, 148–49, 165; Nazi assault on, 15–16, 22, 116–17, 202, 215, 260*n18*;

and Jewish thought, 10–11, 16–17, 22, 88–89, 219, 256; and Jewish identity, 20, 52–53, 57, 104, 117; and die Wissenschaft des Judentums, 67; traded for autonomy, 69–77; and the face, 81, 193, 194; as substance of the soul, 95; as substance of creation, 119–20, 125–26, 153, 205–6; and woman, 126, 285*n23*; and the father, 129–30, 132; and the child, 134; as substance of the body, 145, 271*n113*; and meaning in life, 154–55, 185, 278*n77*; and *tikkun haolam*, 175, 187, 193–94; oneness with God, 205; and Messiah, 234
Tory, Avraham, 139
Tradition, 110–11, 150, 153, 154, 155, 167, 176; and *tikkun haolam*, 177–83; recovery of, 183–89
Trawniki, 214
Treblinka, 134
Tree of Knowledge, 31
Treitschke, Heinrich von, 73
Truth, 129–31, 132, 155, 252; and faith, 238, 241
Tsadok, 221, 222
Tsimtsum, 206, 208, 211, 224, 262–63*n59*

Understanding, 124, 126, 131, 219, 222

Vilna Gaon, 4, 137, 234
Vilna Ghetto, 139, 260*n18*
Vital, Chayyim, 31, 130, 183, 298*n61*
Vittel, 139
Voltaire, 50
Vrba, Rudolf, 145

Wagner, Peter, 274*n19*

Wallach, Luitpold, 274*n19*

Warsaw Ghetto, 82, 134, 141, 213, 214

Wasser, Hersh, 141

Wells, Leon, 141, 142

Western philosophy, 50–51, 131–32, 165; and the holy, 17, 121; and Jewish thought, 23, 36, 53, 64. *See also* Modern philosophy; Ontology

Wielcka, 214

Wiesel, Elie, x, 8, 9, 87, 157, 231, 233, 280–81*n27*, 300*n8*; on the Nazi assault on the child, 12, 135, 136, 141, 199, 254, 286*n43*, 286*n51*; on God, 60, 222, 263*n6*; on time, 100; on the assault on the name, 103; on the Nazi assault on the human being, 104–5, 122, 158, 264*n75*; on the meaning of the Shoah, 114, 116; on the Nazi assault on the father, 131; on the Messiah, 137, 252; on the Nazi assault on memory, 151; on the essence of Auschwitz, 281*n28*

Wiesenthal, Simon, 142, 282*n52*

Will to power, 18, 45, 48

Wisdom, 33, 129, 131–32, 133

Wissenschaft des Judentums, 67

Wöbbelin, 98

Women, 179, 284–85*n19*, 285*n23*

Wood, Allen W., 265*n91*

Word, the, 78–79, 86, 92, 198, 241–42, 252; Nazi assault on, 91, 92–95, 103, 288*n11*; silence and, 102–8,

159; in Hebrew, 104–5; restoration of, 165. *See also* Language

World, Nazi assault on, 108–13

World of Action, 181–82, 206, 224, 227, 228, 234

World of Creation, 181–82

World of Emanation, 181–82

World of Formation, 181–82

World of Shoah, 224–29

World to Come, 234

Wundt, Max, 291*n86*

Wyschogrod, Edith, 47, 49, 270*n80*

Wyschogrod, Michael, 18, 67

Yaakov Yosef of Polnoe, 33, 180–81, 259*n5*, 298*n64*

Yehoshua, 232

Yehuda Hanasi, 135, 239

Yochanan bar Nappacha, 87, 168, 178, 200; on the holy tongue, 206; on the Messiah, 239, 250

Yochanan ben Zakkai, 13

Yom Hashoah, 231, 239

Yom Kippur liturgy, 209

Yom Kippur War, 200

Yonatan, 248

Yose, 222, 223, 226, 257

Young, James, 139, 286*n56*

Zalman, Schneur, x, 127, 183, 203

Zebul, 221

Zionism, 11, 83, 200, 202, 272*n117*, 279*n101*

Zunz, Leopold, 67–68, 85, 274*n19*

Zyskind, Sara, 140